The Coming of Tan

PEACE

Riley L. Martin

DATE

The Coming of Tan

Riley Martin
&
O-Qua Tangin Wann

HISTORICITY PRODUCTIONS

NEW HOPE PENNSYLVANIA

 Published by Historicity Productions, Box 531, New Hope, Pennsylvania, 18938, USA
Second edition

Library of Congress Cataloging in Publication Data

Martin, Riley L. 1946-
The Coming of Tan / written mid 1988 to early 1990

ISBN 0-9645745-0-0 10 9 8 7 6 5 4 3 2

1. Past, present and future of humanity
2. Extraterrestrial attention
3. Environmental catastrophe

Historicity Productions ~ Historical authenticity books may be purchased for educational, business or sales promotional use. You may order books on line using our secure order form, or write/call: Historicity Productions, Box 531, New Hope, Pennsylvania, 18938
telephone: 609-397-8446

Publisher: Curtis Cooperman

http://thecomingoftan.com

Contents

Foreword 1

A Poem Recited by: O-Qua Tangin Wann 5

1. The Coming of Tan 6
2. The Seven Intelligent Life Forms 12
3. Time, Space, Propulsion 27
4. Biaveh 38
5. Question and Other Things 52
6. Inside the Alien Mind 64
7. Back in Time 82
8. Of Men and Gods, Recent History 97
9. Eastern Shore Maryland ~ August 1975 109
10. The Targ Terror ~ May 1988 127
11. Mass Mind Control ~ Truth or Fiction 141
12. Let's Look At This Thing Objectively 161
13. Artificial Intelligence and Robotics 190

14. Statements of Reflection ~ Logic & Other Stuff 213

15. On the Future of Humanity 229

16. What Is, Is Not ~ Reality Transcended 258

17. The Omega Zone 280

Illustrations 316

Biaviian Symbol 340

A Selection of Biaviian Symbols 342

A Symbol in Color .... inside front cover

Photograph of Riley Martin .... inside back cover

FOREWORD

In 1953 at the age of seven, near the St. Francis River in Arkansas, I was abducted and taken aboard a UFO or flying saucer and kept for three days before being returned unharmed. Since then I have been visited by the same extraterrestrials every eleven years.

This association has been an ongoing one for the last thirty-five years. During that time a kind of intimate rapport has developed between them, the Biaviians (pronounced BE-AH-VEANS) and myself. I do not believe that my experience has been unique owing to the fact that a considerable number of earthlings have been and are contacted, and also the fact that I personally saw a number of humans, via telescan, living on the home planet of the aliens, and at least one man who also appeared to be in their confidence as I have thus far been. I further believe that three levitating, domed gardens aboard the great mothership are peopled by humans or hybrid humans, though I never had the chance to view them close up.

My formal education does not exceed a G.E.D., and I have spent time in several county jails and one prison during my life. I won't attempt to go to any extraordinary lengths to try to convince the reader of the first hand truth of my knowledge. Instead I will leave the contents of this book to your own scrutiny and sense of logic, be you scientist or layman.

Since I am not a scientist, I know that much of the information that I've been made privy to is beyond my ability to comprehend and my over-all assessment of the character and motivation of these aliens is, no doubt, handicapped by my intellectual limitations, but it may not be beyond yours.

During my life I have pursued a varied number of vocations, most of them legal, some not so legal and nearly all of the physically menial sort. I left home before my fourteenth birthday and have traveled extensively about this country and some others. I have worked as a farm hand, a migrant worker, whiskey maker, bare knuckle fighter, bodyguard, soldier of fortune, construction worker and other minor things.

I have no history of mental problems or blackout spells, and I've never before this time come forth with this knowledge that I've gained of the aliens. I do so now for several reasons. First, as with many abductees, the conscious memory of these experiences has been a fragmented haze up until recently, second, I've learned through recent hypnosis that I had made a promise to these visitors not to divulge our association until I was given the go ahead to do so. I've recently been given that permission. Even so, there is at least one other species of aliens who do not wish this information to be spread and who have actively sought to curtail my revelatory activities of late and with some success. These negative type aliens are called Targzissians and appear to me to be of reptilian origins.

I wish I could tell you that these celestial visitors have come bringing only good neighborly cheer and some universal message of perfection, but sadly this is not the case. The aliens are not perfect, they are not infallible, and they do have technological, psychological and spiritual limitations. They do not have, in my opinion, a good understanding of the human psyche and are often perplexed at the fickle illogic of humanity's modus operandi.

To some they have appeared as angelic all seeing, all divine apparitions from heaven, while to others they have been perceived as unfeeling, uncaring and terrifying automatons. The truth is that they are some of both, depending upon the individual, the incident of contact and the physical treatment remembered from the encounter. As I have come to know them on a more conscious and intimate basis, having spent as many as nine days in one stretch in their company, I have found them to be fascinating, strange, logical, silly, funny, loving, offensive, careless, ignorant, wondrous, fragile, ominous and momentarily terrifying, but never unbelievable.

The extraterrestrials are real. They have individual personalities, tastes and subtlety differing philosophical opinions. They eat, sleep, have sex of a sort, defecate, burp and even die, either by the rate techno-accident or eventually by choice.

The ones I'm most familiar with, the male and female called Tan and Nela, have even learned something of the concept of bullshitting or joking, as well as amusement expression, via the smile. I have smelled them with my nostrils and touched them with my finger tips, held long and in-depth conversations and at the age of eighteen made love to from nine to a dozen hybrid females for purposes of procreation. Though I've not always been completely satisfied with the answers given to me, I've never yet asked a question of my alien friend, Tan, that he did not answer. And I asked many questions.

Of course, numerous sightings have transpired simply by chance, but I have learned that seldom if ever have there been chance abductions. The subjects are chosen for a reason, even though this reason may not be one of esoteric or revelatory meaning. The reason is often a matter pertaining to genetics and other scientific procedures.

Inasmuch as it is possible for an Earth person to penetrate the inward motivations and intentions of these celestial visitors, I have slowly come to the realization that the human animal is unique to the aliens simply because they feel responsible for a living experiment of their own formulation, if not creation. To allow the human species to perish from the universe would be a sad thing. Therefore, the human race must be preserved as a species in spite of itself, just as numerous other species of creatures have been preserved though we believe them to be extinct.

While the Biaviians, I believe, look upon Earth man as a

kindred spirit, albeit an inferior one, the sentiments of the Targzissians or Targs, I believe to be a different one, more clinical in its projection. I further learned that common reasoning as we have come to know it and our set of values, which, with minor nuances, may be considered universal on Earth, need not necessarily apply to these aliens.

I personally saw numerous forms of life aboard the great mothership, but I learned that there are but seven different species of intelligent technological life forms aboard the huge egg-shaped craft and these are: (1) the Biaviians, (2) the Targzissians, (3) the Stagyians, (4) the Dorians, (5) the Nyptonians, (6) the Insectillians and a (7) the Seventh Form for which I could not learn a name or the nature of their origins.

I'm sure that many people have suffered grievously, more psychologically than physically, and some have probably developed different kinds of psychoses which have on occasion landed them in an asylum, yet I do not feel as if I have undergone any major psychological alterations as a result of my experiences with them. Perhaps this is because I have known of them for most of my life and thus have never been subjected to the preconceived notion that man is the only intelligent life in the universe. It has never occurred to me to believe that extraterrestrials do not exist, thus I simply thought of them as strange and different beings who for some reason of their own chose to befriend me at the age of seven.

This book definitely contains a message for all and erstwhile secret revelatory information for others. Some of the things that I will reveal during the course of this book will serve as a key to unlock the unconscious doors of the minds of other contactees who are not yet consciously aware of the fact. This book will also serve, I am told, as a beacon instrument for those who shall ultimately be chosen as the ones for the great airlift which will transpire in the not too distant future.

Further, this book will serve as an instrument to at least superficially acquaint the masses with the knowledge that the aliens do exist. Thereby helping to psychologically condition them for the mass overfly, which must inevitably happen if the mass airlift is to transpire. It is not the aliens' wish to cause mass panic with their temporary presence, nor to be construed as an invading force.

If you should measure my life as most people measure this existence, that is by education, position, material possessions and tangible accomplishments, I'm afraid you will find me sorely lacking in sociological substance or even pinpointed religious zeal. However, the nature of this fantastic dimension of reality that I have been made privy to tends to supersede what most consider to be the tangible accumulated norms of society.

I do not consider myself an outcast of society, and I'm certainly not a loner. On many occasions in my life, I have been as actively involved in what I believe to be worthy causes, such as the Civil Rights marches and the picketing of the South African Embassy.

I am in empathy with conservationists and all manner of human suffering.

The fact that I have thus far neglected to become stationary and put down roots may have something or much to do with the fact that I consider all the trappings of human society as fleeting, transitory things of little value in comparison with the universal order of reality.

The fact is that most of man's ideology, politics and religions are composed of just so much false and rhetorical bullshit. His politics, wars and professed sense of moralistic worth are but a simple fabricated facade blanketing his true primordial bestiality. His esoteric motivations rarely go beyond eating, defecating and fucking. All exalted position is nothing more than varying stages of the license to steal. Philosophically and spiritually man is a potential God, while realistically he is nothing more than a naked predatory ape with a gun.

Human society, I've come to believe, is composed of two predominant kinds of people, the predators, who through various forms of subterfuge or outright dictatorial tyranny, feed their gluttony by controlling the stupid, bigoted masses which thrive on hate much more than common sense, and the smattering of philosophically prominent ones in between from whence all the rest draw the bulk of their religious and moralistic pseudo persuasion and fleeting inspiration. So I don't attempt to delude myself that my revelations will change the nature of humanity.

But this book will, I hope, reach the ones for which it is intended and also serve to enlighten humanity at large as to the reality of physical things far beyond the scope of our commonly realized dimensions.

I won't dwell unduly upon those portions of my life which do not deal with my time spent in the company of the aliens, because the subject matter covered during my time with them is quite sufficient to fill the manuscript of this book.

What you will gain in knowledge from this book coupled with what you already know will no doubt serve to speed up and bring to maturity the purposes for which it is intended.

A Poem

OMSA LA' JUWANN O-QUA TANGIN WANN

As recited to Martin by Tan 26 September 90

I have traveled far and swiftly, Across yon deep and leaning sky:
I have witnessed a nova's burst, and saw a living planet die.
Across to voids of space unmeasured, Oh yea, Omsa-La-Juwann:
I have pierced the quantum octaves, mastered hyper warps in time.

Vaulting onward o'er the spiral, on a journey here to save:
Fellow beings wrought of madness, from yon weeping, living grave.
Nestled there upon the ether, as a jewel among the stones:
Earth the precious orb of legend, soon your glowing shall be done.

Children of the living waters, possessors of the staff of reason:
Beings of celestial promise, doomed to perish in mid-season.
From the stone axe to the heavens, lo' the vision did not fade:
Still that pulsing seed of hatred, lay thy fate beneath the spade.

Before me the planet lay in shambles, eco-destruction beyond repair:
By the greed of false controllers, acids now permeate the air.
Pristine waters from the mountains, die en-route down to the sea:
Thus to hasten soon the horror, the sapien race may cease to be.

All my dreams of bio-perfection, was but just a futile deed:
Seeking to create a pure utopia, we unleashed a monster seed.
Still within them lay the spirit, to transcend the rabid beast:
And to comprehend the Omsa of the elements of peace.

Oh ye' marvels of creation, why have you not sought the light:
Must you fade into the shadows, of that still, cold, azure night.
Unto you my sign is written, there upon the living fields.
Lo' the circle is eternal, though you perish, you yet shall live.

Interfacing with the acids, beneath some new Jurassic sea:
To turn again and scan the heavens, and to learn again to be, to be.
If I did not breach your stratos, you would surely some day breach mine:
Tis a factor without question, tis a factor but of time.

I have not returned to conquer, nor to alter the flow of fate:
But simply to gather a certain number, soon before it is too late.
Too unstable to embrace, yet far too noble to cast away:
Beautiful life form though unsuccessful, might succeed another day:
There upon the flowering meadows, Oh, shining precious Biaveh.

Chapter 1

The Coming of Tan

I was but seven years of age in November of 1953, when I first saw the strange lights above the river near my home in Northeastern Arkansas. At the time my family lived near the western bank of the Saint Francis River, which is one of the tributaries that feed into the Mississippi.

The lights had appeared above the river for three nights straight at around the same time in the late night or early morning, coming closer with each successive visitation. On the third night the brilliant lights were close enough to our house to cast the glow of their presence onto the walls of my bedroom. It was on this third night that I decided to go out and investigate.

Strangely, my two brothers, who shared the room with me, never awakened to witness the lights. Even when I tried to awaken them, I was never successful. Perhaps this was by design, because ordinarily I would not have been awake at that hour of the morning.

There were four of the lights, and I had watched them, fascinated by their acrobatic displays. They would shoot across the starlit sky from the west and come to an immediate standstill above the river. Then slowly they would circle in a follow-the-leader manner. Or the fourth one would remain stationary while the smaller three circled it. After a time, the fourth light would disengage itself from its companions and descend, glowing ever larger, toward the treetops near the river.

I could not detect any sound. The lights would often change in color and intensity from yellow to white, to red, green and shades of blue. And when they departed, they always buzzed the house, all four following in a row. It was on these occasions that I could feel the vibrations of their engines. The vibrations would grow in intensity as they passed over and diminish as they went away. They would circle back over the opposite direction, move away for a few miles and then just stop and shoot straight upward until they disappeared into the night sky.

On the third night the lights were very close, and it seemed to land behind the trees less than a quarter mile from my home. I put on my jacket and went out. Having explored the river bank on many occasions, I was thoroughly familiar with that area. I was accompanied by faithful and fearless mixed breed dog, Brown Boy.

We soon approached the spot where the ship had landed. Peeking through the bushes, I saw the saucer. It stood in a clearing suspended about twelve feet above the ground, and, though it was moored by three flexible legs, it slowly danced about, like a cork bobbing on water.

Shortly, the ship pulsed pinkish, and I found myself focused in a light beam emanating from the ship. Out of the light strode two little people. They were dressed in shiny blue jump suits and wore bubble type helmets. I was only seven, but they were hardly as tall as me. My faithful dog, Brown Boy didn't make a sound of protest as the two beings took me by the arms and led me toward the ship. When we stepped directly beneath the saucer, there was a blinding white light, and the next thing I knew we were aboard. I found myself laying nude on some kind of table, similar to an operating table.

I can now speak with clarity upon that first encounter because the memories were reawakened in me through hypnosis in early 1988 by the UFO author-researcher Barbara Simon, whom I had met shortly after my 27 December 1987 sighting over the Ozark mountains in Arkansas, during which time I managed to take several Polaroid photos of the craft, before being taken aboard for the fourth time. Since Barbara and I started those regressive hypnosis sessions, my memory of those past incidents has been returning to me with a flood of recall, so much so that it is no longer necessary to undergo the hypnotic sessions in order to key up my memory.

Further, I've learned that the alien Tan told me on that last occasion that all of my memory would shortly return. Possibly engineered by my meeting with Barbara. Certainly a great number of things have transpired since our meeting to substantiate this belief. I will rehash these things in detail later in this book.

When the little people first approached me on the river, I was momentarily terrified. My fear was the result of my not being able to physically resist when they laid hands upon me for the first time and by my inability to move my arms and legs as I lay on the examination table aboard the ship. The presence of a third and fourth alien, whom I later learned to be Stagyians, didn't help matters either.

After we entered the craft, the two small aliens had removed their helmets, and I could now see them clearly from the waist up.

The male was about four feet tall, and the female was a few inches shorter. In actual appearance, male and female differed just slightly in features. The heads were noticeably larger than normal in proportion to the body. The eyes were large, unblinking ovals. The male's eyes were a light to deep gold color, while the female's eyes were blue. The shades of their eyes tended to change depths, depending upon the light and perhaps the emotion.

Their arms were long, the fingertips reaching almost to their knees. Their feet looked flat and kind of splayed. Their hands were long and delicate and had only three fingers and a thumb. The forefinger was longer than the middle finger. They had no outward ear flaps, but tiny holes where the ears should be. The nose had no cartilage and was almost flat against the profile. The mouth was thin-lipped and looked like a slit on the face. The teeth were tiny and uniform, like baby teeth. The chins were sharp and receding and gave the face an egg-like shape.

The female's skin tone was a gray white, and the male's complexion was yellowish brown or golden. The skin colors also changed at times, not in basic color but in subtle tones. They did not look like dangerous monsters, but I could not call them cute either. They did not articulate with their mouths but communicated via telepathy.

The actual physical examination was left to the Stagyians. I could see and feel their long spindly hands. Their touch was cold and clinical. As I've said, I could not move my body, but I could move my eyes and my head with effort.

The Stagyians, by any stretch of the imagination, are very ugly creatures indeed. They stand nearly six feet tall and have dark red leather-like skin draped loosely over their skeletal-like frames. The head is long and prune-like, and the eyes are tiny, black and close set.

Even aboard the craft, they both wore some kind of breathing device over their mouths, and at times you could hear their rapid shallow breathing.

I was later to learn that the Stagyians, in spite of their physical appearance, are considered to be the Pacifists even among the aliens because of their ability to store and retain vast amounts of data and recall and disseminate the same. The Stagyians hold many scientific and other brainy positions among the Biaviians, with whom they are affiliated.

I further learned that the Stagyians are the ones who perform most, if not all, of the physical examinations for the Biaviians on abductees. It is apparently the sight of these ugly but harmless beings that has caused many abductees to remain terrified of the experience, even though I am told that the Biaviians have never physically harmed an abductee, yet I can't truthfully make the same statement in regards to the Targs.

The Stagyians also communicated via telepathy. However, I could never comprehend any of what they were saying. On the other hand, neither could the Biaviians understand the Stagyians except by replaying or filtering their transmissions through some kind of electronic devise.

Strangely, I could hear and communicate with the Biaviians telepathically even as a child. Of course, they had to revert to English from their native tongue, if it can be called that. I was told that most human beings have the dormant ability to communicate telepathically, but it is more pronounced in some, especially the ones who still maintain a greater portion of the original Elohim gene. Apparently I'm one of the gene retainers, and telepathic intercourse with the aliens comes easily to me.

During my physical examination, I was touched from head to foot, scanned with some kind of light probe that resembled a giant eye. The Stagyians may have taken hair samples, toe nail, skin scrapings and saliva from me. It was while I was on the table that I started to communicate with the Biaviians. Tan and Nela spoke to one another in words I couldn't understand as they stood near my feet, and I butted in to their conversation telepathically, saying something like: You better turn me loose, 'cause my daddy's got a big ole shotgun, and he'll shoot you with it. At which they both looked at me with interest. Then they started to converse with me in English.

Tan said that they were not going to harm me but were obligated to momentarily restrain me because I was big and strong and might try to hurt them. Soon I got over my fear of them if not of the Stagyians and convinced them that I wouldn't harm them if they let me up. Initially I had called him a "big head Doodie dog", to which they looked at one another and repeated the phrase "BIK-ADE-DOOEY-DOK". They weren't familiar with the phrase or its meaning, and I didn't bother to explain it to them at the time.

I cannot say exactly how long I remained on the examination table, but after a long while they allowed me to get up and move to a kind of translucent recliner. They didn't seem to be bothered by my nudity at all, and both Nela and Tan seemed to enjoy exploring my body with their hands. Their touch was cool but gentle. They seemed fascinated with my hands, my kinky hair and my sex organs. Even though I could move, my strength was greatly diminished. Tan stuck his finger in my mouth and ran the tip over my teeth, and I bit him slightly, to which he said, "Ooow", and snatched his hand away. I told him that it wasn't polite to put his finger in some one's mouth, and he said something about highly developed verbal resonance.

They spoke to me on occasion and about me to one another or others. I could hear their exchange inside my head, not understanding them.

After a while they stopped examining me and walked over to converse with the Stagyians. It was then that I started to take a good look at the circular room or flight deck. The dome of the room was completely transparent, and you could see out on a 160 degree radius, even though, depending upon your point of focus, the objects outside were distorted by the curve of the dome. I remember that when I was outside looking at the ship the dome had appeared a solid metallic. A console, banana or hot dog shaped, covered about a quarter of the room's outer circle. I didn't see any protruding buttons or levers or even dials on the console, just different spots of pulsing color. The ship was actually piloted by a robot, that is a metallic thing with arms that seemed to float about in front of the console. In the center of the room there was a round disk-like table on which were some neon configurations like a star chart. The exam table and other examining instruments had completely disappeared, and the Stagyians now stood near another console-like thing and seemed to be working.

Presently Tan and Nela returned to me and pointed out of the dome. I saw the Earth small and shining in the distance, about the size of a golf ball, and the moon which was much larger. I could tell that we were going away out into the void of space, and I started to cry.

The alien Tan touched my check and retrieved a teardrop, which he then rubbed upon his brow. He said, "Oh, Martin, I can experience your emotion, yet its meaning is lost unto me. It is well that I may once again relate to sensations long un-recalled. Do you understand?"

But I didn't understand at the time. Over the years I have come to realize what he meant. Apparently the Biaviians, or certain Biaviians, are able to telepathically mesh or interface with certain humans to the extent of actually being able to experience all the earthly emotions and physical sensations that the human feels. I understand that this state of intimacy between the alien and the human is not a common occurrence but a rarity. Yet to actually feel the emotion is not necessarily to know its meaning or the nature of the emotion's logic. While numerous human beings could probably communicate telepathically with the Biaviians, few aliens and humans can achieve the symbiotic state of emotions transmutation. This is sad because I believe that if all the aliens could experience the emotional anguish that most humans go through upon abduction, they wouldn't have made so many mistakes, been so unfeeling or used the same techniques of contact. Over time I believe that I was able to communicate much of this to my alien friend.

I also found that I could transmit some emotions to the female, Nela, but we never achieved the rapport that existed between me and Tan. She seemed more attuned to the sensations of joy, mirth and, perhaps, sensuality, while my occasional attempts at humor or joke telling seemed for the most part to be lost upon Tan. To this day, the little alien remains almost machine-like in his analytical reasoning, most of the time.

Then he turned and pointed out into space and said, "Look, Martin". I looked and saw a brilliant comet shooting out through space and crossing the path of the other three saucers that accompanied us. I forgot my sadness as I watched the great comet. Then one of them said, "Martin, sing me the song". I guess that I had inwardly been singing a song that my mom wrote for me to sing in church, and I began to sing it with my mouth:

I dreamed that the great Judgment morning,
Had dawned and the trumpet had blown!
I dreamed that the nations had gathered,
To Judgment before the great throne.

From the throne came a bright shining angel,
And stood on the land and the sea!
And swore with his hand raised to Heaven,
That time was no longer to be.

And oh with a weeping and wailing.
As the last ones were told of their fate:
They cried to the rocks in the mountains,
They prayed but their prayers were too late.

As I finished the song, the ship moved over near the fiery comet and then began to pace it. Suddenly the ship started to move in a clockwise fashion around the comet, and as we were doing so, the ship began to play the melody of my song. It sounded wonderful and was composed of flutes, trumpets and a host of other magnificent instruments, filling every octave with scores of melodious harmonies.

I don't remember when the aliens dressed me in a fine blue robe or placed the clothlike blue slippers on my feet, but when I noticed myself again they were there.

I saw that we were coming up to the planet Saturn with the great rings of ice and was told that the planet had twenty-three moons. The planet and its rings appeared to me to be devoid of color like a black and white photograph. Then as we passed one of the largest moons I saw it, shining like some great bejeweled egg upon the azure background of the endless sky. "Behold, Martin", said Tan. "This the vessel of our origins". This was the first time that I laid eyes upon the great mothership. I was to visit it again on at least two future occasions, and it would take the contents of the latter visits to reawaken the memory of that first visit at seven years of age. Bear with me, dear reader.

Chapter 2

The Seven Intelligent Life Forms

I left home and went out on my own in the big world at the age of fourteen and because regular employment was denied me at that age, I did what so many before me had done. I joined the migrant hordes that gathered the produce crops seasonally up and down the Eastern seaboard. I was always tall for my age, and my upbringing on the farm had conditioned me to hard work so it wasn't difficult for me to do a man's work. When I gave my age as being eighteen, it was rarely questioned.

Among the migrants two new worlds were opened up to me. The factor of actually making money of my own and sex. My first sexual consummation was with a lady at least twice my age. She was about thirty. After finding out that I was indeed a virgin to the sensual arts, I became, for her, a most precious commodity and she sought, albeit unsuccessfully, to deny my prodigious attributes to other women. She attempted this in two ways, one by literally inundating me with sensual activity, and by whipping the living shit out of any other woman who got too close.

It fascinated me to find myself the focus of so much feminine attention and made me aware of the rawest forms of human aggression concerning these matters. With the cunning and stealth of some obsessed pride of lionesse, the women succeeded in luring me away from my claimant and sampling my adolescent treasures. With equal stealth and complicity on my part, I might add.

It further seems, though I wasn't aware of it at the time, that the women had discovered something extraordinary about me. If I perchanced to make love to a certain lady several times, this lady seemed to grow visibly younger. Of course, it may be reasoned, and with some justification, that a woman in love tends to feel and act younger. However, I've had a number of women show me and tell me of the disappearance of facial lines, wrinkles and the renewal of youthful skin texture, as well as the inner knowledge of past youth, etc. At that time such things were lost upon me, and I didn't put much stock in these revelations. However, I would find out the truth of them during my second visitation and time spent among the aliens at the age of eighteen in 1964.

It is a fact that at the age of fifteen and sixteen I sometimes made love to eight or ten different women a day and was not unduly overtaxed in doing so, but even the novice Casanova must eventually reach his limitations. I found it expedient to literally escape my admirers after a time on many occasions.

It was during one of my self-imposed spans of abstinence at the age of seventeen that I discovered that I possessed another more profitable talent, the art of fist fighting, bare knuckled fashion.

At six feet two inches and 170 pounds, I became a most formidable and deadly foe in the timeless art of one-on-one combat. Because of my string bean physique and obvious youthful inexperience, the other fighter, being bigger and older, was always the odds on favorite, thereby giving me and my trainer, Big Manuel, an opportunity to make good money. With all due modesty, I can say that during the year and a half of my pugilistic career I never lost a fight, but these victories were not all won without paying a price, and I still have the scars to prove it.

In October of 1964, I had decided to quit fighting, take my nest egg and return to Arkansas. Big Manuel concurred with this decision after my last opponent up East had died of injuries sustained during our bout.

Truly remorseful for my part in the man's death, I gave about half of my nest egg to his wife and four children and went on my first drunken spree over in New York City. I awakened a week or so later in a cheap hotel with an equally drunk middle-aged lady in bed beside me. Of my hard-earned fortune, I still had sixteen dollars and change. This is why I agreed to stop in Alabama on my way south for one last fight.

On November 14, 1964, in the red hills near the town of Oneonta, Alabama, I fought a man called Grutch, and I took him down in the 33rd round. In the process I suffered a broken nose, two fractured ribs, a sprung thumb, the loosening of several jaw teeth, a black eye and numerous bruises and contusions.

When Big Manuel departed for his home in Tennessee, I decided to stay on in the camp a while and recuperate. The camp contractor's wife and three daughters took on the job of ministering to my wounds. To show my appreciation for their angelic care, I was obliged to make love to all but the youngest daughter. It was for this reason that the camp contractor and four of his henchmen, two of whom were married to the two oldest daughters, set upon my person with frightful aggression, and dumped me, injured and penniless, in the hills several miles from the camp with instructions under penalty of death to make myself scarce in those parts.

It was after midnight when I saw the lights come flying silently across the sky from the northeasterly direction. Passing directly over me, close enough to brightly illuminate the surrounding area and to cause the hair of my head to crackle with static and the bushes to tremble, the craft set down in the weeds off to my right.

I went to investigate and saw the ship standing nearly immobile just above the ground in a clearing. The hum of the engines was barely audible, but I could feel its vibrations. As I walked toward the ship, I could feel the static electricity all over my body and see the leaves trembling and moving about on the ground all about me. The ship was about thirty feet in diameter, flattened on the bottom and domed on the top. A line of blue lights circled the perimeter, and a blue, red and yellow light shone from the undercarriage. The body of the ship was a dull metal that glowed with a varying blue-white intensity.

The dome cleared and I could see two small beings standing and looking out. Then I distinctly heard a voice saying, "Come forth, Martin, for we must leave in haste." I literally ran beneath the ship and looked up to see a spiral door open, a dazzling white light, and I was in a tube shaped chamber, which nearly touched my shoulders. The chamber was lined with thousands of tiny lights of many colors. I could feel the lights play over my body like the ripple of warm water. I was acutely conscious all the time. Then I smelled a very strong perfume-like odor for a moment. A door in the chamber whisked, and I was blinking in the soft light of the command deck. It suddenly occurred to me that this experience was not new to me and that I knew the two aliens that were awaiting my arrival.

"It is well to see you, Martin", said Tan. "And it's good to see you again", I said.

This time I was not subjected to the extensive physical examination of my childhood but was led directly to the translucent recliner type chair. I noted that the material from which the chair was made tended to cleave to the curvatures of my body, like jello, and would give to my hand-print wherever I touched it. It was cool but pleasant. The interior of the ship was also cool, not freezing but naturally cool.

Once again Tan and Nela started their hands-on exam of my nude body. Where my clothes had gone, I cannot say. I was still experiencing sharp stabs of pain from my last encounter with the contractor and his men, and every time I felt a sharp pang, the alien

Tan would flinch indicating that he was attuned to the sensations, so much so that he was forced to snatch his hands away, recoiling from the pain.

I looked out and saw the lights of a city off to my right, perhaps it was Birmingham. Then I saw the four dimensional video projections of two jet planes approaching at high speed. The form of the planes was displayed on the dome glass like modern day computer images composed of schematic type graphic lines.

I said, "Tan, we'd better get the hell out of here, because those jets have missiles". And he said, "Fear not, Martin, for we are but little more than apparitions before their capabilities". At that very moment the ship shot straight up through the clouds. Within ten seconds I could clearly see the outline of Florida, the eastern coast and South America. In another ten seconds the entire planet was a basketball sized marble, visibly growing smaller before my eyes, yet I did not feel any physical sensation of motion.

I can only venture to guess, but I had the distinct feeling that Tan was really enjoying the painful sensations that he picked up from me. It was almost as if he was in ecstasy. However, Nela didn't seem unduly affected by those sensations. After a while she asked, "Martin, you are feeling a great discomfort?" And I said, "Yes, Nela, can you give me something for the pain?", at which she took an instrument that looked like a small flashlight and touched my left big toe. Almost immediately a numbing sensation moved up my leg and soon encompassed my whole body and the pain went away. Only then did Tan cease his writhing and humming.

"Oh, Martin", says he, "these are marvelous sensations, where did you acquire them, what are they called?" I said, "What you are feeling is pain, which was gotten as a result of a 'whipped ass'."

"A whi-ped hass", he repeated. "Martin, how does one acquire a 'whi-ped hass'?" "Well", says I, "the best way to get a whipped ass is to say something about my mama or in this case, to get caught screwing a contractor's wife". "Oh, and what is a mama and a con-rac-dar?"

"Jeez... What a puddin' head". I thought aloud. "Pud-don ade" said Nela. And so it went for a good while. I actually felt quite superior to these little people because they didn't know from shit about the most ordinary things. I came to the conclusion that they really didn't have any conception of what a mother is. Oh, they knew that humanoids bi-peds gave birth after approximately 270 days of gestation, but of the bond of motherhood, they had no true knowledge.

I was to learn that these aliens were very ignorant of the human experience, the human senses of love, hate, jealously, envy greed, conscience, etc. I concluded that were Tan a human being he would be considered somewhat freaky as he seemed to get off on pain.

Slowly it began to dawn on me why he had chosen me as his conduit into the human order. It seems that there is a faction among the Biaviians who have decided to try to learn through hand-on intercourse the nuances of the human factor. Certain ones among the Biaviians are highly sensitive, telepathically and emotionally, to certain humans, and these are the ones chosen to gather the data and attempt to pass it along to others of their species.

"Martin, these sensations are very forceful. We must acquire them again and to a greater degree", he said. I kindly explained to him that it would be much better if he personally gained the experience by getting his ass whipped, thereby not having to trouble himself with picking it up from me. Furthermore I suggested that he could easily participate in this ecstatic experience by setting down in Birmingham and shouting "General Lee is a punk", to wit he would be shortly blessed with an ass whipping of scientific proportions.

Now with my pain gone, I felt a kind of esoteric buoyance, and I really started to enjoy playing with their heads. It occurred to me that by hanging on to my every word these aliens could conceivably be led astray. So I started to use more care in my explanations to them. It seemed to me that their ability to separate seriousness from general bullshit was nil. Yet time and experience slowly led me to conclude that these beings, though naive to much of the human equation, were by no means fools. It is only that their way of rationalizing things is different from most of ours, only to the extent that they don't clutter the obvious or falsify the facts. No Biaviian could ever be an Earth lawyer, preacher or politician. Also, logic exceeds honesty in its straight forward context. Logic is both divine and cruel.

I asked them where they were from, and they said that they were from the planet Biaveh (be-ah-vey), which is 4.6999 travel years from Earth. It is a constellation consisting of eight suns, seven planets and nine moons. That is, in this star system there are seven intelligence bearing planets, which are presently working on this joint venture of exploration. They all share a common mothership, which is of Biaviian origin, though their scout ships are of different dimensions and origins.

Tan tells me that the Biaviians and Targzissians have been visiting this planet since the Jurassic era of the Mesozoic period. He also tells me that these seven intelligences are not the only ones who have visited the Earth. However, the Biaviians and the Targs are the two principal species who have foremost scientific claims to the planet.

I asked Tan, "How many living planets are there in the Milky Way Galaxy?" He said, "Martin, should you visit a different living planet each day for the duration of your physical gestation, you should not even begin to tax the number. Nor could I". And I've learned that Tan is about ten thousand years old as we measure time, which is young for a Biaviian.

Further, he told me that not even the Biaviians know the

true number of living planets in the cosmos but could only theorize. Nor do the aliens possess what we consider to be supernatural powers, such as foreseeing the future of knowing tomorrow's lottery number, for these things depend upon a lot of unforeseen variables. However, their collection of physical data and knowledge of all historic circumstances puts their deductive technology far beyond our own. Thus they have ventured to theorize as to the future state of the planet. Their findings lead them to believe that they will most probably find it necessary to save the human species from extinction in the not too distant future, just as they have preserved specimens of all other living things which have thus far existed upon this planet since their first visitation perhaps 600 million years ago.

He also tells me that none of the seven intelligent life forms visiting here actually evolved upon their present home planets, but instead colonized those planets at a later more technological time of their evolution. Yes, it is possible to technologically destroy all life upon or even the planet itself. I understand that this very thing has been done on many occasions before some where and will no doubt be done again. All intelligent life forms will, without fail, seek to travel beyond their planet of origin, either by choice of by necessity or both, providing they don't self-destruct before this can be accomplished. The Earth, unfortunately, has reached the critical zone on the self-destructive probability scale.

All of these things and much, much more I learned during the course of my many long conversations with Tan and from assumptions and intuitive knowledge gained during my stay among them. Tan had a kind of strange way of speaking. In many cases I simply had to surmise what he meant, that is, on many occasions the meaning far exceeded the spoken words. As we progress through this book, I will attempt to indoctrinate you in these revelations to the foremost depths of my ability to do so, and I must beg your indulgence in excuse of my limitations.

From what Tan tells me, the human being or the Homo sapien was not the first intelligent bi-ped to inhabit this planet. Of course, the Biaviians and Targs themselves were here long before man evolved and began to introduce a number of hybrids strains upon the young planet. I'm told that at that time the journey from his home to Earth required thousands of Earth years and most of the introduced strains did not fare well and a number of factors contributed to their untimely demise. Some were so biologically at odds with the planet that they died out before developing immunities to infections, and some to natural disasters, coupled with predatory invasions. I'm told that some were giants, while others were very small, that is only inches in height. Still others devolved instead of progressing in intelligence. The factor of inter-breeding disseminated several strains to the extent of self or necessary experimental failure destruction.

A few managed to actually achieve a notable state of

technology before some great calamity befell them. There were those who endured for a longer span than the homo erectus has thus far been credited with. However, none before were as successful in numerical reproduction and diversified adaptation as the human species. The human being has an advantage over the first colonizers in that the human being is composed of indigenous as well as alien chromosomes, while the first ones were all foreign transplants. To this day, I am told that the full-blooded Biaviians cannot live long in the Earth's atmosphere without the aid of artificial life support systems. Even the mixed breed hybrids so recently introduced among us find the factor of infectious organisms quite deadly and are forced to continually consume many kinds of medicinal compounds. Generally the hybrid's stay among us is limited to short spans of time. I was not told just what their purpose was in doing so.

Yes, the aliens do have and have for thousands of years maintained permanent bases on the Earth and on some neighboring planets. Do the aliens take anything from the Earth? Yes. They are forever collecting things like plants, insects and a host of other living specimens of creatures, including man. However, with man it is more than just a scientific specimen thing, as is exemplified by my relationship with them. I do believe that we are afforded such privileges as one intelligent species bestow upon another. For instance, I saw numerous examples of Earth creatures of the lower order in life and in frozen animation aboard the mothership but never an example of man like so treated.

The Aliens, I'm told, some times take large quantities of fauna and sea water in order to preserve certain living creatures in their natural habitat. I once saw a large quantity of fresh water fish ejected into space encased in a huge liquid filled bubble. I was told that the numbers aboard the great mothership were kept constant in this manner.

Also, the great ship accumulated large quantities of by-products or trash, which were rendered into dust via disintegrators and then ejected into space. I learned that the Biaviians are vegetarians and consume no flesh. I believe, though I can't swear to it, that they don't consume any solids. In all of the time I spent with Tan, I only once saw him drink about two ounces of a red liquid, the color of red wine. Nor did I ever see him urinate or defecate, though I'm sure that they must at some time.

I saw and was at times in the same proximity of some of the Targzissians, but I couldn't learn much of them from Tan. That is, we never discussed them at length. I was never permitted to go in to one of their V-wing ships nor in to their particular area of the great ship. However, I saw a few of them close up in other parts of the ship, as well as a small group of black-haired oriental looking men, dressed in black suits that some times accompanied the Targs. They always wore dark glasses, but once one of them removed his shades and looked directly at me. His eyes were reptilian or cat-like with only a slit for a pupil. These creatures and the Targs always gave me an uneasy feeling akin to fear.

The full-blooded Targs look to me to be of reptilian origin, and their insignia, which I saw upon the great door to their sector, is a rendition of a winged serpent. The Targs have space ships of different shapes, the most common of which is a V-winged design, which may be a hundred feet across, while some might be a thousand feet across. They also have the saucers which are flat topped instead of domed and may sport two tiny tail fins. I once saw a Targ tanker as big as a football field harvesting ice from the rings of Saturn. It was shaped like a giant loaf of bread.

During the course of my conversations with Tan, I learned that the Targs have done some not so nice things on Earth. They caused a blackout on the east coast some years ago when one of their craft expended a large charge of electrons too close to power lines. Their electromagnetic field may sometimes cause engines to malfunction. The Targs, I am told, have taken organs and hemoglobin from domestic animals and then carelessly left the animals' carcasses laying around for the owner to find. This is a no-no, and they no longer do it.

A few Earth people have suffered detrimental radiation burns from the Targs' decontamination procedures, which for a time did not make allowances for the different tolerance levels of the individual human. The Targs may be flesh eaters, consuming muscle protein, though I can't say for sure. Many of them carry a plastic and metallic-looking stick-like instrument on their waist belt, and I can only guess as to its purpose.

A Targ stands about five feet tall and is slender. The forehead slopes and the skull is pointed. The ears are sculpted into the head, small, pointed flat. The nose is a sharp close setting beak, and the mouth is wide and frog-like with no protruding lips. The arms are long and bony, and the hands are webbed with five fingers. The neck is bony with perceptible notches down to the spine. A tail is visible on some. The legs are bent forward at the knees, and the feet are too long and encased in a kind of heel-less boot with rubberlike soles. When they walk, it is a kind of mechanical gait.

The Targs also communicate via telepathy, and later in this book I will explain how the only physical pain I have thus far suffered at the hands of aliens was done to me by a Targ. Yet that encounter with the Targs gave me the answer to a question that had been plaguing me for a long time, namely why it is not possible for the aliens to subjugate man through mind control and why it would be very dangerous for them to even try it.

The Targzissians, or at least some Targs, are able to communicate telepathically with man. I know this because I have personally communicated with one of them. The resonance and texture of that telepathic exchange was definitely different from that which I experienced with Tan, but nonetheless a definite fact.

I'm sure that on occasion the Targs also abduct humans, but I don't know how well these captives fare while in their possession. There may be some hybrid experimentation by Targs upon humans, as is exemplified by the existence of the white-skinned oriental-looking men seen with them. These men, if they never removed their glasses, could pass as human without much trouble. Yet, while it is easy to attribute some human qualities to the Biaviians, I could never detect such qualities in the Targs, but then I never had an opportunity to associate with them.

The third form of intelligence with whom I came into proximity, though I did not develop a rapport with, was the Stagyians, whom I have spoken of before.

Among the seven intelligences, the Stagyians are the only ones I know of who do not have shuttle craft of their own creation. Thus they are not an independent force but are instead obliged to work in close collusion with the Biaviians, and should you ever see a Stagyian, it will be aboard a Biaviian ship. Further, I'm told that the Stagyians do not possess interplanetary space ships even on their home planet but are visited by and protected by neighboring life-bearing planets. On their home planet the Stagyians are great horticulturists and herbalists. Stagyians are educated and used on Biaveh because they naturally possess the extraordinary ability to store, disseminate and recall vast quantities of information and therefore make the best doctors, physicians, mathematicians and other brainy professionals.

The Stagyians effectively conquered physical aging in Biaviians and now humans, as well as overcoming the problem of faster than light speed travel and hyperspace trajectory. It is the brain chromosomes of the Stagyians that form the central brain of the largest Biaviian computers, in which data is stored and disseminated by living matter. Stagyians perform most of the physicals on human abductees and are working with Biaviians to duplicate an Earth-like ecology for the transplanted humans on Biaveh and for those who have yet to be transplanted there.

Teleportation from one point to another has not yet been perfected to the galaxy to galaxy status but is some times used over distances of less than a light year. Suspended animation, brain transplants, cloning and lab controlled birth are already perfected things. The transplanting of the living brain into bi-ped mechanical skeletons or bodies has also been accomplished. The ultimate in Bionics, which are called the Ancient Ones, I shall speak of further in this book.

By nature, Stagyians are docile and pacifist and constant in emotions. If working on a particular theory, a Stagyian may lapse into a dreamlike contemplative state and not emerge until another step in the equation is found, even if it takes a thousand years.

From the human standpoint, Stagyians are very ugly

creatures. However, I do not believe that humans have anything to fear from these beings. Apparently the Stags are not able to breathe an Earth-like atmosphere as I never saw one moving around, even on the mothership, without wearing some kind of breathing apparatus, which covered the mouth and nose. Therefore, I never got a chance to see exactly what they look like. A Stagyian's body movements are slow and fluid. They never seem to get in a hurry, and they communicate telepathically in short bursts of sound. I understand that so much information may be compacted in these short bursts that not even Biaviians can comprehend them without recording and decoding transmissions.

The fourth group of aliens are very interesting, both in mannerisms and physique, but unfortunately I was unable to learn much about them. They are called Dorians, and they are definitely Caucasian in appearance. The Dorians are tall in stature, about six feet tall. They are all blonde and they wear their hair in a kind of Prince Charming style. The hair doesn't quite reach the shoulder, and the bangs are clipped across the forehead. The forehead is very high, and the eyes are large and wide set and may be blue, gray, green or brown. Their nose is tiny but well-formed, and the lips are pouty and full, though the mouth is not very wide. The chin is pointed and small in comparison with the wide upper face. The skin tone is almost chalky white in color.

The upper body is long and the neck is small and slightly elongated. The waist is very narrow and the hips flared. The thighs are strong looking, the lower legs are slightly bowed and skinny and the feet are flat and rather long.

The Dorians are able to articulate with their mouths as well as communicate telepathically. I saw male and female Dorians aboard the mothership, but I got the impression that the females were the pilots, while the males held other positions like caring for the ships on the ground. I'm sure that the Dorians saw me, but we never communicated beyond making eye contact.

I saw at least two kinds of Dorian space craft. One was the domed saucer-like ship with a very sharp outer rim, as opposed to the curved outer rim of the Biaviians saucer. The Dorian saucer rested on four legs with round pads at the bottom, and they disembarked via a walk ramp. The ship was an aluminum metallic color and not as smooth as the Biaviian ships. You could see thin seams and rivets, which set smooth with the hull's surface. Instead of the transparent dome, there was port holes around the top of the ship and in repose the ship made a hissing sound.

There was another saucer shaped ship which was literally coated with shiny silver balls of different sizes. I was told that this particular ship was capable of making the intergalactic journey from the mothership to the home planet. There was a third Dorian ship which looked like a number of metal donuts, beginning large and tapering to smaller sizes in a beehive configuration.

Dorians all looked alike in general terms. They were not identical in height, eye color or color of dress, which was brown jump-suits with yellow gloves and boots for the ground crew, to light green, blue with red outlines, red with black stripes and a number of other color combinations for the females. However, they all wore the same hair style, and the hair was approximately the same color. The facial features were too much alike to discount a common genetic kinship, and the milky white skin complexion was unvarying.

When working on the ships, the crew wore life support helmets with small backpacks, but inside a glassed-in recreational lounging area, none of them wore the apparatus. I was never taken into this area but could see them clearly from the great spiraling causeway of the mothership as we passed.

One thing seemed common among all of the aliens and that is the lack of laughter and revelry one generally associates with a group of soldiers or workmen. Everybody always seemed either serious or simply passive. Maybe these things transpired, but I didn't witness them. I feel as if the presence of a human being on the great ship was nothing new as none of the multitude seemed to pay undue notice to my presence. In fact, the closest thing I ever had to human companionship in character and mannerisms was a furry creature who remained a constant companion to me during my stay aboard the mothership. I named this creature 'Question', though I never learned what his species name is. I will speak more extensively on my friend Question later in this work. I know that the Dorians are visiting the planet Earth regularly, but I don't know to what extent they have associated with human beings.

The fifth form of life is a strange one indeed, but I'm told that they have a long history of earthly contact and intercourse with humans. They are called Nyptonians and are very bizarre in appearance.

The Nyptonians are about five feet tall and are nearly as wide as they are tall and though wearing a life support suit and helmet, I could see that their skin was blue. The inside of the helmet, was coated with drops of liquid. This is because the Nyptonians are more at home in water and can live on land only with support of the life suits.

The head comes to a peak, and the eyes are a vertical slash instead of the horizontal slash of humans. A configuration resembling gills can be seen following the contours of the jaw-line. They have no noticeable neck, and the shoulders are square, super muscled and powerful looking. The arms and legs resemble elephant limbs and even the feet are broad and almost perfectly round. I saw several of them from time to time. They were never walking but riding on the transport disks, which were much in use aboard the great ship.

The Nyptonians are also called Nomos or Namons and maintain several undersea bases on Earth. They come from a very large planet and live beneath the waters of that planet, yet they breathe air, perhaps like a fish. The Biaviians and the Dorians also have underwater bases on Earth, as well as subterranean bases, and one each near the poles of Earth. However, neither of them is adapted to the water like the Nyptonians. I'm told that the Targs prefer more temperate climes like the tropics.

The Nyptonians are great explorers and teachers, according to Tan, and have stayed to oversee a number of scientific experiments on various planets in the cosmos. I saw one of their ships in space near the mothership, and it was a huge thing that reminded me of a dirigible, lined with port holes from whence a number of smaller ships departed and entered. I was told that this mothership was the kind that would stay in orbit around a given planet as a support or home ship for the scientists on the surface of the planet. However, this ship was not capable of making the intergalactic journey back to the home planet or a least was much too slow to do so. It would be brought back aboard the much larger Biaviian mothership for such an extended journey.

I gathered that the Nyptonians do not literally live in the water like a fish but instead live in fabricated underwater structures from whence they venture forth. I noted on an Earth atlas type map that I saw aboard the great ship that there is a large underwater base some ninety miles off the East coast of Florida. However, the largest aqua base by far in this solar system is located at the northern polar region of the planet Mars.

Further, the Nyptonians are great authorities on sea creatures, and are I believe, in charge of over-seeing the facet of the combined mission. On two occasions I had an opportunity to view the fauna and living sea creatures in the Hyborian garden, not the levitating gardens, aboard the great ship. Many of these creatures I have never seen before on Earth; a long-necked monster with flippers which must have been forty feet in length, a scorpion-looking shellfish which was about ten feet long and a monstrous shark maybe sixty feet in length.

In this garden there was also a family of hairy apelike people or creatures, male, female and two younger ones. The male must have been eight feet tall, and they were eating raw fish. Yet the number of living examples was tiny in comparison to the numerous specimens in frozen suspension. I could view the familiar and unfamiliar creatures along a section that I call the corridor of ice. I could have spent months just looking at all the different species of things in this area, but of course time would not permit it.

The sixth form of intelligent life still gives me bad dreams on occasion even though they have given me no direct cause to fear them. They have another name, but I call them the Insectillians because they are, by any stretch of the word, from the insect order of life. Even under hypnosis I found it difficult recalling this creature.

Its description is thus: the lower body is that of a locust or large grasshopper, while the upper body is indicative of the praying mantis with four arms equipped with thorny claws like a scorpion's. The head is similar to a praying mantis's head with two short antenna. The lower body is encased in a prismatic plastic bubble, while a similar apparatus fits over the head leaving the torso exposed.

I saw this creature in the Great Chamber of the Council of the Seven. Upon this council sits one representative from each of the intelligent species. I was taken before this council on two occasions, once when I was seven and again when I was eighteen.

There was a beautiful book in there which lay open and suspended upon a levitating disk I was told that my genealogy was recorded in this book, going back for untold ages. In explanation, Tan told me that each individual's genetic code will undergo numerous spans of biological diffusion but will, either by design or mathematical progression, eventually be duplicated with little change from the original again and again down through the ages, and this genetic journey will take us across nationalities, race and sex. In controlled circumstances, the proper genetic combination will recur approximately every fourteen generations, while in uncontrolled circumstances it may take longer and cannot be pinpointed or projected even by the extraterrestrials.

I don't know exactly what Tan meant by controlled circumstances, but I've gathered this much; those things we consider of unique value are in themselves a kind of imposed control. Everything from race, religion, social customs and practices, lifestyles, language and prejudices tend to create a state of genetic pooling that resists unchecked biological diffusion. Wars of conquest, the explorative and transient nature of humans as well as migratory lifestyles have caused a great mixing and diffusion of the gene duplicity recurrence, so much so that the Biaviians have not managed to make the easy relocation of catalogued genetic patterns an exact science. In other words, about fifty or sixty percent of the time they abduct a party who doesn't check out. However, once having located a desired party, they have no problem keeping track of them for the duration of that life span. Does that make sense to you?

Throughout the universe, the insect order of life is by far the most abundant, and according to Tan, it is the most tenacious, diversified and adaptable order of life, the most synchronized and prolific. However, it is also the slowest order in coming to technologically intelligent fruition. He told me that the insect order, or Skreed, aboard the great ship is the oldest member of all the intelligent species there, even predating the reptiles by billions of years. Even now their rhythmic biological synchronization does not foster individuality, and yet they have achieved a state of technology which is far beyond our own in many ways, while in others it still remains in realm of lower logic.

The Skreed are at present mining one of the moons of Saturn

and live in below ground modules. However, they don't employ robotics to do their work, even though many of them perish as a result of accidents and faulty design.

As far as I know, the Skreed have no interest in the mammalian order on Earth, and any close contacts with humans are purely accidental. They do have ships of their own which resemble a barbell with two large balls, one on each end, and one smaller ball in the middle, with numerous port holes or round windows along the surface of the balls.

I saw a video scan of their home planet once and saw their living structures. Can you imagine termite mounts a hundred stories high, leaning off center with numerous smoother prism surfaces, like grotesque, upside down carrots, sitting in a moss-carpeted valley with thousands of below ground earthen domes poking up from the soil, winged insects as big as helicopters gliding the skies and a red sun casting shades of blue over a foreboding panorama?

According to Tan, the insects generally end up inheriting most living planets, not because of technological conquest but by simply surviving all the destructive efforts of other higher forms. The mere thought that man could one day have to deal with six feet tall armed locusts is enough to give you nightmares. I began to understand the aliens reluctance to accept man into this celestial coalition. While man might possess the ability to accept the Biaviians or Dorians as superiors, he could never begin to accept the Targs or the Insectillians.

The seventh intelligent form of life is odder still in its dimensions. I know less about them than all of the others yet I find them less repulsive and threatening than say the Targs or Insectillians. In physical description, the seventh form may be safely called formless. It is a glob of life consisting of two hearts, various intestines and a single large translucent eye, floating in a pink liquid. All of this is encased in a clear test tube looking container with a curved bottom upward and the open mouth downward. The life form sits on a polished metal base and remains levitated about a foot above the floor. Visible blue arcs of static electricity continually play about the form. There is no body structure or visible appendages.

When I asked how this form could possibly build and maintain a technological order, Tan explained to me that to these creatures such things are simple by virtue of their telekinetic abilities and their extensive use of robotics. Either I cannot recall or was never given a name for them. However, I had no problem recalling what they looked like.

I understand that this form collects data from the Earth and neighboring bodies by dispatching numerous small electromagnetic modules or globes. These luminous spheres are the eyes and limbs of the seventh form. Just precisely what part they play in the scheme of things I could not discover. I do remember that a blue electrical arc from the lips reached out and traced the outline of my body, leaving me with a peaceful, happy feeling.

These are the seven forms of intelligent life aboard the great mothership. Let me reiterate. These are by far not the only forms of intelligent life inhabiting the Milky Way and other galaxies nor are they the only intelligent forms who have visited Earth or perhaps have yet to visit this planet.

Regardless of the scientific calculations on the theoretical probabilities of life bearing planets, all of these theories will have to be rewritten with future revelations. There is an unknown but large number of intelligent life forms which are much older than our own, and there are many other forms still in the earlier evolutionary stages.

While many of our foremost scientists tend to believe that the brain and opposing thumb and forefinger of the Homo sapien makes it the greatest proponent of intelligent probability, this is true in one sense only. The mammal is the rarest form of intelligent life in this galaxy, but is by far not the most abundant form of intelligence here. Insect, reptile, fowl and other forms we haven't even conceived of are out there. Some of these forms conception of reality is so far different from our own that we would escape their presence by virtue of simply being of no scientific interest to them.

Chapter 3

Time, Space, Propulsion

The great Biaviian mothership is an awesome and beautiful thing to behold. At seven years of age I'm sure that I did not possess the faculty to truly appreciate the magnanimity of this wondrous craft and even now the proper words of descriptive force tend to elude me.

During our journey to the great ship in 1964, I was taken on a quick tour of our solar system. Tan spoke to me as having lost a subspace whisper craft and its four crew members a few years earlier in the southwest. The ship exploded as a result of a malfunction in the electromagnetic propulsion system, and he told me that the remains of the crew members and the debris of the ship were collected by Earth men.

A few years before that a Dorian remote controlled disk malfunctioned and crashed on the Pacific Island of Japan and was retrieved by the Japanese almost intact. From this find came the first great leaps in their mini-electronic technology.

You see, the principles of electronic transmission and computer data dissemination are relatively the same and must conform to the numerical laws of mathematics. Man has not yet learned to circumvent, alter or manipulate these laws as the aliens have. While man may theorize on quantum physics and time travel, he has not yet managed to devise the mechanical means to do so nor to develop the proper materials. Should he endure long enough as a species, he would eventually accomplish these things, some of which could only be executed in the vacuum of deep space using materials and robotics which are yet beyond his means. The aliens do not underestimate man and recognize the fact that should humanity pool its collective intelligence without regard to race, sex, nationality and political or religious idioms there is no limit to what he can accomplish. For instance, certain metals and composites thereof, which are rare upon the planet Earth, may be found in abundance on certain uninhabited bodies in space. The Biaviians have the technology to work on the surface of Saturn and to relay solar rays from the sun in abundance, as well as to utilize numerous kinds of energy rays.

The mothership is a great egg-shaped craft with both ends equally curved, instead of the one smaller end of a true egg. It is forty kilometers across the center or about twenty-eight miles. We had just finished doing an aerobatic thing through the rings of Saturn when the first sight of her assailed my senses. At first, I perceived her as a pulsing silver star surrounded by a cluster of three much smaller stars that flashed a host of different brilliant colors.

At that distance I couldn't possibly imagine its true size, and yet, as we drew closer, she continued to grow and to grow. Only then did I begin to realize the hugeness of the mothership. To my right I saw a number of V-winged Targ ships heading in, and to my left were a number of saucers coming away. Some of these ships were anywhere from thirty to a thousand feet in width, but they would appear only as black specks when I first noticed them coming away from the great egg. In this manner did I start to conceive its true dimensions.

I didn't know what our air speed was, but it must have been thousands of air miles per hour. When the ships before us approached the mothership, they seemed to simply disappear instead of slowing down and entering some visible landing bay opening. The skin or hull of the mothership seemed unbroken as it absorbed the incoming or expelled the outgoing craft.

The three small stars surrounding her, I was told were sentinel globes, and their purpose was to protect the mothership from all outside danger. No matter if this danger came in the form of fabricated projectiles or meteor showers, it could not approach beyond a certain distance without suffering total destruction. I estimated each of these globes to be about seven miles in diameter.

When you approach a thing the size of the mothership, after you get close enough, it appears to be just one endless flat wall, and you cannot see the curvature of the ship looking up, down or to the side. Since Tan didn't seem to slow his air speed upon our approach, I panicked and said, "Tan, slow this mother-fucker down! There's no door. We're going to hit!"

Yet even before I could form a decent blood-curdling scream, we were upon it and through my fingers I saw it happen. Like the super swift spiral shutter of a camera, a circular door opened just enough to accommodate the width of our ship and closed behind us in less than a heart beat. This procedure transpired two more times in blinding succession, and we were sitting motionless within the bowels of the great ship, from ten thousand miles per hour to zero in one second. According to the laws of physics, this is not supposed to be possible but tell that to the Biaviians.

The only physical sensation I noticed was a momentary blurring of vision. Then, as my vision cleared, I looked out to my right and to my left and viewed what appeared to be miles and miles of space ships of various dimensions as far as the eye could see and beyond. Biaviians by the score and a smattering of Dorians, Targs and Stagyians mulled about and literally thousands of robots of all descriptions.

We exited through the bottom of the saucer, which was bobbing just slightly while being anchored by three metal rope type legs. Then we walked a good distance, accompanied by the animal I call Question, before entering a hall. We stopped upon a translucent disk type thing, which lifted gently from the surface about six inches and moved along at a brisk walking pace.

After about two miles another door whisked open, and we stepped from our disk onto an even larger disk and moved onto the great spiraling causeway. What I saw took my breath away. I was standing and looking upon another world, a world which was fashioned by the hands of intelligent beings, breathtaking in its dimensions and seemingly impossible to the human conception.

On the causeway were hundreds if not thousands of other Biaviians of all ages and skin complexions, male and female. They were all short of stature, the males being around four feet and the females a few inches shorter. They ranged in skin tone from chalk white to olive black, and their eyes ran the spectrum of colors.

They were also dressed in a number of different colored garments, though no jewelry. Every color from silk black, numerous shades of blue, with a smattering of oranges, yellows and reds thrown in. I also saw two obviously very old Biaviian males pass us. They did not use the transport disks but were levitating along, and they were dressed in purple robes. Two of the only four robes of this color I ever saw there.

Most wore the light toga type robes similar to my own, but I saw a number of others who were dressed in the skin tight pilot jumpsuits like Tan, and Nela wore. A few had the 'H' symbol inside of a star-burst like Tan, while others had Chinese character symbols or nothing at all on their chests. None of the robes had symbols.

The Biaviians seemed overly shy in the Oriental fashion, seldom making eye contact or just staring at you like Westerners are prone to do. However, if I did catch an eye and waved, they would always wave back. I never waved at the Targs, and they didn't wave at me.

The great causeway was as wide as an eight lane highway and circled the inner surface of the mothership, gradually climbing toward the top. Looking up or down, people became as small as ants and eventually diminished from sight altogether. Out in the central expanse, scores of transport vehicles, open topped, glided silently by, carrying dozens of Biaviians from one place to the next.

Birds flew free in the expanse, but the most fantastic sight of all was that of three great levitating gardens, each covered with a soft blue dome and tended by a glowing orb that served as a sun and a moon. To picture the gardens, imagine a giant saucer perhaps ten miles across, which is covered with a glass dome. In the closer garden I could see what appeared to be plowed fields, fruit trees, a meandering stream, small homes and animals. I could also see a number of tiny people, but I couldn't tell if they were Biaviians, humans or mixed. I would loved to have visited them but it was not allowed.

If I could have spent every waking moment for a year consuming all the sights of this great ship, I'm sure that I would still have left much unseen. For a person to be exposed to such a thing suddenly would probably be a most shattering experience. Even now sometimes I experience shudders when I think about what I have seen. If I were not of stable mind, it might be possible to convince myself that all of it was some kind of complicated dream or delusion, but I know better.

You see, aliens have smells and sounds, taste, texture and feelings. I didn't have any problem breathing the atmosphere aboard the great ship, but the temperature within the craft was not constant in all places. For instance, along the corridor of ice where the many thousands of specimens were frozen in suspension, it was shivering cold, but heat welled up from the transport disk to compensate for it. Near the Targzissian zone, it was notably hot and stuffy so cool air welled up to compensate. In other places the temperature would vary from one point to the next, and some times an easy gust of wind would take you by surprise. Within the great Hyborian garden, you could experience all of the water smells. The smell of flowers, other plants and fallen fruit was in the air.

I don't think the Biaviians wear any kind of fragrance, but they do have a faint odor and it's not the exact same from one to another. The foods served to you, mostly liquids, have a taste, and if some one or some thing passes by you, you can feel the movement of the air currents. Once back on Earth, I found breathing labored for a short time and the surrounding odors to be offensively harsh. I found the climate crude, and human beings somewhat odd acting.

Did I tell you about the scribe disk? This was a little disk that followed me around wherever I went and transcribed my every word or utterance. Even when I went to sleep in my personal quarters, the disk stood immobile in the air a few feet above me. When I walked or rode about, it maintained its position just out of reach above my left shoulder. Most of the time you would forget it was there. Trying to jump up and catch it was a futile gesture. You see, Tan and I communicate exclusively through telepathy, while I always spoke verbally with Question, my constant companion. Apparently Tan had other things to do and was not with me every waking hour but Question was and would venture off sometimes only when Tan and I were together.

Since I've never actually seen Tan or any Biaviian sleeping, I can't truly say that they require it. However, the aliens are well aware of the fact that humans need sleep and provide for it. No matter how excited I was, when I laid down on my silken bed I went immediately to sleep and awakened refreshed. Question slept near me, and sometimes I would have to shake him awake to which he would say something like, "Buzz off, moose breath", before grudgingly arising.

There was a bedroom consisting of a commode, wash basin with real water and a shower, mirror and a non-motorized toothbrush. If you weren't aware of where you were, you could momentarily forget that you were out in the cosmos, but for this you had only to look at Question brushing his two huge beaver-like front teeth and you immediately knew that you were off in some strange shit.

Most men think of time as a precious commodity, and they set out to accomplish great things during their life spans and this is as it should be. For the human being, life is short, and the active youthful part of life is shorter still so it's no wonder that most people are in a hurry. Unfortunately, in man's quest to gain the riches and power of the world, he will find it necessary to often destroy the lesser in order to become greater.

The adage that time waits for no man is true when it comes to earthlings, but time, as we consider it, holds no such desperate significance for those who have conquered the elements of physical longevity, biological rejuvenation and time travel.

What tremendous changes do you think would transpire on Earth if each mortal knew that, barring some unforeseen catastrophe, he would live about twenty thousand years, give or take a couple of centuries? Well, this is the actual life span of the average Biaviian, and when the original body is too worn to be rejuvenated again, it is not too difficult to literally transfer the original brain to a brand new young cloned body. Theoretically it is possible, I am told, to live indefinitely, yet, with rare exceptions, the mortal being always reaches a point which may be called 'consciousness fatigue' and will, by decision, choose to no longer continue as a mortal entity and will depart this plane of reality by one of a number of different means.

One may choose molecular dispersal, that is having their living forms scattered into the endless void of space by a kind of disintegrator ray. Another may choose to drink of the dream nectar and be cast adrift in space while instruments on board record their dream sequence unto death. And yet another may choose the one which is most fascinating, to be encased alive in a kind of translucent crystal and then be cast upon a journey into the eye of the sun, a black hole or even a neutron star. Their telepathically transmitted words, thoughts, reflections, fears and poetry are recorded all during the conscious phase of their journey. The Biaviians, I discovered, are just as concerned with life after death as is man, and their knowledge of the other side, I believe, exceeds man's in only one respect. The Biaviians have gathered enough recordable data to substantiate the fact that the life force per se is eternal and cannot be nullified. However, as to the extent order and workings of the world beyond, the Biaviians, like man, can only speculate. So you see, they don't know everything. Thus the recording and cataloging of all information pertaining to the experience.

Tan and I had a long discussion on mortality, and I learned that he was just as interested in my concepts of life and death as I was in his. I told him that the quest for physical immortality has been a preoccupation of man's throughout all recorded history. I went on to explain that extreme longevity and immortality have generally been associated with magic elixirs, fountains of youth, supernatural beings and other intangible things. In other words, historically, superstition has far exceeded scientific reality in the quest for immortality. However, many medical advances over the last century have succeeded in extending the life expectancy on most parts of the so-called civilized world.

Yet any true expectations of physical immortality would seem to be centuried in the future at least. Anyway, if such a thing became common to man, it would prove catastrophic due to the already runaway growing in humanity's population.

He listened intensely as I continued my oratory on the human order. I went on to explain that in much of the world, religion, social tradition, lack of technology, necessity and just plain ignorance have thus far ruled out the acceptance of universal contraceptive practices. Therefore, the stronger nations have found it expedient to both create and to support all sides of armed conflicts between traditionally warring factions in a host of third world countries in the hope of keeping the world's population in check as well as preventing any numerically dangerous coalition between these countries.

Diseases and natural catastrophes also contribute to slowing the population growth, but all of these things combined do little to contain a lemming-like reproduction quotient of humanity as a whole. So I can't see where the gift of greatly extended life spans would be beneficial to mankind.

After I concluded, Tan reflected for a long moment before responding to my erstwhile negative assessment of the thing, and then he said, "Martin, I do not doubt that what you say is true, yet I think you underestimate the ability of intelligent beings to adhere to logic when exposed to alternate fact". He accented his timeless words of wisdom by jabbing a monster fore finger at the ceiling and lifting his left brow.

"And what the hell", I asked, "do you mean by that?"
"Let me clarify", say he, "Please do", says I.

"Martin, if the possession of mortal extension was contingent upon the agreement to submit to sterilization, compliance would logically be universal. Eventually the Earth's populace would become manageable by virtue of common discretion. We have learned that rational modus tends to become virtually universal as the reasoning factors gain more data. Knowledge grows in substance with the passing of time. Therefore as the accumulated knowledge of centuries is contained within the original organism, perception cannot help but evolve toward the sensible modus".

I cut in, "Otherwise, you're saying, that even an idiot can't help learning something if he lives long enough". "Precisely", he said.

"Then you're even dumber than you look", I said. "Man has never yet created a single thing that he didn't abuse and corrupt. First of all, if such a medical breakthrough were discovered, it would be confiscated and declared classified technology by the host government. It would then be restricted to a small group of the powerful elite. Then, if possible, to only one race or a segment of one race. Eventually some greedy or idealistic sucker among them would sell or give the secret to the opposing country. If it exists, the underworld would be bootlegging it even before the government perfected it, and the result would be genocidal destruction such as the world has never known before, not even mentioning the con men, quacks and shyster. Tan, if man was prone to common sense surely he would have at least learned to distinguish between his ass and a hole in the ground, which he has not".

"Do you realize that over half of humankind won't even entertain the thought that any kind of life may exist in the universe beyond Earth. Man has not yet learned to cease hating his brother simply because of the color of his skin, so how do you think they could conceivably handle eternal life? Huh? Better yet, why don't you zoom over and lay the secret on him?"

"Your point is well taken, Martin", said Tan. "To give such a thing would serve to alter the present order of the progression of mankind, and such intervention is not permitted by the Council of the Seven. I wished only to reveal that even the Elohim once experienced many of the same states of being which are now common to man. Our past errors have far exceeded our accomplishments. We lay no claim to perfection. In some manners of separate though similar ways, our faults might transcend your own and knowledge just as incomplete".

"But I was counting on you to enlighten me with all your celestial wisdom, oh great melon head", I said.

The Biaviians and some other kinds of aliens are capable of time travel. As Tan explained it, by utilizing ion trajectory combined with the hyperspace frequency, the Biaviians can travel back in time and traverse thousands of light years distance in but a fraction of the real time. However, they cannot travel into the future because of the quantum equational variables. For instance, he can take you back to visually witness the siege of Troy, the crucifixion or Custer's last stand because they are fixed happenings that continue to play back in their proper quantum coordinates even though those coordinates are constantly changing in accordance with the speed of light.

At this moment an 'I Love Lucy' episode which aired thirty years ago is continuing to play in its entirety thirty light years distance from here. You need only plot the proper course, travel at a speed faster than light and literally catch up with the proper time projection, and then maintain a speed or frequency equal to it to see it. Once you reach the desired time, this is easy to do because when you slow to the speed of light, you immediately become a solid part of that particular time and it doesn't require any further effort to stay there. The energy is used only when you actually transverse the time quantum. When you look up and see a UFO, which appears to your sight suddenly out of thin air, it is either utilizing the time quantum or the frequencies of hyperspace.

It was explained to me that it's possible to become lost in time, so the Biaviians generally opt for sending unmanned probes back in time to videotape the desired happenstances. They are not always successful in completing the mission.

Stagyian mathematician have theorized the possibility of traveling forward into time but have thus far been restrained from actually sending a probe there for fear of unleashing something beyond the control of present comprehension. You can go back to yesterday and come back to this moment today, but anything beyond the present is a question. Does the future ever exist in tangible form? That is the question. If Tan knows the answer, then he didn't care to enlighten me. All of his answers were speculative, that is all of his answers as to the future.

However, he was more precise when describing the past. The past, under the proper circumstances, is just as tangible as the present. Therefore time travelers must take care not to physically interfere in the incidents of the past, that is in the major history making incidents. For incidence, what would have been the outcome had Alexander been saved from an early death? Or if Moses had not been assisted by the celestials? I was told that time travelers may freely indulge in social intercourse with some lesser or unknown personages of the past, and these contacts will not noticeably alter the future course of things.

To clarify further. Look up on a starlit night and you will no doubt see a star which had died ten thousand years ago. You can clearly see the light of that star. The light is real. The light can be measured on physical instruments. If you could travel fast and far enough, you could go back and again witness the nova of that star and should you come too close to the solar flares, you would be incinerated.

And Dillinger's bullets are just as lethal now as they were then. Therefore, all incidents which have transpired since the beginning of infinity are yet solid reality. On rare occasions, certain elementals of the past can overlap with the present and physically displace or adversely affect matter. Certain natural conditions sometimes duplicate the proper frequency and up pops an apparition, a moving mirage and even a ship minus its crew. On other occasions, a present day person may simply disappear into the past. The subject is far too complicated for my limited comprehension, but it is nonetheless a fact. The Biaviians have managed to technologically manipulate the past quantum. The same technology is utilized to transverse the immeasurable vastness of space without being restricted by the known laws of physics.

At this point in man's techno-progression, he cannot reconcile these things into theorized limits of his knowledge, yet with his eyes and radar, he has witnessed UFOs perform aerial maneuvers which are impossible. I accept these things for this reason: I have personally been aboard a craft during the performance of these maneuvers and flown through hyperspace back into yesterday. I have seen video-images of people from ancient Earth times living in good health and youthful age in present day surroundings.

Physical death is not necessary. Imagine how much greater would grow the knowledge of an Einstein should he live for twenty or thirty thousand years. If indeed we only use about ten percent of our mental capacity during a normal lifetime, imagine how much more he could learn over that time. No wonder the aliens have developed so many technological and neurological abilities which man has yet to discover and develop. These things are technically possible and genetically inevitable should man endure as a species. The Biaviians intend to see that he does not become entirely extinct in spite of his great efforts toward annihilation.

Tan has more faith in the flexible tenacity of man than I do. I don't believe he really comprehends or has forgotten the elements of greed, hate, bigotry, pride, ignorance and stupidity. He told me that man was on the verge of making the breakthrough discovery of a workable fusion process, and this will set him on the road to creating other quantum leap technologies based upon fusion energy. Only if he immediately begins to utilize this discovery to the fullest extent of his abilities can he possibly hope to avoid the terrible catastrophes that are almost upon him. There is not even a decade left to squander let alone a century.

If man follows his normal course of action, as I think he will, he will probably buy up the rights and then suppress the process of fusion abundance in favor of the powers that be. We shall see.

Fusion energy, I am told, is the ultimate power source in the universe when it comes to the transportation of matter. I know that the aliens use fusion cores extensively, if not exclusively to power their inner, outer and hyperspace ships. Fusion is used in a number of different forms by the aliens. There are manners in which fusion energy can be generated at room temperature by utilizing a sodium hydrogen solution. Other processes involve a super-heated core, which is suspended in mid-chamber by utilizing sound waves, like the Targs, or by using a system involving temperatures far below absolute zero like the Biaviians. In other words, not even the aliens have managed to improve upon fusion propulsion in its many forms. Electromagnetic generation and manipulation is the end result of the fusion source.

In huge lumbering ships like the Targ tanker, I'm told that the crude form of propulsion called anti-matter thrust is sometimes used to escape the gravitational pull of some large planets before switching to pure electromagnetic power in deep space. While the fusion core is virtually safe when it comes to fissionable contaminants, the same cannot always be said of the electromagnetic currents that fusion is capable of creating. For instance, a momentary malfunction of the core or a glitch in the electromagnetic field can cause a discharge similar in power and potentially destructive force to lightening bolts.

All of the aliens make extensive use of unmanned probes or remote controlled devices. The drones may be of a number of sizes and shapes from miniature saucers only six feet in diameter to glowing orbs or small V-winged ships. Set upon a pre-plotted computer controlled course, the drones zoom through our stratosphere busily recording and transmitting data back to the mothership. Some times they are seen by people when they descend to very low altitudes to collect some localized info. These drones are not always perfect or infallible and may some times be adversely effected by radio waves, variables in the Earth's electromagnetic field, thunder heads and other things. The drone may momentarily lose the line-up with the master computer and have been witnessed performing weird acrobatic maneuvers by humans. Then, after a moment, the link is re-established, and the drone continues on its way. Some times the drones are manned by robots which are programmed to abduct and examine life forms, including humans. I'm told that this method of human abduction is being phased out and is now rarely utilized and then only by the Targs.

In preparation for the great airlift of the future and the resettlement of a large number of humans on the planet Biaveh, the Biaviians have been closely observing a number of Earth towns and small communities for generations. Among the places observed are the towns of Searcy, Arkansas; Monroe, Louisiana; a town called Oak or something similar in Wisconsin; places in Africa, South America, Europe and China, both primitive and advanced.

The object is to duplicate as closely as possible the natural fauna, climate, animal life and living structures of the natural habitats. Even motorized vehicles of a sort will be adapted identical in all physical dimensions but utilizing a non-polluting form of propulsion. It's not clear whether they will actually take only members from the observed communities or are simply using them as a cross-reference to represent all human beings.

This I do know, the best intergalactic traveling age for human beings is the early to mid thirties. When these people are taken aboard, those older will be technologically regressed to the proper age, around thirty-three or four. Those younger will be allowed to age normally to that age before being stopped at that point in the aging process. These people will live on the planet Biaveh for approximately one thousand years before being returned to re-populate the Earth. Some won't return, by choice, but most will. These people and their offspring, once back on Earth, will once again begin to age but at a much slower rate than present day people.

These returnees will be different in many ways from present day man in that they will all possess a thousand years of conscious knowledge. Telepathy and kinetic abilities will be standard for many and no doubt many kinds of technological advancements would have been learned while on Biaveh. These wayfarers will have access to all of man's literature and the sum of his mathematical and technical knowledge since the beginning, and they will probably pick up many other wondrous things of value from their Biaviian hosts.

Some will spend a lot of time going on deep space expeditions and visiting other life bearing planets with Elohim. Biaveh is somewhat smaller than the Earth in circumference, and thus the gravitational pull is about a third less than that of Earth. A Biaviian year is about 960 days Earth time.

Roughly every eleven years, two moons of Biaveh are perfectly aligned and the gravity pull is at its least. I'm told that under the proper psychological conditions during the moon alignment it is possible to literally levitate via mind power. For some reason, children seem to be able to accomplish mind flight much easier than most adults. This is also a religious or festive time for the Biaviians, and many babies are born shortly after this time, or should I say incubated, as the Biaviians no longer practice sexual copulation in the human fashion.

In 1975, during my third stint aboard the mothership, I was escorted into a circular room and shown a holographic scene of the mother planet Biaveh. So realistic was the view that I could feel the blue grass beneath my feet, feel the gusting breeze upon my face, hear the songs of the birds and the laughter of a group of children, six of whom were my own offspring, fathered at the age of eighteen. I could even smell the odor of the wild flowers and see silver and gold-colored fish jumping in a nearby crystal stream.

Chapter 4

Biaveh

At some point in the not too distant future, a large number of humans will be transported from Earth to the planet Biaveh. These wayfarers will be composed of pre-chosen volunteers and some members of their immediate families. The aliens understand that for various reasons many who have been called will not respond to the invitation, yet the number will be sufficient to assure the continuing survival of a cross-genetic social pool of humanity.

In their extended observation of human beings, the Biaviians are of the general opinion that the common person, the farmer, the rural dwellers are more desirable as candidates for re-settlement on the home planet. That is not to say that all professionals and wealthy people will be discounted, however, their number will be very small. Leading religious figures, politicians, military personnel, police, lawyers and doctors are not considered essential to the transplant community.

Tan and I spoke extensively on the Biaviian way of life and order, and in many ways it parallels many of the aspirations that man has held down through the ages, and I don't believe that their way is beyond the capabilities of man. In practice, mankind would be limited only by his technological boundaries, and yet I don't think that the Biaviians are even close to understanding the true nature of man. If they did, then they would know that mankind would hardly accept the Biaviian way without finding some way to corrupt and ultimately destroy it if given the means and opportunity.

When compared to Earth in size, Biaveh is a small planet

barely eighteen thousand miles around its equator. The planet is located about ninety million miles from its sun and has two moons that orbit close together and become aligned every eleven years. However, the Biaviian year is equivalent to 960 Earth days. Strangely, the Biaviian day is about the same as Earth's, being twenty-four hours in duration.

The combined gravitational pull of Biaveh's sun and dual moons, together with its small size, of course, make the 'g' force pull of the planet quite a bit less than that of Earth. The density of the planet is somewhat greater than that of Earth, thus holding the gravity ratio at a level which is nicely tolerable for human habitation.

The atmosphere of Biaveh is ideal for humans, and the purity of its climate is unexcelled by any spot on Earth. There is no industrial pollution owing to the fact that all of Biaveh's technical production is done out in deep space or on uninhabited bodies.

Fusion power in its many forms is utilized almost exclusively in transportation, communication and farming, and electromagnetic propulsion is used in the great space ships, as well as in individual transport pods and vehicles.

Most of the plant and animal life forms on Biaveh are transplants from other living planets including Earth. I saw blue grass and purple apples and all kinds of flowering plants. Vegetables tend to grow much larger and faster on Biaveh: red, green and blue melons. Pink bananas and yellow tomatoes with red vein-like stripes. Basketball-sized oranges and cannabis plants as large as live oak trees, with leaves twenty-four inches wide. Grapes the size of large plums growing on purple vines and corn with three feet ears.

I saw great birds with wing spans of forty feet gliding through the skies casting swiftly moving shadows over streams and lakes filled with crystal clear and onyx green waters. Sea turtles as large as small submarines and fish of megaton size. The Biaviians are not meat eaters, yet I saw large Earth type bovine animals, ground fowls and wild meat animals inhabiting the forests and plains of the planet.

Some humans are already there and have been there since Biblical times. I saw a woman playing with some hybrid children. I recognized her as a famous lady pilot who flew around the time of Lindbergh. She was still young and beautiful. I saw a few other people as well of various races, and a few full blood human children in various stages of growth. One little boy was busy stacking play blocks with telekinetic power, while a hybrid child stood watching and clapping her hands.

When the Biaviians first came upon the planet, it was still in the earliest stages of the evolutionary processes, and this was about four hundred million years before their first visitation of Earth. So the Elohim actually controlled the progression of the planet by suppressing, destroying or altering any unwanted or unessential portion of its ecology and introducing more desirable planet and animal life forms to the topography.

In keeping with the order of nature, there are predatory as well as non-predatory animals in the waters, on the land and in the air. Certain pests have been left out, and the animal life is not as numerically extensive as that of Earth but the array of birds and other creatures is marvelously impressive. Outer settlements and individual homesteads are protected around their perimeters by electromagnetic force fields, and robots are used extensively in agriculture and other menial tasks.

The polar regions of the planet are much smaller than our own and the temperature of the planet is consistently more moderate than Earth's. There are snow-capped mountains and rolling hills, tree-dotted plains and white sand beaches. There is even a high escarpment of huge reptiles composed of Earth and other kinds of dinosaurs.

Oceans and seas cover about fifty percent of the planet's surface. The planet has four great continents and many islands. It is a beautiful planet and has the appearance of a well manicured theme park, due to the ceaseless activity of robot drones that dart about clipping, pruning, damming, draining, harvesting, etc.

I once said to Tan, "My friend, if you have it so neat, why don't you smile a lot more?" And he said, "Martin, I know of no perfect instrument. There is a variable schism that seeds the marrow of infinity, and we ever raise our lips to suckle the nectar of its Omsa".

And I said, "Me, too, on what you said", and then I asked, "Do you believe in God force?" He retorted, "Do you?"

I said, "Tan, I asked you first like a nice person, so why are you laying this big shit on me? Could it be because you're flying around in a big upside down type dip dish?" To which he responded, "You first".

I said, "I want to warp to hyperspace and stuff. Maybe then I could see a little clearer". "Agreed, when we meet once more", he said.

I said, "Aw, shucks", and then I continued, "The ways of decency hold true without changes among all people. Only the customs are different. Yet conceptions of God, no matter how noble, are superseded by human personal emotions of various prejudices toward their fellow beings. Even so, this doesn't dissuade me in the least that the omnipotent force jams like two bats fucking. The proof is that I feel it sometimes and I look good when I smile".

"To many people of the Earth who are not oft given to inner confrontation and esoteric flashes, you could be considered a God. Don't get me wrong, I am impressed almost to the thin shits with your superthing, but Gods don't wear funny looking boots like those", I said, pointing at his ample flat feet.

He said, "Such boots would last you a life span". And I said, "Well, you couldn't hang out with me with no boots like them, that big head is bad enough. Small miracles happen all the time, if you're looking for them, and a baby will sometimes tell you some deep shit, if they like you and you don't try to get too slick. Miracles do transpire, and a life force is common and inextinguishable among all things. I think that all humans are aware of this, and their many religious beliefs, philosophies, supersaturations and practices are mostly an attempt on their part to give order to what they don't understand. Yes, I do believe there is a great force that governs us all". And with this I concluded my short recitation on Earth religion, "Now you, Tan, please keep it simple".

After a rather long moment of reflection, he began to speak telepathically. "Martin, it is true that once the state of logical deduction is attained, it follows that the possessor will seek to discover and master all knowledge. From the consumption of lesser organisms to the destruction of planets is but a tiny step in the quest for omnipotence. It is also true that simple yet destructive creatures such as you and I shall foolishly proclaim ourselves supreme above all else. Our concept of God force, we believe, is limited only by our inability to master all knowledge. The Elohim spawned forth from the saline broth just as you have gone forth to partially chart the dimensions of six galaxies. Yet we know that tens of thousands of other galaxies do exist. Thus our true knowledge is restricted to but an isotopic measure of the whole".

"The recorded history of the Elohim encompasses the evolution upon and the destruction of the useful life span of two other living planets before the settlement of Biaveh and the future is but a theoretical infinity. There are those who are much longer of history than we, both lesser and greater, and we cautiously approach yet others yet unknown".

"We have come to know of life forms which are the least rudiments of molecular modus, while others do possess mammalian metabolism and yet a few have evolved beyond the necessity of material form. As the progression span is based upon seven states of order, we the Elohim have yet to conquer the third stage. You see Martin, we have not yet discovered a thing so great as to consider it supreme unto reverence. Yet it is generally accepted among us that a force supreme does possess the source of all Omsa, and for want of a better expression, we call it 'Light'. Light from whence all things must have come to be, to be and to forever be. This that you call photosynthesis is the only constant throughout all of infinity, and its many components form the basis of all progressions, both material and mathematical, even as we utilize solar, infra, alpha, gamma and other rays for organic nurture and propulsion. It is but certain spectrums of the nuclea-Omsa".

So the aliens are religious beings of a sort. I learned that it is only natural that man would go through his present phases of religious philosophies and destinies. However, I'm given to believe that man's very survival could very well depend upon his ability to alter his original concepts to conform with the even-changing realities of life and knowledge gained. Even these space travelers, who have conquered galactic travel and the quantum of time, are forever seeking a greater, more timely state of omnipotent comprehension. Because of the religious power base, mankind has historically been held short of his true potential, and it has just about led to his own undoing. We are truly on the very brink of self-destruction and sink deeper with each passing day.

The Biaviians, I find, are very practical in their social, ethical and philosophical outlook and actions. Crime as we know it does not exist on Biaveh. It is a society in which nothing material or organic is denied its citizens. They are not all automatons, and they don't all think alike. Lodging, food, medicines, transportation and access to all educational materials are not denied anyone, because these rudimentary things are essential to the peaceful progression of any society.

Full blooded Biaviians no longer procreate by copulation in our manner, but are nurtured in incubation pods. Materials for the cloning of younger future bodies are extracted from each originals. However, the Biaviians do make love and form close relationships.

In 1975 during my third stay aboard the mothership, I had the opportunity to observe two younger Biaviians making love, and they do it in this manner: The male and female stand facing one another with a kind of dazed or dreamy look in their eyes and a kind of visible glow seems to engulf them. They both raise their hands as if to hand wrestle or to give the high five, and, as the glow seems to build in intensity, their hands come together, palm to palm. When this happens, the hands glow brighter. Then their little bodies seem to sway as if they are hard pressed to keep their balance. Slowly a kind of pink dot of light appears on their foreheads, and the big heads begin to bob inward toward one another. Now they seem sorely intent upon keeping their foreheads from touching, but they are fighting a losing battle. Like two pink-tinged melons, the heads are slowly drawn together by some kind of meaty magnetic force. Their diminishing struggle to keep those heads apart causes a tiny yellow arc of power to jump from one forehead to the other. Now they can prevent the inevitable on longer, and a blue flash accents the touching of the foreheads, at which they both collapse as if they've been pole-axed and lay swooning on the floor, their hands still locked. After this, I'm told, matter will be extracted from her and him and a baby will be born. If they were just doing it for fun, which is seldom, then no offspring would come of the union. Only the truest of mutual vibration wish will produce the love-child.

When Tan asked me what I thought of the Biaviian way of procreation, I said that the whole thing was very cute and nifty, but you people don't know nothing about fucking. He said, "Even as our way seems odd to you, Martin, I tell you truly that if you could but once know that sensation, you might perish of its force". And I said, "Well, kill me. Give me head, till I am dead". To which he replied, Oh Martin, again you shit the bull (bullshitting)".

Just like humans, I'm sure that a number of Biaviians bump heads a lot just for fun. While there are groups of Biaviians who like to explore the properties of various drug compounds, that is get high, I learned that just about all of these drug compounds are synthesized in a manner which is organically acceptable to the body.

The old adage that birds of a feather flock together holds true even out in the stars. Those who like certain things tend to gather in special surroundings or communities, both on and off the planet. The Biaviians learned long ago that it is futile to deny a person access to any substance. To do so would be to lay the ground work for dissension and crime. Instead they set about to duplicate or mimic all drug compounds in a manner which would have the least detrimental organic effects on the body and make them available to the users. Then these users were required to live in certain separate communities. They are not permitted to produce offsprings while living there until such time as they may desire to leave that life style. It is not a prison, but you are not permitted to bring any substance or paraphernalia out, nor to possess the substance anywhere but at home. Out of these communities have come many creations of art, music, philosophy and practical science. Some of the greatest Biaviian minds have lived in these communities.

These restrictions of separatism only apply to those who indulge in the stronger or habit-forming compounds and not to a number of natural non-addictive herbs that grow wild or are cultivated on the planet.

I also understand that there are some Biaviians of less than exemplary life styles who may be of loose morals from the Biaviians standpoint. As far as I know, no restrictions are placed upon adult sexual pursuits and habits.

A Biaviian may have any number of head bumping experiences with various other Biaviians and not incur the wrath of his or her chosen companion. Perhaps this in part because once a certain sensation is experienced, it can be passed along to another of similar vibrations, and if one gets bored, he can always hop on a ship and tour the home planet, visit space installations or take an extended journey out into the cosmos. Or simply go fishing. If one should decide that all of this has no more to offer and opt for leaving this plane of existence, a number of disintegration stations or booths are to be found at various locations. The question to live or not to live is left to the individual.

Biaviians, in as much as they are able to show emotions, seem to love children and animals, and everyone tends to view every child as his own, responsibility-wise. In 1964, aboard the mothership, I saw two young Biaviians playing a game which was fascinating.

Sitting at a round table facing one another, they were attempting to disassemble and rebuild a pyramid structure of crystals telekinetically. The object was to move your pyramid from his side to your side, piece by piece, while hindering his process of moving his own. And all of this transpires while both of you levitate the table and chairs and yourselves above the floor. The whole game doesn't last any more than a few minutes, and the players are assisted by a high tech power source. I am told that some of the older Biaviians can play this game using nothing but their own kinetic abilities, though I never saw them do it.

The Biaviians also love music, of a sort. I've heard some of it, and I wouldn't submit it for a Grammy. However, it's not completely unpleasant to the ears or the mind and with a little tutoring they might even learn to jam.

Though they are high tech star travelers, surprisingly, on the home planet many Biaviians live in the countryside and assist their robot drones in plantings and harvesting, etc. Some even shun all of the high tech conveniences for the rough, back to nature sort of existence. I understand that a rather large colony of humans and hybrid human Biaviians also live there.

There was a time in Biaviian history when a criminal or antisocial under society did exist, but I understand that this is no longer a problem. During those days, such individuals were committed to a prison planet or moon or asteroid, both male and female. They lived in a self-contained domed city and were given the rudimentary instruments to sustain themselves. Each individual wore a signal device and could not commit a crime without being caught by guardian drones and summarily destroyed. Nor could they produce offsprings or undergo the close transplant transition at the end of their days.

The prison colony was guarded by sentinel globes orbiting the planet in order to prevent any unauthorized traverse to or from the prison. By all logical reckoning, the inmates could live a relatively normal life span without the Biaviian supervision or intervention. They were forced to work together in order to survive.

Eventually they were able to do away with the antisocial elements via technological and social means.

There is no medium of precious metal or emerald exchange, because when you have the run of the galaxy and such advanced technology, no known substance is precious any longer. Gold, diamonds and other materials are so common on Biaveh that they are utilized in all kinds of necessary and decorative ways. Children play with uncut diamonds, and the entire infrastructure of a dwelling may be fashioned of or plated with gold and inlaid with various emeralds.

The shuttling of various produce products from in-season to out-of-season areas work like clockwork.

Biaviian computers and robotics are far in advance of our

own, but they do have limitations. This is because of a bad experience the Biaviians once had with artificial intelligence. If you give a machine the ability to reason beyond its designed purpose, it may, after due consideration, decide that it doesn't need you any more.

It is hard for us to envision some things that the Biaviians do with some regularity. Exploratory crews lying in suspended animation were dispatched from the mother planet as long as several thousand years ago and are yet en route to a pre-charted destination, perhaps in another galaxy. Long ago, one such expedition was en route to some distant point. The on board guardians for this crew was a new kind of artificial intelligence. Somewhere between the home planet and the destination, on board computers, upon assessing the situation came to the conclusion that the ship would not be able to reach the destination, complete the mission and return to the home planet.

Obviously some of the non-essential things, equipment, etc., would have to be sacrificed for the sake of the mission. The artificial intelligence further reasoned that certain building materials, plant spores, organic food stuffs and the fragile crew members in suspension were non-essential ballast and so were forthwith jettisoned into deep space. By the time the home planet received light speed transmissions explaining this, the crew had long since been destroyed. The self-destruct sequence was sent out forthwith.

The artificial intelligence was correct in its assessment of the situation, but its actions were of clinical machine sort, devoid of true compassion or benevolent improvisation. The Biaviians never made that mistake again. So in reality artificial intelligence actually underwent a kind of techno-regression to its present state. Now all robots are designed and programmed for one specific task and are thus immutably restricted to that function, whether it be horticulture or neurosurgery.

Some Biaviians are natural explorers, while others are content to stay at home. Many will undergo the clone-brain transplant procedure in order to maintain eternal or very extended physical youth, while others are content to just grow old in their original body and to die a natural death.

While school may encompass a very wide range of subjects, the curriculum is not structured except as per the wishes of the individual student. Just as water seeks its own level, so does the intelligence aspirations of the individual. For instance, a Biaviian historian has access to hundreds of millions of years of recorded Biaviian history, as well as that of a hundred other living planets including Earth's. No one is in a hurry, so to speak. Considering the very short life span of earthlings, they do very well actually.

While on the other hand man can do more damage in one hour than he is capable of correcting in twenty years, and the imperfection of his creations and his gluttonous disregard for future planetary damage will do more than any other factor to bring about man's imminent destruction, if he doesn't alter his ways of doing things completely, immediately.

Just like the great mothership, the planet of Biaveh has a true space defensive umbrella protecting the planet and its deep space installations. Neighboring intelligent life forms are always visiting the mother planet, but at a certain point of approach in deep space, all functions of an incoming craft are taken over by the ever-vigilant sentinel globes. No armed craft may enter into the home space zone without suffering total and immediate destruction. They are also able to generate force shields around individual cities and installations. This leads me to believe that the peaceful Biaviians do not consider themselves completely safe from the elements of warlike aggression from parties known and unknown.

Of course, the reason given for the space defense units is primarily one of meteor and other space debris watch. I must also accept Tan's statement to the effect that Biaveh has not suffered a war in tens of thousands of years. I have never personally witnessed the sentinel globes in action, but I was told one incident involving Earth in which the destructive force of the units played a vital part.

In the year 1907 or thereabouts, a large meteor was deflected away from a collision course with the planet Mars. Had it struck it would have destroyed an alien installation on that planet. I'm told that a sizeable chunk of that meteor broke away from the main body and headed for Earth. In order to correct a mistake of their own making, the meteor was literally disintegrated just outside the Earth's stratosphere, but the recoil or sound waves of the blast still did considerable damage at a point on Earth. I believe it was in Northern Russia. Fortunately, none of the actual meteor got through.

According to the aliens' sky charts, I learned that the Earth is due to be visited by another great meteor in the latter part of the year 1998. Its present trajectory will definitely bring it through our solar system. Should it make physical impact with the Earth, it would be most catastrophic. So great would be its destructive force that it could actually wipe out most of life on this planet. The meteor will be about six miles in diameter. The precise trajectory, I'm told, cannot yet be pinpointed by the aliens, because the meteor is subject to a number of unforeseeable influences, such as dimensional dissipation and gravitational influences by planetary bodies, sun flares and other forces I'm sure. In any case, the technology of the Earth is not advanced enough to deal with it. Tan would not give me a position as to whether the aliens would take a hand in the matter if necessary.

The exact point or the full extent to which the aliens are prepared to participate in the affairs of Earth has remained somewhat obscure to me, even unto this time. I know that the Biaviians could give man the technology to completely alter the course of his destiny, but they seem to have rules against such intervention. Yet, judging from the rather extensive part that they have played in the ascension of the human species, I would think that a higher level of intervention would be acceptable by the celestial.

After considerable thought on the matter, I've come to the conclusion that the aliens, while willing to save man from extinction as a species, do not consider us ready to be accepted into the galactic community as equals technologically. I did find out that the Biaviians have had past experiences with high tech, war-like intelligences and have had to fight several inter-galactic wars long ago.

Further, a war or at least a territorial skirmish was waged between the Biaviians and the Targzissians over possession of Earth long ago. Apparently their disagreement was eventually settled. However, I sense an abiding unease or distrust between these two species even now.

True, the aliens have rules which must be adhered to by all the seven, but like the social rules on Earth, the actual application of some are subject to subtly varying interpretations. Where the Biaviians' relationship with contactees tends to be one of a friend-to-friend thing, the Targzissians don't seem to dwell upon the friendship factor, giving more emphasis to the collector specimen state. Yet it is permissible for them to collect a certain number of Earth creatures, including humans. It is not permitted to physically harm other non-combat intelligent creatures, but moral feelings concerning this treatment are not stressed. So, as a result, many abductees, though not physically harmed, may be permanently psychologically damaged as a result of the experience.

As far as I know, only the Biaviians, the Dorians and the Targs actually make Earth contact with humans. The Nyptonians and the Stagyians participate in the program from the scientific data level, but are not the ones who choose the subjects. I'm told that the Insectillians are not permitted any form of contact with the human species, mainly because the insect and the mammal are so totally different. The Targs, though being of a reptilian predominance, can yet claim some historical evolutionary kinship with the human species. It sounds awfully strange to me, but I'm told that the human came through a reptilian phase of evolution and also has a definite kinship with the fowl.

Humans seem to thrive on the planet Biaveh, and don't usually take long to fully adapt to the gravitational and ecological difference. A combination of Biaviian medical technology and unpolluted ecology causes humans of that planet to live many thousands of years. For some reason, cloning of extra bodies and brain transference is not permitted on the human subjects of Biaveh. However, the full blood humans are permitted to raise hybrid children and to live with cross-bred mates. Full blood Biaviians do not live in the community of humans and hybrids. Perhaps this is because the aliens may fear picking up some germs from the humans to which they have no natural defense.

The human community of the future on Biaveh, I'm told, will be left relatively pure and will live in habitat settings that have actually been transplanted and duplicated in almost every detail from Earth. The human settler will be able to eat the same vegetables and meats and live in structures which vary little from what he has been used to on Earth. The dual moons and the gravity being the most pronounced differences.

Let me reiterate what I said before of the inter-stellar re-settlers. Any earthlings who travel to Biaveh will do so strictly by choice and will in no way be kidnapped or physically forced to go on this journey. The Biaviians are well aware of man's propensity toward violence and are prepared to weed out the obviously dangerous individuals. Exactly how this is done, I can't say.

For instance, if you've read this manuscript thus far, you are aware of the fact that at points in my life I have been involved in physically dangerous circumstances. However, I've never gained any inner satisfaction from hurting people or things, and I would be perfectly content to live a peaceful and loving existence. Even though my manners cannot be called refined and I used to threaten to skin and eat my sidekick Question, the aliens seem to know the real truth of my nature and can distinguish between character logic and evil for evil's sake.

So I suspect a true cross-section of the various human personalities among us will go. In other words, they are not trying to seek out and segregate the dyed-in-the-wool saint-like pacifists among us. So they aren't as dumb and unfeeling as they may seem to the un-discerning. Aside from the fact that he doesn't have a very healthy sense of humor, Tan is acceptable as a decent fellow.

Man uses all kinds of machines to assist him in agriculture and transportation, and I'm told that he will have such things on Biaveh. However, the propulsion system in his tractors, pick-ups and motor bikes will not be of the Earth gasoline combustion type. Perhaps they will be identical in looks only. They may even mimic the sound of this machinery. There won't be any insecticides or other pollutants, as all pests will be controlled via sound waves and other non-polluting means.

Also humans on Biaveh will be allowed to adhere to, create and alter their own governmental life styles as they so choose. However, the factor of poverty and inequality will be virtually wiped out by means of a state of existence which lacks the quest for essential things, housing, health, food, clothing, transport, etc. Nor will there be any kind of weapons among the earthlings, because no weapons will be needed. Those who harbor strong racial and sociological prejudices probably won't be chosen in the first place.

It will be a society in which a person's intellectual and esoteric attainments will be his measure. Also I believe the aliens will choose a number of people who will form a numerical counterpart to their like states on Earth, so they will not discount a person because of their sexual preference or orientation. I suspect that about one in twenty will be homosexual, lesbian, bisexual and so forth. There will be whites, blacks, Asians and Spaniards and a cross mixture thereof.

Further, I understand that there will be more females than males, at a ratio of about four to one. As it was explained to me, the monogamous relationship, one man for one woman, is not the natural or normal order of nature. No doubt many women, who read this book will consider this a rather chauvinistic outlook in the alien's part, but I'm sure that this viewpoint is based upon a natural fact.

In nature, all mammalian fetuses begin life as a female and only the introduction into the system of a certain chromosome will alter the gender of that fetus toward the male physiology. Nature knows that in substance one male may conceivably produce tens of thousands of offspring, while the individual female can gestate but a few. So nature compensates by producing less males and more females among all mammals, including humans.

The survival ability of the female exceeds the male, and females will always exist in greater numbers than males. Accepted values and practices of society will not alter this fact. Should Earth survive, you may be sure, that in the not too distant future, even western society will have to face the fact that virile males are a commodity which must be shared by a number of mates, or a greater number of woman will simply be left out. Even at this moment, if a vast proportion of the virile males of society were somehow prevented from having access to a large number of female companions, a workable society would be impossible. It's simply being done in a clandestine and sneaky fashion, that's all. A virile, healthy male should be able to perform sexually all of his natural life, yet a great proportion lose it for lack of proper stimulation and restrictive social impracticalities. Use it or lose it.

In contrast, I'm told that among the Insectillians, a single female can produce thousands of offspring during their fertile life spans. As a result, only about one in a thousand of their females are born fertile, while a greater proportion of the males are virile. There is a great deal of sexual activity but no offspring results from most of it.

I never saw a female Targzissian and never gave it much thought at the time. Tan was always evasive to my queries about the reptiles. When I passed by the Targ zone on the mothership, I got a feeling that I could not explain. This is only speculation on my part, but I got the ominous and foreboding feeling that something, something huge and alive, was behind that great spiral door. Further, I picked up an inkling or intuitive thing which has led me to feel that the Targs may be destroying all but a very few female offspring. I don't like the Targs at all. Maybe I judge them too harshly, yet one chilling experience with these beings in May of 1988 in Tulsa, Oklahoma, has only served to reinforce my very first opinion of these creatures.

I understand that Earth plants grow swiftly on Biaveh, and generally on a much larger scale. Because of the different nutrient composition of the soil, plants may also change in coloration and potency. When a human being arrives on Biaveh, it generally takes awhile for the person to get over the initial fascination of it all.

The Biaviians mastered the science of suspended animation many thousands of years ago. During the time of transportation of historical characters like Elijah and Ezekial of Biblical fame, it was necessary to lay those wayfarers in suspension for the return journey to Biaveh, because the journey at the time, even at near light speed, required many years, as we measure time. Biaviians and Stagyian scientists eventually developed the technology to transcend light speed, to conquer ion trajectory and to wrap the quantum into hyper-space, and in the midst of all of this is the factor of time displacement or time travel.

While the land areas of Biaveh hold no uncontrollably dangerous and predatory animal life forms who prey upon the citizens, the same cannot be said of the waters of that planet. Owing to the high oxygen content, the lesser gravity and the abundant nutrients of that planet, I'm told that a large number of sea creatures grow to reach megaton proportions.

If travel upon those waters was crudely conventional of the Earth sort, then ocean travel could prove a very dangerous undertaking. While many life forms have evolved naturally in the oceans of that planet, many other more evolved forms have been introduced into those waters from the Earth and from other life-bearing planets. The never-ending predatory struggle for survival in nature can be observed in its awesome and most nightmarish forms beneath the waters of Biaveh. So people are able to frequent beaches, swim and otherwise enjoy the seashores only in certain designated controlled areas.

In many ways the present day aqua life of Biaveh resembles the Jurassic period sea life of our own planet's infancy, yet on a more grotesque and larger scale. The new human settles, the lovers of oceanography, would be able to explore this monstrously beautiful underwater wonderland literally for years and years, while observing the life forms from the safety of special Biaviian aqua-space ships, not even to mention the numerous living sights on land. I gather that the planet is a living kaleidoscope of life and plant forms, which have, to a great extent, been introduced there from other celestial bodies by the Biaviian settlers.

As I have said before, the Biaviians do not eat meat, and I have not personally witnessed or detected any inclination toward violence from any of them. Yet I am not deluded into thinking that these peaceful little aliens are not capable of self-protection. No doubt they have the means to conquer via technological aggression, to destroy planets if they should so desire. They don't do such things simply because the need has not arisen again.

My friend Question has said on several occasions, "Don't let them big heads and cartoon faces fool you. If push comes to shove, they know how to do some 'zap shit'."

Chapter 5

Question and Other Things

From my first physical contact or abduction, if you will, with the Biaviians at the age of seven in Arkansas, I vaguely remember the furry intelligent animal from that time. Through the years prior to my second visitation and intergalactic trip at age eighteen, my recollections of and feelings towards the animal I named Question were mixed to say the least. The fact is that he stuck out in my subconscious memory much more prominently than most other facets of that experience, save for my first visual contact with the Targs. So Question must have made a great impression on me.

You must understand that prior to 1987, my literal and clear recollections of these past experiences were fleeting, fragmentary and, in many cases, jumbled. I can easily see where this lack of structured recall can and does cause a kind of mental exasperation among many former abductees. To be sure, some have ended up in mental institutions, while a few others in desperation have taken their own lives.

After giving considerable thought to this factor concerning abductions, I've come to the conclusion that the earlier in life the abduction, the least likely the abductee is to lapse into a psychotic state. Why? I'm not a psychiatrist, but this is roughly the conclusion I've reached.

Most Westerners are born into family structures that either believe in or practice some denominational manner of the Christian doctrine. Socially, culturally and religiously, all of known life is restricted to and focused upon the Earth with mankind as the sole possessor and keeper of the conscious knowledge of infinity. The general consensus leads the average person to assume that we alone are uniquely the uppermost forms of God's creation. To even seriously consider the possibility that more advanced life forms than our own may exist somewhere in the cosmos is an anathema to all basic human conceptions, and after all of this life long orientation toward being the only celestial master to suddenly be faced with the living breathing evidence to the contrary is more than many humans are able to contend with. So they freak out. Even the most educated among us are often unable to consciously accept this fact, because to do so would require a complete reassessment of all that we have come to believe and accept.

It's not that the ancient Biblical and historic writers have tried to hide past visitation because they haven't. It's only that shortsighted religious interpretations and mistakes in logic have suppressed this evidence. To have such a preconceptual bubble burst before their eyes and their sense of reasoning would, for most, be an unbearably traumatic thing.

On the other hand, children are not generally as traumatized by such encounters. A number of factors contributed to this. Age. The child is yet too young to have assimilated and developed a definite conviction upon religious and philosophical things. Orientation. Most children, especially modern day kids, are used to movies, books and tales of things with a high fantasy content, so children are much more likely to accept and deal with the reality of other worldly visitors. From the extraterrestrial standpoint, the children have a less physically dangerous wish or capability and if handled gently are much easier to communicate with. For the most part, children are honest in their emotions and opinions so the aliens are able to gain some insights into the human experience which are rarely possessed by the adult abductees and physically open sensations which are unique to children.

My experiences with Question and the time we spent together are more vivid from my second visit to the mothership in 1964 at the age of eighteen. When I first saw him tagging along with Tan, Nela and myself, I asked Tan what he was, as I could not attribute his looks to any one Earth creature. Tan did not give a species name for him, but simply said that he was a friend animal who would keep me company and talk to me and see that I didn't get lonely.

Later, when the creature and I got to know one another better, I name him Question, mainly because his origins are to me a question and because he has the needling habit of answering a query with a question of his own, and also because I find his personality to be basically one of an offensive, wise-assed sort. I'm sure that I considered murdering him on a number of occasions.

When I first set eyes on him, my attention was tuned to him immediately, probably because he stood out from the other beings by being the only one of his kind around. In description Question is definitely a mammal, who is of the marsupial order, a pouched animal. He stands about three feet tall and probably weighs about forty pounds. His lower body is shaped something like a kangaroo or jack rabbit, with the huge feet and an upright posture. His upper body is equipped with short simian arms with four-fingered hands, which he uses in a human-like fashion. He has a large flat beaver-like tail, which is covered with bushy hair. With the exception of the tail and the shaggy floppy dog-like ears, the body is covered with short smooth gray-brown hair, while the protruding stomach and waist level pouch are covered with short smooth white hair.

His head is somewhat long, sloping forward into a rather broad wrinkled forehead. The eyes are large, deep brown with drooping eyelids, one more than the other, thus giving the eyes a perpetually sleepy and subtly devious expression. The beagle type muzzle is adorned with a moist black hound's nose on a floppy lipped muzzle, which is accented by two large protruding beaver style upper front teeth. From the side profile you can clearly see the huge overbite and weak receding chin.

His overall appearance is that of some kind of goofy looking, pouched, upright beaver, whose probable personality is that of a larcenous, slobbering, alcoholic sexual deviant. However, according to Tan, Question is to the Biaviians what the parakeet is to humans, that is, he is a creature capable of mimicking the speech of his master but knowing nothing of the true meaning and complexities of intelligent reasoning.

From the Biaviians point of view, this assessment might be considered acceptable, yet from my point of view, I beg to differ with them. To me, Question's intelligence quotient far exceeds that of the Earth parakeet, and in deduction reasoning, I would place him on a level equal if not in some cases superior to my own.

Tan told me that every word and thought that came from Question would have been gleaned from my thoughts, so in a cryptic kind of way, Question became a weird reflection of myself. I don't know if it was done on purpose, but the creature seemed to have focused upon that part of my personality which tends to grate on peoples' nerves, the sarcasm and the crude humor, sprinkled with smatterings of grudging comradeship.

I'm one of those people whose bark is for the most part worse than his bite. To the narrow-minded or un-observant person, my cutting jibes and wise cracks have an unsettling effect and may make them angry, but it is basically my way of testing the nature and fortitude of their inner beings. If they pan out, then they really get to know me, and in their eyes I become lovably hilarious, which makes me want to puke.

Unfortunately, depending upon one's point of view, it can be said that Question, for the most part, never picked up on many of my truly lovable qualities. Therefore, he had the ability to piss me off considerably.

For instance, Question has a bad habit of stealing things, any thing that someone is careless enough to leave laying where he can get it, and it will fit into his pouch.

Once he rushed up to me and handed me a little shiny tube-shaped object, saying that he knew how bad I wanted a memento to take home and due to the heartfelt closeness of our friendship, he simply felt compelled, even against the rules, to make me a present of a priceless heirloom which had been in his family for twenty generations.

As he passed the object to me, he was almost on the point of tears, and I was truly touched. I honestly felt contrite and somewhat ashamed at having threatened to kill him on a number of occasions. As I stood reassessing my formally negative opinion of this veritable saint among space beavers, a large and obviously disgruntled Targzissian pilot appeared and stood glaring at me through his beady snake eyes. Suddenly it dawned upon me that he had come looking for the gift that Question had just given me, and as I handed it over, I tried to explain to him that Question had brought it to me, saying, "Go on, Question, tell him that you took the thing, tell him". To which Question replied by making a noise which sounded like "Three-pit, Threep.t".

The Targ just took the thing back and walked away in disgust. I turned around sorely intent on strangling that thieving, lying animal, but alas Question had anticipated my wrath and was even then turning a corner about twenty yards away. Only later would he weasel his way back into my grudging good graces, perhaps by letting me hit his space pipe.

I could never pin Question down on hardly anything, such as his true species name or his point of origin. His answers to most questions were sarcastic and always evasive.

"Question, where are you from?" "Kansas City". "And what would a space beaver be doing in Kansas City?" "Drinking good whiskey and playing the blues". "Playing the blues?" "Ain't you never heard of Sonny Blues Boy Beaver?" "You are a sick animal". "Thank you kindly".

Now that I think about it, I must admit that Question was a refreshing counterbalance to Tan's aloof seriousness. Also, Question and I communicated verbally, so he also served as an exercise object for my human articulation. Perhaps the aliens realized that it is also necessary for a human being to be able to articulate, even though he may be adept at telepathic communication.

I never really gave it much thought, but I have caught myself trying to communicate with people via telepathy, without having been immediately conscious of doing so. Sometimes it works momentarily.

For instance, a person may turn and say, "Beg pardon" or "Were you speaking to me?", even though I hadn't verbally spoken a word, and it also serves to confirm the fact that I'm probably not crazy.

It is difficult to explain all of the nuances of telepathic communication, but I shall try. When Tan and I are conversing, it is a compilation of words and visual as well as emotion stimulus. In order to speak to another person on a walkie talkie, you must press the button, then release the button to hear the caller. A third party may be able to hear and even cut in on your transmissions, but to do so would be impolite. The same holds true of telepathic communications. If you don't desire to communicate with a party, then you don't press the button of the mind that opens the channel.

In other words, you don't stand around listening to everything that everybody says. Tuning out undesired transmissions swiftly becomes an involuntary mind reflex action. So a kind of neurological privacy is assured.

I hear Tan in English when we talk, but should he be conversing with Nela or someone else, if I cut in, I hear them in their own language, which I cannot understand. When you are speaking to another person using your voice, some times what you say is not really what you mean, but with telepathic transmission it is very difficult to hide the true meaning of what you are saying. This makes it a much purer form of communication than is verbal. For instance, if I say to Tan that most politicians are full of shit, he immediately perceives my meaning which is that I don't consider most of them to be honest or forthright individuals. It also means that they are primarily concerned with manipulating, while enriching themselves.

One short expression via telepathy can convey a lot of things, yet if I should attempt to comment upon subject matter the complexity of which is beyond my ability to decipher, then he will probably also be left wanting. It is hard to explain bigotry to Tan because of the subject's complex motivations, and because he himself has no natural predisposition toward sentiments.

In order for him to comprehend the sensations of an ejaculation, he had to actually tune in to my feelings as I made love to a number of hybrid females aboard the mothership in 1964. He could pick up on the meaning of pain if I pinched myself while speaking on it. Pinpointing colors is easy if something bearing the color you are describing is around for visual stimulus. If I say that I am feeling blue and at that moment I have the emotion, he is able to equate feeling blue to the emotion of sadness. This is the manner in which I have literally taught the human experience to Tan over the years.

Once Tan has satisfactorily learned something, he will not forget it, and he has the irritating habit of starting a conversation at precisely the point that you left off, perhaps eight or ten hours before. Maybe I've forgotten that conversation altogether, because I may have considered the subject matter dumb shit in the first place. Yet in order to refresh my memory, Tan will give me a rerun of the dialogue, his and mine, leading up to the point where the conversation was terminated. Sometimes he would crack me up, rerunning some part of our former conversation, because when I was younger, dear reader, I was not adverse to the occasional use of what may be termed 'expletive deleted'. The word itself may not have been funny, but to watch him say it with all seriousness was funny.

Strangely, or perhaps not so strangely, Question can comprehend my meaning much easier than Tan can. Yet I mustn't forget that Question's personality is just a derivative of my own, and to this day, I can't truthfully say that Question cares one way or another or if my friendship actually means anything special to him.

In fact, Question was the one who suggested a number of things which could have gotten me in trouble with my hosts. He stole things and was not adverse to lying, which he could do with a straight face. He is greedy and stingy, not to mention selfish and unfaithful.

For instance, I saw two Targ pilots sitting together and commented on how fortunate I was to be able to witness such highly evolved creatures of a different sort. To which Question retorted, "Yeah, big shit, a couple of lizards wearing tennies". Question was never serious about any thing. Or was he?

The elastic capability of Question's pouch is considerable, and he may have it crammed with any number of things at any given time. However, he was more likely to have a cache of food items than any thing else, the most common of which being a kind of flat, dry, brown, yellow or green wafer. Every once in a while, when he thought you weren't looking, he would pop a wafer in to his mouth and consume it making a crunching, smacking sound. If I would turn and look directly at him, he would quit and try to look innocent. He used this surreptitious method of eating in a sickening attempt to keep you from asking him for one of his wafers. If you press the point, he will say something like, "You'll spoil your dinner", "This stuff is too scientifical", "Sorry but that was my last one" or "These wafers are deadly to humans and born-again preachers". On one occasion, I startled Question as he attempted to pop a wafer into his mouth, and he dropped a piece. Swiftly I picked it up and tested it. The taste was similar to an unsalted cracker with a slightly onion indication. I found the wafer not unpleasant, but it certainly doesn't warrant a sneak eating habit.

Once Tan, Question and I were passing a complex of different sized spiral doors. Tan explained that their purpose was a system of depressurization which enabled them to launch delicate instruments into deep space. That day Question had been particularly obnoxious, so I tried to get Tan to flush Question out into space, for purely scientific purposes. I explained that I wanted to see if their instruments could pick up space beaver screams as he tumbled violently toward the sun.

On another occasion, I tried to get him to demonstrate their quick freezing process on Question. I even went so far as to say that it was a universal custom of friendship on Earth to turn little furry creatures like Question into Davy Crockett hats. But, try as I may, I was not successful in getting him tortured and killed. Furthermore, I'm certain that I will have the misfortune of seeing him again when I return to the great ship.

Another factor of Question's personality is his insatiable curiosity. It seemed that he was forever exploring surrounding machinery or antagonizing the numerous robot drones that constantly skittered about performing some menial or technical task. Particularly active are those little drones that go about changing the numerous booster rods in various places.

These energy rods are about a foot long and are cylinder shaped. They resemble an arm-sized glass tube that glows a dull blue, green, red or yellow and has notched metal couplets on the ends. A kind of utility drone goes about at a rapid clip, removing the used and replacing them with fresh rods. The drone would whiz up to a group of three or six rods, give a 180 degree turn on the rod, and change them one by one. It would remove one rod and set it in a pre-programmed spot, pick up and replace the fresh rod and then pick up and store the used rod. The whole procedure takes about fifteen seconds at each rod group.

Now, this is where Question comes in. In several occasions I've seen him swiftly jumble the new and used rods during the drone's operation. Apparently the drone is not programmed for the contingency of someone messing with its process, but it can distinguish between a new and used rod. It also seemed puzzled that the rod is not in its proper slot or sitting on the prearranged spot. After about a minute or two of this perplexing unaccountability, the drone goes into something which can only be described as an electronic tizzy, bordering on an electro-nervous breakdown. It then seems to send out a distress signal, which causes a more complex autobot to presently appear, at which point Question cuts out like a mad space beaver on wheels. On two occasions, the complex autobot attempted to follow him, but Question lost it in the jungle of the Hyborian Garden. If Question suddenly slid around the corner and ducked behind me, saying, "Cheez it, the heat", I knew that he had done more dumb shit.

Can you imagine how this made me feel. Here was I, a noble and humble representative of my species sworn to uphold the exalted principles of humankind, liberty and justice for all and all that good shit, and through no fault of my own I was stuck with a klepto psychotic space beaver as a sidekick, whose main preoccupation seemed to be to try to get me in trouble.

Question might have been funny if he hadn't been so pathetic. The closest Question ever came to actually getting me in trouble was the time that he deceived me in to getting high on his space pipe. Then while I was under the influence of the mind-boggling space drug, he talked me into helping him steal a flying saucer. It happened in this manner, and I caution the reader to bear in mind that, though honest to a fault and self-effacing in my humble refrain, I was at the time under the influence of a terribly good substance and in the clutches of an insidious minded goofy looking, drunken slobbering space beaver.

One day as we lay on the grassy slope smoking his space pipe and observing the aquatic antics of a couple of water monsters, Question approached me with the suggestion that we should 'borrow' one of the saucers and do a trip. "I don't know a thing about flying a saucer", say I. "No sweat, just leave it to me", says he. "You're not shitting? Are you sure you can handle a ship?" I asked. "Is bear shit brown?" says he. "Okay, but even if we did get the ship where would we possibly go? Would we venture out into the far reaches of space, shoot across the uncharted voids and go where no man and space beaver has ever gone before?" "Nope". "Then where would we go?" I asked. "Vegas", says Question.

I couldn't help from laughing in his face at such a preposterous suggestion. "Are you out of your little maggot mind?" I said. "I can't just show up in Vegas in a stolen saucer accompanied by a drunken space beaver". "No sweat, we just park the ship out in the desert and you go into town". "For what", I asked. To which he retorted. "Marty, I know you're just a human, and a mentally retarded one at that, but even you should know what to get in Vegas. You pick up a couple bales of money, some booze and some girls". "And just how am I going to get this money?"

"From the slot machines", says he. "Do you know what the odds are against winning at the Vegas slots?" "Not to worry. I got a gizmo to fix the machines", at which he pulled from his pouch what appeared to me to be a small claw hammer. "Hey, man that's a fuckin' claw hammer", I said. "Tsk, tsk au contraire, poor funny faced human. What you are looking at is a specialized, synchronetic, tapered, precision cast, manually operated, metallic percussion instrument". "No shit", I said, "I could've sworn that it was a cheap claw hammer. Did you steal it from the master tool room or have it specially fashioned by the greatest technological knowledge in the universe?" I asked. "Nope", he said. "Then where, pray tell, did you get it from, I asked. "The Pentagon", says he and we both collapsed in guffaws and slobbering snickers like two maniacs.

"Okay, okay, say I manage to get the money, the booze and the girls. Not even yours truly, with all of my suave persuasion, could convince a chick to mess around with a space beaver". "No problem", says he. "How so", says I. "Did you ever try to walk home from the moon?" says he, and once again we cracked up.

While still in the dizzying grip of drunken dementia, we were both busted crawling through some off-limits zone, giggling like snot nosed banshees, and summarily confined to quarters, where we might have remained forever had it not been for the benevolence of Tan.

A day or so later, being a young Earth man and sorely afflicted with the wants of sensual nature, I asked Tan if they had anything aboard this dump to get high on and also if there were any females around that didn't look like cartoons. His answer was affirmative to both queries.

A small serving disk whizzed up, bearing a little vial of a greenish liquid. Upon drinking the liquid, I immediately went into a woozy state, which can only be described as a kind of sexually gluttonous fantasy.

He led me into a softly lit circular chamber and laid me nude upon a kind of levitating bed. I don't know where he went, but I sensed that he remained near. Presently a kind of highly fragrant mist was released into the air around me. At first it stung my nose but quickly became mellow. Then I saw three females enter the chamber. They too were completely nude.

My mental state at the time was one of a blissful sexual hunger, the force of which I've never attained before or since that time. The ladies were obviously alien in origins though not unlike Earth woman in basic appearance. They were above five feet in height and had straight waist-length hair parted in the middle. One had raven black hair, the second had snow white hair, while the third one's hair was a flaming red in color. Their bodies were somewhat thin, like models. The breasts were small and firm like grapefruit halves, the waists small and the hips flared. The thighs were appealing, and the lower legs were a bit small while the feet were kind of flat and flared. The eyes were large and wide set, while the nose was small but well-formed. The lips were small but definitely human shaped. The whole face was egg-shaped with the small end being the chin, the forehead being broad.

The red haired one's skin was a deep red, the white haired one's skin was olive black, and the black haired one's skin was pearl white. Red skin, black eyes. Black skin, golden brown eyes. White skin, gray eyes.

In body proportions and facial features, they could have been triplets. The skin of the face and shoulders was smooth and unblemished, but they all had oval coloration marks covering the entire body from the breasts and upper arms downward. These skin configurations could clearly be seen as the ovals were of a deeper or different pigment coloration to the rest of the skin.

The pubic hair, though not identical in coloration to the head hair, was short and formed perfect triangles similar in tone to the hair of their heads. By Earth standards, I couldn't call them beautiful. However, while under the influence of the liquid and the odor of the fog and their bodies, I found them most desirable. The fingers of their hands were long and may not have had fingernails. Neither did they have eyebrows.

They made coo-ing sounds and massaged my body all over. I was immediately erect. We did not kiss. Then one after the other the ladies climbed atop me and made slow and noisy love. One did not replace the other until I had reached a climax, and I must tell you that these climaxes were marvelous in intensity. After this experience, I slept. I don't know how long I slept, but when I awakened, three other females had joined me.

The second group of three was more alien in appearance than the first set, being broad of body and quite muscular. Their breasts were larger but firm, the shoulders broad, as were the hips. The lower legs were strongly fashioned but shorter in proportion to the upper leg. The hair of the head was upswept and tightly curled like a fine Afro. Their eyes were wide set and slit in an oriental fashion. The nose was almost flat to the face, and the mouth was wide with full lips.

The thing that stands out more than any other about these females is the fact that they all had small sharp canine teeth, or vampire teeth as I call them. During our love making, they bit me with these teeth. I could feel the sharp tingle of their bites on the inside of my upper arms and the inside of my thighs. I don't think that they drew blood, as I couldn't find any obvious bite marks or skin breaks later, but I can't be sure.

All the females assumed the dominant position in our sexual activity. There were two sets of the long haired ones and two sets of the short broad lush ones, equalling twelve different partners altogether over an estimated period of seventy-two hours or there about. Later Tan told me that he had also experienced the sensations of my climaxes but had to tune out after the sixth one.

This was in 1964. When I was taken back to the great ship in 1975, I had the pleasure of being shown at least six of my offspring, not in person but via video scan from the home planet Biaveh. They looked more human than their mothers, but still possessed enough of the extraterrestrial characteristics to make them look lovably weird with big heads, large round eyes and small tweety bird mouths.

There were three boys and three girls, and they were all dressed in jump-suits and slippers of varying colors. They were accompanied by adults, who appeared to be full blooded humans including a white lady whom I recognized as being a pilot back during Lindbergh's time. She hadn't aged at all. The children were a bit shorter than their ten year old Earth counterparts. Some were playing with what appeared to be rather complex toys, and at least one boy was stacking play blocks using telekinetic power. Watching them brought tears to my eyes. I was told that I would some day be able to see them again in the flesh. However, they will no doubt be adults at that time.

I explained to Tan that it would be considered rather freaky on Earth for a person to get off on watching another person screw. I understand that the pleasure he sustained, paralleled my own, and he didn't even have to do any of the work.

After we got busted trying to steal a ship, they shook Question down and confiscated all of his non-food trinkets including his space pipe, which he said had been in his family for many generations, but which he had probably just recently stolen from some unsuspecting space junkie.

After that he couldn't even get near a robot drone without setting off some kind of alarm, and this made him a repulsive companion to be with for a while. A Targ busted him with his hand in the Targ's carrying unit and sicked the drones on him. They put him temporarily in a force field cage, and Tan had to get him out. When I tried to lecture him on the error of his ways, he said something about my momma, and I tried to choke him. But we soon forgot our differences as Tan took me about on a wider ranging tour of the mothership.

We even took a trip out to the huge planet Neptune, which is the furthest planet out in our solar system. The rings of that planet are composed of black chunks of matter, which I was told is carbon in varying forms. Robot units are on the surface of the planet and are mining that planet for a type of super pure carbon deep beneath the surface, which is harder than the Earth diamond. The substance is used in certain high tech instruments and is also used to coat the moving joints of the bionic beings called the Ancient Ones. The metals titanium, platinum and herculeneum are also found in abundance upon Neptune. Some metals, I'm told, have to be extracted from the superhot core of the planet, and this process is difficult to accomplish, even by the Biaviians.

While remote drones may be controlled in the Earth's atmosphere by a master guidance system out in space without much difficulty, this is much more difficult on or beneath the surface of Neptune because of the violently powerful electromagnetic forces in the atmosphere of that planet. So the robot units are sometimes almost entirely independent during their preprogrammed operations. Saturn also presents problems in this respect because of the violent turbulence on its surface.

Also, deep space is not always neutral in action and reactions. Out in the voids, there are huge electro-carbon zones where a great amount of electromagnetic and fissional disturbances occur. On occasions a remote or even a manned ship will lose contact with the mother base while exploring these zones or 'creation clouds' as the aliens call them.

The Biaviians have successfully charted at least six other galaxies and know of various life forms inhabiting them. Yet, as I have stated before, even the Biaviians have not discovered or communicated with all of the life forms in the Milky Way Galaxy alone. So in this sense their knowledge is quite limited.

Let me tell you, I personally met a true galactic traveler, who is from a galaxy other than the Milky Way. He, as close as I can remember his name, is called 'Agynmum' or the Great Agynmum.

Tan told me as I awakened one day that he wanted me to meet someone and that I shouldn't be afraid as his appearance to me would be fearsome. He was right. When the great door spiraled open and our transport disk whizzed in to the dim softly lit interior, I felt the rippling tingle of the decontamination lights, then the lights came up slowly, and I found myself standing before a huge sixty feet tall glass globe. Encased within this wondrous globe was a huge aquatic creature that resembled an Earth octopus in many respects. With a tall bulbous head and huge eyes and tree trunk-like tentacles, the Great Agynmum was blue-black in color with great gray dots. He was floating in some kind of blue liquid and great bubbles rose slowly through the mixture.

Suddenly I felt dizzy for a moment and then the picture started coming through to my inner sight. I saw a great planet surrounded by seven moons and a red sun. Some great cataclysm caused that planet to literally be torn apart. Agynmum escaped in a great ship and appeared to have traversed the vast distance between the two galaxies by utilizing a black hole or anti-space corridor.

He explained to me that he was the last one of his kind, and I shed bitter tears for him. It seems that the Biaviians are using his scientific knowledge to learn more of his mode of galaxy to galaxy travel. Even Agynmum's knowledge is limited by the fact that his method of coming to this galaxy was uniquely a one shot deal, and when he entered the corridor, he had no way of knowing where or even if he would emerge. They theorize that somewhere in the cosmos others of Agynmum's kind may exist. It is also hoped that they will be able to keep him alive until this can be accomplished. This magnificent creature who has journeyed here from the infinite distance of space, it seems to me, must be a loving and caring entity. Yet I can conceive of no happy existence for him even among the many aliens I saw aboard the great ship, and I feel a great tinge of sadness even now as I think of him. Even Question seemed to have been somewhat sympathetic to the plight of Agynmum. When I spoke of the creature to him, he said, "Yeah, tough shit".

Chapter 6

Inside the Alien Mind

For many years people have witnessed flying saucers cruising our skies, and on more than a few occasions, certain people have actually come into physical contact with the occupants of these ships. Generally the extent of the being-to-being communication between the abductee and the space men has been quite limited so any information as to the nature and purpose of the aliens' minds and motives has been fragmentary and speculative. Where did they come from? What do they want from us? These questions have plagued mankind down through the ages. Yet, to be truthful, we have indeed been given some insight into the minds of these visitors from time to time.

The book of Genesis tells of a time when angels or aliens walked the Earth and procreated with the daughters of man, and the offspring of these unions brought forth the first great kingdom builders on the Earth. Successive members of the blood lineage from the originals lived a very long time by Earth standards. When reading the biography of these generations, we find that this longevity diminishes with the infusion of more and more human blood.

The story of Lot and the destruction of the four cities on the plains, of which Sodom and Gomorrah were two, should be attributed to alien intervention into the affairs of man. The angel with whom Jacob wrestled and Elijah's fiery chariot are also recordings of extraterrestrial beings. Scriptural recordings in other ancient books also speak of these visitors from the skies.

In most civilizations, advanced or primitive, living or dead, legends and recordings of space visitors are an integral part of their history. Even in those ancient times, we find that these sky visitors generally chose to contact and communicate with the common man instead of with those who were rich and powerful, and the same holds true even unto this day.

The aliens don't seem to be interested in the political and position aspirations of man nor are they interested in literally preserving most individuals from those privileged walks of life. The future survival of the human species will not lie in the hands of the dictator or the privileged dynasties but in the propensity of the common man to assure mass survival by the sharing of available resources. Those who hoard and control any commodity of necessity to the masses are the cause of most of man's ills and are of no present inspirational or spiritual value to the aliens and are of no real future value from the practical sense.

To be sure, there has always been and there will always be a definite need for leaders among humans, just as there are always leaders among the animals of nature. If prehistoric leaders among the human species had been of the same quality as are the leaders of today, the Homo sapiens could not have survived. If the strongest hunter had hoarded all the meat and fruit from the rest of the clan, then the masses would have starved. If the stronger males had killed all of the weaker males, or failed to protect all the members in sickness and in health, they would have died out. In order for any race or society to endure and prosper, each member of that society must be given or have unhindered access to at least the bare necessities of life.

The aliens look upon this planet as just one world community and tend to measure the worth of man by how he treats those the least among his kind. They do not recognize country, state and city boundaries when observing the planet. This great imbalance in the possession of natural resources is a thing restricted exclusively to man on this planet.

The aliens revere the wisdom of the aged and view all children in a common parenting sense. No Biaviian would ever permit another of their kind to live in want of the common necessities of life. It would be, to them, an unbearable shame, which would reflect upon them all. In their eyes, when compared to all of the other living orders of above animal intelligences, the human species must be placed at the very bottom, not because humans are technically or even spiritually inferior to all other intelligences, because we are not, but because of man's willful perversity of moral character concerning his own.

During the course of our extensive conversations Tan asked me a question which I've never since forgotten. He asked, "Martin, if all humans were given those things essential to survival, would the rich be made poorer or the strong made weaker?" I said that I didn't think so. "Then the humanoid bi-ped is a most repulsive species indeed, for not even the Targs are guilty of such a thing nor the Skreed".

Of course, the overall situation on Earth is not that simple but the concept of a global community free from the want of food and shelter is clearly within our agricultural and technological capabilities, and it wouldn't necessarily alter the balance of social and economical power. In other words, the rich would remain rich, the famous famous and the powerful powerful. Bearing this in mind, the aliens have concluded that such negative circumstances are the results of man's willful inhumanity toward his fellow beings.

If I were a person formally schooled in the study of the mind, no doubt I would be better qualified in attempting to learn and then explain the inner workings of the extraterrestrial mind, but since I don't happen to be a trained psychiatrist, I'm afraid that you are stuck with me as I, beyond most if not all other known human beings, have had the rare opportunity of spending substantial spans of time in the company of these beings. So, in as far as my perception goes, I will give you my opinions and thoughts along this line.

Our first recorded rules or laws governing the workings of a communal society were probably of extraterrestrial origin. These first rules and laws were not born of divine inspiration but were simply a structuring and humanization of a more primordial method of progression. No philosophical or spiritually exalting doctrine has yet managed to improve upon the simple premise of "Do unto others as you would have them do unto you". If this rule alone were followed as closely as possible, it would nullify most of the greater problems afflicting humanity. The common elements of decency and fairness are truly universal in their application and hold true on Biaveh just as on the planet Earth.

I am truly awed at the technological capabilities of these extraterrestrials. If they so desired, they could take over this planet militarily in a matter of hours. They could cripple all communication networks, and literally stall all combustion engines should they so desire. They could develop and introduce special and deadly germs, alter the weather, destroy the ozone shield or literally blow the entire planet to smithereens. Those people who believe that the aliens are waging a covert war against humanity are rudely mistaken. Materially, man has nothing of necessitative value to the aliens and little of spiritual value to offer them.

True, there has been an on-going program of genetic cross-breeding which involves human and alien genes, but the aliens do not have to wage a subjugating planet war in order to acquire these genetic materials. Nor is it necessary to literally implant electronic devices in the bodies of individuals in order to keep track of them as study subjects. Should a subject person meet an untimely demise, they will also know this.

I believe that the aliens already have enough preserved genetic materials to re-populate a dozen planets the size of Earth with humans and hybrids if they so desired, just as they are able to reproduce any species living or extinct in the chronology of the planet Earth since its living origins. Think about it. The aliens aren't doing anything in this respect that we wouldn't do if we possessed the technology. Our scientists have managed to clone salamanders and frogs, and it is only a matter of time before more complex creatures, including man, are cloned. The aliens have perfected such things.

The extraterrestrials have also made great strides in the techniques of creating 'genetically specific' creatures for transplantation on to planets that have a different ecological order than the planets from whence they originated. In this way, certain aliens are continually adding to the already abundant life in the cosmos.

The Earth is but one among many celestial bodies which have been altered in this manner. The experiments aren't always entirely successful. The Homo sapiens are the end result of a number of mammalian bi-ped attempts, and one of the most successful. Yet on the vast scale of time, man is thus far the shortest-lived of any species which has ever dominated this planet. In other words, humanity is yet in its infancy as an evolutionary subject. In man's favor is the fact that, technologically, his advancement has been phenomenal. Yet if we had access to all of the historical recordings and knowledge that have been deliberately destroyed in the past by one set of consequences or another, we would even now have established ourselves on other planets. Or we would have already succeeded in completely destroying our species via one destructive means or another. The miracle is not that we have come to be but that we are still here.

On a number of occasions down through history, the aliens have found it necessary to intervene physically into the affairs of man in order to insure humanity's survival, both morally and physically.

The celestial rule of non-intervention as is presently practiced by the Biaviians has not always been in effect. There was a time when man, or the most civilized and advanced segments of humanity, was genetically closely intertwined with that of the celestials. The first great leaders, pharaohs, kings, priests, physicians, astronomers, seers and scribes were direct descendants of the full blood alien visitors.

The next chapter will speak more extensively on the specifics of this alien blood lineage, but now we will deal more closely with the alien, the Biaviian mind, more specifically their sense of logic and inner being as I perceive it at this time. Upon close scrutiny I have found that most of the aliens' actions are easily comprehended when we take into consideration their sense of reasoning.

1. Q. Why are nearly all human abductees restrained or otherwise temporarily incapacitated during their captivity?

A. Human abductees are initially restrained for a number of reasons, the most prominent of which being that the Biaviians are quite small in size and physically much weaker and fragile than the average human. So human beings are potentially dangerous, and even a human child has the physical strength to main or kill an adult Biaviian and so has to be restrained. However, drugs are rarely if ever used to restrain the human. Instead, I'm told that certain nerve centers of the brain are technically altered to control the physical prowess of the subject. The comprehension and the logic factors of the person are the last things to be interfered with. However, it is sometimes necessary in order to inhibit the horror factor or prevent a psychological or nervous breakdown in the subject. Generally the elements of touch, sight, hearing and even speech are left intact, the extent of which is governed entirely by the ability of the subject to adapt to the experience. For the highly emotional or potentially psychotic, a kind of dream or trance state is induced.

2. Q. Why are abductees taken?

A. In the case of the Biaviians, abductees are almost never chosen at random but are taken for some specific reason generally related to the genetic biology of the person. There are a considerable number of humans who yet retain a pool of the genetic inheritance of the originals and are considered relatives by the aliens. Also these individuals are the best subjects for biological cross-breeding with the aliens. The possessors of the gene may be of any race or sex, as the gene has migrated across racial and cultural lines through the prolific cross-breeding of the races through conquest, travel and general social intercourse between earthlings.

The migration of this gene cannot be consistently plotted except under an encapsulated circumstance, which is almost non-existent at this time on Earth. Even the enforced purity of a certain race does not guarantee the continued purity of the gene, but instead may eventually alter or destroy the gene in a given case. The infusion of new blood instead has contributed to the unaltered continuation of the gene in many cases. Also the retention of this gene may pool in the biology of a single member of a large family while being of insignificant measurement in the rest of the family members. Further, possession of this gene does not automatically make the carrier smarter or stronger. It does generally make the subject more capable of learning and retaining what is learned, provided that person is exposed to the means of knowledge gathering. These potential geniuses may be of aboriginal, black, oriental or Caucasian origins, and if the means of formal educational materials were equally distributed among all earthlings, there is no limit to what mankind could already have accomplished.

3. Q. Why haven't the aliens contacted more world leaders instead of the common person?

A. There was a time historically when the political leaders of men achieved their positions through their strengths of character, benevolence, common judgment and contributions to the general welfare of their subjects, but this element of worth has since been lost, corrupted or forcefully taken over by the most ruthless elements of mankind and therefore is no longer considered worthy of the aliens' personal confidences.

The same holds true of literal knowledge potential. While the original cherubim or leaders possessed most of the scientific knowledge, their knowledge has since been widely dispersed among the population at large. The enlightened one does not find it necessary to subjugate, intimidate, oppress and rob his fellowman in order to fulfill his inner nature. As a result, they rarely seek politically forward positions. Think about it. Nearly all good inventions and discoveries of world impact have been perfected by little known or otherwise obscure individuals, though the results have generally ended up in the hands of the leaders who are ruthless. The re-inventors of gunpowder, airplanes, firearms and other implements of destruction were not the ones who advocated or sought to use these inventions for world conquest.

No doubt the discoverers of nuclear fission initially sought to use this discovery for the benefit of man. Had they known the extent to which evil men would go in the aggressive implementation of this power, they probably would not have been so free with this knowledge.

So the aliens have no desire to allow the rulers access to their technology or into their confidence. In their opinion, there is no such thing as a world leader. There are tyrants, dictators and political manipulators, but not worthy leaders in the foremost positions on this planet. This is the heyday of the beast, the tyrants and deceivers, the gluttonous and the planet killers, so much so that humanity's destruction is almost imminent.

4. Q. Why is communication between the abductee and the aliens generally limited to little or no language communication?

A. This is mainly because most physical contacts are not made with verbal communication in mind, but more often are done for purposes concerning genetic testing.

Rudimentary communication such as assuring the abductees that they won't be hurt and that they are friends is standard operating procedure for the aliens. On rare occasions when a particular subject overcomes the initial shock of contact and is easily susceptible to telepathic reception, the alien may communicate at some length with the subject, and fewer still are taken into confidence and allowed to take journeys and spend time among the aliens.

Apparently there has of late been a movement among the Celestials to gain a closer rapport with the human psyche and motivations. Thus the prolific rise in close contact like the relationship between Tan and myself. For some reason, I think it is very difficult for most human beings to accept the reality of these aliens presence and then reconcile this knowledge to the human experience, to maintain a sane perspective in the face of it all. Even I find it difficult to accept the equality let alone the superiority of some of the creatures I've seen with my own eyes, and I have no desire to be a servant to a lizard or a giant mantis insectillian, though I know that it could conceivably happen. The force of it all is simply too fantastic for the human species as a whole to accept or endure, so most close contact between the aliens and humans is purely scientific instead of social.

5. Q. What do the aliens think of man in general? To what level of social esteem does he hold humanity?

A. When we see a chimpanzee, we immediately recognize a biological and genetic kinship, and our inner feelings toward them is generally one of benevolent guardianship. We know the animal to be of some intelligent worth and believe that it has the potential, no matter how slightly, of expanding this intelligence into something similar if not equal to our own, given the time and instruction.

Now then imagine that the chimp has learned to build crude living structures, build a fire and use sticks as weapons. We know that such small accomplishments on the chimp's part could not truly threaten us technologically, however, the creature now warrants a closer observation than say the baboon. We don't even consider accepting the fire building monkey as a social equal, but we can no longer rule out that eventual possibility.

In order to ascertain the latent potential of the creature, we start to scrutinize it much closer. We prepare experiments which will include everything from simple logic operations to genetic crossbreeding possibilities, while one segment of scientists may view this chimp as a brother of the future, others will explore the possibility of a futuristically cheap and controllable work force.

One thing is for certain, the chimp must not be allowed to advance so swiftly as to become a physical threat to us humans, and though benevolent and protective we may be, we must be prepared, if necessary, to destroy this upcoming species or certain dangerous parts thereof. Perhaps we will decide to scrap the project altogether and destroy only the fire builders while allowing the original jungle ones to endure, or the meek ones.

Perhaps this is not the best description of how the aliens look upon us, but it is probably close. However, owing to the great diversity of intelligent life forms in the universe, the aliens are no doubt more flexible in their propensity to accept extremely different kinds of beings than we are. Hell, we haven't yet learned to accept another human of a different race, tribe or skin color.

Man is far too dangerous to be accepted by the universal community, but not so insignificant as to be totally disregarded either. There is always the chance that man may chance upon some scientific breakthrough that could make him a threat to his neighbors in the Milky Way Galaxy.

6. Q. Why don't the aliens step in and prevent man from literally destroying the ecology of this beautiful planet?

A. The aliens, in my opinion, do not hold any dictatorial aspirations toward any other intelligent species in the cosmos. To do so would be to set a negative precedent for other powerful intelligences in the cosmos. Perhaps in some far quadrants of this galaxy far away from the seven who are here, there are interplanetary civilizations at war with one another, but just like here on Earth have come to treaty agreements with our fellow man and cleaned out certain territorial spheres into which others may not enter and beyond which we will not go, then on a larger scale, so has the universe been so dissected.

If you are a warlike life form, do not tread on this part of the Galaxy lest you be utterly destroyed by the seven. The Earth falls into the Biaviian sphere of protection and territory, and in this part of the Galaxy, we do not conquer and subjugate lesser evolved planets like Earth. We wonder why in the face of all of the war, famine and pollution on Earth don't the Celestials step in and change things.

This is the impression I get. As I have said, the aliens take the rule on non-intervention on the global scale seriously, and the aliens do not look upon time in the same manner that man does. Tan was a young male adult when the cities of Sodom and Gomorrah were nuked and is yet a young man by the Biaviian measure of age.

Man's preoccupation with the destruction of his fellow man is as old as the primordial order of the survival of the fittest, and yet this is the first time in man's evolutionary ascension that he has within his grasp the technological power to destroy all human life on this planet. The aliens are well aware of this, and so they have decided to save a portion of our species via direct airlift. Tan tells me that the A-bombs dropped on Hiroshima and Nagasaki were not the first incidents of nuclear destruction on this planet, but it was the first time that the human species itself had learned to split the atom. This great destructive power has been in the hands of man for only the slightest moment on the scale of measured time.

It is no secret that man gained this power while at the very depths of his inhumanity towards his fellow man. But for the racial hatred of the human monster Hitler, this awesome power would almost certainly have been developed first by the Nazis, in which case the plight of humanity would have swiftly reverted to one of nightmarish dementia. If Hitler had embraced the Jewish ethnic sector of his society long enough to take advantage of those Semitic scientists' knowledge, what would ultimately have been the destiny of all humanity?

The aliens seem to have a good grasp of the fickle and potentially explosive evil of man. They know very well that the element of mass psychosis lays dormant in the hearts of whole nations and can be reawakened with the changing of the wind. In times of famine and economic depression, the very structure of humanity's ethics and laws of universal rights can be successfully challenged and corrupted through popular hatred, bigotry and stupidity. With his own eyes, Tan has observed the rise and fall of a number of civilizations on this Earth. He also knows that the next one will be the big one from which no nation shall emerge intact.

At certain points in history the mixed breed offspring of the aliens did intervene militarily into the affairs of man, and this practice, though well meant, ultimately led to the destruction of that ruling society. They were called the Elohim, but the world has come to think of them more commonly as Atlanteans. So the pure bloods of today simply refuse to interfere in a military manner, even if it means the end to life as we have come to know it, nor will they extend to us that technological knowledge which might or would exalt one nation over the others, because none are without the inner predisposition towards tyranny.

7. Q. Do the aliens have the power to actually stop a global nuclear confrontation which is in progress?

A. If every nuclear warhead on Earth were aimed at the Biaviian mothership, which is situated in deep space, the aliens would have little trouble neutralizing the threat. This is because they have the home-based apparatus to do so. They could deflect the missiles, take control of the trajectory or detonate the warheads at a safe distance.

If they knew that a nuclear confrontation was imminent on the Earth, they could prevent the initial firing of the missiles on both sides, but in doing so they would be forced to disrupt the electronic communications network over the entire planet without discriminating between the military and cities, etc., and the computer network upon which all of civilization is run would be literally wiped out or glitched beyond reasonable repair. All commerce, communication and transportation would be knocked out.

If the rockets were actually launched, not even the Biaviians could safely deal with the problem. Even if the warheads were exploded after they breached the stratosphere, the resultant damage would irreparably injure the ozone layer and still disrupt the electronics of the Earth. Smaller, lower trajectory warheads and cruise missiles would also wreak havoc. The aliens are very powerful, but they are not all powerful. There are limitations even to their technology.

I got the impression that the aliens are not nearly as worried about the possibility of nuclear war as they are about the imminence of nuclear accident, disease, chemical pollution and ozone destruction. The combination of these things at their present level of contamination assures a terrible fate for humanity in the not too distant future. Scientists on Earth estimate that about fifty percent of the Earth's fresh water supply has been contaminated by pollutants, but the Biaviians put this percentage at about ninety percent of the water presently in use by humans, and this level of chemical contamination is growing daily.

The aliens know that we have the technology and the brain power to develop alternate and cleaner sources of energy, the ability to scientifically control the population explosion and the agri-resources to feed the starving nations. Yet they also realize that our varying differences in religious, political and social orders would make such an undertaking very difficult, not in materials, but in logistics and psychological alterations. Nonetheless, as they see it, we are surely doomed if we don't expend every possible effort in accomplishing these things.

Rome would not have been so easily conquered by outside forces had it not first been undermined by the continuous influx of starving aliens and the deterioration of ethical social order among the Romans themselves.

The bomb is the least of the threats facing civilized humanity. The extraterrestrials are aware of the fact that man is the only species of creature upon this planet that does not fit into any natural niche of the evolutionary and ecological order, and by all logical reasoning, all other facets of natural order would be much better off should the extinction of man occur. They have estimated that should man disappear from the surface of the planet via nuclear holocaust the Earth would repair itself within a thousand years or so.

I know that they plan to airlift a large number of humans from this planet within the not too distant future and return them after a thousand years, but I don't know how much of the Earth-bound population will continue to survive to witness their return. Nor do I know if the aliens plan to make sure that those left behind do not survive or to what extent a natural or man-made catastrophe will contribute to the extinction of humanity. Tan told me that under no circumstances would they personally contribute to the destruction of man, but I further realize that even space Gods can lie.

I do know that the Targs have historically been a war-prone species, and because of their aggressive nature, they gained the pre-eminent evolutionary position on their home planet. I suspect that in order to have done so, they had to have eventually destroyed all other ascending species on that same planet, and I shudder to think what might be the fate of Earth man if his destiny were left to the Targs alone.

We tend to view society on the person-to-person level. As a socially viable organism, humanity is in a bad shape indeed. However, from the aliens's point of view the human species numerically is a very successful life form. The insignificant numerical value of one-on-one abuse, the mass murderer, robbers and arsonists is lost upon the aliens overview since such antisocial things almost never transpire within their society's experience.

8. Q. What makes mankind so interesting to these aliens?

A. A scientist, no matter what his origins, is always interested in any new or different life form discovered and is compelled by scientific curiosity to observe and examine these plant and animal discoveries.

However, to the Biaviians the human species holds a slightly greater significance. First, because man personally removed himself almost entirely from the ecological evolutionary order of all other living things on this planet, and secondly, because man is one of the few species in the Galaxy who is genetically close enough to the Biaviians to actually be crossbred to them. Third, man is destined, should he survive, to some day become an intellectual and technological member of the intelligence community of the Milky Way Galaxy.

The very existence of modern man poses for them an enigmatic question, namely does man owe his continued existence to the fact that he has learned to predominantly overcome his social, political and religious differences, or does humanity yet thrive simply because he, prior to this time, did not possess the means to completely destroy himself?

Historical data tends to support the fact that humanity would have destroyed itself long ago or at least have subjugated and enslaved all weaker humans had the means been possessed. Now that man has the bomb is his continued survival owed to the fact that the possession of this technology is not yet universal? The aliens data is yet incomplete on this question.

Because of the abundance in the cosmos of all manner of precious metals and emeralds, and because they have no difficulty producing enough food substance or building living structures for all of their fellow beings, the aliens are hard pressed to decipher man's sense of logic concerning fellow humans. When they have a social or logistical problem, they immediately get together and solve it. Hunger and abject poverty are to them anathema to all logic, when one has the means to solve the problem. To them it would be ludicrous and totally unworthy of rationality to allow a Biaviian to live in want of medical care, shelter and proper education. Remove all elementary wants, and crime becomes a rare anomaly instead of a socially malignant phenomenon.

The Biaviians realize that an intelligent society essentially is run or kept prominent by a relatively small number of individuals who form the nucleus of the scientific and governmental order, while the greater masses are the ones who physically fashion the dreams and inventions of that nucleus. In the Biaviian society, this small nucleus is not a totally exclusive club in the sense that any Biaviian who makes the grade in technological or mechanical accomplishment automatically becomes a member of this club. As I have said before,

Biaviians come in various skin colors but intelligence knows no pigment.

The Biaviians see man not only as illogical, impractical and stupid, but also evil in his ways of motivation. He is at want to comprehend why man finds it more fulfilling to build more prisons instead of factories and guns instead of schools. Bombs instead of bread and apathy instead of care. The Biaviians' viewpoint is not born of some celestial benevolence but of simple common sense. What manners of fools are we that we would live as prisoners in our homes while being constantly victimized by those who commit crimes in order to acquire drugs, when we could solve the problem tomorrow by simply making drugs accessible to the user, thereby wiping out the incentive to commit the crimes. Which is more costly to us, the production of the drugs or the building of more prisons and the hiring of more armed protectors. If they knew the meaning of the emotion, they would find man contemptible and not worthy of continued existence. In their eyes a beautiful planet is being scrapped by a living intelligence malignancy called man, and to make matters worse, this creature called man knows better.

In the minds of evil greedy men, the reasoning is that if the world should gain universal peace and freedom from hunger, the population would expand at an even greater rate than at present. But this sense of reasoning, upon scrutiny, does not hold water. On the contrary, the highest birth rates are the exclusive happenstance of the poorest nations, while the lowest birth rates transpire among the most advanced societies. Better educated and well fed people are far more inclined to see the merits in practicing birth control than are the poor and ignorant segments of all societies.

The aliens don't understand the logic of denying a man a job and then condemning him when he steals. Stay locked in the creeping rot of transmitted diseases while withholding medical care or making needles easily obtainable to slow the spread by this manner. Spending billions on research to cure a host of cancers which are caused by the use of manmade chemicals in the first place. Deny all children a quality education and then gloat in the fact that they're ignorant. Express the wish for a cleaner environment while refusing to support research in the discovery of alternate fuel sources. The great farce of legal justice and political application. And they see religion as the one greatest hindrance to sanity upon this planet. When Tan asked me the way of these illogical preoccupations of mankind, I could only shake my head and say that I am sometimes truly ashamed to be a member of such a repulsive species. I personally do not entertain the belief that man shall ever rise above his gluttonous and gullible dementia. I can't think of many reasons to justify the continued existence of human kind. The negative reasons outweigh by far the positive, and yet I'm not too far gone to harbor the belief in miracles. Unfortunately, the aliens do not give sway to the credence or logic of such things as miracles. For them there is no greater crime than to do 'dumb shit' when you know and have the means to do better.

9. Q. Describe the alien mentality?

A. The aliens are critical of man's obviously foolish short-comings only in the analytical sense, while my assessments are more emotional in context. While I am repulsed at the bestiality preoccupations of humankind, the Biaviian tends to view the whole human organism as a shabbily run operation, which does not adhere to the common flow of logic.

I can see the collective and concerted corruption, bigotry and evil in man, but the Biaviians see him as a fickle enigmatic creature. They are not angry with man, nor do they hate him. They seem to get a lot of amusement, if not fun, in trying to figure out what man's next move will be or even to figure out why nations or governments choose to do a certain thing when it obviously calls for another.

These aliens are not very astute in the philosophic sense. They hold firm to the premise that for every problem there is a solution. Often the solution is too simple for the rational mind to miss. Then when, as usual, man cannot or will not respond correctly to the problem, it disconcerts them no end. So Tan asks me to explain the why, and often my explanation is not sufficient to clarify the matter to his satisfaction.

For instance, Tan observes a new building going up. A rudimentary scan of the structure shows the obvious flaws in the fabrication process. The concrete in the foundation and slab-work is subgrade and lacks the proper steel binding. The super structure of the building is composed of a low grade and flawed steel. The electrical wiring is too fragile to carry the projected load, and an Earth tremor of five points on the Richter scale will cause the building to collapse. Within ten years electrical fires will be common, and the foundation will be rife with cracks.

His questions to me is why would someone build such a death trap when the knowledge of doing it right is literally thousands of years old. Then I begin to explain to him about the kickbacks to town politicians, the bribery of building inspections and the greed factor, which supersedes the care for human safely, and other unsavory dealings.

On the extraterrestrials' view of human sexuality, a hypothesis: As I have stated a number of times before, the Biaviians do not experience emotions in the same manner that humans do. Their emotional plane seems to run on an even frequency, and their way of viewing things might be considered more machine-like in comparison with a human's way of viewing things. Yet they are able to experience the sensations of emotions second hand by telepathically tapping into the human's emotional frequency. However, it is a different story to figure out the inner meaning of the emotion.

For instance, if you walk into a dark hallway and one of your friends jumps out and says "Boo", initially it may induce within you a strong emotion of fear, the pulse races and the adrenaline flows, but the emotion of fear quickly degenerates into the emotion of anger at the friend for doing such dumb shit. Then a mellow feeling of relief follows because you are now glad that it wasn't a real threat to your safety.

If the alien were presented with the same scenario, he would view it differently from the inception. His first reaction would be evasion, as he assesses the probable danger of the situation. He would by now have recognized the friend or used proper force to nullify the threat. He would not have experienced either fear, anger or relief as we conceive them. He would not have felt any measurable emotional thing one way or the other.

The average person can watch the same movie over and over and still re-experience many of the same emotions he felt upon watching the same film. A Biaviian could never be impressed twice by the same scenario, because he knows what's going to happen, yet if he were tuned into your emotions, he too could feel the same emotions again and again, the difference being that you, as a human, can probably recall some of that same emotion again and again by simply thinking about the part that brought it on in the first place, while the alien cannot.

For all intents and purposes, after the initial emotion has diminished in the alien's mind, it is gone for good, unless you are there to resurrect it for him. Strangely telepathic transferences seems to be a one-on-one thing, in the sense that you can transmit the emotion to only one alien at a time, and he in turn can pass it on to another, who can pass it on to another in a rippling effect type manner.

I've seen this done by Tan in the great circular chamber as I lectured to literally hundreds of aliens. I could visually see a certain strong emotion passing among them and follow its progression as each alien responded with a shudder or some other visual sign in turn. If it was a really strong or interesting emotion then it might make two or three or even four circuits through the crowd with a kind of domino effect. Then they would discuss its meaning among themselves.

The emotions of fear, anger, sadness and delight are strong and distinct emotions, but the crowning emotional sensation of them all is that of the sexual climax, and the aliens dearly love to absorb this emotional sensation. All emotions fascinate them, but sensual emotions seem desirable to them.

The act of copulation in one form or the other is essential to the reproduction of any species. It is a biological function that comes as naturally as breathing, yet the Biaviians have advanced technically beyond the necessity or ability of physical copulation. However, I believe that their ritual of two loved ones bumping foreheads produces within them sensations which are similar to the human sexual climax, but a Biaviian may live for hundreds or thousands of years before performing this reproduction ritual once, if ever, and not even the forehead bumping ritual is essential in the reproduction of Biaviians. The laboratory cloning of Biaviians is universally practiced among them, so the practice of experiencing the human sensual release via telepathy is apparently a way for them to practice safe sex, or at least reproduction free sex.

I've never seen a male Biaviian completely nude, but judging from the close-fitting contours of their flight suits, the presence of substantial outer reproductive organs is not evident. Ergo, the aliens seeming fascination with human reproductive organs.

A scientific researcher is a scientific researcher regardless of his origins. The foremost intent of the researcher is to learn the manner by which the creature or thing under observation reproduces. Earth scientists are not capable of picking up the sensual sensations of the copulating subject telepathically, but they would if they could, and the sexual sensations experienced say, by a bull, might easily become addictive to the observer, as the bull's sensations may far exceed those of man's in intensity and thus in desirability.

I believe that I can safely say that the Biaviians have a collection of sensual human material which easily far exceeds that of any one known earthly collection of same. The common explicit sex film found on Earth is a staged, choreographed affair, but the alien tapes are all candidly recorded examples of the sexual methods practiced by every race, creed, ethnic group, gender and tribe on this planet. They also have taped examples of all manner of sexual fetishes and perversions not directly associated with or essential to biological reproduction.

I was shown excerpts from numerous sexual scenarios. I found a number of them to be highly to moderately stimulating, while others I considered repulsive. In the end, the assortment was narrowed down to the ones that stimulated me the most.

First of all, I want to impress upon the reader that the holographic reproduction technology of the alien tapes simulates reality to a factor exceeding ninety percent. The images are real to every sense but that of actual touch. If you stood within six feet of a couple making love without them knowing you were there, you could feel the air waves of their motions, smell the aroma and feel the heat from their bodies and hear every word, sigh and groan. This is the technical presence of the alien tapes. Only when the images fade before your eyes do you again realize that the subjects were not actually there with you.

Within hours of having observed a large variety of sensual material, I was recruited for the three day sexual marathon with a number of hybrid humanoid females. This was in 1964, and I was eighteen years old at the time. I can't say that the sexual participation was forced upon me against my wishes, as I was truly in a ravenous sexual mode at the time. However, I'm sure that I would not have found those females so sensually alluring had it not been for the introduction of a strong aphrodisiac mist and fragrance into that love chamber by the extraterrestrials at the time.

On the other hand, once I had initially agreed to participate sexually, entered the love chamber and inhaled the mist, I was no longer capable of physically or psychologically backing out of the deal. Because the mist served to magnify my sexual desires while rendering me physically weak, the females were obliged to assume the dominant role in the sex acts.

I feel as if the Biaviians deliberately sought to magnify the sensations of the sexual climax to the very pinnacle of its strength just this side of fainting and cardiac arrest so that they could pick up on it like so many celestial mind leeches.

The aliens can visually record the sex act, but they don't have the power to record the emotions and sensations for playback. Thus they have to have live subjects to experience emotions. In them, once the sensation is felt and passed, it cannot be recaptured with their imagination. Maybe they don't possess the power of imagination to any strong degree.

On several occasions I literally achieved telepathic interface with Tan, and in that state I could actually see the surroundings through his eyes. Somewhere in the mind link crossover, residuals of our thought processes got intermingled, though not enough to make me a space genius or to make him a human bare-knuckle fighting lover. Yet enough of his personality lingered to give me a tangible concept of how his mind works. I swiftly came to the conclusion that it's much more fun being me than being him. Tan has the technical power to destroy planets, but I could detect none of the haughty omnipotent attitude of his personality during the mind links that the possession of such power would induce in a human.

I also believe that, if given the opportunity, I could operate one of their ships, because I felt as if I understood the mechanism of the machine while in his mind. For instance, I instantly realized that the saucers do not use the power of engine thrust as do engine jet craft, but instead use a method of magnetic attraction and magnetic repelling power to move about. By manipulating the electromagnetic forces, the craft is able to go up, down, backward, forward or sideways, and the gravitational field within the craft remains a stationary force, almost completely un-effected by the surrounding centrifugal forces of gravity. Any kind or frequency of radio or other waves can serve as an invisible highway in the sky. To go to the moon you simply switch the magnetic poles to push the ship away from the Earth and then at a certain distance away you switch to the magnetic pull of the moon. You can literally slingshot yourself through solar systems without raising the engines.

I later learned that my sexual tryst aboard the mothership in 1964 served a purpose beyond allowing Tan and crew to get their jollies. The sexual session also produced at least six hybrid offspring, which bore more distinct human physical characteristics than did their mothers. They were shown to me on the vid-screen in 1975, and to me they looked strange but cute. They even had sparse hair on their little Mr. Potato heads, and, I believe, five fingers on their hands as opposed to their mothers' four fingers.

I have never been able to fully reproduce those sexual climax intensities again with Earth women, but the alien females did not spoil me on Earth women. Why? Because my sexual experiences with the extraterrestrial females were different. Extremely good, but different in a spiritual sense. The alien women didn't love me, and I didn't particularly like them. It was purely a case of drug induced lust. I resent the fact that they used me, that they performed sex upon me instead of making love with me. I'm not keen on the idea of having been rendered physically incapable of assisting or preventing the sexual activity. Still, all things considered, I still think of it as having been a very pleasurable experience.

How widespread is this cross-breeding program, and what is the numerical value of the earthlings so used? I really can't say, but I know from first hand experience that it is still being done. What is to be the future purpose and destiny of the hybrid offspring that result from the cross-breeding? This too, is a question that I'm unable to answer at this time.

I'm sure that the females I had sex with were part human. I gathered this opinion from their physical appearance, which was similar to humans in more ways than they were different. They were not mental automatons but had distinct and different personalities. Of the twelve females I had sex with, not one was to return for a second session. Physically the six lean ones were very similar in appearance, yet I had no problem distinguishing the unique differences in their personalities. As any woman or man who has experienced a number of different intimate partners knows, no two individuals feel or make love in exactly the same manner, not even identical twins, so I could tell the difference between them.

The whole three days was like one long sensual dream, because the effects of the mist, as well as possibly the liquids they fed me, may have continued to induce the mellow torpor of the sensual high. When it was over, I was noticeably weak in the knees for hours, and upon my return to Earth, I could not achieve an erection for a month, no matter the stimulus. My problem was that at the time I had no conscious recollection as to the why of my temporary impotence, and it disturbed me grievously.

That was twenty-six years ago. Sometimes I find myself wondering how those females are and what my offspring look like now. I truly believe that I will see those kids again in this lifetime.

I believe that the six offspring I was shown on the screen in 1975 were the progeny of the six slender hybrid women. I was not shown the offspring of the heavier females, if indeed any offspring resulted from those unions. I could tell that the heavier ones were of a differing racial genetic order than the slender ones, but I couldn't see any resemblance between them and any of the seven known intelligences aboard the ship. Could they be of some celestial race not represented in number aboard the mothership? With a little imagination I could easily conclude that the slender ones were of Biaviian and human stock, just like the Biaviian features were still visible in my alien offspring, though not as pronounced as in the features of their mothers.

Aside from being humanoid bi-peds, the heavier ones bore no true resemblance to any of the known intelligences aboard the great ship. Then I stop and remember that Tan told me that different species of life are abundant throughout the galaxy and no doubt the many other yet uncharted galaxies as well. Still I would like to see those kids, if they exist. I could love them, even though, judging from their mothers' looks, they've got to be some ugly little bastards.

When I stop to think about it, I must inevitably come to the conclusion that the human gene has already been dispersed throughout the cosmos, if not in Homo sapien form, then certainly in the form of hybrids. I know that I have at least six offspring on the planet Biaveh, and I also saw other hybrid children there.

During the study they will ultimately know how much of the human population is heterosexual, homo or bisexual, and to what extent certain fetishes prevail. From this study, they can correlate the relationship between sex and aggression, prejudice and the underlying nuances of what we call moralistic persuasion.

They will learn what sexual practices are acceptable on the mass level and which ones are frowned upon. They realize that man's sexual nature serves as the catalyst that motivates and controls the greater portion of his actions. Perhaps they are attempting to breed a more logical thinking and less aggressive man, an attempt perhaps to incorporate the physical strength and tenacity of the human being with the more astute mental faculties of the aliens.

The subject of human sexuality did not occupy all of our discussions there, but it was definitely a subject that was given priority exploration.

Chapter 7

Back in Time

There are Biaviians living today who are forty or fifty thousand years old. This is meant literally. Fifty thousand years ago a bouncing baby Biaviian was born on Biaveh and yet he lives in the physical form. He has been physically cloned several times, that is his original brain has been surgically transplanted from one aged body into a new youthful one, which was grown from genetic materials taken from his own original body.

However, the numerical value of the Biaviian population is strictly enforced. This is the way it works, and it is not without some complications. It may be noted that genetically flawed fetuses, which cannot be medically corrected, are all terminated in early growth on Biaveh. True, literally every Biaviian citizen has duplicative bio-matter stored or frozen in anticipation of the time in the future when the duplication process will be necessary should the citizen so desire. Of course, it would not be practical to begin the clone growth process too early in the life of the original lest the planet's storage capacity be overextended with adult sized clones lying around waiting.

So the birth and growth process is started only when medical examination foretells the imminent necessity for this transference. Those ready to receive the operation must remain on the home planet for the sixteen to eighteen years that are required to bring the clone to trans-status, and there are no exceptions to this rule. Not even the foremost scientists, pilots or artisans may leave the home planet during this time period, and though it is possible, the cloning materials and technology are not permitted to leave the home planet. I'm sure that this is for security reasons to prevent the possibility of this technology being abused, stolen or duplicated. However, the necessary equipment for freezing new materials can be carried on missions. Should a particular scientist of great knowledge meet some untimely and mortal fate away from the planet, his original being or spirit is lost because the Biaviians are not able to preserve the original brain for extended periods of time without damaging it.

If the clone is permitted to develop naturally, it will produce another brain identical in all biological respects to the original, but it will remain an empty vessel, which must be taught in the manner that all children are taught. Though biologically identical to the original, it won't automatically inherit the conscious properties and content of the first. Ordinarily the brain of the clone is medically suppressed in growth and will weigh only several ounces even when the body matures, and it will have no conscious awareness of its surroundings. If the cloned body is allowed to develop naturally, complete with brain, it is in essence, a totally separate entity with rights of its own and thus cannot be used for brain transference. This is the law.

Any one person may have enough genetic materials in storage to clone a thousand separate bodies. However, only one duplicate of any Biaviian, even a high council member, may be in the developing stage at one time, and then only when the transference procedure is imminent and necessary. Otherwise, you're not allowed to order up a hundred of yourself at will.

In order to keep the population in check with topographical availability, the birth rate is strictly controlled. Each couple is allowed two children, of which the gender is left to chance. If for some reason the parents die, the orphaned children will be placed with childless couples and will supersede the birth of new babies. There are no orphanages on Biaveh. The birth rate is also governed by the number of deaths or willful terminations. Since death is to a greater extent by choice, the birth rate fluctuates with time.

I'm told that the Biaviians sometimes experience a euthanasia fad or flap, in which a large number will choose to die in a given time span, and these flaps cannot be anticipated. They just seem to happen. At these times, new births are encouraged. Other happenings may entail a burst of new births, such as the rehabilitation of some new found planet or the decision of many to simply live out their present life span and die a natural death. Once this decision is made, the stored genetic matter is forthwith terminated, so your decision is final.

All over the planet at any given time, a Biaviian has decided to end it all. A computer records the termination and destroys the corresponding genetic materials, cross references and duly alters the new birth quota.

A child or animal cannot enter the disintegration chamber. Should a child attempt to enter, the eye of the computer duly records the attempt and someone is dispatched to investigate the matter. If the child attempts to enter again, he is allowed into the chamber and is simply held until the authorities arrive to pick him up for tests. Should a child or other non-terminate status person opt to kill themselves by some other means or meet with accidental death, the sensors will also record their death, even though it did not have the power to prevent it.

Since the gender of all children born on Biaveh is left to chance, more females than males are born, so males are valuable, pampered beings and polygamy is standard. However, if a male has more than one wife, the average is about four, he can only produce one offspring to each wife beyond the two children to the first wife.

By law, each wife must have a separate residence of her own, apart from her husband's and the other wives. In most cases the wives' homes are built in a circle around the husband's house, which is in the center of a wagon wheel configuration. The children are common property and have free run of all the houses. Actually the children are spoiled rotten, even by Earth standards, and are prone to manipulating the parents, as are all children.

Strangely, a woman does not have to go through any legal procedures in order to leave her husband, but is required to inform him of her departure via computer before or after the fact. The divorce is duly recorded. Should she decide to return, she needs only his permission. If he refuses, then she can take him to court. Infidelity is not legal grounds to prevent her return, but refusing him her sexual favors is. Her inability to bear an offspring for him is not grounds to prevent her return, but her refusal to adopt is. And like Earth customs, in a separation, the child generally remains with the mother, and so do her personal servants and companion robots, since their programs have become closely attuned to her wave lengths.

I further learned from Tan that Biaviian males are in many ways just as perplexed as to the actions of their women as are Earth men. They have their dominant and docile female personalities, busy bodies and gossips, fidelities and infidelities, schemes and intrigues, no doubt on a much more subtle level of expression in comparison with their Earth sisters.

It would be a mis-statement to say that the Biaviian individual is always above reproach, because there have been, and on rare occasions there may yet be, an anti-social or renegade Biaviian. There is no guarantee that a seemingly normal individual may not at some point, for some reason, go haywire.

The Biaviians have long known that it is dangerous to place too much power in the hands of any single individual. The checks and balances involved in taking a major action are so extensive and complex that it would entail a major collusive conspiracy in order to bring it off, so any notable deviation from procedure is nearly always detected and corrected early.

Fortunately, the Biaviians don't have a major organized

under-world or subculture like that of Earth, because of these checks and balances and the lack of the material and social incentives that foster gangsterism.

If you're a Biaviian and you have a yen for soldierly combat, you can participate in the combat games or exercises. This game consists of you against an opposing team of lifelike robot fighters. During these games you can destroy these robots with your lasers, and they can stun, wound or literally knock you out with their weapons should you get hit right. The combat is non-lethal to you, but memorable. There are numerous ways to satiate the needs of nature on Biaveh, and regardless of skin color, all Biaviians look upon themselves as one person, one race.

Biaviian culture is hundreds of millions of years old, as we measure time, and I'm told that the first Biaviians set foot on this planet called Earth, along with the Nyptonians and Stagyians, some six hundred million years ago. Of course, at that early date in our planet's history, there was no existing creature which could conceivably be called intelligent on its surface.

I'm told that at that point in time the young planet was simply charted on the log as just another planetary body which was capable of sustaining life. It was but one among many such heavenly bodies.

In those days the Biaviians had not yet developed a mode of space travel even close to their present capabilities, and a journey from the home planet to Earth would have taken hundreds of years. On that first expedition, the wayfarers spent a few years on the planet's surface, collecting samples and other scientific data, before departing for home.

Tan also assures me that the Biaviians were not the only space travelers who knew of and visited the young planet Earth. Biaviians continued to stop by on occasion over a period encompassing literally millions of years. During that span of time the Earth did not hold a position of prominent interest to the Biaviians. The universe is filled with scientifically interesting planets. Earth's initial discovery was claimed by the Biaviians, and if they desired to keep possession, it would be necessary for them to actually start some tangible development on the planet's surface.

Back in that far away time, Biaviian technology and social order had not yet been refined to its present state, and there were unlawful elements of society to be dealt with. Since banishment to planetary colonies was preferable to capital punishment, the planet Earth became Biaveh's Australia. So a substantial group of Biaviians and other species of intelligent undesirables were shuttled off to Earth.

The great prison colony airlift transpired about a hundred and fifty million years ago as we measure time. The new settlers must have found the Earth to be a terrifying and a nightmarish place, because by that time the scaly megatons had crawled from the ocean on to the hot steamy shores and the dinosaurs ruled the land.

Perhaps the captain of the great transport ships did not have forewarning of what manner of life forms they would find here, but once having reached their destination across several hundred years of space and not having the on-board supplies to return the prison hordes, decided to off-load them on to the now forbidding planets. They would have to survive as best they could by their own wits and resourcefulness. Thus were the first intelligent bi-ped life forms introduced on to the planet Earth. The home planet would not know of their success or failure for another fifty million years or so.

Such fantastic time spans tend to boggle the minds of most people, yet I'm told by Tan that there are living planets which were discovered and visited hundreds of millions of years ago, which probably shall never again be visited by the Biaviians even though they remain aware of their existence. When we pause to reflect upon the tens of billions of stars in the universe, most of which boast their own solar system, then we realize how insignificant this grain of living sand is in this infinite sea.

As time passed through eons of measure and the Biaviians succeeded in conquering the time quantum and to exceed the light speed equation, multiple visits to out of the way planets like Earth became a more practical reality. Had those first settlers succeeded in conquering the natural obstacles of this violent planet and risen to their former technological level, perhaps they would have one day returned to their home among the stars. As it was, those first settlers, though they survived fifty times longer than man has been a bi-ped creature, ultimately failed and melted into oblivion, leaving nothing behind but a few foot prints in the Mesozoic clay.

During the time of the first intelligent inhabitants, the planet Earth was a much different place geographically and geologically than it is at present. I'm told that the planet goes through varying ages of warming and cooling, and at that time the Earth was experiencing a warming period the intensity and duration of which has not been equalled again. Even unto this day the Earth is in the process of warming and cooling. Think of a great mud ball, which has a hot bubbling core. From time to time the core of the ball flares up and literally heats the crust all the way to the surface. When this happens, a kind of greenhouse effect prevails over most of the planet. By and by, the core loses fuel and starts to cool. When this happens, drastic and swift changes occur on the surface, the oceans cool, volcanic activity subsides, the polar ice flows advance and much of the fauna goes through a transition of adaptation. So do many forms of animal life. It would be safe to say that a volcanically active planet eventually will turn itself inside out. As the magma from the core continues to boil to the top, the regurgitated material is eventually replaced with new material, some of it organic. During the Jurassic period of the Mesozoic era, the plant and animal organic fuel period was very rich, and the seething core of the planet reacted by bringing forth the hot, moist and steamy surface conditions which were ideal for the nurturing of numerous megalithic forms of life, among which the reptile rose to ascendancy.

It was a time that was tropically ideal for the incubation of reptilians eggs, which were hatched in profusion. Many reptiles will continue to grow for the duration of their lives, and many of those creatures boasted life spans of literally hundreds of years.

The reptiles were so diverse in size, habit and diet that no other species of vertebra could compete with them on their turf. Some were land dwellers, while others lived in the sea. Some were vegetarian, while others were carnivores, some omnivorous, amphibian, gliders, scavengers, crawlers, runners, jumpers, ground and tree dwellers and all of them were hungry and dangerous to some link in the living chain. Some dinosaurs were a hundred feet in length and weighed many tons, while others were mere inches in length. Many developed various forms of body armor, while others possessed poisons. Size protected some, while speed protected others. Some laid their eggs above ground, some buried their eggs, some swallowed their eggs and hatched their young internally. Some actually guarded their nests or their young, others did not. The reptile's greatest enemy was other reptiles, the scavengers and predators.

Yet in the midst of this awesome reptilian nightmare, other less prominent species of animal life struggled to find and hold a survivable niche in the rippling cracks of this reptilian empire. Nearly two billion years before the thunder lizards reached ascension, the same melting pot of electrically charged nucleic acids from whence they came also brought forth slightly different kinds of life forms, which would slowly evolve parallel forms of warm-blooded creatures. A small number would endure to gaze in awe and fear upon the awesome and deadly lizards through large expressive myopic eyes from beneath the twisted and grotesque roots of great swamp trees.

No larger than small rodents, possessed of hyperactive metabolisms and covered with tender sparse hair, the little creatures found it necessary to consume two-thirds of their own body weight each day in order to stay alive, so nearly all of their waking hours were spent hunting food and avoiding the predator reptiles. Some of these little creatures lived in underground burrows or in the hollows of rotted trees. Others had learned to climb and make their nests in the canopied tops of the tropical trees.

As the warm-blooded creatures gradually evolved into more tenacious and adaptable forms, so did the reptiles continue to multiply and diversify, until there came a time when the line separating warm-blood from cold-blooded species grew thinner among some species of reptiles, and the warm bloods found it harder and harder to survive when pitted against such awesome adversaries.

Different species of animals tend to evolve under specialized conditions and may be restricted to one particular geographical area.

Should this area suffer some great cataclysmic upheaval or disaster, an entire species or sub-species may become extinct in a very short span of time. During that terrible far away time, some vast part of the surface of the Earth was always in the process of awesome upheavals. Huge fiery volcanoes thundered and blew magma ash into the scarlet evening, and the seething surface moved like some great steaming water bed, bringing scalding gaseous destruction to millions of scampering, screaming creatures.

Scorpions eighteen inches long and praying mantis more that a foot tall skulked through the night and prayed upon lizards twice their size. Sometimes during the warm tropical rains great sea crabs would seize the chance to leave the foaming waters and raid the shores, scavenging and even preying upon the unwary and the slow.

A seventy foot brontosaurus trapped in the grasping quicksand will not live to perish of starvation before falling prey to swift carnivorous ostrich-sized pack lizards. A number of lizards, while being light in weight, possessed great folds of leathery skin stretching between the forward and rear legs. Sometimes a sudden gust of wind would catch the skin and momentarily lift the lizard aloft. By and by these lizards became conscious of and sought to utilize these updrafts in clumsy attempts at flight. Some kinds eventually succeeded and because quite dexterous at gliding. The abundance of warm currents welling up from the seething surface made staying aloft easy for some, so much so that some like the pterodactyls become predatory masters of the Mesozoic skies.

During this span of evolutionary adaptation, warm bloods were also devising more complicated and specialized methods of survival. The warm-blooded creatures had always been nocturnal and retiring, ever scrounging in the shadows of the true masters of the Earth, the Dinosaurs. Instinctively some of them came to realize that the reptiles could not exist in the cooler regions of the higher altitudes, and so they retreated to these zones.

The seasons at that time were not so pronounced as they are today, but there were definite seasonal changes and the snow or frost lines of the mountains advanced and receded with the seasons. By following the ice line closely, the warm bloods were able to avoid much contact with the terrible lizards.

Some of the warm bloods, vegetarians and carnivorous, started to grow in physical size and to develop specialized means of survival. Some still retained the ancestral habit of laying eggs, while a few developed marsupial traits. Yet another had developed the ability to fly. One kind possessed six feet leathery wing spans and reposed upside down from the ceilings of caves, emerging only at night to drink of the blood of other creatures.

Yet as time went by and the wheel of evolution continued to turn, certain kinds of saurians started to develop metabolisms which were similar in working to the warm bloods. This biological transition enabled some of the reptiles to invade the cooler zones and to pray upon the warm bloods there. This infiltration of the mammalian zones by the reptiles eventually decimated the species value of the warm bloods. The competition for survival between these opposing species was clearly being lost by the mammals.

Archaeologists have long been of the opinion that the evolutionary process is a long drawn out procedure of subtle alterations, which are directly influenced by the creature's environment. To a lesser extent this is true, but to the greater extent, it is a matter of genetic defects.

The same is true of numerous plant species. Frequently the fossilized remains of some extinct creature is discovered, to which scientists can attribute no transitory kinship with other known species.

Today the genetic pool among the species is more specialized and individually refined. As a rule, the species rarely interact to the cross-breeding level, and the creation of entirely new species as a result of the cross-breeding is not nearly so common or possible as it was at one time.

There was a time when the genetic differences among reptiles, mammals and fowls were not so different as to prevent the cross combinations.

Two large lizards hatch a clutch of eggs, and among the hatchings are several runts, genetic deficients. If these runts survive, they may seek out other genetic runts in the same commune and proceed to birth a new order of smaller lizards. This same scenario can be applied to certain fowls and mammals, so, in many cases, the link is missing. I realize that my assessment is very simplistic in its expression, but it is nonetheless true. How else could all domestic dogs have come from the wolf, or domestic cattle from several wild kinds. Look at your thoroughbred horses and various breeds of swine. Today we have reached the point of designed animals through various methods of cross-breeding.

It may be noted that for every successful species of animal who survived, perhaps a hundred other new species didn't. In the ruthless ages of the evolutionary melting pot it seems that nature embarks upon an unrestricted creation campaign, bringing forth a great profusion of life forms, but time, environment and happenstance will cause this number to dwindle accordingly until only the most tenacious and adaptable remain. The best kinds of survivors have always been those species who are able to swiftly adapt to any kind of ecological or food source chance. For instance, the cockroach, the coyote, the rat and the human being, to be able to live anywhere and to eat anything, meat or vegetable, rotten or fresh.

Some six hundred million years ago when the first forms of intelligent life were delivered here from the stars, the creatures I've just spoken of had not yet evolved to any prominent level. Yet the planet was still populated with a profusion of lesser life forms, many of which were deadly, and volcanic upheavals on the planet made permanent location settlements a most precarious undertaking indeed.

Nonetheless, these first interplanetary life forms, who possessed some rudimentary technology, managed to settle in and survive for eons. They built cities and advanced to the level of producing combustible motors for transport and power. When they first arrived, I'm told, there was a sense of comradeship between them, and they proceeded to work together in the re-creation of much needed technology and mutual protection from the surrounding animal life and the elements.

Primarily, there were three kinds of beings: the Biaviians outcasts, who were about four feet tall and fragile of physique. The Porons, who were a warlike species of giants from some far off planet in the galaxy who had fallen prisoner to the Biaviians. They were about twelve feet in height, weighed a thousand pounds and walked on elephant trunk like legs. The third group were the Nilts, who were a race of tiny people, who were about six inches tall. I'm told that the Nilts were very valuable because of their expertise in micro-electronics.

This partnership lasted for centuries until difference of origins and other innate jealousies eventually drove the coalition into different opposing camps, and ground wars ensued. Over a period of time wars, disease and the ecological catastrophes literally brought these species to extinction. I'm told that they even used biological warfare on one another. If any survived at all, they are not in evidence at this time. It is theorized that some of the Nilts may have managed to survive by moving underground permanently and may exist in a primitive form even unto this day, but this is pure speculation.

Then about seventy million years ago a new and very dangerous intelligent life form entered the picture. The Biaviians had known of the existence of these intelligent reptilians for many thousands of years. They had followed the Targzissians' technological process for many centuries and were aware of the fact that the Targs had developed anti-matter propulsion rockets and ruby lasers.

By peopling one of the solar systems around a neighboring star, the Targs fell into the territorial chart boundaries of the planetary federation. Yet close social and diplomatic relations with the Targs had never occurred, not because the Biaviians didn't wish it but because the Targs were very secretive and mistrustful of all others known to them and even though their technology had reached an advanced level, the Targs were still warlike and primitive in many things.

Their differences in genetic origins, social order and cultural reasoning were too extreme to be desirable to the Biaviians. It was noted that on their home planet the Targs had quite literally destroyed all other primitive but intelligent reptilian species and has conserved only those food animals they desired for sustenance.

The planet Targ is rich in precious metals and jewel stones

and continuous volcanic hot springs and gaseous geysers supplied a readily abundant natural source of energy. A kind of greenhouse effect pervades the planet, making the atmosphere undesirable to soft-skinned warm-blooded life forms due to ultraviolet rays penetrating the stratospheric level. However, the atmosphere is ideal for the reptile. By and by, the Targs advanced to the stage of space exploration. Even with the advent of satellite planetary exploration, the Biaviians didn't feel as if they had anything to fear from the warlike Targs. However, when the reptiles, with the scientific aid of another unnamed life form, gained access to fusion electromagnetic propulsion capabilities, the Biaviians began to take notice of them.

Within a century the Targs began to raid Biaviian industrial installations on off plant moons and asteroids, destroying the then rudimentary sentinel systems and stealing the refined materials and finished products, which were peddled on the planet Targ and to other smugglers in the star system. Initially the Biaviians only made diplomatic inquiries, then protests. The Targs denied any involvement in the raids.

Then a manned industrial installation was raided, and all hundred of the male and female scientists were executed by the Targ raiders, but not before video-scan recorded the actions there. It was decided by the council federation that a punitive strike should be made on the Targs.

The results of the strike wiped out the Targ interplanetary fleet and literally paralyzed the industrial production capacity of the planet. Several thousand Targs were destroyed. The Targs were cowed but unrepentant. They agreed to cease all aggressive activity in the future and not to rearm their off planet ships, but they had no intentions of honoring that agreement. They had learned some important lessons from that first campaign. They learned the true military capabilities of the peaceful fragile Biaviians, and they would try not to underestimate them again.

In order to reap the benefits of the numerous industrial installations that the Biaviians already had operating, it would be necessary to take the factories intact, along with their robotic technology. In order to assure the success of this take-over, it would be necessary to nullify the source of the sentinel systems, the planet Biaveh itself.

So then the Targs made plans to build a war machine of a great enough magnitude to attack and destroy the planet Biaveh. Though the Biaviians were not definitely aware of the reptiles' intentions, they did know that the birth rate on Targ had increased drastically and that numerous supposedly non-combat ships were being built, not to mention a huge network of underground installations. It was suspected that great quantities of fissional materials were being mined by the Targs on the home planet and on various uninhabited space bodies.

The reader may perceive the impression that these things happened in a matter of a few years, but in actuality it took a few hundred years. The Targs have long memories, so the whole process was slow, clandestine and calculated. The Biaviians found true reason for apprehension when it was discovered that the Targs had developed the technology for near light speed travel and were dispatching ships out into deep galactic space. During one of these deep space jaunts, and perhaps using star charts stolen from Biaviians, the Targs discovered the planet Earth. This was about seventy million years ago.

Then back on the home planets, it is recorded that the Targs struck in force. The Biaviian suffered great losses in deep space, but not so great as the Targs. In our solar system near Venus the Targs attacked the Biaviian exploration ship and were almost wiped out.

Back home, the planet Targ suffered something akin to a scorched Earth destruction before capitulating to the Biaviian visitors. The Biaviians then turned their attentions to the young planet Earth. They were not pleased at what they saw.

Before them lay a beautiful young planet, which was teeming with life forms. There were fowl, insect, aquatic and mammalian species in large numbers, yet among all these creatures the obvious maters of the Earth were the terrible lizards. The dinosaurs in their many diverse sizes, habits and forms completely dominated the natural direction of things. This would not do.

If left to its own evolutionary direction, it was agreed that the reptiles would continue to rule the young planet and would eventually displace and completely wipe out all other aspiring species of warm blooded creatures. The Biaviians had experienced more than enough of the reptile form. Should the Targs eventually be able to gain control of the new planet with its abundance of natural resources, they would have another base in this sector of the Milky Way from whence to launch future warlike campaigns. The Earth was still considered frontier territory and being outside the accepted space region of the seven intelligents and yet bearing no intelligent life of its own, was basically up for grabs. They might be able to lay claim to the Earth by virtue of genetic kinship with the dominant species on the planet, the dinosaurs.

It was soon decided what must be done. The Elohim came to the decision that the reptile dynasty upon the Earth must be destroyed. Furthermore, the ecological progressive rhythm of the planet must be altered so as not to remain an ideal atmosphere for the future nurturing of such an unrestrained and numerically diverse habitat for huge reptilians.

The manner in which this was accomplished was shown to me on a huge vid-screen aboard the great mothership in 1975. I stood and watched in awe at the terrifying reality of the true technological power possessed by these wondrous beings from the stars. Imagine if you will, being transported back through the trembling eons of time, back beyond the conception of conscious intelligence as we conceive it.

From a birds-eye view, far below you see what appears to be a pack of small animals surrounding a much larger animal and its two cowering offspring. At first you get the impression of a pack of hyenas attacking an elephant, but as you draw closer, through the steaming mists, you are amazed to see that it isn't an elephant at all, but a desperate horned triceratops mother and her two offspring locked in mortal confrontation against a determined hunting band of much smaller ostrich-like meat-eating lizards.

A great and chilling chorus of grunting, clicks and hissing rent the air as the mother triceratops turned, charged and turned in a desperately futile attempt to keep the hunters from reaching her young. Numerous bloody scratches, bites and lacerations covered her back and shoulders, as well as those of her two siblings, who crowded close to her, emitting high-pitched screeches of fear.

Two of the hunter lizards rushed under her, trying to get at the tender belly of the great lizard only to be trampled to death, at which their still trembling corpses were immediately set upon by others of their group and literally ripped to pieces. Though a number of them were tossed about and injured, the hunter pack was relentless. Before long, first one and then the other of the triceratops young fell under the onslaught of the predators. Then seeing that all was lost, the mother charged through the pack and lumbered off, but judging from the extent of her wounds, I felt that she probably would not survive.

Now from out of the scarlet sky several kinds of winged reptiles descended and started vying with the predator lizards for their share of the spoils. Suddenly there was a thunderous roar, and the pack lizards, as well as the winged lizards, scattered in fear for the king had come. Standing nearly thirty feet tall and weighing eight tons, the awesome Tyrannosaurus Rex has arrived, and it didn't take long for the king lizard to completely consume what was left of the two young triceratops.

The panorama was dotted with distant active volcanoes, and the swampy landscape was dotted with great steaming tar pools and deadly bubbling suck holes of hot quicksand. Through these perpetually steamy tropical rain forests roam the great vegetarian brontosaurus and other swamp vegetarians of an even greater size and a host of other megatons and smaller reptile species. Huge armed snapping turtles, twelve feet across the back, plowed slowly through the mud-like moss covered tanks.

Boa constrictors the size of oak trees and measuring sixty feet in length hung lazily from the overhanging tree limbs. Dragonflies with two foot wing spans came to rest upon the ridged backs of sixty foot crocodilians. Pink skinned lungfish crawled from the muddy waters and sunned themselves upon leaning tree trunks and the loops of shallow twisted roots, while great twenty pound bull frogs chorused their deep thunderous voices from the moving shadows. This monstrously benign scene is marred occasionally by the dying hiss or scream of some hapless creature falling victim to the fangs and talons of some greater predator.

Moving back from the scene, we can now see the curve of the planet below. Before us lay the great tropical expanses and the much smaller than present north and south poles of the living planet. I'm told that every available trans-space ship was dispatched from the mothership with two purposes in mind. One, to collect specimens of numerous animal and plant life forms from the surface of the planet and two, to plant a large number of high megaton nuclear bomb devices at certain designated spots on the planet.

I'm told that these preparations took about ten years Earth time before the Biaviians were ready to execute the action. Of course, all of this was condensed for my benefit, down to about two hours of viewing time. The Biaviians have a great habit of visually recording all of their operations, and I have no doubt that in their archives is an audio-video recording of every historically significant event on Earth and of every human abduction. Also I am aware of the fact that the aliens are intimately familiar with all technological accomplishments on Earth, having monitored all bomb tests and rocket launches. They have physically retrieved and closely examined some Earth satellites. They also have methods of observing certain individuals and are able to predict a number of scientific breakthroughs in advance. A later chapter will be devoted exclusively to some of these revelations in particular.

You must understand that the aliens didn't just set these fissional explosions indiscriminately, but did so only after extensive scientific, geological, topographical, ecological and atmospheric data. It was never their wish to completely destroy the planet, but instead to change its future ecological procession and to change the evolutionary order of species ascendancy.

As I sat and observed the primordial Earth floating gently, a soft blue sphere nestled upon a deep purple azure sky, Tan explained to me what was taking place. It was hard for me to comprehend the fact that I was viewing a videotape which was recorded about sixty-seven million years ago, as we measure time.

The destruction sequence was started with the simultaneous detonation of two multi-megaton loads a few miles above the surface of the north and south poles of the planet, and though I had been told by Tan that the brilliance of the recorded blasts would not harm my vision, I still found myself momentarily shielding my eyes from the light.

According to Tan, these blasts would literally melt much of the ice tonnage of the poles and also literally reverse the magnetic field of the planet. Even before the ice blue light of the initial blasts had diminished, the sequence of mega-blasts, which has been planted in a chain running north to south began to detonate, starting from the equator and moving outward toward the poles.

The process had been sped up on the screen, and I actually saw the planet slow and stop its revolution, such was the force of these explosions. From my viewpoint, the process seemed like slow motion. When the planet's revolution stopped, the shifting waters of the oceans would not be restrained and governed by the awesome centrifugal force of gravity, continued to move inland.

I heard myself saying, "My God", as before my eyes, the entire planet slowly tilted from its previous axis. Now the cameras panned in swiftly, and I beheld what, from a great distance, had appeared to be slow-moving waters. I saw a great wall of thundering water, standing hundreds of feet tall, rushing over the land, undeterred by even great mountain ranges. As the awesome deluge swamped active volcanoes, rain forests, valleys and geysers, the liquid struck the glowing magma and terrible reactions occurred.

Great chunks of whole continents heaved upward and dissolved into the churning waters. Huge herds of terrified dinosaurs stampeded before the coming doom and were swept away like ants before a thunder storm. Soon oceans lay where prairies had been and dry expanses where seas had been. Connected portions of continents became islands and mountains now protruded as small islands surrounded by oceans. All of this time a great nuclear cloud was swiftly spreading over much of the planet, turning day into night and temperate zones into frozen wastelands.

The planet settled into its new orbital position and the nuclear winter, which was wrought by technology, held the planet in its chilling talons for several centuries. Then as the atmosphere slowly settled and cleared, a kind of new atmosphere and ecological circumstance emerged. The resultant electro-magnetic waves from the blasts coupled with the ecological and atmospheric changes of the planet had accomplished the alien's wishes.

The lizard dynasty was no more and numerous other species, both land and sea dwellers, had been destroyed. The planet's new revolutionary axis had caused the temperate tropical zone to become restricted to a narrow band, which followed the equator of the planet. The poles had grown much greater in size, and the notable changes in the seasons had become entrenched.

The aliens knew that some enterprising and tenacious species of creatures would survive. For the most part, these were physically small, ground dwelling types of mammals and reptiles and insects. They also knew that radiation would not harm certain kinds of creatures, and that others would suffer chromosome damage but would still continue to breed until the altered genes reverted to normalcy.

A great number of the larger species of fowls, mammalians

and some reptiles had been previously retrieved from the planet's surface for reintroduction later. A few ocean and lake dwelling saurian species initially survived the cataclysm, but they had to come to the shore to lay their eggs, which were so affected by the fissional magnetism in the atmosphere that they never hatched, and the adults eventually died out.

After about a thousand years the Earth had renewed its ecological vigor enough for the preserved species of plants and animals to be reintroduced to the surface of the planet, and this is how the dinosaurs were destroyed as the supreme species of life upon this planet.

Then, aside from an occasional scientific expedition for the collection of specimens and the observation of ecological and evolutionary progression, the Biaviians did not place another permanent settlement on the surface of Earth until about forty thousand years ago. As I have said before, even though it may be hard for us to imagine leaving this beautiful planet alone for many millions of years, we can better understand it when we realize that this is but one of scores of living planets that the aliens know of, and Earth remains of interest only for its ongoing scientific update value and because it has come to the brink of ecological and fissional destruction.

Chapter 8

Of Men and Gods
Recent History

Perhaps, before I am obliged to leave this planet, either in body or through the transition called physical death, I will learn more of and write in more detail about the vast expanses of time which are not covered in this book. The knowledge passed on to me by my friends, the Biaviians, concerning the history of this Earth and mankind was restricted by my own inability or failure to put the necessary questions to them within the time allotted me in their presence. Had I been an archaeologist, a historian or some other highly educated personage, no doubt the knowledge gained would be more encompassing and precise. So I must beg your forgiveness on this score.

Many other things were revealed to me that I'm sure I've forgotten or simply was not capable of understanding and retaining. Also, and purely for the sake of science mind you, I was obliged to partake of certain esoteric and mind-altering or enhancing substances that were in the possession of my alien friends or had been feloniously pilfered by my side kick, Question. There is also the possibility that I witnessed some things which were so repulsive to my psyche that I deliberately blotted them out of my forward memory.

Even while moving along the great spiraling causeway of the mothership, the awesome kaleidoscope of activity that assailed my eyes could not possibly have been consumed and retained in its entirely during my passing. I might pass some great slimy tentacled creature of many eyes and even get a whiff of its repugnant odor, and I did not have the nerve or wish to know what it was or if it was considered intelligent.

Once I saw a family of hairy ape-like upright creatures in the Hyborian garden and upon inquiry was told that these creatures were genetic relatives of man and that several races of them still live upon the Earth. I consider myself open-minded, but I would not want to invite one of them to lunch, and I'll never forget the smell of these creatures.

Over the eons of time following the first great space wars, the Targs had eventually taken their earned place on the Council of the Seven and had begun to team up with the Biaviians and others on joint exploratory missions. So it came to pass that about forty thousand years ago another colonization mission to Earth was formed and executed by the Biaviians, the Targs and the Nyptonians.

The purpose of that mission was to scientifically ascertain the probable intelligence factor of the Homo sapien and his ability to make the transition from predatory savage to homogenous stationary societies. Genetic experiments would be performed to ascertain to what extent the human creature could be cross bred with other forms of intelligent life. These experiments were supposed to be strictly controlled, and none of the hybrid specimens of these experiments would be permitted to leave the control area.

In order to assure the complete segregation of the colonization experiment from the rest of humanity, the colony was started on a large island, which was located in the Indian Ocean, and was, at the time of their coming, uninhabited by humans. I'm told that the island was some forty kilometers wide and sixty kilometers long and was formed from volcanic action in the past. The volcano that stood near the center of the island was still active.

By forty thousand years ago the Biaviians, the Targs and the Nyptonians had attained the technology to reach near light speed in inter-galactic space travel but arrived on Earth in a common mothership of Biaviian design. That mothership was large but not nearly so large as the present one, and as a result was able to bring along only a limited amount of technology.

Each of the three groups possessed the materials to fabricate self-contained living structures and several saucer ships, each of which was capable of solar system exploration but did not have the power capacity to return to the home planets. The superstructure of the mothership was dismantled and used to build the self-contained cities for the three intelligent life forms. Ships, submarines and transport vehicles would be fabricated out of natural alloys found on the Earth.

The Nyptonians are from a high gravity planet and chose to build their permanent living emplacement beneath the ocean off the southern tip of the island. The Targs built their dwellings on the northern tip of the island, while the Biaviians raised their city at the center of the island and this city encompassed the land stretching from the western foot of the volcano to the seashore on the western shore of the island.

Human beings tend to think in terms of resettlements of any nature being accomplished in a matter of decades, and where human settlers are concerned this is generally true. However, I'm told that these extraterrestrial settlers kept their activities and their presence restricted to their island for over a thousand years Earth time before making the first contact with human beings. No doubt that time was spent in construction and the building of suitable vessels and vehicles for Earth traverse, as well as in scientific studies of the Earth's ecology and of its indigenous humanoids. These are, of course, the Negroid, the Mongoloid and the Caucasian.

The aliens also found that even with the purity of the Earth's atmosphere at that time there were numerous organisms against which they had no natural biological defenses. A large number of the Targs and the Biaviians were afflicted with various forms of infections and a number perished. The Nyptonians were more fortunate because initially they lived under very controlled circumstances.

Living in a city beneath the ocean the Nyptonians lived in an atmosphere which was segregated and virtually pure. Over a period of time the Nyptonians developed various serums and antibodies to protect themselves from Earth organisms by utilizing the immune properties in the blood and organs of the dolphins, with whom they could communicate, and which is a species native of Nypton, the home planet of the Nyptonians.

Dolphins were transplanted to Earth millions of years before by the Biaviians at the behest of the Nyptonians. The physiology of the dolphin of forty thousand years ago had evolved some, and the language had advanced to a more complex level. However, the Nyptonians were able to swiftly develop a communication rapport with them.

I'm told that the dolphins were used in many constructive ways by the aliens, to seek out ore deposits, pinpoint human groups along the shores, harvest fish and even protect Nyptonian workers from shark and other predatory sea life.

Dolphins are friendly creatures, and the Nyptonians taught them to always look upon humans as friends and even protect and save man in times of peril. To my knowledge, they are the only sea dwelling species on Earth so inclined.

I'm told that there are a number of species native to Earth which have similar counterparts out in the cosmos, and the biological similarities of these various species are not the result of the interplanetary seeding by space travelers, because in the overall picture of the numerous life forms in the cosmos, species seeding plays a minute role. The greater portion of the interplanetary biological similarities among species is a matter of evolutionary and genetic happenstance.

For instance, the basic aerodynamic design of the bird's wing and the digestive system of the fish is quite similar to that of creatures on Biaveh or Nypton or Doria. Of course, there are many other life forms which are radically different from anything which may be found on Earth, yet I'm told that, over all, the physical and biological similarities of creatures from living planet to living planet is quite notable. I have spoken of these things so as to reveal the fact that the genetic similarities between Biaviians and earthlings are not a rare occurrence between mammals from planet to planet throughout the cosmos.

The full extent of these genetic similarities became apparent as the Biaviians started to abduct individual humans from among the various racial and tribal groups. It may be noted that the original Biaviian settlers never fully overcame the immunization problems of Earth's biology. After the first thousand years, the aliens found that not even their on-board technology could arrest the aging process indefinitely, nor did they have the technology on board to perform the necessary brain clone procedure, as this technology was not allowed off of the home planet. Even so, and with all of the natural perils of Earth, the Biaviians or Elohim as they are called, could expect to live perhaps twenty thousand Earth years before physically dying.

Yet it was soon learned a most extraordinary thing. It seems that each successive generation of Biaviian born on Earth lived shorter and shorter physical life spans and even the medical knowledge of their scientists could not preserve or extend their children's life spans beyond five thousand years, and then forty-five hundred years, then four thousand and the genetic stability would continue to diminish until it could no longer reproduce in the Earth's atmosphere. But how was this circumstance to be rectified? Thus, before the death of the original generation, the quest to overcome the genetic obstacles of interbreeding with humans began in earnest.

With the passing of the centuries, the original Elohim began to die off, leaving the continued existence of their species to their mixed breed offspring. The Nyptonians worked in close proximity with the Biaviians in gathering the proper human subjects for the hybrid experiments. In those days, on the whole, the human species was nothing more that roving predatory bands of hunter-gatherers.

In order to ascertain their mental possibilities and to pick the best subjects, it was necessary for the Nyptonians to start to practice human husbandry, so they literally started to teach humans the first semblances of stationary community agricultural life. They introduced unto man a Biaviian grain, which we have come to call wheat. They taught man how to breed and to domesticate milk and meat animals and to structure a social order based upon that of the Biaviians.

The Nyptonians traveled in submarines and would disembark from these ships and teach the people on the land near shores, and the people came to know them as Namons or Nomons. The most astute among the humans and some of the most beautiful females were taken back to live on the Isle of the Gods and to bear of them offspring.

As time continued to pass, the memory of the home planet Biaveh started to recede into the distant catacombs of past legend.

Unfortunately, or fortunately, the Targs could not find a reptilian counterpart capable of bearing their seed to any intelligence level, and as the original Targs began to die off, they reawakened the age old primordial hatred of their former enemies, the Biaviians.

The differences in social structure, philosophy and ethics have always been and still are obviously quite different between the Targs and the Biaviians, and on the Island of the Gods, these differences became pronounced with the passing of time. For the Targs to have considered attacking their mammalian neighbors outright would have been foolhardy, as the Biaviians numbers grew, even as the Targ numbers dwindled. Yet their hatred of their neighbors continued to grow and to fester within their hearts.

Any kind of social intercourse between the Targs and the hybrids offspring of the Biaviians was forbidden and strictly enforced. Inasmuch as the Targzissian mind is capable of intrigue, they set about to undermine the social structure of the Biaviians by seeking to bribe and corrupt the minds of some of the rural hybrids against the central authority of the Elohim.

As the original pure blood Biaviians died off, much of the original technological knowledge died with them, and as a result, the level of technology deteriorated with the passing generations. We must understand that the growing number of hybrids in procreating with the human species further diluted the original blood.

By and by, those who were the original scientific God leaders, through successive generations, eventually evolved into a kind of religious priestly caste. With the dilution of the original blood also came a dilution of the ability to decipher and retain a true knowledge of the original science, and the Biaviians began to take on many of the emotional and primordial weaknesses of man.

When it was discovered the extent to which the Targs had managed to influence the minds of a few of the Biaviian males and females against the central authority, I'm told that the Elohim went forth and destroyed the last remnants of the Targs' technology and forbade them to build any more aircraft of any kind of machines which could be used in a warlike fashion. Forbidden to attempt cross-breeding with humans, the Targs were doomed to die out and be reduced to the common non-intelligent forms of natural reptilian life. The corrupted and rebellious hybrids were expelled from the Island of the Gods and sent to dwell among their lesser brothers. Without the protection and medical care of the Elohim, they would be doomed to short mortality life spans, which would be shorter still for their future offspring.

As time passed and the settlements of humans continued to spring up in Africa, the Elohim began to send forth emissaries and teachers to develop more stable social orders and to develop trade networks among the human. It was there in the valley of the Tigris and Euphrates Rivers that the sons of Gods took unto them the fairest of the daughters of man and produced the offspring who would form the first great kingdoms and dynasties among man. They were the original founders of the Kingdoms of the Sumerians, the Thebians and formed the base blood lineage of the original twelve tribes of Nog. Eventually their offspring traveled to various parts of the globe and started civilizations in the Americas, Asia, Europe and other places. Along the way, the original scientific knowledge was lost or corrupted.

Splinter groups from the Ancients moved about and settled in many places and started their own orders. One group was those who started to build the nuclear cooling towers in the Valley of Shinar, but were thwarted by the forces from the mother Isle of the Gods. And some who escaped that destruction, eventually founded the fabled and notorious cities of Sodom and Gomorrah and their sister cities on the plains. Others formed the first dynasties of Egypt and built the first great pyramid and the Sphinx, using laser and levitation technology.

Because the original authorities on the Island of the Gods continued to monitor and sometimes destroy the works of the dispersed, there eventually developed a loose confederation of beings who were avowed to the downfall and destruction of that central authority. If you have read the book of Genesis, then do so again while bearing these things in mind. The scriptures of this book quite literally parallel the chronicles of the writings of the Elohim scribes, omitting few details. If one is aware of present day cloning and artificial insemination methods, then the significance of these scriptures become more revealing.

In order to follow the diminishing of the life spans with the crossbred dilution of the blood through successive generations of the infusion of human blood, you must read the fifth chapter of Genesis in its entirety. The chapter chronicles the generations of the house of Adam. But do read the entire book. The chronicles of the blood lineage of the original Elohim is highlighted all the way down to the House of Abraham, Noah and Lot.

During the course of my stay among the aliens, they did not refer me to any particular scriptures or writings, but from time to time certain familiar names were mentioned, names like Abraham, Noah, Lot, Menes, Ahkenaton, Aaron, Jacob, and some others. A number of present day researchers have become convinced that extraterrestrials played a major part in the recorded history of mankind. They have searched and in some cases found the deserted remnants of lost civilizations. Modern day archaeologists, paleontologists and historians admit that they are greatly impressed at the level of architecture, medicine, mathematics and economic proficiency of those societies. They have also noted the structural similarities between the pyramids, pottery and philosophical traits of various people in Africa, Asia and the Americas. They are amazed and perplexed in their attempts to figure out just how these ancient people were able to accomplish such a great engineering feats without the aid of modern day technology and equipment.

The researchers cannot reconcile the advanced accomplishments of these ancient people with the known order of technological progression among other indigenous people of the same geographical regions. In essence, these points of enlightened realities were true enigmatic anomalies in a world dominated by stone age barbarism. Even though some of them have come to theorize the extraterrestrial connection, structured peer limitation and persuasion, coupled with their own misconception of their uniqueness, the inability to explain has caused them to simply cast aside the hard physical evidence which is staring them in the face.

Yet, as I have said before, it is not my wish to try to shove the reality of extraterrestrial intelligence down the throats of those who would have to be mental deficients not to have reached this conclusion long ago. Perhaps the researchers could better understand if they knew that the great structures like the pyramids and the sculptures and other artifacts left by those lost civilizations are the handiwork of distant relatives of the original Elohim, instead of the Gods themselves. The last vestiges of the central power had passed away about seven thousand years ago with the cataclysmic destruction of the Island of the Gods.

From the time when the sons of the original Elohim thrice removed started to establish earthly kingdoms among mankind, there arose dissenters to the central authority. Those great leaders through intermarriage with humans soon became more man than alien in their physiology and concepts of social order, and all of those elements possessed by mankind eventually took precedence over the more aloof and objective logic of the central code.

Greed, envy, pride, gluttony, slothfulness and sexual depravities literally became the order of the day within many of those mainland kingdoms. Before long, the numerical value of the wayward dissenters and their offspring became too great and widely dispersed to either keep them under central control or to efficiently destroy them all. So it boiled down to simply keeping the stronger ones under surveillance and monitoring their social and scientific progress.

From time to time, a considerable number of those who still possessed some of the true knowledge of science, medicine and weaponry would band together and form social orders which, if left to their own designs, could eventually overcome all less advanced peoples and infect them with norms of depravity which were anathema to all logic and decency.

Thus it came about that a group of these renegade hybrids,

while languishing under the titles of priests, came in among the indigenous people of the plains and formed the settlements, which would become the five cities on the plains, the greater of which were the cities of Sodom and Gomorrah. Now these cities became the center points which controlled the bulk of the commerce and trade of the plains and achieved a reputation for a time as the cultural center of the middle eastern world. Drunk with power and other human weaknesses, the two greater sister cities eventually devolved into the foremost dens of depravity and iniquity in the ancient civilized world.

What the researchers of today do not yet know is that the original ruling priestly caste who founded the cities were beings of immortal status in comparison with the indigenous peoples, because their lives were centuries long. These long-lived priestly beings were also genetic scientists and experimenters, and they had literally an endless supply of experimental subjects in the common people.

I am told that those priest scientists did not restrict their experiments to the human species, but also sought to incorporate the animal and human genes. They sought to incubate the human spermatozoa within the bovine, the sheep and the goat's womb. The monstrosities brought forth from these indecent experiments became worshipped fixtures of the inner courts of the rulers. I am told that sexual practices between humans and animals became a norm, and slowly a caste of biological freaks and monsters came to be in those two unholy cities. And among them, there could not be found ten men or women who were not given to the most perverse manner of deviate license.

The time came when trading caravans would not dare enter the cities' gates, but would languish near the city walls and do their business, and upon completion thereof would hastily depart. Un-indoctrinated slaves sold at a premium in those awful cities, where young males were preferred over women by other males, and dogs were preferred over men by wealthy females. Disease, insanity, human sacrifice and rape murder were rampant in those cities, and cults which practiced cannibalism skulked through the fire lit nights. It was a place and a time when sexual deviation was the norm, and normalcy was not condoned or even tolerated.

Now, near the gates of the city of Sodom lived a wealthy trader named Lot and his family. Lot was of the family and the religion of the powerful nomadic sheep and goat herding tribes of the House of Abraham, and he served as a middle man between the trading caravans and the people of the cities. Lot was allowed to remain unmolested by the people of those cities for several reasons. One, he was the only trustworthy trade representative near about, two, he supplied the cities with meat animals and grain, and three, he was under the protection of the powerful tribes of the House of Abraham, whom the Sodomites feared as a military force.

It is also known that Lot was a distant relative of those people of the cities, as his blood lineage could be traced back to the original Elohim on the Isle of the Gods. It was unto Lot that the central rulers sent three of their emissaries, who could rightfully be called advance scouts for the coming strike force, which had been ordered to completely destroy four of the five cities on the plains.

Lot was instructed to immediately flee the area with his family. He petitioned the central power to spare the cities or at least to wait until he could recoup some of the debt that was owed him. Then, upon the promise that he would be compensated for the loss of his properties, he grudgingly prepared to depart.

Lot's wife who had for some time chose to maintain liaisons in the city, stole away from the fleeing family group during the night in an attempt to warn the city of the coming holocaust. I am told that one of the emissary scouts followed her and rendered her rigid with a paralyzing ray when she had come within several miles of the city. At sunrise, the four nuclear bombs, which had been hidden in traders wagons in or near the cities, detonated and within a matter of minutes, the four cities on the plains were utterly destroyed.

Yet, remnants of the ancient knowledge of the Elohim scientists survived in the minds of a small number of those who escaped the doomed cities by being away on business journeys at the time and yet some others who had escaped the notice of the central authority on the Isle of the Gods by literally crossing the oceans and settling among the indigenous peoples in Mongolia, northern and western Europe and the jungles of the Americas. In truth, the rulers on the mother island were having problems of their own.

Over the centuries all of the original Gods or Biaviians had died off, and the human factor in the blood lineage of their offspring now greatly outnumbered the purer rulers. Many had traveled the distant parts of the world and were aware of the human ways of ruling. Thus differing factions began to form among the inhabitants of the Island of the Gods, and by and by the various factions on the island began to fall into the decadent practices of those they had destroyed not so long ago and the central authority began to lose its hold on the populace.

Soon there were mutinous rumors and some set about forming conspiracies against the central authority and plotting campaigns to literally take over the rest of the world. The only thing that prevented an outright takeover was the fact that the central city authority still possessed the well-guarded knowledge of the atom bomb and utilized laser technology to protect the entrances to the central city and its gardens.

But the central authority knew that the hand writing was on the wall. They rightfully concluded that their initial efforts to civilize the savages and to assure eternal life through genetic experimentation had failed. It was decided that the secret of the atom and other advanced technology must not fall into the hands of their humanized and corrupt subjects.

They did not have a personal standing army, and they knew that it was only a matter of time before some enterprising group would manage to either penetrate or sabotage the city's defense systems. Even as they reached the fated decision, they were aware that some powerful leaders on the outer island were busily building ships and weapons which would be used to conquer the world.

Then, there in the great temple, the elders all gathered and drank wine from golden goblets, and as they lifted their voices in an ancient song which spoke of the glory of Biaveh, the eldest angel pushed the button which detonated the nuclear pile hidden deep in the caves of the volcanic mountain.

The resultant blast turned Atlantis into liquid fire and sent Tsunami waves crashing into the mainlands hundreds and thousands of miles away. So great was the force of the Armageddon blast that the very elements were torn asunder, and great storm clouds formed of the seas' waters and poured down upon the Earth flood rains of near universal proportions.

Far out in the cosmos, travelers from the home planet Biaveh picked up the frequency waves of the blast and communicated this to the mother planet. Thus, the destruction of Atlantis, transpired some seven thousand years ago as we measure time.

Now my explanation of the history of the extraterrestrial intervention into the evolution and the affairs of mankind is of course, quite incomplete and only touches upon the true magnitude of it all. The lost technological knowledge of the original Elohim is just now re-emerging in the present day science of man. Our computers, micro-electronic, jet propulsion, hydrogen fission and the first rudimentary breakthroughs in cold and hot fusion are all products of the genetic legacy of the Elohim. To be sure some portion of that genetic heritage can be found in some measure within all races and nations. If given the opportunity, the Aborigine or the Carib Indians or the Westerner could be a physicist or a mathematician or a surgeon.

The extraterrestrials have always been aware of the knowledge potential of the human brain. I was further informed that the human possesses neurological powers that even the Biaviians no longer hold en masse. The psychic power to levitate and to heal the sick or to alter the bio-molecular order of other people's physiology, the power of clairvoyance and other paranormal attributes which escape the elements of scientific logic. The Biaviians find these things fascinating and are ever seeking to find scientific explanations for them. They believe that these paranormal attributes are powers retained from a time even before man became a bi-ped Homo sapien.

For instance, many kinds of lower creatures in nature have seemingly inexplicable powers. Some animals know when a storm is coming, can find their way home from thousands of miles away. A wild duck hatched in captivity and raised away from its peers still possesses the urge to fly south in the winter. Animals can read feelings and may know exactly when they are going to die. It is believed that the more primitive a human is the greater his retention of those inherent powers.

Correct intuition is to some extent a kind of clairvoyance, but the modern day human in general is not rigidly structured nor his modus operandi born of common species compulsion or universal necessity. The human mind's true complexity lies in the fact that it cannot be accurately plotted or anticipated either by themselves or by the technology of the all powerful Biaviians. Personally my opinion is that most people are so busy thinking up dumb shit that they literally don't know what they are going to do next.

In contrast, the Biaviian mind is quite analytical, to the point and is rarely if ever given to flights of fancy. During all of my time among the aliens, I discovered the fact that they don't have any industrial fantasy factor, things like movie studios which are dedicated to entertaining fiction films, nor do they have superstars of music, stage, screen, sports or politics. I never saw cartoons, comic books or toys which did not serve some practical purpose other than just fun.

This doesn't mean that they are ignorant of our movies, superstars and preoccupation with amusement. Tan spoke to me of several notable films in December of '87, which was the last time that I was physically in his presence. He spoke of the movie, 'Close Encounters', and was impressed with its special effects. I believe that the Biaviians aided in the fabrication of the production by seeding the dreams of Steven Spielberg and many of the technicians. They may also have played some part in rounding up the proper personnel to act as advisors on the picture and helping to see that they were available.

He mentioned the movie, 'The Color Purple', and was of the opinion that it should have received an Oscar. He expressed an artistic admiration for: Robin Williams, Oprah Winfrey, Whoopie, Richard Pryor, John Belushi, Cecily Tyson, Sally Fields, Lee Van Cleef, Lisa Bonet, Charles Bronson, Redd Foxx, Richard Burton, Brando, Dustin Hoffman and some others. He liked Eastwood's picture: 'Play Misty For Me', and he spoke at length of Stevie Wonder. He especially liked the album; 'Songs in the Key of Life'. I was mildly surprised to be sitting there discussing show business with a little big-headed alien.

I said to him, "Tan, if you like Stevie Wonder so much, why don't you cruise by his crib and zap him some eye balls". And he said, "Martin, if I should give him sight, might it not take away his ability to see?" And I said, "Tan, you're not as dumb as you are funny looking".

He also spoke of Kennedy, King, Mandela, Dick Gregory, Claude Pepper and Jimmy Carter with admiration. These aliens are well aware of the state of things, socially and politically on this Earth, but they don't seem to be noticeably impressed by the shape of things.

It does fascinate them to witness the mass falsity of the great machine and the ease with which the silly masses are manipulated by pure bullshit. It is hard for them to realize that even humans could be that dumb.

If humanity is not yet aware of their presence in our stratosphere, then it is no fault of their own as they make hundreds of solid appearances each year. They have a policy of not appearing en masse and just freaking everybody out. However, during the course of everyday movements, they will be seen if only by chance.

I was told that perhaps seventy-five percent of UFO sightings are of remote guided drones. Biaviians have several kinds of robot drones, the most common of which being the small saucer. Just like mankind has begun to send out information gathering satellites, so have the aliens. Of course, their techno-capabilities far exceed those of man, but the end results are relative, and it is upon this data that the aliens base their knowledge of the present and projections of the future. We do the same things in many ways every day, in stock market speculation, retain business, property purchase, weather forecasting and market analysis to name a few.

Unfortunately we do not place a premium on many aspects of life which are vital to the continuation of the human species. What are the projected ecological damages of a major oil spill, acid rain, chemical pollutants in our lakes and rivers, nuclear accidents, etc., etc. These things are played down by the manufacturers and the paid-off politicians.

I am informed that auto emissions alone virtually insure the destruction of our atmosphere to a point of mass death within the next twenty years and this without even getting into the millions of tons of inorganic chemical poisons from other sources. What we have to stop and realize is that the literal extinction of an intelligent species through ecological pollution is definitely possible and in the case of humanity, quite probable should things continue as they are at present.

Because we live in a society which has raised lies, deception, unreality, falsity, bullshit and mass apathy to an art which approaches a way of life, by simply suppressing or ignoring these awful facts they seem to assume that it is not true or that it will go away.

We live in a time when the few voices of dissent are raising in defense of this dying planet. They seem at best a noble oddity and at worst a pathetic nuisance. Sodom and Gomorrah were Sunday Schools in comparison with the perverted dementia that now infects civilized society and not even the murderous hordes of Gengis Khan could strike a light to the murderous damage done by your major corporations.

Unfortunately the wealth and the social and economic policies of this world are not controlled by the will of the caring, but by those who only care about what they can get out of it. Foresight and proper preparation are odd phenomena, and those obscure scientists who are busy working to create the process which could stave off the coming doom are at present fighting a losing battle.

Chapter 9

Eastern Shore Maryland August 1975

In 1975, once again I had joined up with a Blues Band, and we followed the migrant work season up the eastern seaboard. The produce gathering season starts in south Florida in May and moves progressively up the East Coast as the produce crops ripen in planned sequence. We played the juke joints in the migrant camps generally on the week-ends and by August of that year we had reached the state of Maryland along the eastern shore.

My last physical contact with the extraterrestrials had been in 1964 at the age of eighteen. Approximately eleven years had passed since that last encounter, and it seemed like a long lost dream, a lifetime ago. During those eleven years I can't remember even having discussed UFOs at length with any person. The experience had remained in the back of my mind and on occasion I had experienced flashbacks but the order and depth of these reflections were overshadowed by the everyday happenings of life. At no time did I ever consider that my reflections were just a figment of my imagination, because I never read, nor do I now like to read science fiction magazines. I had gone beyond the point of doubting the existence of alien life forms. I knew for a fact that I had at some point been contacted by them, I just couldn't remember all of the details of that contact. I simply took the track that they would let me know what's happening when they are ready to.

How, you may ask, had I come to this conclusion? The answer is that things happened in my life which can not be explained by rational standards. I know for a fact that I had gained the power to heal pain and illness in others by simply touching them. Common sense persuaded me that this power did not emanate from any great religious or saintly qualities on my part. I've never been and still am not a devote anything where denominational religion is concerned.

In those days, in order to alleviate a little of the loneliness in the world, I found that it was incumbent upon me to do my share by making love to a vast number of lovely ladies, some of whom neglected to tell me that they were married, most probably to a three hundred pound homicidal psycho, who would cherish the opportunity of causing a nice person like myself extreme pain and mutilation unto death.

I was not adverse to partaking of games of chance like cards, dice, dog racing, mumbly peg or foot racing, and on several occasions my good reputation had been besmirched by accusations of cheating, thereby causing me to be forced to shoot out the light and dive head first through the nearest window. To this day I don't know what dastardly villain planted that extra ace up my sleeve.

I also like to partake of an occasional medicinal six pack of beer or pint of good sippin' whiskey, and even with my docile, self-effacing personality, hardly a week passed without my having to defend my honor with a fist fight, which on occasion might involve knife play. Hard drugs were never my forte, but I've always smoked an occasional joint of cannabis as an esoteric appetizer. So my healing gift obviously didn't come from clean living.

And there was another inexplicable phenomena connected to my person which yet strikes me as strange but fascinating. I found that I am able to cause clearly visible biological aging changes in the women with whom I've had sexual intimacy at least twice. For some reason the aging process is halted and in some cases reversed in the women with whom I've had intimate relations, and the effects seem to be long lasting if not permanent. Some changes tend to transpire within days, and I know of former loved ones who yet retain residuals of that liaison from twenty years past and are aware of it. Therefore, I've been cursed with many short relationships even unto this day. It seems that on many occasions the side effects of our union is that of extreme personality changes in the ladies, such as burning jealousy, possessiveness and sexual hyperactivity which soon turns me off and drives me away. Many never realize why they feel compelled to give sway to these extreme emotions. However, I believe that the psychological aberrations subside after a time following my clandestine departure.

I always have been, and no doubt shall always be, a man who loves women. There are some imperfections in this biological phenomena. For instance, the alterations do not occur in every woman I've loved, at least not noticeably so. Perhaps a few are immune to the process. Also the biological process does not occur in these women who fail to or are unable to reach a climax, while the effects seem to be compounded in those marvelous ladies who are given to multiple orgasms.

From what I know of sexuality I would, with due modesty, classify myself as a good to excellent lover, as I truly do love each and every woman I make love to no matter the age or race or duration of the encounter. If, for some reason, I do not have this love vibration for a particular lady, no matter her physical beauty, I find that it is literally impossible for me to perform sexually. Fortunately, I rarely meet a lady that I don't or can't love, at least for a time.

I've been told by the aliens that this sexual anomaly is caused by a certain genetic trait which I possess as a biological legacy of the blood of the original Elohim. Furthermore, this genetic trait I have is rare but not unique to me alone. Actually a considerable number of people all over the world possessed this genetic trait, and the trait is often stronger among a certain isolated group of people who haven't dispersed their gene legacy too widely because of that isolation.

Males who possess the trait, barring injury and lack of stimulation, generally remain sexually active very late in life. My father, for example, sired fourteen healthy children at home and is still sexually active though he is well into his eighties. My mother bore children to the age of fifty, and then said, "Enough already", by choice, not for lack of physical fertility. Tan named a number of people who possess this gene, and some of them you would immediately recognize if I called their names, but I won't.

I also believe that I've always possessed a real measure of precognition, which has served me well down through the years, and has no doubt saved my life on more than one occasion.

Tan tells me that I am telepathically sensitive who can communicate with him at almost any time without effort, but remember that not even the Biaviians can give you metaphysical properties that you don't already possess. They can teach you to recognize and channel it or to enhance the workings of such attributes, but only if you are psychologically capable of consuming and retaining the instructions.

The power to heal sickness and relieve pain with a touch is a factor you must already possess and cannot be controlled or explained by the workings of science. I am convinced that is indeed a spiritual thing, but I do not attribute it to any particular written religious doctrine or philosophical rendition. Instead I attribute it to the force of the spiritual wish which emanates from the inner being of the giver. No doubt any number of miraculous healing have been accomplished by non-Christians and insincere evangelists, witch doctors, soothsayers, loving mothers and well wishers, not to take away anything from those truly sincere denominationally religious people.

There is another anomaly connected with the factor of telepathy, I believe that when a person succeeds in overcoming the nuances of telepathic communication, he also opens channels or frequency doors through which out of body spirits may sometimes enter. For instance, when Barbara places me in a hypnotic state and starts to regress me in time, I often see and even speak to out of body spirits who, for all intents and purposes, have nothing to do with the aliens, and sometimes their voices may be channeled through my body. But for the most part during the hypnotic state, I try to pass these spirits by without pausing, though I can see and hear them clearly. It's rather complicated so I won't dwell on that aspect of the experience.

Since December 7 of 1987, I have managed to take several sets of photographs of the Biaviian ships, when they came within visual range. I was able to accomplish this because for years I was always given forewarning of their appearance.

In August of 1975 I was instructed telepathically to leave the place I was in and to go to a secluded spot for the rendezvous. They don't always announce their coming via telepathy, but there is a certain sensation of inner resonance that is unique to their presence that I learned to recognize. Of course, they may sometimes pass over, while having no intentions of contacting me personally, but I can still feel their presence.

Lately when I get the feeling, I immediately get my camera and start to watch the sky until they appear or until the sensation passes. There have been occasions when I was at Barbara's house that things, small inexplicable things, would happen: a video tape of one of our sessions would disappear from where it was placed, the lights might go out, all the dogs in the neighborhood might begin to bark, the temperature of the house would change and consistent manifestations would appear in the development of photos which were taken during these times, no matter the camera or the film brand, which we had developed at one of the retail chain stores. We feel that the configurations are deliberate because the shape and dimensions of the etheric forms was duplicated from film roll to roll and camera to camera.

I believe that all these things were deliberately done in order to assure us that we were not suffering any delusion, but were experiencing a tangible reality. I attempt the writing of this book at the behest of those same extraterrestrial beings, though I am aware of the fact that the Targs do not wish the work to be done. Certain inexplicable accidents have happened to relatives and some other people close to Barbara, and the Targs have gone so far as to physically amputate the last joint of my right little finger as revenge for my having telepathically injured one of their kind. I will speak further on that incident later in this manuscript.

It was a Friday, and the band was engaged to play a dance at a camp near Salisbury, Maryland that night. We reached the camp around seven that evening and set up the equipment. Our scheduled gig was to start at 10 p.m. Around 9 p.m. and just as night was falling

I was told to get up and walk away from the camp.

The spot I was drawn to like a homing pigeon was about three miles away from the camp at an even more isolated place. As I passed through a stand of trees and walked rapidly deeper into the woods, about a hundred yards in I came to a large clearing. That's when I felt the titillating vibrations of the ship's engines, through I hadn't yet made visual contact.

Then I felt the hair on my body stand on end and static electricity in my clothes. The leaves of the trees were trembling, and static was all around me. I felt a kind of sensual vibration growing and growing within my body, and it caused my vision to momentarily blur.

By this time I had reached the center of the clearing. I looked to my left and saw the blue orb approaching me at a fantastic rate of speed. Orange, green and red lights flashed on the undercarriage. I remember ducking down and saying to myself, "Oh, shit, it's going to hit!" A dazzling white light, then a low hum, and I was standing in the decontamination chamber being cleaned by thousand of multicolored lights. I started to say, "What the fu", and the door whizzed open and there stood Tan and Nela. "Damn, I know them", I said as if to myself.

Behind them on the dome of the saucer, I saw a computer graphic display of two jet fighter planes being rotated and graphically dissected. I stepped out onto the command desk and looked out through the seemingly transparent hull, and I saw the eastern coastal region of America going away at a fantastic rate of speed.

"Friend Martin, it is good to be in your presence again. Welcome. Come and sit. Forgive our swift departure. It was necessary to evade contact with the angry thrusters", said Tan by way of explaining the swift pick-up and the jets.

Since this was the second occasion on which military aircraft were in pursuit of the alien craft even in my personal experience, it is inconceivable that the military and the government couldn't know of the extraterrestrial presence in our stratosphere. I'm sure that the aliens have the technology to become invisible to radar or to project false images at a different location should they so desire, but in many cases they don't bother because they know that we don't have the technology to either fly with them or to penetrate their protective shields. The aliens also have the power to literally disappear by fantastic acceleration, by in-place vibration or by jumping to hyper-space.

But all of these high tech powers are not possessed by all kinds of alien flying implements. Some, like the remote guided drones, must rely on speed alone to evade cannon and missiles. It is conceivable that man could fabricate high powered multi-frequency instruments which could override the robot electromagnetic guidance system of one of the more simple drones. The technology does exist, but the time, place and kind of target would have to be just right, and to my knowledge that hasn't yet happened.

Also I am told that the government actually has listening devices, which are powered by a vast eight acre computer complex located between D.C. and Baltimore, which has actually picked up a number of extraterrestrial ship to ship transmissions which they have not yet been able to decipher. The duration of some of these transmissions may be no more than a nano-second. If they had a key from which to work, they would soon unravel the messages.

Rockets, lasers, particle beams and sound bombardment have all been used by the military in unsuccessful attempts to shoot down the alien craft. Of course, the government and military have been attempting to communicate with the extraterrestrials for years through Project Ozmos and other means, but the Biaviians are not foolish enough to open up channels of communication with the kinds of people who govern these societies. They have nothing to gain and too much to lose by doing so, and if my own sentiments are a good representation of that of other friends, then we have all advised them against such a move, not that they needed my advice.

As we moved away from the Earth I saw the body of a man floating in space. When they punched him up on the dome screen, I saw that he was a Russian cosmonaut, and the name on his helmet, I believe, was: A. Kamarov or something very similar.

Of course, I have no way of verifying this to your satisfaction, so I won't try but somebody knows. I was told that the aliens beamed him out of a space capsule at the very moment of its destruction, but he died immediately of space vacuum exposure. So the alien technology is not perfect.

It was on that trip that I had the opportunity to see the planet Neptune, which is the furthest planet of our solar system from the sun. Neptune has rings similar to those of Saturn, except that Neptune's rings are composed of carbon chunks as opposed to the ice chunk rings of Saturn.

The aliens actually harvest pure carbon materials from beneath the surface of that planet, utilizing robot technology. Should man survive, he would some day be able to accomplish similar operations. The aliens concede the fact that should man survive there is no limit to what he can accomplish.

We circumnavigated the planet Venus, and I was told of a subterranean base there which is operated by the Dorians, who make extensive use of robotics and also have manned stations there. The Skreed or Insectillians also have a mine network on Venus, and most of the work is done by Skreed personnel. It seems that there are several mineral sources there which are found only in rare quantities throughout the universe. The aliens also told me that the planet Venus could be rejuvenated via technological means, but at present they don't consider such an undertaking to be of any great importance to them.

If man had been able to lay aside his racism hatreds and differences no more than fifty years ago, he would already have established permanent launch bases on Mars and the moon. His failure to utilize all of his brain power resources, which is possessed by all the races collectively, has held him far short of his true potential and has probably assured his destruction as a structured civilized order.

At the rear of the command deck of the saucer I saw two Stagyian scientists sitting in the shadows and the realization that I also knew them immediately came back to mind. As I settled back into the comfortable translucent recliner, I saw a computer graphic of my own form appear on the dome screen. The graph revealed first my skeletal structure, my vein network, inner organs, heart and lung action, brain, eyes, etc. This whole process was accompanied by numerical and linguistic symbols, which I could not understand. The graph also revealed the coins in my pocket and the structure and weave of my clothing.

After we had left the planet Neptune, Tan told me that he would now fulfill his promise and grant my wish to experience a hyperspace ride, and this is the experience as best I can explain it.

The robot pilot programmed a number of color and tone sequences on the console, and I felt a kind of vibration that went through my whole body. Then the inky blackness of deep space began to exude a deep purple, which gradually lightened into a brilliant red and then a golden orange, that gradually pulsed into a blinding white light, which caused me to shield my eyes. Then suddenly a quietness, no sound no movement. Slowly, so slowly the area was engulfed with a green light, and I felt a sensation in my ears like being under water. I moved my hands without undue effort, but all action registered in slow motion. I was startled to discover that my hand had become translucent like lime jello and the veins and skeletal structure looked like black ribbon veins and shiny blue crystal bones.

As I looked around me, it seemed that the entire ship was composed of invisible glass, which gave me the sensation that I was sitting un-encased out in the void, and the void was composed of cool thick nectar through which we moved like lazy bubbles.

Tan and Nela were transparent gummy bears with big heads and the robot pilot was silver tinted glass. I can't say how long this state of slow motioned translucence lasted, but if I had to guess, I would say fifteen minutes before I felt a pop in my ears and saw the green glass bubbles start to mesh together and slowly revert to a purple color then a bright red that turned to orange, then yellow, then a brilliant white flash which again caused my eyes to blur momentarily.

I blinked my eyes several times and gave a defensive startled jerk as I saw the great shining mothership right in front of us. We were approaching a solid mass at a high rate of speed. Before I could gather my wits, we were once again inside the landing area of the awesome egg. From ten thousand miles per hour to zero in one-tenth of one second. Mind blowing.

Don't ask me how, but at some point between the moment that we jumped to hyperspace and the moment we came out of it, I had changed from my regular clothing into the familiar blue sheer robe and the woven cloth footsies or slippers, if you wish. Everything around me, the glowing globes and the hundreds of docked ships was both familiar and newly fascinating to me. In other words, I never overcame the awe and magnificence of it all.

I noticed that my arrival didn't seem to concern the many beings around in the least, with the exception of one Targ who stopped working for a moment and looked in my direction. No others seemed very interested. Obviously a human visitor was not a novelty to them, so common was the happenstance.

As we neared the transport disk for the short journey deeper in to the interior of the mothership, I saw a strange furry creature waiting for us. He was busy digging in his stomach pouch. For a moment I stood confused, then recognition suddenly dawned on me. I snapped my fingers and said, "I know you, you're Question, aren't you? You're my friend, good to see you". Then Question said, "Oh, goody, now the universe is safe again. I'm so happy I could just shit", and kept digging in his pouch. Then it dawned on me that I probably didn't like this animal very much at all. It kind of hurt my feelings that Question didn't seem happy to see me again. I resolved to control my temper and not let him get on my nerves. After all, he was only a dumb animal. Then I heard a familiar crunching, smacking sound and looked around to see Question munching on one of his eternal wafers. He noticed me looking at him and said, "Oh, I'm sorry, would you care for a wafer?" "Thanks", says I. He held out half a wafer, and I smiled and reached out for it. In a flash he flipped the wafer back into his mouth and shook my hand all in one motion, munched a few times, swallowed loudly and the belched. It was at that moment that I decided that Question must die.

Once again I saw the great domed levitating gardens floating in the vastness of the mothership sky and immediately noticed that something was different about them. Then it dawned on me. What I was now witnessing was winter in the gardens. Except for the evergreens, the trees were devoid of leaves, and the Earth was blanketed with snow. The stream was frozen over, and the roofs of the little houses were blanketed with snow. Little lights shown in the windows, and a small herd of deer moved through the tiny trees.

If I were closer, I'm sure that all things would appear normal-sized instead of like snow in a glass bubble from such a distance. Obviously the seasonal changes inside of the gardens were controlled technologically, and I wondered if the beings who lived in the gardens were aware of this.

Surely if God should look down upon the Earth, it would appear like this. For a fleeting moment I was struck with a trembling chill at the implication of it all. I remember looking back upon the Earth from deep space and thinking how small and fragile it looks. In a larger sense the Earth is only a self-contained levitating garden on a larger scale than the ones aboard the great mothership, and if I had possession of a single Biaviian whisper craft or saucer, I could easily dictate my wishes to all of humanity and they would have no choice but to obey. No, if there's one thing I know with certainty, it's that the Biaviians are telling the truth when they say that they have no desire to conquer the Earth.

While mankind is preoccupied with building what they call a Star Wars Defense Umbrella in space, they don't realize that even if such a system were possible at this time, which it is not, it would only serve to assure an attack from those who could not afford to allow its implementation.

For those who haven't witnessed the awesome power possessed by those aliens, it would be very difficult, if not impossible to imagine just what a single sentinel globe could do were it employed above Earth's stratosphere with instructions to enslave mankind to the wishes of some controller. Such an instrument could be programmed to take out a city or a certain parking meter, an entire missile installation or to explode a cigarette lighter in a certain soldier's shirt pocket. The sentinel could be programmed to incinerate every organic thing on the continent of Australia or to cook a slice of toast in Chicago.

Just imagine what the world would become if control of such a weapon would fall into the hands of man. Let us be thankful that the Biaviians are the ones who possess the technology instead of Saddam Hussein or George Bush. It is no accident that the aliens have chosen not to socially interact with the governing factions of this planet. It would be suicide.

I must admit that it bothers me to know that similarly destructive technology is also possessed by the Targzissians and quite possibly the Skreed, not to mention the less intimidating Dorians and Nyptonians. I have been told that none of the intelligent species aboard the mothership has any designs upon Earth which involve conquest of any sort. I believe this, not because I believe the aliens to be endowed with any great saintly qualities, but because I know that if such had been their desire, they could easily have accomplished this long ago. Also, I believe Tan when he tells me that such actions are against the Celestial directive.

If a Biaviian should read our Constitution and believe its words, then they would no doubt attribute to man the most noble of attributes, but we know different, don't we. In actuality, the factors of freedom and equality play little part in the applied policies of our society and indeed in the world as a whole. So I can sleep peacefully at night in the knowledge that we need not fear the beings from the stars.

And what about the beings in the levitating gardens. I have never seen a single Biaviian enter or leave these gardens. Could it be that the beings within are not aware of the true dimensions of their world? Do they believe that the world does not reach beyond the impassable glass shield of the sky dome that covers them? Or do they voluntarily choose to live in the gardens because they are similar to their home planets? Are they Biaviian, Dorian, Hybrids, humans or some other form of intelligent life? The questions concerning those mysterious gardens are endless, and at this point I do not have the answers.

On this trip I did get a chance to ride aboard one of the inner ship shuttles and passed within perhaps a half mile of one of the gardens, close enough to see the deer and recognize them as a species indistinguishable from certain deer or Earth. The living structures, as far as I could tell, were identical to some homes on Earth. I never did see one of the garden dwellers close up, so I still cannot say exactly what manner of species they are.

After a rather extended tour of parts of the great ship that I had never visited before, Tan took me in to a large chamber which was practically dark. Then he said, "Martin, close your eyes (COZE-R-ICE)". I did so, and after a long moment, he said, "Now open them", which I did. The magnificent vista that assailed my eyes nearly took my breath away. I heard Tan say, "Behold Biaveh".

For all intents and purposes I was standing on the planet Biaveh. I stood on a rolling meadow of carpet-like blue grass, really blue, which was in full bloom with fragrant purple, orange, red, yellow and green wild flowers. There were also many shades of blue blossoms. The flowers were being harvested by golden honey bees with iridescent pinkish red heads. The bees were larger than Earth's varieties, being about the size of your big toe, and their wing beat was more relaxed in pace.

Butterflies of all descriptions created a kaleidoscope of casually moving color. Some had wing spans easily a foot wide, while others were the tiny purple variety. I couldn't even begin to describe all the marvelous colors of the butterflies, for the wing colors ran from shiny black to blue dappled with pink, red sprinkled with yellow, gold, orange, yellow, flaming red, iridescence, etc.

I saw the Biaviian version of the hummingbird, and I chuckled at their seemingly slow wing beats, beautiful. Forward of me I saw the multicolored Biaviian forest stretching away to the slopes of a truly majestic gray, purple and pink hued mountain range, whose peaks were lost in billowing white clouds. Off to my right was a grove of fruit trees, which for want of a better description, I will call apples. Certainly the fruit of these trees was identical in shape to apples, except that it was as large as small pumpkins and purplish red in color. The leaves of these trees were canary yellow with red veins, while the trunks of the trees were a golden brown with shades of green and pink.

Down the sloping meadow to my left was a slow moving, crystal clear river lined with trees of various colors. Occasionally a large gold, silver, black or green fish would leap from the water and hang suspended in the air before splashing loudly back into depths.

Near the closer bank of that river I saw a number of children and several adults. The kids were cute and obviously of mixed alien origins. I noted that the adults were humans of the Earth variety, and I saw one lovely lady who looked familiar to me. I couldn't remember her name, but I know that she was a pilot back during Lindbergh's time. She had not aged at all. There were about a dozen children there, and they were doing what children do everywhere, playing.

In my fascination at it all, I had forgotten that Tan was there with me all the while, so it startled me a bit when he spoke, "Martin, is Biaveh not beautiful?" "Yes, Tan, it's beautiful". "See there, Martin, of the children, six are of your seed". And I said, "No shit. Which ones?"

He then proceeded to point out to me three boys and three girls, who are the offspring of my sexual experiences aboard the mothership back in 1964. As I looked closer at the children, their characteristics became apparent.

The children were somewhat shorter of stature than Earth children of comparable age. Their heads were noticeably larger, and the eyes were wide set, rather large expressive. They all had hair, though it was thin and fragile. The noses were small but well-formed. The mouths were small and doll-like, and the children apparently had the power of verbal speech. The ears were notably small in relation to the head size and the chins were small but firm, giving the face an egg shape. The hands possessed the five fingers of the human and were long and of the classic sort. The length of the arms was a bit longer than usual but not grotesquely so like the pure blood Biaviians. The feet were good-sized but not as splayed and as flat as the pure blood. If you have seen the drawings of those adorable kids with the large eyes, then you have a good idea of how these kids looked to me. Strange but undeniably cute.

One of the boys was busy stacking geometrically formed crystal play blocks using the power of telekinesis. One of the little girls was playing with a flock of butterflies. This would not have been so unusual had it not been for the fact that she seemed to be literally controlling the flight pattern of the butterflies. In response to her hand gestures, the butterflies flew in various formations, forming circles, crosses, etc.

Upon querying Tan about these things, he explained it to me in this manner. It seems that the offspring of human and Biaviians and other aliens are naturally endowed with neurological powers, which are not generally possessed by the pure blood alien or human. For some reason the powers of telekinesis, levitation and who knows what all are often greatly pronounced in these offspring. Perhaps it is because the aliens have lost the ability to dream and to escape into fantasy. Perhaps they are devoid of all those flippant elements which are characteristic of the still evolving human.

Without a doubt, the aliens find these hybrids fascinating but not so much that they would allow them into the mainstream of Biaviian society. I understand that the humans and hybrids on Biaveh are segregated to a geographical location which is away from the alien metropolises. This is done for the protection and well-being of the aliens as well as the hybrids. One could only speculate what might happen if these mixed bloods should ever gain widespread access to all of the awesome technology of their hosts. We might safely guess that those beings who are in most cases more genetically human than alien would no doubt retain many of the pure human psychological characteristics, and we know that human are prone by nature to anger, greed, envy, pride, etc. Such emotions simply could not be permitted to run unchecked among the docile host.

Tan said as much but in different words. Instead of voicing the probable negative aspects of such a thing, he seemed to take relish in pointing out the marvelous freedoms offered the new Biaviians. For instance, the new Biaviians, according to Tan, could walk for ten days in any direction and not come in contact with a pure Biaviian settlements. Their sphere of habitation includes rivers, lakes, parks, forests, hills and mountains, valleys, fruit groves, video screens, horses, dogs and all of the amenities which the most prosperous of human beings enjoy on Earth. So the apples are purple, what the heck! You want to sky dive or water ski, you got it. Want to camp out, horseback ride or fly fish? You got it. Want to do a five year space vacation? You got it. Plus, you will live for literally thousands of years while remaining sexually virile and disease free. While the world of the new Biaviian has some restrictions, they are certainly not imprisoned by a long shot.

As I stood there and scanned the living vista before me I can only say that no description I could possibly give you of the seeming reality of the experience would suffice. The outpouring of love that I felt while looking at my offspring caused me to shed big soggy tears.

I could clearly hear the squeals and laughter of the children, feel the texture of the grass beneath my slippers. I could smell the river and the wild flowers and the over ripened fragrance of wild-fallen fruit. I felt the Biaviian breeze on my face and heard the rustle of the leaves as well as the drone of the honey bees, the splash of playful fish and the call of distant birds. The shadows of the clouds passing overhead moved lazily across the meadow. It was midday, and I felt an overwhelming urge to just run over and join the kids and the rest of the people and just refuse to return. But before the urge overtook me, the scene began to fade out, and presently I was back in the large circular chamber aboard the mothership with Tan, Nela and

Question standing beside me.

"Tan, is it real?" I asked, being still somewhat choked up. "Yes, Martin, it is quite real". "Will I ever get to meet my kids in person?" I asked. "Yes, Martin, you will, providing you survive the dangers of your earthly modus".

In explanation, he informed me that the Biaviians are no longer allowed to interfere in the destinies of man. However, it was known that an element among the 'fellow wayfarers', which I took to mean the Targs, and said as much, which he didn't deny or confirm, did not feel that I should be allowed such access to the sights of the mothership of such close interrelations with the aliens in general. But this sentiment on the part of the Targs applies to all human contactees. I suppose that their opinion of human beings holds some merit in the sense that nearly every contactee in the past has used any information gained to try to cleave out a demagogy for themselves on the Earth or to add to and embellish incomplete information.

However, I was told that, be that as it may, I was under the protection of the Biaviians and that the Targzissians would be restrained from physically harassing me providing I never invited their contact through my own wish and concern. Unfortunately they neglected to tell me that the Targs might be able to telepathically influence the minds of other people who might do me harm. I'm certain that these unseen influences have been at work, especially since my decision to renew my knowledge of the aliens, after my last contact on 27 December 1987.

Too many things have transpired which do not fit in to the natural order of things. Of course, any attempt to explain these happenstances to the average person would be futile. Even the person who has been telepathically influenced against you, although unable to explain the source of the sentiment or its justification, will still, in most cases, pursue these actions. So I am never surprised at the broken trusts, the double crosses and the clandestine intrigues mounted against me. I know such things to be real as I have suffered the definite measurable effects of them.

My only defense against such hindrances is to remain aloof and free of close relationships. Remaining a lone eagle and a free unattached spirit is no complete assurance against the wrath of the Targs, but it helps. Now don't get me wrong, the privacy thing is not a psychosis, I'm certainly not schizoid, but I can easily see why some people who have been contacted and who have been so treated would have become so. It is a fact that some former abductees have ended up in asylums.

Before you allude to the words of Shakespeare who said, "Me thinks thou protests too much", in defense of my mental stability I will only say that my life experiences on the whole have not lent themselves to giving sway to fear, and I'm not about to be intimidated by, or live in mortal fear of a bunch of lizards. Besides I am perhaps the only human living who knows how to hurt them, and I can teach you how to do it too should you ever find yourself in their presence.

The first three days aboard the mothership were spent in visiting parts of it I hadn't seen before and holding long conversations with my friend, Tan. When I had last visited the mothership eleven years before at age eighteen, I had spent half of the time in the hyborian gardens, along the halls of frozen suspension, along the upper causeway and in the chamber of love, where I spent three days procreating with a number of hybrid alien females. But on this visit I was taken to see some of the central and lower levels of the great egg.

What these aliens have accomplished in robotics is nothing short of mind boggling. From an area above an operating room, I had the chilling pleasure of watching a neurosurgeon robot perform a brain operation, and the actual operation couldn't have taken any more than ten minutes tops. Using lasers, the machine worked swiftly and silently and never paused a second in the intricacies of its task. Immediately after the operation the patient got up and literally walked away toward the recovery area. I was told that he would return to full duty in about twenty-four hours.

Other robots were busy making what appeared to be microchips and other tiny electric parts in a purified enclosed environment, while others did things that required intense heat but not on the scale of a steel mill. The parts they were making were small and individual. What fascinated me so was that the fabrication of one of these pieces required dozens of processes and literally thousands of geometric moves. There were robots that cut diamonds and wore invisible nets using superthin strands of gold or platinum.

I have spoken of small globes or light spheres that darted about the docking area and other areas of the ship, seemingly under their own power. What their tasks were, I do not know, but I had the unforgettable opportunity of seeing one of the globes actually being fabricated by a specialized robot. The robot and its fabrication materials were encased in a large bathysphere shaped metal module. The interior of the chamber was a pure vacuum, and the inner atmosphere was alive with jagged blue-white fingers of electrical charges. The robot was shaped like a half loaf of bread with a dozen arms protruding from it, and so complicated was the machine that each of the arms seemed to be performing a unique function, and it continually levitated around the chamber, ever busy.

First the robot bombarded a piece, which seemed to be composed of some kind of metal which had been incorporated into some kind of crystal. The piece looked some what like a child's play jack only with more arms or points. The piece was set into a spinning motion, rose into the air and stood there suspended. The robot then took a superheated wad of some kind of materials, so bright it nearly blinded me with its brilliance and placed the glowing wad in a cavity of its outer chest or mid-body. Presently it started to feed the material out in a very fine glass thread, which started to circle the suspended spinning piece, and as it did so, the globe began to form.

The entire process took about thirty minutes, but I was told that some of the more complicated and finer spun globes could take many hours or even days to fabricate. A Stagyian scientist sat in a soft blue chamber nearby silently programming information into the individual globes and possibly the robot also. When the process was finished, the globe took on a life of its own and zipped away to begin its programmed functions. Fascinating.

Tan told me that the globes are used for a number of purposes. Some are used for planetary reconnaissance and to protect manned ships. Some are used for returning information to and from the home planets, while yet others are utilized to travel back in time to record certain incidents. I'm sure that the globes have many more applications that I wasn't told of.

Alien in-ship shuttle craft as well as the large interplanetary ships do break down, because I saw a number of them undergoing repairs in the landing zone and the in-ship shuttles in an area deep within the ship.

I also had a chance to see the chamber of the sleepers, where literally hundreds of Biaviians lay in a kind of suspension. They were lined up in neat rows, resting on levitating translucent slabs and were being watched over and cared for by a number of quietly mobile robots. I was told that an individual's sleep span might last a hundred years or just a few days. We didn't go into the in-depth reasons for these varied sleep spans, but I was told that the dreams were recorded.

As far as I know, the Biaviians are not troubled with any uncontrollable diseases. However, their lack of sickness, while being wonderful on the one hand, can be a deadly affliction on the other, because it makes them easily susceptible to the many kinds of natural and unnatural infectious organisms they will be exposed to from new life forms. Even though the aliens visit Earth, they don't drink the water or breathe the air, and as I think back, I realize that even though I saw thousands of extraterrestrials of various origins, I never came within touching distance of any but Tan, Nela, Question and the hybrid women. Apparently those who were near me have somehow been inoculated against my germs. Of course there was always the decontamination stage I went through with each contact. So in spite of all the things I did and the places I visited aboard the mothership, I was still kept in a kind of subtle isolation. I'm sure it was for my protection as well as theirs. Even with all these extraordinary precautions, I'm told that infection of some kind still manages to slip through on occasion.

Did I tell you about the universal drink that was served to me? It looked like a glass of pink lemonade, but at first it tasted flat or had no flavor at all. When I mentioned this to Tan, he told me to simply think of any flavor I was familiar with, so I recalled the taste of strawberry soda and immediately the liquid took on the color and taste of strawberry soda.

There is no limitations on the number of flavors that the liquid could mimic. Your own imagination was the only limitation. After that I would create wines or beer, and once I did a pretty good imitation of good corn whiskey.

Question kept bugging me for a taste, so I created a glass of vinegar for him. He took a sip, spit it out and said, "No wonder you mother fuckers are an endangered species."

Tan also liked to taste my creations. According to him, this was his way of experiencing the human tastes. He looked silly sitting there with his little glass straw waiting to get a sip of my next creation. For the sake of science and as a proud representative of my species, I immediately set about creating all the various flavors of alcoholic beverages I had ever imbibed, most of which were of the cheap, hard or illegal variety. In a short span of time all three of us were duly zonked to the slobber factor. I saw Tan's big head bobbing and bet Question that his awesome melon would flip him over in six more bobs. He lasted about four before flipping backwards. His little feet went up, and we thought this was funny as hell.

The last thing I remember before waking up with a dry mouth was attempting to order a full barrel of the liquid so that I could turn it into Napoleon brandy. Apparently the robot didn't know what I was talking about and failed to fill my order before I passed out. Strangely I didn't feel any great hangover effects. Tan never asked to sip my drinks again, but Question kept trying to get me to taste the lake in the Hyborian Garden and zap one up. I explained to him how ridiculous and irresponsible an act that would be and expressed my shame at his shameful gluttony. Anyway, I had already tried the waterfall at the lake, and it didn't work.

Onward into this visit, I spent approximately three days counselling or teaching the human experience to an entire circular auditorium full of Biaviians and composing 'mind music'. The teaching sessions were held in this manner. Of course all Biaviians are telepathic, as this is their primary method of communication. However, the vast majority of the Biaviians have never had any direct contact or social intercourse with humans. Secondly, all Biaviians cannot easily communicate telepathically with the average human, and few have actually experienced the human emotions and sensations as Tan has through me.

As a result, the average Biaviian has little idea of the true emotional, cultural or spiritual level of the human being. Instead, perhaps, they tend to view the human as just another mammalian biped animal who possesses the rudiments of technological promise.

So in order to convey my meaning to the mass before me, it was necessary for me to funnel the message through Tan. If he comprehended it, he would then pass the meaning and/or the emotion along to the crowd. Most of the time it would take a while for one or two among them to get it. Then these few will pass it along to their peers, and the rippling effect soon encompassed the whole host. There is much head bobbing and foot shuffling, and it doesn't matter what the subject matter is. The whole thing, I thought, was really stupid because I could say just any old thing, and they would take it and blow it all out of proportion. For instance, "Never ever get your nuts caught in a bear trap". Now wouldn't you say that's stupid? Then me and Question would just crack up laughing, and after a while they all would be shaking and bobbing.

Then Question would say something like, "What a bunch of dick heads", which would set us all off again. It was fun. They never wanted to know about politics, religion, prejudice, etc. They seemed satisfied with just picking upon the human emotions as I conveyed them. I must admit that it was fun.

On this trip I also learned that the aliens are capable of video recording human dreams. They demonstrated this by recording my dreams and showing some of them back to me. They are also capable of beaming images into the dreams of people on Earth.

For those former abductees who remain consciously unaware of their experience, the aliens, for reasons of their own, sometimes beam images into those peoples dreams. I suspect that may be the aliens' way of sensitizing those people to places, beings and situations that they will physically experience in the future when the time comes for the great airlift.

Also, dream probes may be another way of learning more of the human experience. As I stop to think about it, I realize that the aliens probably recorded all of my dreams while I was in their presence and have no doubt recorded some of my dreams down through the years. Wouldn't it be marvelous if we had the dream technology here on Earth. When I asked Tan how long they had had the dream penetration technology, he said that it was possibly for fifty thousand years as we measure time. The possibilities of the applications of such a technology are astronomical, and I can easily see how it could be abused or corrupted were it to fall into the hands of man.

Just before my departure from the mothership in 1975, I spoke for an hour or so without interruption to the assembly and though I do not consider myself a great orator, I am proud of this parting speech I gave. Near the end of my oration, I became choked up with emotion and was near tears. Then I heard Question say, "Oh, oh somebody get my boots, somebody get my boots".

Still I went on to complete my speech after being so rudely interrupted by this deplorable animal. Yet before I boarded the whisper craft, I attempted one last time to say goodbye and to express my sadness at parting from my friend Question, to which he said, "Cut the crap, slim, and get the fuck offa my egg". As we boarded the saucer I said, "Tan, okay, I'll go back and save the world and all that good stuff, just so I can get the opportunity to return to the mothership and choke the shit out of that beaver".

Judging from my sleep cycle and other experiences, I estimate that I spent at least nine days aboard the mothership, yet when I returned to the camp in Maryland and my pissed-off band members, I found that only three days Earth time had passed since my disappearance or departure. Just a small example of the time warp factor.

Chapter 10

The Targ Terror
May 1988

I've spoken of the Targzissians before, and my personal opinion of them is for the most part negative. I base this opinion upon what I have learned of them and their actions toward man in the past, as well as upon a personal and chilling experience I had with these creatures in the recent past.

Like the Biaviians, the Targs also communicate telepathically and are capable of conversing with humans. I know this because I personally conversed with a Targ via long range telepathy in early 1988, not long after my last visit with the Biaviians on 27 December 1987.

Tan has always been rather close-mouthed about the present day activities of the Targs. However, over the years I did manage to glean a certain amount of information on them during the course of our many conversations. I learned that a major blackout of the east coast some years back was caused by a huge charge of electrons which were emitted from a Targ ship's malfunctioning fusion core.

The Targs are carnivores as opposed to the vegetarian Biaviians, and do on occasion supplement their diet by taking living animals from Earth. I learned that the Targs have been reprimanded for taking domestic animals, such as sheep, cows and an occasional horse, removing the blood and some internal organs and then leaving the carcasses around for the owners to find. Understand that the Targs weren't reprimanded for taking a few animals here and there but for leaving them where they could be found. This is a no no.

Wild animals are also taken, but those carcasses are rarely

found by people. Generally when an animal is killed or dies, the carcass is swiftly consumed by predators, insects and natural processes. The creatures that have been harvested by the aliens have a slower deterioration rate, and scavengers tend to leave them alone. I'm just guessing but do you think that the slow deterioration could be due to the radiation used by the aliens to decontaminate them and that scavengers bypass them because of the Targ scent that remains with the animal.

As I've explained before, the Targs come in several forms that I know of. The original form is that of an upright lizard, which stands approximately five feet tall and whose skin appears to be scaly and may be gray blue in color. The eyes are prominent and reptilian in appearance. The hands are long, thin and claw-like. Small notches are noticeable down the neck and spinal column, and the whole upper body tends to lean forward when he walks. The mouth is thin lipped and wide with small sharp teeth.

Another form of Targ, or hybrid, could pass for oriental or perhaps Hispanic human. They are short, around five feet, sallow white skin, black hair with the vampire peak in front, and they tend to dress in black suits that appear to be made by humans.

I believe that there is a third kind of Targ, which is very huge, but I cannot swear to this as I have not seen such a creature with my own eyes. I do know that the Targs are born from eggs, and that they have been among the Earth's visitors for thousands of years.

As to any genetic cross-breeding between Targs and humans, I have no proof nor confirmation from Tan. However, the white skinned black haired beings in the dark suits tend to suggest that there is some form of biological intercourse between the Targs and humans. Yet even if the Targs haven't biologically crossed with humans, I am certain that the aliens have had physical contact with human beings.

The Targs are more secretive in their wish to avoid discovery of their activities upon the Earth. In the past, certain people who saw things, or perhaps were abducted, have been visited by some mysterious men dressed in black, who literally sought to warn or scare them out of attempting to reveal what they know. And with some success, I might add.

It is known that electrical motors and appliances may experience shut down or blow out when an alien ship passes near. This anomaly is typical of Biaviian, Targ and Dorian craft, but tends to be more pronounced in Targ ships than in others.

From what I've lately learned of other abductees, it seems that most of them tend to look upon their abductions as a horrifying experience, yet very few of them have any recollections of pain or ill-treatment in the physical sense from the aliens. However, some people have suffered scars and other physical complications as a result of the decontamination radiation and physical examination processes of the Targs.

Unlike the Biaviians, the Targs seem unfeeling in their dealings with Earth people. I believe this is because the Targs really don't look upon humans in the same manner as do the Biaviians. They may see humans only as experimental objects and not attribute any spiritual qualities to them.

I can imagine what a terrifying experience it would be for a person to suddenly find themselves in the clutches of these cold creatures. Some abductees have complained of having been probed with huge needles or of having skin and blood samples taken from their bodies. Woman have complained of missing ovaries and aborted pregnancies and other medical complications all as a result of having come into contact with these aliens.

In my opinion, the Biaviians are light years ahead of the Targs in human feeling and public relations. I get the distinct impression that the Biaviians don't hold any great affection for the Targs either.

When I was leaving the mothership in '75, I passed close to a Targ V-wing craft that was still humming, and I noted that the ship had wads of some fine materials on its hull and landing gear that looks similar to spiders webs. I grabbed a bit of it in my hand, and it slowly melted away. Also from the open hatch or ramp way of the V-wing ship, I saw and smelled a kind of humid fog coming from within, indicating to me that the interior atmosphere of the ship was warm, damp and humid. There was a kind of orange glow emanating from within the ship, as opposed to the soft blue interior of the Biaviian saucers.

The Targs also make use of robotics, but I don't think that their technology comes near that of the Biaviians. For example, I saw a Targ maintenance robot working on a ship. The machine seemed aged and worn, and a Targ was standing near it with what appeared to be a remote control unit.

The Targ ships were not as clean, unmarred and as smoothly constructed as the Biaviian ships. The power drive of their ships is louder than that of the Biaviian ships. The only other alien technology which comes close to matching that of the Biaviians in sleekness and beauty is that of the Dorians. However, the Dorians seem to do a great deal of their own work manually, while I've never seen a Biaviian do much of a manual nature. I once saw a number of Dorians sitting in a R & R area, and they were retrieving their meals and drinks from dispensers around the wall. The Biaviians have only to think of what they want and almost immediately the desired object or material appears borne silently on a levitating disk.

The Biaviians are the least physically imposing among all of the intelligent life forms. However, I have no doubt that these diminutive beings are the pre-eminent power force over them all. Yet when it comes to the factor of actual physical danger to humans from an extraterrestrial source, the Targs are the most likely perpetrator.

It may also be noted that in the history of man, the Targs have not always remained an unknown quantity. Even while the Biaviian Gods were taking mates from among the daughters of mans, there were other groups of men who also gained a kind of civilized prominence that was more violent and warlike in its context. It will be found that all of these groups, no matter their geographical origins, have a common persuasion. They all worship the snake, the crocodile or some other reptile.

Just as a number of Biaviians escaped the destruction of Mu or Atlantis, so did a few Targzissians, and while the Targ survivors may not have had the technology to accomplish crossbreeding with man, they did have the tech magic to influence or control the rise and direction of those cultures. This world-wide worship of the reptile or the dragon is no fluke or coincidence.

And what of the Nyptonians? As near as I can learn, some Nyptonians did survive and continued to people undersea installations beneath the oceans of the planet. The offspring of the original Nammons still survive even unto this day. No doubt they are visiting on a regular basis by wayfarers from home and are sometimes seen doing so by lone ships or passing aircraft. It gives us cause to wonder about the many mermaid legends, which have been told by sailors down through the ages. I know for a fact that the Biaviians sometimes visit undersea bases, and it never occurred to me to ask just who was maintaining these underwater bases. But who would be better suited for the job than the Nyptonians.

Once I saw an open atlas representation of the Earth in a chamber aboard the mothership, and upon that map were pin light indicators which I believe pinpoint the location of alien bases on this planet. I noticed that a blue light indicator showed a location off the southeast coast of Florida, another off the northeast coast of Florida and a third due east of central east Florida. There was a red indicator for the North Pole and a yellow indicator for the South Pole. There was another blue indicator in central Africa and another blue off the southern tip of Africa, a yellow in central Australia and a red in northcentral Russia, a blue in northern China and a few other points. Oh, yes, I saw a triangle representative for a pyramid in Egypt, the Americas and Europe. There were other indicator symbols dotting virtually the entire planet, but I could not consume all of the information.

Whether the Biaviian language also consists of recognizable symbols, I can't say, However, these are some of the symbols I saw from time to time: and all of these symbols are connected to the Biaviians.

The following are symbols connected to the Targs: 
The following are the only symbols I glimpsed of the Nyptonians: 
The Dorians did not wear symbols on their suits, but I did see this symbol in their recreation area: 
As to the Stagyians, the Insectillians and the Seventh Life Form, I saw no symbols which I could definitely attribute to them. Most of the on-screen writing or symbolic representations of the Biaviians, strangely, reminds me of Chinese characters.

When you pass close to a Targ pilot, you can feel the heat emanating from his body or life support system, and you can also feel a rise in temperature when you pass near the Targ zone of the mothership, or indeed, near one of their V-wing ships. You can also smell an odor, ever so subtle, that reminds one of humid swamp land, like warm mud, while a Biaviian exudes a fleeting body odor which reminds one of honey-suckle, a pleasant smell. I didn't get close enough to a Nyptonian to smell them, nor to the Dorians. The only place that I ever saw an Insectillian or the seventh form of life was in the Great Chamber of the Council of the Seven, that is I never saw either of them moving about among the populace.

I learned that the Targs once actually captured an Earth jet fighter along with the pilot. The reason I know this is because Tan told me that the pilot of the plane was turned over to them and chose to go to Biaveh instead of return to Earth. He is still alive.

In February of '88, not long after my last contact with the Biaviians, I started to receive a different kind of telepathic transmission late at night, and the voice was saying, "Friend Martin, we know of your greatness and have need to speak with you". This message was at first almost as faint as a passing thought, but I left my receptive mind open to it, and it became progressively stronger over a period of several days. I finally responded by saying, "Who are you and what do you want?"

So the answer came, "We are of Targ, most high greetings do we bring, and seek council with friend Martin". And it seems as if the softer resonance of Tan's voice cut in and said in effect, "Martin, don't do it. Your trust is to me only. Only by your wish may the Targ approach". In other words, he was telling me that if I chose to commune with the Targs, I would do so at my own peril.

On one hand I somewhat resented this telepathic intrusion into the privacy of my psyche, while on the other hand I was fascinated at the possibility of broadening my knowledge of these extraterrestrials. You see, it was around this time that Barbara Simon and I had begun to make great progress through our regressive hypnosis sessions. It was also soon after the time that a local television channel had run an interview with me and the Polaroid photographs that I took on my 27 December 1987 contact.

Perhaps it was only coincidence but the television antenna of that particular station inexplicably fell on the day or the day before my segment was to be aired, and as a result the segment could only be seen by those people who had cable.

Things began to happen around Barbara which could not be explained in the conventional sense, and several people in the media whom I had contacted concerning the materials suddenly chickened out. One radio announcer even left town. So publicity of the event was quite limited by this train of coincidences.

And now I was being personally contacted by the aliens. There are those among you who, at this point, may say that this guy was just hearing voices and is therefore some kind of nut. Had I not been consciously aware of the existence of these beings, I may have drawn this conclusion myself. However, I had no doubts whatsoever as to the reality of the situation.

Deep within I knew that the Targs were nothing to play with. I've learned that some contactees have ended up in asylums, while it is possible that others have met violent untimely ends. Even though I am not a cowardly person, I also do not consider myself foolhardy. Yet I am well aware of the fact that if I have an addiction, then the most prominent of my afflictions must be my insatiable quest for knowledge. My compulsion to learn something new was and is greater than my fear of the unknown. So, against the advice of Tan and the echoes of my own better judgement, I instinctively knew that I simply had no choice but to pursue the matter. Even though I inwardly knew that I would eventually bow to the inevitable, I still spent most of my time contemplating the situation.

I had always been inquisitive to know more of these aliens, of their sense of logic and self-esteem. To what extent have they been involved in the history and affairs of man. What are their present and future plans concerning humanity, and to what extent have they already incorporated the genetics of man into their own biology. I wanted the answers to all of these questions and more, and who could better supply the answers than the Targs themselves.

Before that time I had never had any verbal communications with these creatures. However, I was aware of the fact that they had previously had dealings with mankind. The fact that the Targs were able to locate and contact me indicates that their tracking technology is quite advanced, and the fact that they were able to duplicate my neurological brain frequency and initiate communication clearly indicates their skills in this field, even though their technology cannot compare with that of the Biaviians, it still dwarfs that of man.

Barbara knew that I was in telepathic contact with the Biaviians, and I had mentioned the Targs to her. However, I decided not to inform her of my impending communication with the Targs, because I knew that she would insist upon being present and I didn't wish to expose her to any danger that might be connected with the visitation. If anything detrimental was going to happen then, I didn't want any innocent bystanders involved. Also I didn't want the presence of others to possibly prevent the Targs from making the next contact.

In early March, I had decided and started to leave my nights open for the next contact. On the night of March 14th, or should I say the morning of the 15th, the telepathic contact came. It is difficult to explain what the sensations of the transmissions felt like. While the transmissions between me and Tan were performed, I lay in a kind of somnambulistic state between open consciousness and sleep, and the sensations were quite pleasant and didn't require any great effort on my part. The words are nearly always accompanied by sharp images, and these images are composed of what Tan is seeing through his own eyes during the transmission. I believe that he can also see what my eyes are seeing.

But with the Targs it was different. First of all, the telepathic exchange caused a feeling which is similar to the sensation of being under water, with the voice echoing deep within the brain. Instead of seeing through the Targzissian's eyes, it was as if I was sitting ten feet in front of the Targ and looking directly in his face. It was like seeing him through tunnel vision, but his face was clearly distinct.

"Greetings, friend Martin", he said. "It is well that we may meet at last, that you have bade me come and speak with you". And I responded by asking, "and just what the fuck do you want from me?"

"Friend Martin, your eyes beheld such wonders as must be denied most of your kind. It is not well for them when you say it over", he said. And I said, "I have the blessings of Tan that it must be told. I know that most will not believe me, but some will understand", And then he said, "Tan does not lead and the power is not of Tan, but of the host, You will yield to me and speak not of these things". And I said, "Fuck you, lizard". I'm not sure, but I think this is what made him mad.

Suddenly I felt it. It is hard to describe what it was, but it started in my temples just in front of my ears and slowly moved toward the back of my head. Then it started to ease down my spine like a hot cube of ice. I discovered that I could no longer move my hands or my head. My mouth hung open, and I could blink my eyes only slowly and with great effort.

During my lifetime I have felt fear, but never before or since have I felt such helpless fear as that I felt on that occasion. Now I understand the terror that an abductee feels as they lay on an examination table, conscious of their surroundings but totally helpless in the face of it all. The super lizard was taking over my very body with my knowledge and defying me to do something about it. I could feel myself losing it, and it was causing my chest to tighten up. The Targ was either going to kill me, or worse, destroy my mind and leave me one of the thousands of the mentally crippled.

Suddenly it dawned upon me that the Targ was inducing this state in me through psychological-induction. Could it be that he is also vulnerable to physiological influence or imagery? Bearing this in mind, I rallied my mental faculties and started to lash out at the Targ. I conjured to mind two claw hammers driving nails into the Targ's skull. This seemed to surprise him, and I felt his grip loosen, so I escalated the attack and began to saw into his body with a revving chain saw, then to shoot him to pieces with a pump shotgun.

He turned me loose and vainly tried to defend himself, but the saw, the hammers, and the gun continued to destroy him. Then I compounded this torture by dousing him with gasoline and setting him aflame. At this, the Targ started to flail about and to scream, and I heard a voice say, "Release him, Martin, release him".

But I was like a scared pit bull who has tasted first blood, so adding an imaginary hand grenade to this, I proceeded to blow his shit away. With that, the telepathic screen went red, and I felt my mental and physical factors return to me.

Ten days later I spoke telepathically to Tan, and he told me that I was a subject of discussion among the Targs and my situation might now become perilous. He didn't say it in these exact words, but I got his meaning. Apparently my mental barrage had actually done some great irreparable damage to the Targ, and they were pissed off. According to Tan, it was no longer a question of would I have to pay some price for my dastardly deed, but what exactly would that price be.

Now under these circumstances, a great percentage of people would become extremely paranoid, and I'm no exception. However, I didn't allow my fear of the Targs to incapacitate me. I tried to assess the matter realistically. I had beings mad at me who were capable of retrieving a jet fighter in flight or destroying a city with the touch of a button, so if they wanted me, there wouldn't be much I could do to prevent it, so why lose any sleep over it. That's not to say that I wasn't apprehensive at all times.

On the 7th of May, 1988, Tan told me that a decision had been reached. This was it. Since I had willfully and maliciously destroyed the mental factors of a benevolent Targ, who was simply attempting to extend a friendly hand to me, it was obvious that I was by nature an aggressive and violent being. Since it was against the council's rules to physically destroy a human, it was decided by the Targs that this propensity toward aggression was inherent in my offspring on Biaveh. Thus the children must be destroyed. However, this could be prevented and their lives spared if I would agree to pay a price. This price turned out to be the last joint of my right little finger. If I would willingly give it up, the lives of these children would be spared.

Now, if this was all a psychosis or fabrication on my part, or if some how I have been a victim of some great lifelong delusion, then agreeing to part with a joint of my right little finger could do no harm. If what I was experiencing was true, as I believe it to be, then this amputation would prove it once and for all, at least to me. So I agreed.

On the night of my 42nd birthday, which was May 9, 1988, at about three in the morning, I looked and beheld two alien beings appeared in my room. I sat in awe as they proceeded to amputate the last joint of my right little finger with a kind of laser scalpel. They had materialized out of nothing and to nothing they returned.

The finger stub did not bleed at all, and I felt no pain until hours later. You will not find any hospital records of my having gone for medical treatment for the injury, because the wound completely healed over in about five days.

I can only speculate as to why they wanted a piece of my flesh. Perhaps it is going to be used to clone other Martins. I know that the Biaviians have this technology, and perhaps the Targs do also. Could this be the manner in which they obtained the men in Black? Possibly they found the ideal subject and proceeded to make multiple copies of the same to get the men in black. With due modesty, it would seem that, according to them, I am something of a unique specimen among human beings. Perhaps they believe that if they can clone another Martin, they can discover what it is about me that has caused the Biaviians to trust me and to confide in me things which quite possibly no other human being on Earth knows. In any case, the Targs don't have to do anything else in order to convince me that they are real.

Since I've never before compiled or published a major literary work, I can't say with any certainty that this work is of literary merit, or even if it is grammatically passable. However, I'm certain that it is of vital importance to those for whom it is meant, and that it could be of vital importance to all of humanity if only mankind would take it literally and start from this day forth to drastically change the way in which we do things.

Should there ever come a time when peace prevailed upon this planet, I'm sure that the Biaviians would be better disposed toward sharing some of their positive technology with man, and no doubt make their presence universally known and without question.

Many people have claimed to know of these aliens down through history, and there have been numerous sightings which have been recorded in writings down through the years. I would venture to say that there is no ancient written language or living culture which has not alluded to these space beings at some point in their history.

Instead of asking yourself, what if I'm wrong, you might better ask yourself, what if I'm right. I will concede the possibility that some of my ideas concerning these beings may be wrong or miscomprehended, yet this does not nullify the fact that the aliens are real. I hope that during the course of this work, I shall be able to cause the skeptic to really wonder and to cause the open-minded to realize even greater things that I have thus far been able to learn.

My first intuitive feeling that the Targs were dangerous has been verified, and I might venture to say that the damage they've thus far done has been held in check only by the edicts of the celestial council and the technological power and moralistic strength of the Biaviians. Still I'm certain that they have done enough on the isolated and individual level to have painted a negative picture of the extraterrestrials as a whole, especially in the minds of those who have suffered the terror of having been abducted.

Barbara, who is herself an abductee, has a skeptical and basically negative opinion concerning the over-all intentions of the aliens, and I have not been able to dispel these sentiments in her, not that I've tried very hard.

I myself am a true skeptic by nature, and I have not developed my conclusions lightly. Even though I truly do trust the Biaviians, I freely admit that I've not yet learned to accept anything one hundred percent in all its projections. Though I am impressed with the things that the aliens have shown me, I remain inquisitive about the things that they have not revealed to me. Let me put it this way, even though I truly don't believe that the aliens wish to conquer or subjugate man, suppose I am wrong, and they do have some negative plan for humanity. Will simply ignoring their existence change anything? Of course not. And if we should look objectively at the history of human kind, we might begin to wonder if man wouldn't be better off in the long run under the leadership of the aliens. If they treated us like we have treated our less powerful fellow men, then our plight would be rough indeed.

There seems to be some kind of agreement between the different alien species as to which humans may be abducted and by whom. Apparently I fell under the Biaviian umbrella by virtue of my genetic inheritance. This hands off rule apparently can be circumvented on occasion because I have been granted visual and physical access to the reality of the Targs, as well as of the Biaviians. Also, because I willfully allowed myself to be approached by the Targ emissary, I personally removed myself from the usual modus operandi, and thus contributed to the Targ vengeance that was perpetrated against me.

The Targs probably knew that I would be speaking extensively of them in this book, which was at that time only in the planning stages. Eliminating me as an individual would, of course, be a simple thing, but since I am under the wing, so to speak, of O-Qua Tangin Wann (Tan), my life has thus far been spared.

Before the confrontation of the minds between the Targ and myself, I used to receive a number of telepathic intrusions almost on a daily basis. However, since the incident of the amputation, I haven't received a single telepathic molestation from those beings. I'm sure that some other people are not so fortunate. Who knows how many lives and sanities have been drastically altered or destroyed by the experimentations of the Targs.

Why, you may ask, are the Targs such cruel and uncaring entities, and my answer is this. First of all you must not logically assume that technological advancement goes hand in hand with exalted moralistic principles and divine aspirations. We have only to look at the history of humanity to dispel this notion.

As I have said before, I don't think that the Targs are evil in the calculating or sadistic sense but in their inability to comprehend the ethical workings of the human mind. For instance, a Targ may look at a certain city and see that the female population exceeds that of the males by several thousands, so what's the harm in taking a few females samples from that populace or a few children, etc. The fact that the family of that individual or the mental stability of that individual may be devastated by their actions is a concept that is lost upon them.

While the Biaviians are capable of taking such things into consideration, the fact that a number of abductees have suffered temporary or even permanent physical and psychological damage as a result of radiation burns and surgical procedures in their hands is dismissed as minor imperfections of ongoing research. I'm sure that a Targ would no more restrain and torture a human for pleasure than a naturalist researcher on Earth would do with some lower form of life.

Where humans are concerned, you find the factor of individual personality and fetishes, et al., is a thing of prevalence, but among the Targs I don't believe that such individuality exists. If given the task of collecting one reindeer, one bear and one human, the Targ so assigned will perform the task without sentiment one way or the other.

Apparently the Targs do have the presence of mind to duplicate certain human phrases which have proven successful in calming the abductees down, phrases like: Don't be afraid, we won't hurt you, we are your friends and so forth. Since Targs do not communicate easily with humans on the telepathic level, the phrases are probably synthesized by computer.

The Targ abductees, like the Biaviian abductees, are anesthetized against physical pain, but the Targs, I believe, fail to realize that in the case of humans much of pain is psychosomatic.

The sight of a large needle penetrating the abductee's stomach will cause psychologically induced pain in the subject and as I've said before, the radiation decontamination process will have differing effects on different individuals depending upon their biological tolerance level to the radiation. Also, in the case of the

Targs, and because of the organism contamination problem, most, if not all, of their abductees are handled by smart machines instead of by the Targs themselves. I realize that I am probably simplifying what are much more complicated procedures, but I will devote a later chapter to these more bizarre aspects of the alien experience.

While the Biaviians have been exposed to human beings from the hands-on level for thousands of years and have succeeded in learning more of the psyche and motivations of humans, the Targs, I believe, have never reached any human state of socialized intercourse. Historically, while the ancient people were starting to adhere to the more democratic principles of the Biaviians, the Targs were content with human and animal sacrifices. While those societies who were Biaviian motivated were toying with things like universal suffering, the Targ motivated groups evolved warlike religions and values.

This play and counterplay with the human species by the different alien factions went on for thousands of years and continues to this day, only on a more subtle and surreptitious level. Much of the Targs present technology was developed by or pirated from other forms of intelligent life, so the intelligence of the Targ using the machine need not be scientifically advanced. In fact, I get the distinct impression that the average Targ foot soldier is little above some kind of mindless automation, not given to individual decision making.

Any actions taken by these aliens comes directly from a central control, and if that central control were somehow knocked out or nullified, the whole system would collapse or be cast adrift without meaningful direction.

Yet with the Biaviians the factor of individuality is not a lost concept, but like the Targs, much of the Biaviian's technology is developed or co-developed with the aid of other intelligent forms, namely the Stagyians. As we said before, the Biaviians and the Targs have retrieved and examined Earth satellites, and I feel certain that they are abreast of all significant technological developments, both military and non-military. No doubt they also monitor radio, television and telephone transmissions on Earth. I don't believe that they would hesitate for a moment to take and use any tech-advancement of man's creation and adapt it to their own use.

As a self-contained living laboratory, the Earth is a great source of fascination and research for the aliens. The great diversity of life forms on this planet and the relatively unique eco-system make it an endless source of scientific interest to the celestials, not to mention the fact that the Earth would be an ideal departure point for inter-galactic expeditions as it sits on the very outer perimeter of the Milky Way spiral.

Human research programs are rarely planned to exceed the life span expectancy of the originators, but the aliens think nothing of starting research projects which may span thousands of years. So the fact that you and I are living in a time frame which coincides with revelations of universal import and with the coming of the aliens on a visibly mass scale can be attributed to the inevitable and coincidental culmination of events, which consist of sociological, ecological and technological peak fact.

Such a thing could have served no great purpose fifty years ago and will be of little value fifty years from now. Most people on Earth at this moment are really ignorant of the fact that humanity has literally touched the ecological point of no return.

As far as I know, the Targs have no interest in saving, moving or rehabilitating the human race, and for some reason, which eludes me, I believe that the Targs are dead set against the human airlift planned by the Biaviians.

It is a fact that most human beings have an instinctive fear of and dislike for reptiles, and I'm sure that the Targs know this, so developing any form of social rapport between themselves and humans is out of the question. At this point no effective means of mass human mind control has been created, either by the Targs or the Biaviians. In the next chapter I shall explain in greater detail how and why I've reached this conclusion.

Abductions of human beings by the Targs, I believe, have drastically diminished in recent years or stopped completely, and the Biaviians have assumed the dominant role in hands-on dealings with earthlings. That's not to say that the Targs don't still cruise our skies and collect other scientific data, nor even if they still don't collect a human specimen on occasion.

Tan assures me that the Targs have been forbidden to abduct any more humans or to begin experimentation upon any that were not touched prior to the stop order, but I get the impression that the Biaviians are not privy to all of the Targ actions in this and other respects.

By international law, the embassy of one country, though situated in a host country, is sovereign territory and cannot be invaded by host authorities. So theoretically what goes on inside that embassy is private and secret. The same concept holds true concerning the various intelligent species aboard the mothership, so though they all share a common ship which belongs to the Biaviians, their individual zones on the ship are considered sovereign territory and respected as such. So it is conceivable that the Targs are still performing clandestine experimentation on heretofore untouched human beings.

In closing this short chapter, let me reiterate some of the facts concerning the Targ-Biaviian social and political relationship. As before stated, the Biaviians beat the Targs in their last interplanetary war many centuries ago, and I've concluded that the Biaviians, while having accepted the Targs into the Council of the Seven, still play a major role in the content and direction of the Targs progression.

There are certain kinds of technological weapons and war use substances which the Targs are forbidden to have or to develop and a guideline of interplanetary actions to which the Targs must adhere. Other known intelligent species of beings must follow certain trade guidelines when dealing with the Targs.

Biaviians do not physically occupy the Targ home planet, but I have no doubt that they are closely monitored. The Targs do maintain a modicum of autonomy on the surface, but they are by no means free agents. The Biaviians hold no illusions as to the warlike potential of the lizards.

So then I don't think that the human race as a whole has anything to fear from the Targs, but we must not ever completely discount the possibility that political and possibly interplanetary situations are capable of changing. For want of a more tangible thing, let us all wish the Biaviians well lest, the Targs become preeminent.

Chapter 11

Mass Mind Control Truth or Fiction

Perhaps since before the advent of stationary, agricultural and fishing societies, men have attempted to practice various forms of mass mind control with varying levels of success. It began in a consciously planned sense in the cave dens of pre-dawn humanoids. The male who gained leadership of the group through his hunting skills and physical strength ruled his clan through a system of fear and respect. In its baser sense, this law of rule with various ideological and technical attributes still prevails among the human species even unto this day.

Perhaps the hunter leader of the cave clan gradually gained a kind of mythical status because of his ability to overcome the most ferocious game and his prowess in combat against upstart males of his own clan and enemies of other clans. By keeping the tusks of the largest boar and the teeth of the bear, he seemed to mystically capture the strength and cunning of those worthy adversaries, thus gaining more overall control over the minds and destinies of his clan.

Soon just the knowledge of what he had done caused others to bend to his will, and if the game was plentiful, he could even afford to be benevolent thus gaining a modicum of admiration and even love. As this leader grew older and possibly because of injuries sustained, he was forced to rely more and more on his mental dexterity to maintain his exalted position in the clan. Coupled with his accumulated knowledge of game habits and his tracking skills, as well as his intuitive attributes, was his grasp of the persuasive power of ritual.

Today a person who possesses this intangible touch of mysticism is said to have charisma, and such a person makes a successful politician, actor, minister or salesman. Unfortunately, charisma, intelligence and fairness don't always go hand in hand. This a maniac as well as a saint can possess this ability to control the emotions and even destinies of masses of believers. There have always been a few individuals who possessed charismatic leadership abilities which far extended those of others, and who were able to gain the influence to control the minds and actions of the masses.

Jesus of Nazareth accomplished this feat by exuding some great and tangible esoteric saintliness and a philosophical oratory which was and is of the highest benevolent rapport. The prophet Mohammed also possessed a great measure of this saintliness, but the negative aspect of the justifiable murder or holy war was incorporated into his philosophy. The force of the persuasive power of both of those men exist in strong measure even today. Even so without a doubt the religious connection in its many forms has been the most successful method of mass mind control to have thus far existed throughout all of recorded history.

But we would do well to understand that religion itself served only as the catalyst or rallying point of the control, and the driving force of the mass compliance stems from base, raw and uncomplicated compulsions that lay in the hearts of human kind.

When the Christians went to war, all non-Christians were branded heathens and barbarians and were sub-humans deserving only conversion or death. When the Moslems went to war, all non-Moslems were labeled infidels and pagans and were thus deserving only of conversion, slavery or death.

Even with its success ratio in the mass control of the minds of great populaces, the more astute among the perpetrators knew that religion itself was not the basic driving force and that a large segment used the religious precepts only as the catalyst of opportunity toward other ends. In other words, there are Moslems who drink and gamble and indulge in all the other vices surreptitiously and Christians who only pay lip service to the doctrines of their faith. So in the real sense, true mass mind control has never been a reality.

For a time mass population control was accomplished by the Khmer Rouge of Pol Pot, who murdered millions in Cambodia in the post-Vietnam era. Without a doubt, the mass control accomplished by the Khmer Rouge was born entirely of fear and terror. The hearts and minds of the Cambodian masses were never won over, they simply complied with Pol Pot's orders to avoid being summarily murdered. The most heartless and ruthless among the Khmer killers were often young boys and girls.

Here we see the expression of the baser, raw and beastly elements of the human animal in action. The Khmer Rouge never masqueraded under any religious ideology. In their enforced isolation, they swiftly evolved a totally separate and vengeful mentality toward all of the surrounding populace, and they succeeded in attaining and holding the mental state of total enemy to all non-Khmer, so that when their time finally came they were able to slaughter their fellow beings without qualm or remorse.

In the case of the Khmer, their wrath was not born of religious or even coherent political ideological percept, but of an unbridled vengeance upon those whom they had come to perceive as their lifelong persecutors, even though many of the younger Khmer had never come into close contact with or been involved in a military action against the soft ones of the cities.

Unlike many other conquerors, the Khmer did not gain their position through the popular support of the people, but because of the lack of any organized resistance on the part of the ruling factions of the country. Before the rise of the Khmer, the political situation in the country had deteriorated through graft and corruption, nepotism and favoritism to the point of having completely shattered the common people's respect for the government. It is the classic case of a handful of people owning most of the wealth. The cities were dens of iniquity, crime and arrogant decadence.

If the people had respected and supported the government and had possessed a strong sense of nationalism, the Khmer Rouge could never have succeeded in conquering the country so easily, because the guerillas were never very great in numbers. Initially many of the people welcomed the victors, but the awful truth of what the Khmer had in store for them wasn't long in coming.

After the Khmer had succeeded in murdering two or three million people, the Vietnamese invaded the country and stopped the massacre, but after a few years the Viets decided to withdraw and by doing so may have left the way open for the Khmer to return.

In relating the methods of the Khmer and the Viets to mass mind control, it should be clearly pointed out that most compliance to the occupations by the mass of the people was due to their fear of the guns of the occupiers and thus cannot be considered true mind control.

Even lifelong orientations within a certain political or religious structure is no guarantee that the individual will not at some time rebel and challenge the edicts of the central authority. It may be noted that in every recorded society down through history, there always arose a segment of that society which chose to attempt, and in so cases with success, to change the original direction of that society. So in this sense, the ideal form of mass mind control has never existed.

Then there are examples of attempted mass mind control on the microscope level. Case in point, the Jim Jones suicide incident and the Charles Manson cult murders. It is no doubt that both Jones and Manson possessed a certain measure of that intangible factor we call charismatic persuasion.

Manson was able to impose his will upon his cult group through the use of isolation from society, drugs, sex and fear, and his own presence and philosophy. By using these methods over a period of time, he was able to weed out the rebellious and potential usurpers and keep the psychologically docile. Even so, he still never reached the ideal state of mass mind control over his disciples.

Nor did Jim Jones achieve that level, even though he may have come a bit closer than Manson. It may be noted that during the latter part of Jim Jones' infamous leadership, fear had become the strongest element of his control over his isolated cult group.

When a scientist thinks of mass mind control, he thinks not in terms of religious, political or ideological concepts, but in terms of some man-made chemical, electronic or other invention or process, which would be capable of transforming the masses into mindless, servile automatons.

If such a creation should ever be perfected by mankind, it would, of course, immediately be bought, stolen or seized by the ruling factions and forthwith abused to the extreme. I have no doubt there are presently any number of secret experiments going on in universities, chemical company laboratories and secret government installations throughout the world with this end in mind.

Barring mind control, the ruling forces have resorted to and are still perpetrating ongoing schemes to weaken certain segments of societies or countries, and many of these schemes involve the cruelest and most hideous forms of demonic subterfuge.

Back in the 1950s, some doctors in Alabama, under government instructions, infected twenty black men with the syphilis germ and then observed them over a period of twenty years as the infection drove them insane or blind or both before they died in the most terrible fashion. They started the experiment in Alabama for the simple reason that the chances of any of these southern black men ever having sexual relations with women of the Caucasian race was nil, so they were fairly confident that the infection would stay in the black community. This filthy, indecent and ungodly experiment is atypical of the kind of leadership mentality that governs this land. The same experiment in New York or Los Angeles would not have remained so racially controlled. You may rest assured the syphilis experiment was not the first nor the last to be sponsored by the government and other shady organizations.

During the course of our conversations, I spoke to the alien Tan about the Acquired Immune Deficiency Syndrome, A.I.D.S. viral epidemic, and even though he didn't elaborate extensively on the virus, he did tell me that the disease is man-made. It is the product of biological genetic research of some western medical personnel in central west Africa.

It seems that there is a certain species of monkey, native to that area, which transmits a certain kind of virus through its bite, that, when it interacts with the sickle cell trait which is a biological anomaly possessed exclusively by the black race, it metamorphosed into the HIV-3 or AIDS virus.

Now even at this stage in the African's metabolism, the virus may cause the carrier some physical complications but is not generally lethal. Because the species of monkey in question is one that has been used as a pet and in other domesticated capacities by the indigenous people, the simian carried infection is widespread in that area.

The western researchers knew of the virus and its unique properties for some time before its surfacing in the west. They started a research program on the virus with the ultimate goal in mind of concentrating and enhancing the elements of that virus which would make it lethal. They were hoping to tailor its lethal components so that the virus would be deadly to the black race only.

They were eventually successful in culturing a more virile and deadly form of the virus. They then injected it back into the veins of a controlled group of local people, and as hoped, the virus proceeded to break down their immune systems and kill them.

However, at this point they hadn't tried the deadly virus on any other racial group but the pure blood Africans. Now they wanted to find another group of blacks whose genetic metabolism was predominantly Negroid and in which the inter-racial sexual activity was at a bare minimum. After some discussion and geographical research, it was decided that the small island country of Haiti would be the best prospect for trying the AIDS virus.

Why Haiti? Well, for one thing, Haiti is almost entirely black, and the people of Haiti, because of their long isolation from the genetic pool mixing with other races, still maintain more of the pure African genetic metabolism than any other black group which was separated from the motherland. I have no way of knowing if these researchers took into consideration the fact that Haiti has been the un-publicized mecca of retreat for American and European homosexuals for many years. Or maybe they did consider this and chose to sacrifice, if necessary, a number of the western homosexuals community for the sake of science. After all, theoretically the gay community is a relatively closed one, and this would be an ideal chance to study the transmission factor and the biological effects of the virus as it crossed the racial line and without incurring the wrath of the straight community should the experiment ever become known.

For years middle, upper middle and wealthy white gay men regularly vacationed in Haiti, because in the dirt poor, corrupt and desperate economy of that country an American dollar goes a long way and young black males can be hired inexpensively as sexual partners.

Soon the AIDS virus started spreading in the west. It was first thought to be an anomaly that was restricted to the gay community. The researchers who brought the virus to Haiti had not reckoned with the adaptability of the virus. It proved to be lethal to humans of all racial origins and is virile enough to be transmitted in a number of ways.

The virus just happened to hit the Western Hemisphere when the use of intravenously taken drugs is at a peak among all strata of society. Before they caught and started to run tests on the blood bank sales by the drug abusers, a substantial number of blood recipients had been infected. Then there is the bi-sexual and the prostitution factor.

This man-made virus may be the ultimate scourge to have been experienced by the human species since its beginnings. This awesome virus has the chameleon-like ability to literally adapt its structural components to combat any known form of drug yet thrown at it, and in the sexually open atmosphere of western societies, the AIDS virus is at this point one of the most deadly dangers to western human population.

But let's not get side-tracked too far from the subject of this chapter, which is mass mind control. I spoke of the AIDS virus and how it came to be among us not as an example of mind control per se, but to make clearer the fact that man will do absolutely anything, no matter how filthy, inhuman or dangerous, in his quest to satisfy his wish to control the masses or to eliminate certain segments of the masses.

Getting back to the elusive but much sought after method of mass mind control, let me turn your attention to a past mass participation undertaking, which in its inner ramifications yet remains unique and is born of a morbid ghastliness and universal measure of the true worth of humanity, which is un-transcended by any other man-made monstrosity since the beginning of time. I am speaking of the Holocaust, the systematic and concerted effort to exterminate the Jewish race in its entirety by Hitler's Germany between 1933 and 1945.

Within the species family called human, it is universally accepted that self-defense even unto murder is permissible when it comes down to self-preservation, and from what I have learned of the aliens, this same sentiment holds true through the intelligent universe. Self-perpetuity must be protected even at the cost of the destruction of an enemy. Thus the noblest principles of peace known to physical organisms is reason instead of harm, harm instead of maim, maim instead of kill and kill instead of die.

If a greater philosophy exists, then it is thus far unrealized in a practicable sense by any known intelligence. In any war there are excesses to be expected, generally from all sides of the conflict, but these excesses are usually isolated actions by a given group of combatants in their quest to revenge some factual or perceived atrocity upon themselves, which was perpetrated by the opposing side.

But to set about the task of deliberately and completely wiping out an entire chromo-genesis race and seed of a non-combatant racial element, even at the cost of continental and possibly world conquest. It defies all the rudiments of reason, logic and sanity. Such a concept in practice, completely nullifies any possible claim a human society can make toward our animal separation and by proxy condemns all the rest of us for our inactions and mute acceptance after knowledge of the fact.

In any major military conflict, it is inevitable that a substantial number of civilians will swell the casualty lists of the conflict. The common symptoms of total war will, of course, cause much suffering within the civilian populace through the diminishing of natural and agricultural resources, rationing, overburdened medical facilities, destruction of utility and sanitation services and actual physical harm and death from deliberate bombing and terroristic actions.

During the Second World War, the civilian populations Hiroshima and Nagasaki were deliberately singled out for destruction by the U.S. military and government. Those monstrous atrocities cannot be ethically justified. However, as terrible as these actions were, from a militarily strategic and logistics standpoint, these actions made sense. By dropping the atomic bomb on these two cities, the American government was sending a clear and unmistakable message to the far-flung Japanese military which in essence said, either give up the struggle or the homeland for which you fight will no longer exist upon your return.

Without a doubt, if the war had continued via conventional strategic means, tens of thousands more soldiers on both sides would have perished, and the conflict would have dragged on for another year or more as the Japanese were entrenched on dozens of islands in the south Pacific. So even though the destruction of Hiroshima and Nagasaki were reprehensible acts, they are not difficult to comprehend from a strategic standpoint.

No such strategic or logistical rationalization can be applied nor sanely comprehended when viewed in the case of the mass extermination of the Jews by Hitler's Germany. No matter the rabid extent of Hitler's personal hatred of the Jews, he could not have implemented his monstrous master plan of mass extermination without the actual aid of at least tactical approval of the German masses and the apathetic sentiments of the rest of the western world.

After the Japanese attacked Pearl Harbor on December 7, 1941, all of the Japanese people in mainland America were interned in military camps for the duration of the war. Now while this action may have been premature and unfair on the part of the American government, it was not without understandable merit and practicality, and not even the sometimes atrocious treatment of American prisoners of war at the hands of the Japanese caused the American government to commit similar atrocities against the interned American-Japanese populace. Comparatively speaking, such actions of mindless retaliation on the part of the Americans could have been justified in evil logic.

The Germans could not produce any real justification for their beastliness against the Jewish populace of Europe, quite the contrary. By utilizing the economical, cultural and scientific attributes of the Jews in Germany, Hitler could have aided his war effort immensely. In fact, the brain power of certain Jewish scientists in physics and atomic research may have given Hitler the crucial factor needed to emerge victorious in the struggle for world power, because a great percentage of the Jews considered themselves Germans first and Jews second.

No, in the Germany of pre-World War II, something far more fanatic, base and demon-like pervaded the inner natures of an entire race of humanity the likes of which has heretofore not been known or experienced among the human species. It was a thing unique unto a time and a race of man, and the alien Tan and I discussed it rather extensively.

Yes, the extraterrestrials seem to have more than just a fleeting interest in that wartime period, or more precisely the years between 1933 and 1945, which I understand encompasses the initial ascension of and the fall of Adolph Hitler.

In order to more fully comprehend the factors which contributed to the German national mentality, immediately after the First World War, the political and economical agreements which resulted from the Treaty of Versailles did not leave Germany much room for self-determination and economical prosperity. After that war and before the rise of Hitler, the average German citizen lived an economically depressed existence, and under the Versailles treaty the prospect of future prominence was, for the average person, a distant dream. Thus the atmosphere was ripe for political change and the fast rising young national socialists or Nazis proved to be the catalyst for that political and social movement.

Anti-Semitism, of course, did not originate with the Germans or even in Europe. This racial hatred of the Jews by various peoples goes back to pre-Christian Biblical times, and as a general rule, some form of racial hatred is always reserved for those peoples whose social and religious life styles set them apart from the general populaces among whom they abide.

Such a phenomena is not restricted just to the Jews. We have only to look at Northern Ireland and the perpetual hatred between the Protestants and the Catholics or the various factions of the Islamic faith in Lebanon and other parts of the Middle East. It is a case of brother against brother. Religious intolerance it seems has always been with us. From the earliest recordings of history, we find that racial and religious persecution played a part in the sociological shaping of the times. From the ancient Babylonians to the Romans to the tenth century Christian crusaders, we know that the Jewish communities of various places were the victims of pogroms and other forms of persecution.

In Nero's Rome, as in several other places, when times were economically tough, or when certain powerful people found it politically expedient, there was little hesitation in blaming the Jews for these misfortunes, and then sacrificing them as a scapegoat pacifier to the angry public. However, when the initial blood lust of the mobs was satiated after a short period of violence and looting, things generally settled back to normal. Sometimes the pogroms resulted in the expulsion of whole or parts of the Jewish communities in certain places. Further, we find that, in the case of all of these racial persecutions, there were exceptions to the rules. For instance, in Christian countries, those Jews who publicly turned away from their original faith in favor of the prominent religion of the region were spared, as well as many of those who converted at sword point.

In other words, it was generally the religion alone and not the physical origins that dictated the treatment of the persecuted. Before the Holocaust of mid-Twentieth Century Germany, there was never before recorded a massive well-orchestrated plan or movement on a national scale to literally commit mass genocide upon the Jewish race. Generally, we find that beneath the religious persecution there lay an ulterior motive having to do more with money than with ideology.

The ignorant masses may have been driven more by racial hatred than by greed, but the church and political leaders were almost certainly motivated by the prospects of confiscating Jewish property and businesses. Once this was accomplished, they were content to call off the dogs and even be a little more compassionate toward the remaining Jews.

Hitler's persecution of the Jews was unique in the sense that the possession of any Jewish blood was tantamount to a death sentence for those people unfortunate enough to fall into the hand of the Gestapo. Of course, the usual ulterior motives were involved in the murder of the Jews. You see during the years between the First and Second World Wars, the segment of German society who seemed to be more economically fortunate in spite of the depression was the Jews.

To be sure a core elite of the Jewish people had long held prominent positions in the arts and humanities, jewelers, banking, money lending and industrial production. They wore expensive clothes, drove big cars, ate the best of foods and maintained great cultural institutions and synagogues. Of course, as with the German populace, many Jews were poor, but even the poor Jews tended to place great emphasis on education and personal hygiene, thus exuding an air of prosperity even when it wasn't so.

In the eyes of the average German citizen, the Jews were not proportionately wealthy in the face of a universal depression, so envious and hateful sentiments ran deep and raw in the hearts of the average German citizen. Many were deeply indebted to Jewish bankers and money lenders, and many others were envious and jealous because they could not gain acceptance into the Jewish inner social circle. For the most part, the Jewish community maintained a social and economical system which was separate and apart from the larger German populace, and wealthy Jews were just as discriminating, if not more so, than were wealthy Germans, against their children marrying out of their religion.

So when the Nazis arose and started to blame the Jews for all of their social and economic ills, the general populace was quite willing to accept the Jews as a scapegoat and an outlet for their pent-up frustrations. During the Civil Rights marches in the 1960s, we may safely say that the rights of blacks were advanced because of public outrage at the brutal treatment of those non-violent marchers. Yet when far greater atrocities were publicly committed against the Jews in pre-war Germany, there was no such public outcry or popular support for those innocent people. Instead, the average German either participated in or stood back and gloated over the plight of his Jewish neighbors.

As I've said before, the great crime of man is indifference to the plight of his fellowman, and this aberration of character seems to be an anomaly which deeply infects the European mentality, most notably the Germanic people. That same aberration is also dormant in the psyches of the Croatians, Lithuanians, Poles, White Russians, English and Americans to equal and lesser degrees, because for the most part those nationals in the German occupied territories were willing participants in the genocide of their Jewish citizens, while those in countries not occupied by the Germans knew of the atrocities and refused to work toward saving those people or even in broadcasting the facts to the public. The aliens are well aware of this fact and have given extensive study to this particular psychological anomaly among the white races.

The aliens have a sociological research breakdown on all countries, races, tribes and ethnic persuasions of humanity, and they have a comparative chart of modus concerning things like matricide, patricide, incest, pedophile, mass murder, both homo and heterosexual, child molesting, ritual murder, serial killings, suicides and other depravities, such as fetishes, sado-masochisms, etc., and the Europeans win hands down in all categories of these negative aspects. The main focus, however, is on the Germans because the proven expression of their dormant nature forms a tangible base from which to build relevant data.

It is a fact that as a race the Jewish people have been the one most widely dispersed race of people historically on the Earth, and were therefore always available when a racial or political scapegoat was needed in a given place at a given time. While other races have been cast into the role of servitude or slavery, they rarely gained enough economical prominence to be perceived as a social or political threat as did the Jews.

Having always been an educated and professional group politically and economically, the Jews, no matter what their habitat, generally gained some notable political prominence and were thus more likely to be singled out for persecution.

I am told that as a young starving artist, Hitler was denied admittance to several institutions of higher artistic learning by Jewish administrators, and that he was denied the courtship of a young well-to-do Jewess because of her family's disapproval of his poverty and religion. This, the aliens believe, was part of the cause of Hitler's rabid anti-semitism in later years.

Yet, no matter how strong Hitler's personal hatred of the Jews was, he could never have succeeded in putting together his mass genocide machine without the physical, logistical and sentimental support of the masses. Did Hitler possess the personal magnetism to actually have brought about mass mind control? The answer is yes and no. Yes, he did possess a great measure of personal magnetism and the ability to impose his will temporarily upon the most educated and rational of men. But no, neither Hitler nor his extensive propaganda machine could have persuaded literally tens of thousands of common people and soldiers to personally participate in the mass torture and murder of millions of non-combatants, thus the conclusion that this blood lust is an intrinsic factor of the German psychological make-up. In other words, the natural predisposition to murder without justifiable reason is a primordial possession of the German people and possibly mankind in general. The answer to that question could to a great extent influence the perception of the true worth of the human species as a whole.

The great bulk of information which has emerged from the Holocaust has dealt primarily with the transportation and ultimate murder of the Jews, but there were other aspects of that infamous undertaking which have not been given much exposure, These aspects encompass everything from homosexual slavery to pedophilia, sado-sexuality, Lesbianism, sacrificial murder, genetic experimentation, human-animal transplants, cannibalism, rape murder, sado-sensual torture and any known kind of deviate fetishes.

Fetishes and other deviations could suddenly be legally practiced upon an entire race of people at will by any German male or female without fear of repercussions. Suddenly you could have your own basement or attic or secret room full of male, female or children sexual slaves, who were forced to bend to your every perversion under the threat of death.

How many handsome young boys and men met their deaths while being chained in the basement of some middle aged fraulein or burgher? How many thousands of beautiful young Jewesses were held as starving sex slaves to some elderly German farmer? Or babies sacrificed in Satanic cult rites?

Perhaps this sado-sexual syndrome did not even dawn upon the conscious mind of many of the average Christian Germans, yet as time passed, the elements of greed emerged. Why not loot the empty houses or get rid of the man who holds the mortgage on my house. Once having taken the plunge into larceny, many began to formulate plans for satiating their sexual fantasies. When all Jews became hunted beings akin to game animals under the law, it was a simple matter for the German citizen to go out and round up a number of the desired sexual human objects by promising help in one form or another. So the public at large became a direct part of the mass murder cover-up conspiracy. Just about everybody profited either directly or second or third handed from the properties confiscated from the Jewish people.

We are all now partially aware of the genetic experiments performed upon many Jewish children by the infamous Dr. Mengele, but we were not told of the many houses of sexual slavery that were set up by the Nazis to service the military and civilian party elite, male and female or of the carnal houses or camps that were maintained near the death ovens to service the camp guards and other soldiers.

The much used inmates at these camps and houses were subjected to every kind of sexual deviation imaginable including animals and were completely expendable. This mass sexual preoccupation only served to strengthen the mass murder conspiracy. It is a fact that the woman's camps were staffed mostly with the most sadistic lesbians, while the other camps were staffed with the most sadistic males, those mentally twisted people who gain sexual gratification through torture and murder. So then, when considering all of the mental factors involved in the Holocaust, patriotism, idealism, religious zeal, greed and all other motivations, they all take a back seat to the sexual perversion factor.

Yet when it comes to true mass mind control, the actions of pre-World War II Germany are not a valid example of mass mind control. Upon close consideration we must come back to the agreement that true mass mind control would consist of literally controlling the physical actions of people against their will, while rendering them incapable of consciously rebelling against that control. Fear, greed, nationalism and hatred, or even sexual license, are not enough to accomplish mass mind control. Nor has science yet created a chemical or organic compound capable of controlling and directing the masses in some coherent manner. Of course, they could put a barrel of LSD in the New York City water supply, but all they would get from that would be a million uncontrollable maniacs. Or perhaps sedate the city and put everyone to sleep but to what constructive end?

Earth scientists have taken rudimentary steps in seeking to comprehend and utilize the beta-wave factor in relation to the functions of the human brain. It has been learned that the brain's electromagnetic functions can be interfered with or momentarily short circuited by directly bombarding the test subject with beta-waves.

However, the ability of scientists to actually control the motions and thought processes of the subject via remote means is not even close to being accomplished. Technically, according to the aliens, the scientists are on the right track concerning mind control. However, man doesn't yet possess the technology to master this technique.

At this point Earth scientists have been able to accomplish some small things using beta-waves. For instance, they have learned to induce anger or sadness temporarily by bombarding a certain person with rays, and conceivably it might be possible to influence the mood of a crowd of people temporarily, but this could not be considered a viable or permanent form of mass mind control. Nonetheless, the quest for the perfect form of mass control continues.

One of the greatest fears of the human race is that some hostile extraterrestrial species will use their advanced technology to take control of the minds of humanity. The most horrible fate that man can imagine is that of becoming a slave to some other human or thing, yet the thought of enslaving others causes pleasant sensations in the hearts of much of humanity.

There are certain segments of the European race who would rather die than give up their roles as slave masters, as is exemplified by the present racial structure in South Africa, as was the case in America prior to Civil War of the 1860s.

After the Second World War, a large number of ex-Nazis and fleeing German nationals took refuge in the country of South Africa, as well as other locations like Argentina, Brazil and some anti-Semitic Middle Eastern nations. It may also be noted that an even larger number of ex-Nazis found refuge in the United States, either with forged credentials or with the complicity of the American government. So the same blood lineage and ideological concepts still very much pervade these societies.

The aliens know that Hitler still exists in the hearts and intentions of his disciples, and South Africa is the mecca which holds the seed of all that is beastly, inhuman and perverse in European man. It seems that there is something in the nature of the European male and female, Slavic and Aryan, that causes them to literally swoon in the pleasure of holding the power of life and death and sexually deviate dominance over other human beings. The South African, European and American racist would choose war and death over the probability of having to do that which is right and fair.

The Targzissians have argued, and with much justification, that the European race is expendable by virtue of its history and proven inner motivations and that the elimination of this genetic strain might prevent the imminent destruction of the ecology and life chromosome of the planet Earth. I differ with them by pointing out certain selfless examples down through the ages, and I further pointed out that during the Civil Rights marches in the sixties, a substantial number of people of European extraction also put their lives on the line for the cause. I spoke about the abolitionist and the conductors of the Underground Railroad before the Civil War, who aided slaves in their escape to the North. I spoke of the probability that enough of a percentage of these people still exist in the United States and Europe to prevent the domination of Nazi-like elements from gaining control again.

Therefore, I refuse to accept the opinion of the Targs in relation to this race of man. Yet my sentiments will not prevent this ruling segment of humanity from destroying the eco-system of this planet, nor will my opinion cases the South African Europeans to release his slave owning stranglehold on my brothers and sisters. These are the people who tortured, starved, gassed raped and murdered six million non-combatant Jews and who took great relish in tossing truckloads of children alive into great bonfires and who might very well commit the same atrocities again if given the opportunity. The question is are they prevented from doing so by ideological enlightenment or because the Jews now have guns.

I asked Tan whether his scientists have the technological power to enslave humanity on the planetary scale and this is basically the answer he gave me. From the standpoint of military force, the answer to that question is yes. The ever present factor of the fear of punishment or death can be used successfully in forcing the masses to do your bidding in as much as you are capable of enforcing the threat. The criminal or anti-social person on Earth is held in check by such means. However, these elements can persuade only those who fear the possibility of getting caught more than giving way to these compulsions. The law is not strong or fearful or efficient enough to dissuade the determined felon or the wealthy from their dastardly deeds. The astute but violent felon believes he can avoid getting caught, and the wealthy believe, with much justification, that they can either buy or outwit the justice system. So no pure or equal form of social mass control exists among civilized society.

However, the aliens, should they be so inclined, could conquer and control humanity via military might and police action because they have the true technology to do so. It is estimated that they would have to nullify at least a hundred million humans worldwide and completely eliminate all leadership in order to accomplish the proper state of physical futility, docility and fear among the humans. Then it would be a matter of releasing a certain number of sentinel globes and laser-bolts to keep tabs on the activities of the charges, as well as to eliminate any infractors. Population control, agriculture, property dispersal, etc., could be governed in the same manner. Too many people? Zap!

Actually there would be many positive aspects and benefits for humans under alien rule, such as an unlimited non-polluting power supply via fusion technology. Though tens of millions of people now living would have to be put to sleep to prevent the further spread of existing contagious diseases, the ones remaining would live relatively free of diseases. Because a healthy animal is a happy animal and the medical abilities of the aliens are unbelievable, the average human life span would be lengthened perhaps triple-fold.

Hunger and the homeless would disappear because of population control, agri-science and the aliens' ability to reasonably control the weather.

Marriage, as we know it, would no longer exist, and sexual activity totally unrestricted, because the aliens believe that a sexually satisfied animal is a happy animal.

Accidental maiming and physical handicaps would diminish almost to zero, because all transportation would be centrally controlled, and advanced bionics and implants would replace missing limbs, partial paralysis, etc.

According to the aliens, the Homo sapien is biologically a vegetarian therefore meat eating would cease. All kinds of drugs or their organically degradable equivalent would be free and abundant to all who wanted them. All children of a given community would become common property of that community, and so would all resources. A monetary system would no longer be necessary, as all essentials would be supplied.

Education would be restructured to fit the psychological capability of the individual student, so schools as institutions would no longer be necessary.

Natural resources worldwide would be controlled and distributed equally as needed to everyone. Although each person would be granted complete control of their living quarters or homes, no one would actually own anything exclusively.

In other words, the concept of rich and poor would no longer exist. Among other humans, an individual would be measured solely by his character and not by race or position. Religion, as we now practice it, would no longer be necessary. The research and contemplation of the elements of light would be sufficient for all humans. Continued violence between a certain male and female or homosexual couple would result in the nullification of both parties. The same holds true of any excessively violent person.

Manual labor, as we practice it, would diminish almost to zero, and leisure time would be abound, because nearly all of the work would be performed by smart alien designed and programmed machines. For those who decide that life is not worth living. 'Euthanasia Booths' would be strategically positioned around the world.

When life under alien control is compared with life as it exists now for most people, it looks better and better, yet, just beneath the surface of that carefree existence would always lurk the realization that one's destiny is not one's own and that death remains an even-present reality. A great number would go about, literally, seething with inner hatred of their masters and benefactors.

What kind of world would it be if no man had the power to

force his will violently upon others and could not kill without dying or if no person could command fidelity of a mate through intimidation, but only through love, if the formerly rich had to cook their own food and do their own laundry.

I believe that I could easily live with such a system as described by Tan. However, even that system, while being possible and efficient, still cannot be considered a true system of mass mind control. The people would comply with the ruling edicts of the aliens only because they fear being 'zapped' into carbon dust if they didn't.

I am speaking of how I perceive human existence would be under the guidance and control of the Biaviians, but I shudder to think of what human existence would become under the rule of the Targs or the Skreed. Fortunately, and because of the power of the Biaviians, man will not be faced with either scenario. Instead, the emphasis should be based upon the question: do the aliens have the power to subjugate humanity via mass mind control? Let us explore this aspect to a greater degree.

There have been numerous visual sightings of UFOs by multiple witnesses who sometimes number in the hundreds. On many of these occasions we find that many of the witnesses to the same incident have visual interpretations which are different in dimensions from the next witness to the same anomaly. People may get differing conceptions of the shapes, sizes, colors and distance of the ship. One person may see the occupants of the ship as being tall and blonde, while another may see them as short and large headed, etc. And then a few may not remember seeing anything at all.

This leads me to believe that the aliens have been experimenting for quite some time with mass mind control techniques. Of course, there is the quite common occurrence of near total amnesia and missing time in abductee subjects. Yet we know that these attempts at mind wiping are not always successful. I am personally a good example of this fact.

The alien computers are far more advanced than our own. However, a computer is still a computer and is restricted in its functions by precise laws of mathematical and geometric logic. The super intelligent Biaviian and Stagyian scientists are not soothsayers and are thus restricted by their inability to deal with the illogical, and not even their computers are as complex as the common human brain. Speculation on the stock market and in the cosmos is still a matter of chance. The best that the stock broker or the alien scientist can do is to use all available data on a given subject to narrow the odds, yet the unknown quotient and the element of chance remain.

While experimenting on lower forms of life, like fish and insects, the aliens have found that mass motivation control is quite possible. For instance, a certain wave frequency can stop an army ant migration or start it, heard a school of fish in a certain direction or cause whales to beach themselves for no good reasons. However, when it comes to human beings, the process is not nearly so focused or simple. The same vibration or frequency wave which cases one person to experience great sadness may cause another to experience joy.

The aliens have learned that all species of the lower life forms on Earth are rigidly bound by certain lifelong habits and motivations. All lower species of creatures, and indeed some human beings, are creatures of unvarying habit, but the greater percentage of human beings are psychological free agents, and to the aliens this presents a perplexing dilemma when it comes to the factor of mass mind control.

The aliens' study of the prevailing mentality of the German populace historically is an attempt on their part to unravel this mystery, because that particular populace has come closer than any other given ethnic group to possessing a common motivation. The fact that the catalyst of that motivation was born of a kind of sado-sexual negativism is not as important as the fact that it transpired without notable variance. Hitler instinctively knew the right buttons to punch to bring this about.

The same or a similar spontaneous syndrome happened in 1801 on the Isle of Haiti and during the French Revolution. Something similar is taking shape in Poland, Red China and several other locations worldwide. Still, none has yet come close to reaching the purity in force as did the German populance between 1933 and 1945.

The second and closest example to Nazi Germany is the ruling factions in the Republic of South Africa. It is at present the only place on the planet where evil, hatred and sadism have been exalted to spiritual dimensions. In order to maintain and inwardly justify such a system of bestiality, it becomes essential that one learns to literally love the role of slave master and find sensual stimulation in sadism. Throughout recorded time, one but those of the German European extraction has accomplished this and institutionalized this state of human psychosis. This is not to say that none among them possess any decent benevolent human qualities because there are few voices of dissent among them. However, these voices of dissent are relegated to an insignificant quotient by the greater prevailing attitude.

No doubt a great portion of those ruling South Africans will voice the opinion that their racial position is predominantly economic. They simply don't want to share the wealth, but in reality the true motivation far exceeds even the love of money. The fact that ninety-nine percent of the Southern whites before the Civil War were poor did not prevent them from fighting and dying in order to keep the black man in human bondage, and the same holds true of the South African.

The same blacks they hate were the same people who raised their children, who raised them and their forefathers. These are the same blacks who nurtured them in their sickness, served them faithfully during their times of poverty and loved them even when their own brothers turned their backs on them, and yet they relish the power to maim, torture, kill and enslave them.

They would feel the same even if all the gold and the diamonds were to disappear at this moment. The abiding love of and wish to hold the absolute power of life and death over another human being is a thing seemingly typical of the Germanic European race and is thus of an abiding interest to the aliens. If the force of that particular mentality could be harnessed, dissected, altered and focused, it may be possible to find a common denominator in the human mass mind control factor. Is this syndrome atypical of the white race in its entirety? Or has the sociological influence of other ethnic groups brought about a decisive fragmentation of this syndrome among them?

The aliens are not interested in exalting one ethnic or racial group above another, just in finding a common psychological denominator as it applies to masses of people. Fortunately or unfortunately, they have not yet managed to do so. It seems that the variables in human psychological motivations prevent a viable method of inducing mass mind control.

As I have stated before, I do not believe that the aliens have any wish to enslave humanity via military or mass mind control means. However, I know for a fact that the aliens are going to be compelled by necessity to reveal themselves en mass within the next twenty years, and I'm sure that they would much prefer that all of humanity welcomed their coming instead of being afflicted with mass hysteria. They would much prefer that the military of the planet refrain from trying to shoot them down like an invading force, instead of receiving them as the potential friends they are.

On the other hand, they don't want to have to deal with great mobs of people who have not been chosen for the journey. Of course, as things now stand, none of these negative things could be prevented short of military means of mob control. No doubt it would be necessary to destroy some in order to protect the lives of the chosen ones and to assure that they made it unharmed to the pick up points.

Dematerializing or 'zapping' up a few abductees is a lot different from on-loading tens of thousands at the same time. They don't have the means or the time to 'zap' them up one or two at a time and go through individual decontamination. It would require too many small craft and present too many radar targets for military actions. The time factor involved would be extended from a few days to many months, during which time a growing potential mob of human subjects would have to be fed, pacified and otherwise dealt with. According to Tan, any physical harm to humans or military damage to property must be avoided at all cost. Thus the current preoccupation with exploring the possibilities of mass temporary psychological pacification, both for the chosen earthly wayfarers and the population at large. But I don't think that they have thus far had much success.

So, in answer to the question, do the aliens have the power either mentally or technologically to mass control the minds and actions of humanity, the answer is no, they don't. And it is mostly due to the individual fickle and indecisive natures of the human animal and this indecisive nature is more pronounced in Earth female than in Earth male.

In essence, how can the computer anticipate the actions of creatures who themselves don't know what their next actions will be. Plus, there is another even more important factor possessed by the erratic human species. In dealing with the Targs one-on-one and during my telepathic experiences with Tan, I accidentally learned that a human is capable of telepathically barging into the mind frequency of the aliens and doing them telepathic damage. No, it is not the military or even the physical might of the humans that the aliens fear, but the psychological power. They are not mentally equipped to deal with the human emotions of pain, fear and dementia. The potentially destructive force of thousands of humans together is astronomical and much too dangerous to be let loose among the aliens populace.

This potential for telepathic destruction is probably why most abductees are rendered unconscious of their immediate surroundings during that abduction. Because of my childhood innocence and my inner wish to make friends instead of cause harm, I was allowed knowledge of things which have been denied to most Earth mortals since the beginning of time. It is extremely difficult for a human to gain such confidences once they have truly learned the nature of good and evil. This is why, even the nicest people, upon reaching the planet Biaveh, simply cannot be allowed free access to the general populace. For you see, while you are able to telepathically harm or destroy them, they cannot easily do the same to you.

I suspect that this is why the Targs are so adamant against developing close socialization with the human species, and why they have sought to intimidate or scare me out of revealing this truth. They have tried the power of their mind on a human, namely me, and they failed miserably. Of course, not all people are as mentally dexterous or as fearless as myself in this manner, but neither are all aliens as mentally strong as the one they sent after me. So now you know why the aliens could never telepathically control the human species on the mass level.

The aliens' study of and preoccupation with the mentality of the pre-World War Germans, the white South Africans and others gives me cause for contemplation. If all of that collective hatred and bestiality could be harnessed and then focussed, it could conceivably be utilized by one alien faction or race to telepathically disrupt, incapacitate or even destroy portions of some other alien enemy. In fact, telepathic destruction could conceivably be the ultimate universal weapon.

Could this be another reason why the Targs don't want a large populace of human beings on the planet Biaveh. The Targs probably know that they could never persuade a large number of human beings to assist them in such a manner, so they don't want the

Biaviians to have that potentially dangerous advantage.

Since I came to this conclusion on my own, it never occurred to me to put such a question to Tan. When I stop to think about it, it begins to make more sense. I am aware of the fact that the Biaviians have perfected a true Star Wars umbrella protection system. It would be literally impossible for an enemy to penetrate this system and destroy Biaveh via any high tech conventional means, such as fissional projectiles, particle beams, lasers, masers, anti-matter rockets or remote or manned war ships. So the method of attack would have to be some process which could penetrate all known protection systems and do enough immediate damage to prevent retaliation. Theoretically, a mentally destructive force could be fashioned, focussed and utilized without registering on the high-tech protective sensors, and Earth humans would be ideal materials to form the power telepathic nucleus of the death beam.

Let me caution the reader that this scenario is one of my own creation and is not due to any information or speculation to the effect from the aliens. True, the aliens are great students of human psychology and they have carried out ongoing genetic experiments of the human species, but I do not believe and haven't been given any reason to assume that the aliens have any conspiracy afoot to destroy or enslave humanity.

If they are going to have to deal with humans on a mass scale in the near future then it is essential that they learn as much about the human animals as possible, and even though they have tried to hold the psychological impact upon their human subjects to a minimum, it is still unfortunate that they don't seem to have realized the magnitude of the pain and suffering they have caused many of the abductees.

I have tried to impress this fact upon them, and I believe that the Biaviians at least have truly learned from my input.

Some people believe that the aliens have cut a deal with the government to trade technology for genetic materials, but this is not true. Yes, the government and the military powers of the world are well aware of the aliens' existence and presence, but they have never been able to develop any tangible communications with them.

Think about it, and you can easily realize that the aliens do not need or require the permission of the government or military to carry on these experiments. I have ridden aboard a Biaviian whisper craft or saucer on more than one occasion, so I know first hand what these craft are capable of, and I have been shown on the vid-screen a portion of the awesome destructive military potential of these beings. No, they have no wish to conquer or otherwise subjugate man.

I do not question the sincerity of most environmentalists who seek to save the ecology and certain animals species of this planet, nor do I question the wish of these aliens to save the human race from self-extinction.

Chapter 12

Let's Look At This Thing Objectively

Literally millions of tons of deadly chemicals each year are released into the eco-system and atmosphere of the planet Earth, and I'm referring only to those chemicals which are not biodegradable. As with all matter on this Earth, these man-made killers will remain part of this Earth. These chemicals will not go away or lie dormant indefinitely. Many of them have an active kill span of thousands of years.

The active waste from the nuclear power plants must be stored somewhere, and the estimated life-span of this deadly material is twenty-nine thousand years. There have been a half dozen nuclear generator plant accidents that have come to public notice, and there have been a dozen other nuclear accidents which have transpired world-wide that have been hushed-up by the authorities.

The aliens have, of course, done a detailed analysis of all the Earth's nuclear power plants and stockpiles. Based upon the data accumulated in their computer banks, they project a ninety-eight percent probability that we shall experience at least six meltdown accidents within the next ten years, which will result in worldwide ecological and genetic damage.

Their data shows them that even as I write these words thousands of tons of deadly man-made chemicals are constantly contaminating the fresh water table of this planet, and, if at this moment, man ceased to further contaminate the water, it still would not prevent the genetic poisoning and outright deaths of tens of millions of humans because the build-up of deadly chemicals already in the soil will eventually leach through into the water table.

Their computers tell them that the volume of fluorocarbons and hydrocarbons being released into the atmosphere will deplete the ozone layer of the planet to a potentially deadly level within the next ten years. It should be noted that during the initial stages of ozone danger the people of color will fare much better under the onslaught of the deadly infrared rays of the sun.

Then there is the terrible factor of the spread of infectious diseases, which are running rampant through the human population. Everything from food preservatives to growth hormones in meat animals to fiberglass and PCBs are contributing to this influx of new diseases. Also, numerous man-make chemical compounds are having a direct effect upon the lower forms of life and disrupting the ecological chain of the planet. Soon we shall begin to experience plagues of rats, locusts, frogs, tick carried infections and unnatural insect migrations and infestations.

The oceans, after having been literally saturated with millions of tons of non-degradable toxins and other wastes, shall start to regurgitate these pollutants upon the beaches of the planet. An assessment of oil tankers and other chemical transport containers has caused the aliens to estimate that we will experience at least twenty oil spills and chemical plant disasters a year henceforth.

At the rate at which the tropical rain forests are being destroyed, the Earth's atmosphere will undergo drastic alterations within the next decade.

The constant run-off of agri-chemicals and insecticides into the fresh water arteries of the world literally assures the slow poisoning and the genetic damaging of millions of children yet un-conceived. In 1987, industries reported the dumping of some 18 billion pounds of deadly chemicals into the eco-system, but the aliens place the estimated poundage at 180 billion pounds of such chemicals and this volume is compounded yearly. If you think of the Earth as being a giant sponge, then you can understand that the planet has reached the saturation point and is swiftly becoming one giant poison pellet, which is well on the way to being rendered unfit for human habitation.

At present the medical authorities estimate that the AIDS virus anti-bodies are being carried by about a million people worldwide, but the aliens inform me that the true number is approximately a hundred million carriers and that figure is growing daily.

The white man used the small pox virus to wipe out whole tribes of Plains Indians because they possessed no natural biological defense against the virus. The AIDS virus presents humanity with the factor of universal genocide, because at this point no known racial group has a natural biological defense against the virus in its many forms.

(According to the alien Tan, the AIDS virus can be combated using tincture of quinine and also certain genetic properties possessed by a fish called the Moses Sole, which is found in the Red Sea. A certain genetic chemical found in sharks can arrest and even destroy the virus.)

I am telling you of many elements of man's creation that we presently are faced with in order to give you a better over-view of the true planetary situation. All of the aforementioned things must be viewed as one tangible organism instead of in a fragmented manner.

By the laws of physics, the sum total of matter cannot be added to or subtracted from, it can only be refined, concentrated, altered or reformed. Until an intelligent species reaches a point of being able to bio-degrade or off-load all of its garbage from the mother planet, then every ounce of that material shall remain on that planet in one form or another.

Left in their natural state, all materials are biodegradable or re-cyclable. However, the death dealing begins when certain materials are transformed to a form which is no longer biodegradable. It is quite possible for a planet to poison itself, and this is what the species Homo sapien of Earth are doing.

What makes it so insane is that it does not have to be this way. The great oil and chemical monopolies, the auto makers and food producers form a minuscule number of the overall population, yet they control nearly all of the money and resources of the planet. The political controllers are, for the most part, corrupt, greedy, false, sexual deviates. It is the nature of the rich to hate and despise the poor, and for the most part, it wouldn't bother them in the least if nearly all of the poor bastards would just fall dead. They look upon the masses only as living organisms, whose only earthly value is that of consuming the fabricated garbage of and thereby sustaining the rich in their present status. This attitude with insignificant variation has been sustained among the privileged continuously throughout all of recorded history and has undergone changes and upheavals historically only through the advent of civil wars and revolutions which in many cases resulted in the violent deaths or expulsion of much of the elite strata of those countries. They never learned anything constructive from these happenings, nor have they ever voluntarily relinquished any political or economical power. Today they are more determined than ever of retaining all vestiges of power from the hands of the masses and all wealth even if in their gluttony they succeed in literally destroying the eco-system of the entire planet.

It is the general consensus of the Biaviians that few if any rich persons are worthy of being accepted into the celestial host, though it is not a complete impossibility. The aliens have the deplorable habit of looking at things realistically. They are not in any manner influenced by false rhetoric, deceptive promises, media images and such. They can only be moved by results, and as we've come to know such a realistic attitude just doesn't cut it in today's society, a society that is literally built and nurtured upon deadly falsity.

The aliens naturally assume that any rational intelligent being will, as a matter of course, make all things as perfect and efficient as is technologically possible on any given occasion. To have the knowledge and the means to utilize solar power in lieu of highly toxic fuel sources and then not use it is to them an act of insanity.

Since they have no personal conception of greed, I was never able to satisfactorily explain to them that the system of capitalism and free enterprise, in practice, means to make as much profit as possible with the least outlay. From the businessman point of view, it is cheaper to buy a politician or an inspector than it is to add or modify a certain product or part. It is accepted business acumen to falsify, bribe, lie, and circumvent the rules to the extent that he can get away with, and the result is mass death and widespread injury via pollution, poison and faulty implements.

Is it any wonder that the Targs hold humankind in such low esteem? And the fact that the masses have accepted this homogenous crock of shit without substantial rebellion is to Tan unbelievable. In his reasoning, it is like handing a person a live hand grenade and telling him that it is an apple.

It is no accident that the police force is perceived as an occupying force instead of public protectors in minority and low income communities, because this is basically what they are. The concept of equal justice for all under the law is a joke in its application. Thus the police are nothing more than mercenaries and hired killers, whose sole occupation is the protection of the wealthy and the violent pacification of the poor.

A few of them held to the delusion that they are protectors of the public, but the more realistic ones know that they are nothing more than hired guns employed to protect the wealthy from the poor. They know that most of the child porn and other perversions are preoccupations of the wealthy, but they must turn the other way and take out their violent frustrations on the people in the ghetto.

Any high level politician knows that in order to be accepted by his peers he must participate in or condone kickbacks, pork barrel projects, influence peddling, graft, corruption and cover-ups. Otherwise he will soon be put out of business.

Patronizing prostitutes is predominately a middle, upper middle and wealthy person's preoccupation. If the prostitutes had to depend upon the males and females of the ghetto to make a living, they would be forced out of business, so their customers are the ones who will sit on the jury that condemns them. This rampant, almost demonic hypocrisy among humans is not lost upon the aliens. On the other hand, most humans would probably find it difficult to accept and embrace the Biaviians' no non-sense approach to life.

Actually, the aliens' cut and dried approach to reality can be better understood when we consider the fact that the Biaviians are telepathic communicators. Telepathy is felt as well as heard, thereby rendering it very difficult, if not impossible, to lie convincingly. One Biaviian can't just hand another Biaviian an inferior piece of shit and then tell him that the thing is a work of perfection.

Procrastination is not only a waste of time, it is dangerous. The aliens will concede the fact that human beings have not reached the conscious level of truth expression, but they also know that the human being does subconsciously realize the elements of right and wrong, truth and deception, no matter how well it is cloaked in flowery hype. Therefore, they refuse to excuse humanity its preoccupation with universal misinformation and self-delusion. In other words, the wrong doer who says, "I didn't know what I was doing", is simply compounding a willful lie.

On the whole, we, the human race, are trooping along like lambs to the slaughter while the way to greatness and righteousness is so plain that a blind man can't miss it. Once the extraterrestrials led us out of primordial cycle common to the lower animals, so that we came to understand the meaning of good will evil, right and wrong, we were granted the autonomous power to control the direction of our own destinies. They now concede that they may have been premature in their magnanimity toward man, as is exemplified by the fact that we are diligently working toward our own extinction as a species, even while being aware of the probable consequences of our actions.

The bear and the elephant are worthy of being saved from extinction due to the fact that they play no conscious part in the willful destruction of their kind, but man can make no such claim to continuation, nor, in essence, is he deserving of any special consideration in this respect. When viewed realistically, it must be conceded that the planet, its ecology and life forms would be much better off without the malignancy of the Homo sapien genus. (They have decided to save the human species only because they played a direct and vital part in its ascension and are thus ethically bound to preventing its extinction).

Even unto this day, there are idiots who refuse to believe that dinosaurs existed because it doesn't fit into their religious scheme of things, even though you show them the bones. There will be many who will refuse to concede the existence of more advanced forms of life in the universe, even when the skies are darkened with their fleets of ships.

This book is not for them, but for those of you who, through common logic, have reached the conclusion that we are probably not alone in all of these millions of galaxies. This book is for those who would be willing to take on the task of personally contributing to the coming of a brave new world and to the exploration of other worlds, of which I know there are many. In order to even begin to comprehend and enjoy the awesome magnificence of the realities with which we shall soon be faced, it is imperative that we open our minds and dispense with the mindless inhumanities that drive the emotions of most of mankind.

It would serve us well to understand that the selfless love, compassion and benevolence of just a few have saved the lives of multitudes. If someone came to you right now and said, I will spare the world if you can go into the White House, the Kremlin or your own town and find ten righteous, decent and honest men, could you do it? Think about it.

Philosophically men make the sensible argument that no one is perfect. This is basically true. However, the aliens would be satisfied with beings who expended as much energy toward achieving perfection as they do toward attempting to justify their imperfections. The Biaviians will be the first to tell you that they are not perfect and that they make mistakes, yet they continue to strive to reach that state of being where mistakes are not willfully made.

In order to assure a continuous market for their wares, manufactures find it expedient to fabricate things that are sure to wear out or break down within a given span of time. From the businessman point of view, this is logical. However, when he knows that the built-in flaws of his product are going to result in the deaths of some and simply chalks it up to being an acceptable factor in the quest for profit, this is evil.

Why should we except the unconnected observer to look upon life as precious, when we so flagrantly disregard its sanctity and consider a certain number expendable. Is it any wonder that beings like the Targs have dispensed with even considering these ethical questions in their collection and experimental methods upon the human species?

The Biaviians, fortunately, are not as critical of mankind as I am, nor as seemingly apathetic as the Targs seem to be. Tan tends to seek out and compliment the good in people, and he seems to take the track that most of humanity are basically victims of the various subterfuges of the less than honorable controlling faction. Of course this opinion holds merit, but I am unwilling to let humanity off the hook so easily.

No politician or propaganda can compel me to hate one person for the wrongs of another or to condone or remain indifferent to the terrible plight of many of my fellow humans just because of their race, creed or religion. He who politically supports the slave master is no less guilty of that inhumanity. Thus we are all guilty by virtue of association or indifference.

Tan believes that he will succeed in culling from among the masses the great number necessary to assure a higher level of human continua. In spite of it all, Tan remains optimistic and confident in his quest. Once, after I had finished expressing my disgust as to the numerous unjustifiable shortcomings of man, Tan said to me, "Martin, the pain of your care permeates the elements. Surely this thing called love is wondrous in its fearsome complexity". And I said, "Yeah, but sometimes, Tan I get so disgusted with the state of things that I feel like throwing up both of my hands and just saying 'Fuck it' ". And he said, "When you cease to care, time shall be no more". And I said, "Yeah, and Gallo shall make no more wine".

UFOs have been visually sighted on numerous occasions near military installations around the world. Sometimes they show up on radar and sometimes they don't. Still on other occasions the UFOs would project a false image many miles away from their actual position. If it sounds strange to you that a solid object can literally disappear from a radar screen, it really shouldn't as the technology to render a solid object invisible to radar is now within the capabilities of man in the form of the Stealth Bomber.

It seems that the aliens keep very precise data on the nuclear stockpiles of man, as well as the nuclear waste materials, accidents, pollutions and nuclear reactor construction deterioration. No doubt they also keep detailed records of all the numerous sources of pollution and the chemical elements of the pollutants, as well as the effects of these chemicals on the eco-system and animal life of the planet.

UFO sighting witnesses on occasion have noted that the alien craft seemed to literally change shape, fade out or simply blink in and out of vision. Also ships are sometimes visible to the eyes but do not show up on radar. Such seemingly impossible happenings sometimes cause people to assume that they hallucinated the whole thing, but what they saw was real.

As it was explained to me by Tan, just as there are different models of cars or airplanes, there are different kinds of saucer craft, and the technical capabilities of these various ships range from the relatively simple remote controlled drone to the X-6 hyper-space whisper craft, which are capable of jumping to hyper-space and of manipulating the quantum of time. There are also craft whose tech-capabilities range within the middle zones of complexity.

At a certain vibrating frequency, a ship may be capable of literally separating and rearranging its molecular structure or changing its physical shape before your eyes. At a certain vibration frequency, the waves of radar will pass right through the ship like water through a window screen. Meeting no solid resistance, the radar waves will not record as a screen image, or, in some instances depending upon the molecular dispersal, a ghost image may appear.

Man is still a long way from such technical capabilities, but he has developed a viable concept in the stealth technology. The Stealth Bomber utilizes a method of wave absorption. You see, in order for the radar image to register, it has to strike a solid object and then return to the source, thereby revealing the object in question. By coating the low conductive alloy hull of the Stealth Bomber with a petroleum acrylic-based poly-vinyl material, the material has succeeded in nullifying the radar waves by literally absorbing them, thus preventing the waves from returning to the source.

In order to avoid being shot down by heat-seeking missiles, the Stealth is capable of utilizing remote heat decoys, as well as a cold propulsion technology that has not been utilized in such a manner before. This is how it works. The Stealth is cruising ten miles above enemy territory, and though its image is not registering solidly on radar, the enemy is astute enough to realize that something is up there, so a heat-seeking surface-to-air missile is released.

The Stealth's on-board computers pick up the missile image and lock on. Then, at a certain point, the Stealth's computer defensive systems automatically release one or more remote decoys. Almost simultaneously the plane's engines flame out and the cold propulsion system kicks in. The cold propulsion system is a new military innovation, but is relatively simple in its concept. Think of a bottle of cold beer that has a tiny hole in the cap. Shake the bottle vigorously and watch the liquid spew forth through the little hole. If that bottle were a Stealth propulsion engine, the cold chemical reaction would drive the craft forward. Of course, this cold propulsion alternate system cannot replace or match the performance of the hot turbo-thrusters of the craft, but it will perform long enough to evade any known heat-seeking projectiles. When out of danger, the hot thrusters will kick back in.

The Stealth technology is an innovation which is, at best, a military advantage of the most superficial sort, which could not possibly justify the six hundred million dollar unit outlay, because technical radar alterations will shortly nullify its effectiveness. The plane's largest advantage lies in the fact that the Russians will have to spend a lot of money to upgrade their computer capabilities and to modify their detection system to see the Stealth.

The disadvantages lie in the faults in the actual aerodynamics design of the plane, the malfunctioning of its complex system and the fact that the military would never routinely use the craft for fear of one of them falling into the hands of the enemy.

Should a nuclear confrontation ever become a reality, manned bombers wouldn't really be necessary would they? And you wouldn't really give a shit if the enemy did see the incoming warheads. What's he going to do to stop them anyway? You couldn't even hail a taxi in New York or Moscow in the time it takes for the rockets to arrive let alone evacuate any populated area.

It doesn't take a genius to realize that your chances of getting struck by lightning is greater than that of dying from nuclear war between the two greatest powers. Since we already have enough nuclear bombs to destroy every living creature on Earth ten times over, one would think that both of the powers would forego the building of a few rockets and submarines in favor of spending the money to solve the problems of poverty and education, etc. We live in a world where a thousand dollars are spent in creating cancer causing materials for every dime devoted to finding a cancer cure. It is a world wherein a thousand dollars are spent on bombs for every penny spent on bread for the hungry. Not even an insane man would design a more bizarre existence than the one in which we now live, nor has a greater band of thieves, killers and perverts ever before existed throughout the cosmos than the ones who now control this planet.

Even as the planet literally totters on the brink of total pestilence, death and destruction, the aliens are aware that it is the heyday of the gluttonous and decadent rich. While millions perish of starvation, neglect and apathy, the elite faction grows fatter. Bigotry in the guise of conservatism now controls the political and economic might of this country. They achieved this power by catering to the hatreds and prejudices of the greater portion of this country's gullible citizens. Having acquired their political offices, they are now proceeding to economically destroy all of the classes beneath them economically without consideration of race or creed.

Since possession is nine-tenths of the law, they know that by the end of their tenure they will either own and/or control all of the farms, factories, destinies and rights of the people. Their sentiments toward a poor black or white or the elderly or the malnourished children is but the differing degree of revulsion they feel toward each.

Those same small farmers and business people who voted them into power are among the first economical casualties. To rob those tens of thousands who didn't own businesses and farms to steal, they opened several thousands of S & L branches, only to close them when as much liquid capital was collected as possible.

Insurance consortiums and medical procedures are set up and designed to relieve the elderly of their life savings before throwing them to the dogs. Children's school lunch programs have been cut to the bone, and the leader has vetoed a slight raise in the minimum wage, thereby assuring that a third of the population cannot possibly pay rent and eat at the same time.

Most of the major industrial production has been moved to other countries, where labor is cheap, thereby further enriching the owners, while consigning tens of thousands more Americans to poverty. These massive additions to the poverty rolls lead directly to the destruction of the social fabric, feed bigotry and further divide the various ethnic factions of the country.

Still the rich get richer, and this same mentality now infects the highest court officials of the land to a predominating degree, thereby assuring that the rights of the common citizen, women and minorities, are greatly curtailed, while the wealthy need have little fear of just retribution under the law.

Several of the Supreme Court Justices have been bought and paid for by the elite few who got them the job. The future portends of more prisons instead of more jobs, more back-alley butchery instead of family planning clinics and a continuous polarization of the wealth of the country.

Wealthy political homosexuals and child molesters will continue to ply their perversions at the taxpayer's expense, and corrupt judges will continue to hand out long sentences to the black or poor white drug user, while freeing the white collar criminals and fellow child molesters.

Rich drug addicts will continue to be considered as the ones with medical problems, while the poor addicts will continue to be prosecuted as criminals. Poor men's sons will continue to swell rolls of the National Guard, even as the planet writhes in the throe of death.

In discussing these various inhumanities and bestialities with Tan, I was often surprised at his grasp of the nature of the things I was telling him, but then again, I don't consider Tan your typical Biaviian in the sense that his close social scrutiny of humanity and his relationship with me have expanded his comprehension of the workings of the human modus to a greater than usual degree.

The average Biaviian, I believe, tends to see things in absolutes, while not bothering with the subtleties of specific situations and the baser reasons as to why one person may do some awful and unnecessary wrong still tends to elude Tan's comprehension on many occasions. I believe this is mainly because he is personally devoid of such motivations. It takes all of my reasoning abilities to get him to comprehend the greedy logic and total disregard for public safety in deliberately poisoning a whole river in order to save some money on waste cleaning equipment. I tell him that the rich believe that there will always be some un-polluted place for them and their children to drink and to hell with the poor bastards down river who will die of chemical poisons.

Tan and I sat and talked for many hours on the general state of things on the Earth, and the picture from any angle looks bleak indeed. On the scales of intelligent and logical endeavor, we find that the negative and irrational elements far outweigh the positive, and not for lack of the means and ability to do better but by the definite concerted desire and wish to squeeze as much money and power from the masses as is possible. At this demonic preoccupation, the rich tyrannical and dictatorial elements among humanity have been very successful, so much so that they have reached the most elevated height of maggot infected power plant-wide than has ever before been known. Feeding upon the pulsing masses like giant iridescent blow flies and enforcing their omnipotence with psychotic subservient police, rear-sucking prosecutors and bigoted judges, these executioners are well aware of the fact that their very livelihood is owed to the prosecution of the have-nots and their complicity in the sins of the wealthy. Having succeeded in placing a majority faction of bigots and psychotics on the highest court in the land, they feel as if their supremacy is henceforth sanctioned and guaranteed. It has become the classical case of the blind leading the blind.

What they do not realize is that this world is about to undergo such devastating and all encompassing changes that the distinction of wealth and power will be superseded by the primordial ability to simply survive these conditions, and that the Chinese peasant and the jungle pygmy are far better equipped to endure this Armageddon than is the munitions factory owner.

Nature has at this point been poisoned to the extent that a planetary ecological rebellion is imminent. An environmental alteration which ordinarily would have taken several million years has been brought about by man's own doings in just a hundred years. It will take less than twenty more years for this awful cataclysm to be set in accelerated motion, and it will include every aspect from the destruction of the tropical rain forests to the leaking of live nuclear waste, the depletion of the ozone shield to the contamination of the aqua table.

Nature is no respecter of person. When a person contracts a viral infection, the body's immune system goes into high gear in an effort to overcome and kill off the offending virus. In a more complex but similar sense, the whole Earth is such a body, and the planet has been infected to the degree that the planet's immune system is no longer able to fight off the effects of the cancer that affects it. Thus the various vital organs of the planet will begin shutting down, thereby allowing the virus to overcome the entire body. A human being with AIDS is no worse off than the planet Earth in retrospect. This is why it has become imperative for the aliens to start figuring out the logistics of transporting and sustaining tens of thousands of human beings, and this celestial exodus will transpire in your lifetime and mine.

Among astronomers and physicists and others of the scientific community, there is a general consensus that life in some form other than our own does exist out in the cosmos. However, the greater portion of them hold firm to the theory that cognizant or intelligent life forms other than our own are a rarity, so numerically minute that the probability of ever meeting any other similarly intelligent form is virtually zero.

Most are also of the opinion that given the laws of physics, which govern matter and distance, it is highly unlikely that one intelligent species could traverse the light years separating the stars with any hope of returning home, but they are wrong in these assumptions.

I have learned from the Biaviians that life in some form or another is a relatively common occurrence throughout the cosmos, and that the Earth and its sun are by no means unique in the galaxy.

In fact, as near as I can discern, the Biaviians themselves are from the constellation we call Taurus, and while Taurus is about four hundred and fifty light years from Earth, the Biaviians are able to journey there and back in about eleven years, as we measure time. Their sun is of the brown dwarf variety. This means that they are not restricted by the known laws governing speed, light, time and distance, yet I know first hand that they are beings of flesh and blood and that their vehicles are made of metal, glass, plastic, etc. Also, Earth scientists have failed to take into consideration the fact that these aliens have physical life spans which encompass literally tens of thousands of years.

Further, I was told about and shown numerous examples of differing life forms, which were collected from many different living planets throughout the Milky Way Galaxy and in some cases beyond. My understanding of Tan's explanation of differing life forms will, no doubt, leave much to be desired. However, I'll do my best.

The chemical compositions from which the universe is formed are relatively uniform in molecular content, and certain rules governing the evolutionary birth and progression of life are common. Even though intelligent life forms are rare in comparison with the numerical value of celestial bodies, it is not so rare as to go unnoticed.

If you want to find other life forms that most probably resemble those of your home planet, find a star which is similar in age and dimensions to your own there. Due to the variables in gravity, atmospheric composition, temperatures and the ecological predominance of certain vegetation, life forms may be obliged to take on numerous diverse forms, from the gigantic gliders on low gravity bodies to the isotopic fungus of terribly cold bodies.

However, certain requirements in bio-systems must be met. Hollow feathers and bones for flying creatures, a workable digestive system, a central nervous system, and a brain of some sort. There must be eyes or sensors to see and a pulmonary system for carrying blood and oxygen throughout the body.

So similar in biological design are many life forms that the Biaviians have successfully transplanted a large number of them from one planet to another or have actually started new eco-systems on planets yet too young to create their own. A calcite bone and muscle structure are necessary to support the weight of non-aquatic land dwelling creatures.

The ability to survive in the evolutionary order of things makes it imperative for a creature to develop certain methods of defense, and these methods will encompass everything from speed to camouflage to offensive poisons to intelligence. On those planets where the predatory creatures are more abundant, the factor of Homo sapien like intelligence is most likely to arise, while on these planets devoid of many physical dangers, the necessity of higher animal intelligence may never become an imperative factor.

It should further be noted that intelligence need not necessarily be of the warm-blooded mammalian variety, for while mammalian intelligence is more common over-all, it is by no means impossible that an insect or a fowl or fish may achieve technological supremacy if given the time and proper circumstances.

The ecology of a given planet is governed by a number of factors, which are relative throughout the cosmos, that is, it requires photosynthesis, chlorophyll and pollination, etc., in order to thrive. The evolutionary progression of any species of life can be side-tracked or eliminated altogether by natural disasters or drastic planetary ecological alterations. Life is tenacious and is capable of enduring under extreme conditions and of making astronomical adaptations in order to avoid extinction.

Not all intelligent life forms have succeeded in leaving their planets of origin, while some others have been forced to leave by catastrophes of their own making. Still others have advanced no further in technology than has Earth man and like man have just started to make their first rudimentary attempts at space exploration. Just like man, there are forms of intelligent life whose greed and lack of ethical logic are causing them to squander their own natural resources and to literally poison their own eco-system beyond repair, and, like man, some will succeed in engineering their own extinction as a species.

When you read my prophetic words of impending doom, you may be obliged to dismiss my revelations by simply placing them in the category of the many other prophecies of doom down through the ages. Yet before you dismiss my words altogether, stop and think about it. Neither the ancient Hebrews nor the people of the Dark Ages of Europe had to contend with the realities of millions of tons of live nuclear waste, a trillion pounds of deadly pollutants in the water, acid rain and ozone destruction.

Therefore, if everything I've thus far told you about the aliens is a lifelong delusion on my part, it doesn't diminish the fact that we are in a heap of trouble. If you believe that I am being truthful with you, then we are still in a heap of trouble.

Personally I do not believe that there is any chance of mankind altering his ways enough to begin to turn this thing around. Yes, I believe that there are a lot of people out there who are grieving for this dying planet and wishing that it could be saved. Unfortunately, these caring people do not own the factories, the banks or the politicians. Add to this the fact that the American public is probably the most gullible and easily manipulated population of people on the Earth and you have a situation where greed and appearance take all.

A good-looking snake with enough money can lead these people into the bowels of purgatory, while a well-meaning person of principles with little financial backing doesn't stand a chance. The present brand of manipulators, both conservative and liberal, are, upon close scrutiny, indistinguishable from one another. They are all of the same elite fraternity.

In order to assure the continuation of human life as we know it on this planet, immediate and drastic changes would have to be made, and these alterations would have to encompass everything from automobiles to agriculture.

Just to highlight some of the greatest problems, all fluorocarbon manufacture would have to cease. All combustible engine transportation would have to cease in favor of electric engines. All nuclear power and carbon fuels for power generation would have to be replaced by solar, wind, water and volcanic generation methods.

All agricultural insecticides would have to be replaced by natural insect and genetic engineering methods of pest control. All product packaging would have to be biodegradable or recyclable. Further production of nuclear weapons would have to stop. Alternate materials must be developed for newspapers, books, etc., and the tropical rain forest preserved.

Technical advancement are needed in agriculture, new higher yield grains developed and new methods of food animals production should become a major priority with the methods shared with other countries. Vast greenhouse techniques should be developed for arid countries.

Contraceptive and birth control methods should be developed to the highest order and dispensed freely among all the needy countries.

Emphasis should be placed on more advanced methods of salt water and fresh water fish farming. Petroleum products should be utilized extensively in the fabrication of building materials for family units as well as larger complexes.

To ease the combustible engine transportation congestion problem, a new generation of trains should be developed using electric power systems. The existing nationwide railroad network could be altered to accommodate new high speed electromagnetic induction transport carriers all across the country, and the passenger would then use small personalized electric cars to reach his rural destination.

Since America uses about half of the planet's fuel resources, it has to be the one to take the lead and bring in the new age. Of course, the greatest argument against instituting these revolutionary changes is that much of the world's economies revolve around existing power resources and industrial methods.

The cost to make such changes would be astronomical, but I say to you that the cost of change could never come close to matching the price we are paying by refusing to make the initial sacrifice. Let's put it like this: All of these changes I'm speaking of will eventually have to be made anyway, and to hesitate at this point means to be caught in a resource famine in the near future.

The small number of powerful people who control these great industrial consortiums won't do any more than they have to toward making these changes because they believe that their fortunes depend upon the present manner of doing things. These people must come to realize that if things continue as they are there won't be much of a world left for their offspring to inherit.

If it is done right, such a massive undertaking would have the effect of creating universal employment and would expand private enterprise to astronomical proportions. Space technology would expand in leaps and bounds. Space based solar reflectors would beam down the power continually to power whole cities or transportation networks.

Every flowing river and the wave motion of the lakes and oceans could be utilized to generate electricity. Fiber optic technology, if utilized extensively, would greatly enhance all manners of electronic communication and supply systems. The widespread utilizing of drip-water irrigation would relieve the pressure on water reservoirs, and no expense should be spared in the developing of practical methods for the creation and use of fusion technology.

Small manufacturing and home industries should come back in vogue with the production of various components controlled by centralized computers. Gainful employment would not only be universal but would become compulsory, thereby doing away with the welfare system in its present form.

In order to relieve the congestion in the great inner cities, model satellite communities should be built, complete with agriculture and industry, where a job and a home unit are guaranteed to whomever moves there. Of course, freedom of movement should not be restricted so vast networks of underground electronic guidance cables should be installed on certain existing highways. The traveler could move about freely on preprogrammed travel plans.

Drugs should be decriminalized and controlled by the government. This would entail the registration of all hard drug users, the free dispensing of needles and disease prevention literature and compulsory free medical testing of these addicts. The same system should be used on prostitutes. Then only the unregistered would be considered criminals.

Since at least two-thirds of all robberies, murders and burglaries are drug related, as well as two-thirds of all prostitution, the crime rate in this country would plummet immediately. Anyone who wants to kick the habit and become a productive member of society should be given that chance.

Special cities, towns or territories for the drug dependent would not be out of the question, and marijuana should be made legal altogether.

Alcohol related traffic accidents would be virtually wiped out owing to the fact that all transport would eventually be electronically computerized and thus taken out of the hands of the driver altogether.

Having been incarcerated myself, I know that the prisons hold some of the most brilliant and creative minds in the world. In fact, I would venture to say that in no other situation is so much creative power brought together in one place. Therefore, each and every prison installation should have a think tank to which certain technical and engineering problems should be submitted. Every person in prison for less than a capital offense should be put to work earning a salary on one of the many construction, road building, reforestation or industrial assembly projects, preferably away from the geographical haunts from which he came. Upon leaving prison, he would automatically have a nest egg and a guaranteed job, hopefully in a location of his choice, and a place to live.

After high school, further education should be granted to any person without charge if the person can't afford it, to be paid when that person completes the schooling and goes to work. The subject of the education should not be restricted for lack of money but only by the student's mental capacity to master the subject.

The over-all school system should be broken down in to smaller more specialized units, and transportation and school lunch should be free. A child's mental faculties and not his age should dictate the speed with which he advances in grades.

As a prerequisite for receiving our aid, Third World countries would be obligated to develop along these more progressive lines, and all of the major powers would have to work together to quash those dictatorial and oppressive political systems which would not listen to reason. This would not be so difficult as one would think, mainly because all of the major and minor world leaders already know one another on a first name basis and common sense is relatively universal. In fact, you could get all of the people who control this planet in a medium-sized ballroom, and none of them is more than a phone call away from one another.

If all of these things I am speaking of would be set in to motion, it would not cause the rich to become poor or the powerful to become weak. It would, in many instances, require the alteration of productive methods and products and the diversification of more conglomerates, but each and every living human being would be much better off for it.

A world which now lives in fear, danger and distrust would revert to a semi-utopia of common good and the realization of this new world lies in the hands of that small number of powerful controllers.

Ireland suffered a great famine in the nineteenth century because of a potato blight. The entire western world could be practically crippled at this moment if oil supplies were halted. Millions of people are starving in northern Africa, not because of the lack of fertile land but because of warring factions. That entire situations could be changed today if a few people picked up the phone and agreed not to supply either side with any more bullets. This wouldn't cause the warring factions to love one another, but the conflict would swiftly fizzle out and settle back in to a sedentary state.

The state of things in the world is such that any psychotic tyrant can gain military aid from one or the other great power simply by proclaiming himself pro-democracy or pro-communism. The known fact that he is in reality a dope-dealing mass murderer doesn't seem to matter in the least. Only when that upstart dictator thinks himself independent enough to turn on his benefactors do the factors of moralism and human ideals enter the picture.

It is a fact that neither the hierarchy of the so-called democracies nor the communist powers gives a shit about the fact of the oppressed minions. The bottom line is how much money can we make by using those little suckers.

The world has become a very small place indeed, and no single country can endure and prosper without the economical and technological aid of other countries. It is no longer feasible for any one country to become an island unto itself and ever hope to expand its economical horizons. Therefore, it is incumbent upon those countries who profess to uphold the principles of the rights of man to lead the way by standing firm politically and economically upon these principles. But since all of these governments are moved more by greed than by principles, the inhumanities are allowed to continue unabated and, in most cases, even assisted.

The American press is by far the freest in the world and is to be commended for some of its work in the past. However, look at the system of Apartheid in South Africa and its lack of coverage by the major news networks, and you can easily see that the press of this day is predominated by bigots, cowards and other assorted racist maggots to whom little respect is due. Imagine, if you will, what the hue and cry would be if blacks were torturing, murdering and enslaving whites. The western press and the governments would be up in arms until the situation was changed. No, the western press is neither fair nor decent. In fact, this country loves the idea of black people being their slaves so much that three hundred companies are continuing to maintain branches there, while numerous others are quietly supporting and lobbying for that ungodly and demonic regime. So much for Christian ideals.

And to Israel, I can only say that I know the full extent of your business and technological dealings with these enslavers of men in South Africa. It is a fact that unto your people has been given a blood infusion and neurological advantage by the Ancient Gods from space, which collectively exceeds that of any other single nation, but in your insatiable quest for gold and emeralds you have cast aside the ethical principles of your forefathers and given unto the South Africans the seed of nuclear knowledge which will ultimately be used against you in a round about way, because his dormant hatred of you is as great as that he holds for the blacks.

You continue to build warplanes and weapons with him, to purchase his precious metals and agricultural products and to remain mute in the face of all his bestialities and inhumanities toward the blacks. You smile, drink and kowtow to the same Nazis who gleefully sent millions of your brothers, sisters and children to the gas chambers.

You have come to feel as if you are invincible, but you should never forget that, with the exception of some black men, all of the white and colored races of this Earth lay in wait for the opportunity to rend you asunder. Look back upon your history lest you forget the nature of the beast you now embrace.

I can tell you that in spite of these transgressions the aliens still look upon your people as the most stable example of logic and human decency historically upon this planet and that a certain number will be chosen to journey to the new world. The promised land you speak of in the end will not be there among those enemies who hate you but in a place out there beyond the stars.

There will always be those who will refuse to believe that there are other intelligent beings out there, and that they have played such a prominent part in the historical ascension of man, but the rational thinker among us, who are really the only ones who matter, will stop, add up all of the evidence, the sightings, the photographs, the physical evidence and the testimony of many people, including myself, and come to the only conclusion possible... that surely there are other life forms in the vastness of the universe.

With these eyes I have witnessed objects of engineering which exceed the scope of the imagination, have traveled at speeds which nullify the theoretical laws of physics and manipulate the quantum of time. With these hands I have touched the very skin of beings who, should they proclaim it so, would be accepted as Gods, even by me. I have smelled their odor, supped of their food and given up the procreation seed unto their females. I have felt the winds upon my face which emanated from the vastness of a ship so great that it could occupy the exploratory curiosity of a human for a life time and then he may perhaps not see it all nor comprehend the workings of half of it.

Out there, resting in orbital repose behind one of the great moons of Saturn, the Biaviian mothership awaits the imminent day when the great airlift of man shall transpire. The Earth and all of its technological and ecological workings is being constantly observed, and all of the data concerning this planet is being stored in the brains of great super computers.

In reality, the aliens have been quietly taking people from the Earth for many years and even more so in recent times. Most of these abductees have been returned to the surface of the planet within a short span of time. This practice has been necessary in order to study the physiology, psychology and dietary habits and natural bio-rhythms of the human, because the logistics of such a major undertaking must be worked out in advance, how to handle, orientate, feed and occupy the motivational urges of so many people for the duration of the journey to Biaveh.

Regardless of the precautions taken for the actual departure, the aliens know that they won't be able to accomplish this surreptitiously, nor will they be able to conceal their presence from the military, who will by then have a number of particle beams and other space weapons in orbit around the planet. It will no doubt be necessary for the aliens to either render these killer satellites ineffectual or to destroy them outright.

As I've stated before, the government and military are well aware of the presence of other intelligences in our stratosphere, but have long sought to keep this knowledge from the general populace. The government has also sought to make contact with the UFOs for years with no notable success.

I don't think that the military power will take kindly to hundreds of alien ships invading their air space for whatever reason. It would be a fondest dream come true if the military were able to get their hands on an alien hyper-space whisper craft, intact and with a living crew. Given time, they would probably be able to dissect it and duplicate the technology. Then the other peaceful life forms in the galaxy would be in a heap of trouble. According to the aliens, this cannot be allowed to happen, even if it would mean the destruction of a craft and the crew.

The possibility of a ship and crew falling into the hands of Earth military is very slim, but not altogether impossible because saucers have been known to experience mechanical problems or even to self-destruct. As I've stated before, an X-6 Whisper Craft exploded over New Mexico in 1947 and a remote controlled saucer drone crashed in Japanese islands in the fifties and was retrieved with many of its components intact.

It was a simple bit of alien technology, but it was of momentous technical importance to man and gave him a schematic base for the age of micro-electronics. It has taken western man only a few years to have made a quantum leap in the field of electronics. By having successfully miniaturized electrical components, he has achieved a momentous step in preparation for deep space exploration. Now only one thing holds him short of realizing that dream and that is the creation of a practical, long lasting, self-perpetuating power source to drive his space vehicles.

If and when man invents a practical method of containing and utilizing fusion power and propulsion, there is truly no limit to what he could and would accomplish. Out of fusion technology would come a host of new scientific applications, which have heretofore been thought impossible and a totally new vista of scientific endeavor would open unto him.

At this point, the world's power and much of its economy is run on fossil and fissional fuel, and these powerful monopolies have thus far been able to suppress or control any power technology to the contrary. Neither they, nor the politicians they own, are interested in legislating or donating the money to develop these alternate energy sources, which is why this planet now stands on the very brink of ecological destruction.

There have already been major breakthroughs in alternate energy sources and combustible engine technology, which have been bought out or suppressed by the big consortiums. At this moment any major car manufacturer can make a vehicle which gets a hundred miles to the gallon, and new breakthroughs in the fabricating of solar cells could even at this moment be powering whole cities. Microwave and laser technology is now proficient enough to be utilized as a major power source, but these things are deliberately suppressed, unfunded or hidden, even while the planet dies, literally being poisoned to death.

Where energy is concerned, it is the classic case of putting all of one's eggs in the same basket. If and when the western world comes to realize how essential it is to opt for alternate sources of energy, it may be too late. In fact, according to the aliens, we have already crossed over into the critical zone and a drastic ecological and atmospheric alteration on this planet is imminently assured in the near future.

The very destiny of humanity has always rested in the hands of a small number of human beings. These are the ones who compose the monied aristocracy and their aim has always been and shall continue to be that of self-aggrandizement and the common masses have always served as ignorant and emotional pawns in the game of power.

Human beings in the eyes of the elite have always been an expendable commodity. In America, whole communities have been unknowingly used as guinea pigs by large chemical companies and the government to test the long range effects of radiation or deadly chemical poisons. They have done this and are doing these things, while being confident in the knowledge that should they ever be found out (and many times they are not) they can pay off the politicians, give the survivors a few scraps or beat the case in court.

In any case the perpetrators of these terrors, the true murderers, need never personally soil their hands or even look in the eyes of their victims. These killers are composed of just a handful of powerful insiders, who, over cocktails, have decided the fate of hundreds or even thousands of innocent beings. To them it matters not the untold pain, disease and mental suffering they will cause to others, but that their own children are not born without arms or legs. The foreknowledge of what they have done does not interfere with their digestive systems or plague their dreams.

Man, in his ignorance and stupidity, has set himself above and apart from nature and looks upon himself as the master of nature instead of as an integral part of it. He holds the flagrant sentiment that says out of sight, out of mind. Inwardly he has managed to convince himself that the Earth will somehow cleanse itself of the millions of tons of toxic waste he heaps upon it or that he can continue to live indefinitely without paying the price for his own transgressions. The world's masses have slowly come to resign themselves to the fact that ecological destruction is a necessary by-product of civilization, and some even hold to the misguided delusion that their industrialists and their government officials will do, or are trying to do, the right thing by them, and through blind faith or apathy have consigned this beautiful planet to imminent death by murder.

The leading politicians have publicly promised to spare no expense in putting man in permanent space stations on the moon and on Mars, and this dream is neither unreasonable nor impossible. Such an undertaking hardly seems practical when you consider that these same politicians don't seem to be able to get the homeless people off the streets or the unemployed decent or even indecent jobs. To flagrantly spend a trillion dollars to put men on Mars and then oppose a rudimentary raise in the minimum wage, we can gloat over being the first humans to physically collect rocks on Mars, while our children maintain a literacy rate somewhere between a ground slug and a chimpanzee.

We gloat over being the paragons of spiritual virtue on the Earth while our senior citizens are being warehoused, starved, tortured and robbed, and our record of health care is the worst in the western world. Red China, whose population is four times that of America, and whose economy is only a third of ours, still manages to feed and house its entire population.

More people are murdered on the streets of New York City in one month than are murdered in the United Kingdom in a year. Our political representatives have little objection to the Pentagon (who either have to be the greatest idiots or the most flagrant den of thieves on the Earth) spending six hundred dollars for a claw hammer, but can't see their way clear to legislate the money for school lunches or rudimentary housing for the homeless. The President has called upon the charities and the churches to take up the responsibility of assisting the poor and the homeless, the same charities who spent four cents or less of each dollar collected for the purpose intended and the same preachers who can hardly find the revenues to pay off their kept prostitutes or to air-condition their dogs' houses. It's enough to make a God-fearing born-again preacher kick the door of his limousine.

Wouldn't it be nice if the President would suddenly announce that he has decided to build just eighteen instead of twenty Stealth Bombers and will use the one billion two hundred million savings to house the homeless and create jobs for the unemployed? Or if he would suddenly decide that the world could be safe with a few less missiles, or even that $4.50 an hour would not be an unreasonable minimum wage after all, since it would take at least seven dollars an hour to properly feed and house a family of one, providing they didn't waste a dime on luxuries like medicine or school supplies.

Just like those ancient people in the valley of Shinar, who sought to build a tower unto heaven in an effort to impress the Gods and other men of their greatness, so does modern man accept such a project. The Gods were not impressed then, and the Gods are not impressed now.

Man has always sought a short cut unto greatness and omnipotence, but no alien in his right mind is deceived even for a moment as to the true nature of man, and the factor of accepting him as an equal into the celestial host has not been considered. Why? I'm given to believe it is because, upon close observation and from a historic perspective, man has thus far proven himself to be totally untrustworthy in matters of logic and honor and dangerous to the extent that he is capable of being. He has proven himself false to all truth, dishonorable in all promises, distrustful in all written contractual agreements, insincere in all of his religions and gluttonous in his greed.

To trust him would be tantamount to suicide, or at least very foolish. Yes, there are some people who have risen above the lower order of humanity's inequities, but you will rarely find them among the political and the social elite. For the most part they are the rural dwellers, the farmers, the lay person among the religious, the common laborer, the poor, the homeless, with a smattering of artists, musician, poets and so-called primitives.

It should also be noted that where the scientific community is concerned the most open-minded and less vengeful tend to be of Jewish origins. Truthfulness seems to be an anomaly that happens more often among the poor of all races, and the number of females chosen exceeds the males by a substantial number. Age does not seem to play any major factor in the choice of wayfarers, nor religious preferences. Race matters only in the context of numerical value on the planet, and children are prized because of their un-polluted natures.

I asked Tan to explain to me just how so many people could be contained, occupied and housed for a space journey which I understand will take nearly six years as we measure time. I won't attempt to use all of his exact words, because he has a weird way of speaking, but I believe that I did grasp most of his explanation and this is how it shall be:

Among every nation, country, ethnic group and tribe of people, there are gatherers similar to myself. Before the time of the actual airlift, many of these people from all walks of life would have, through telepathic means, gathered together and formed model communities unto themselves. In preparation for the journey, these people would have started meeting, living together, working together, sharing together and becoming as one in sociological principles and brotherly ethics.

They would have learned and implemented novel kinds of self-sustaining techniques in agriculture, energy art and industry, and they will learn to do things, without destroying the ecology around them. They will learn to dispense with jealousy, racism and greed in favor of love and a common good, and they will add to the surrounding society by setting an example of self-sufficiency, psychic healing and the invention of new practical ways and implements for doing things.

They will set a new standard in the kind, nurturing and health giving care for the elderly among them and of charitable service to the community around them. They will set new standards in the care and education of their children because all adults among them will serve as surrogate fathers, mothers, teachers, protectors. They will institute a system of common health insurance and common security by a system of universal profit and work sharing. They will be open and tolerant to all religious pervasions, which preach elements of the positive, and they will not allow any one among them to want for the sustaining necessities of life.

They will protect each others lives and property and tolerate no criminality in their midst nor carry any into the communities around them. They will abide by the laws of the land that prevail in their area as long as those laws do not advocate hatred, racism or statutes which are deemed indecent. Nor will they take up arms against any danger that does not attack them directly.

Among them will be all manner of people from all professions, and through them the world will be shown a living example of what life could and should be. They will be seekers of knowledge and will not ban any literature. They will be realistic enough to utilize any manner of technology around them to enhance their lives and leisure as long as this technology is not of the ecologically polluting kind.

They will be fun-loving people and will always seek innovations to make life easier, as well as ways to produce more abundant vegetables, fruits and herbs and improve the farming of fish, fowl and dairy products. They will have excellent musicians, composers, poets, actors, cabinet makers, potters, painters and inventors, and they will succeed in building self-sustaining communities with new methods and materials for building, air-conditioning and heating. They will patent these inventions for wider distribution.

They will not be stingy with their technology or their philosophy on life, and any person at any time may collect his or her share of the monetary pool and leave that community in good standing. In their community all elders are considered mothers and fathers and respected and cared for as such. Once a person is accepted into that community, he or she assumes full rights, and past lives are not questioned. Prestige is gained through a person's own possession of inner strength, decency and esoteric spirit and shall not be based upon race, creed or sex. They will treasure new ideas and support the creators of new innovations and inventions. Through their common spirit of love, they will often succeed in giving youth to the elderly, wisdom to the young and health to the sick.

Having proven that they can live together in a common bond

of love and fellowship upon this Earth, they shall then be ready for the coming of the Elohim. I am told that the aliens will appear on occasion through the years so that none of the chosen shall forget the promise.

When the time is upon them, the great ships will descend down from the clouds and gather up the multitudes, and they will not tarry long in this stratosphere. The multitudes so chosen will then be taken to the great mothership near a moon of Saturn in preparation for the journey to Biaveh, which is four hundred and fifty light years away.

All of these people who are of advanced age will repose in rejuvenation chambers and will undergo a reversal of the aging process. This rejuvenation process may take several months but to the person it will seem as only a few hours of sleep. During this sleep, they will be shown everything that those awake have seen, as if in a dream.

Those who remain awake will follow a regimen, which appears to them to fit their sleep cycles on Earth. However, when they lay down for the night, their naps may encompass ten or twelve days.

To occupy their time, they will have all of the amenities of Earth, games, showers, television, gymnasiums and a nice variety of foods. They will be shown vid-screens scenes of other worlds, as well as the planet Biaveh, for which they are bound. I am told that they can be shown a different living world for every waking period of the journey and never see them all. They will have a great space observation auditorium and will be able to watch the cosmos passing by, as well as the psychedelic fantasies of hyper-space spans when they jump the quantum of time.

Because of the lower gravitational pull of the planet Biaveh, they will be slowly and almost imperceptibly conditioned for it. At about thirty-three no one will age further but the children on board will continue at age as usual.

The adults aboard will become familiar with Tan's famous thought liquid. This drink assumes any flavor that the adult mind can recall, everything from a chocolate milkshake to the best champagne, from tomato soup to a cold draft beer. The children will have to drink what their parents prepare for them as the aliens recognize the fact that children would probably create only kool-aid, if given the chance.

You want Disney movies or toys for the kids, you've got them. Babies have a habit of waking at all times of the night, and so they shall. The aliens wish to keep things as earth-like as possible.

There will be some things which are not common on Earth like levitating beds and weightless rooms which the kids will no doubt immensely enjoy. There will be dream recorders, so that a person can rerun their dreams and ultimately learn to control them.

The earthlings won't be allowed to free run on the entire ship, they will have a few full blood Biaviians and hybrids among them so as to familiarize them with their sponsors. They will have an opportunity to sample many kinds of fruits and nuts which are native to Biaveh, and also shown the true part that the aliens have played in the history of man. The children no doubt will enjoy watching actual footage of real dinosaurs or being entertained by a circus of robot animals and silly clowns.

There should be more than enough diversions and amusements to occupy the people for the duration of their journey to the stars. They will be able to make mind music and to worship in the all-faith temple. Many men and women shall meet for the first time aboard the mothership and become friends and lovers. Language deciphering machines will immediately translate every known language into your own or vice versa for the benefit of the many different linguistic groups aboard. Just put on the head phones and you can understand Chinese, Greek, Spanish, etc. The technology enables one person to speak to an entire auditorium of people of different languages and be understood.

One thing must be understood. Once a person is aboard the great mothership, there can be no turning back. If the longing for home becomes unbearable, that person can choose to sleep for the duration of the journey. To them it would seem just like a single night's rest.

Once on the planet Biaveh it will be at least a thousand years before any humans are returned to Earth, but remember that you won't age beyond the mid-thirties during that span of time. I have no doubt that some great human minds would have created drugs which will prolong human life once they return to Earth. However, I'm told that once back on Earth, the humans will begin to age again probably at a slower rate, but still they will age.

The Biaviians are of the opinion that these long-lived earthlings will advance to great psychological and technological levels during that thousand years and reach a level of awareness that will place them on the level of the celestials. They will be the inheritors of a great new world.

Of the ones who are left behind, will they survive in part or all perish? What will the wayfarers find in other humans when they return? I cannot say, and Tan has not seen fit to tell me, but I do know that the returning number will be far greater than the number that originally left due to new births.

Just what will be the true extent of the new man's developed neurological powers. I can only speculate. I would think that he would have developed the power of telepathy and tele-kinetic levitation, as well as far greater mathematical and other scientific, as well as philosophical attributes.

Heed well these words and get ready for the coming and the sojourners. Be prepared for the coming of Tan.

The alien finds it almost impossible to comprehend these political and gluttonous factors, probably because they are not afflicted with the elements of monetary greed or political intrigue. On Biaveh, you actually have to know what you are doing in order to be allowed to do it.

At this moment there is enough nuclear bomb throw weight to kill all life on this planet ten times over, so why continue to add more bombs to this multiple absolute? When I start to explain to Tan the tens of thousands of jobs connected to the arms industry, the rampant bribery, national paranoia, etc., I generally lose him somewhere between the two hundred dollar Pentagon light bulb and the pork barrel contract.

In his mind, these things are imminently lethal to the human species, and fissional materials in their dormant form literally guarantee so many millions of birth defects, deaths by cancer and permanent ecological pollution, even under the safest precautions that man has yet devised, so the continued expansion of the nuclear stockpile on Earth, for whatever reason, escapes his understanding and does not fit into the theoretical scope of logic. Suicide by greed transcends the elements of sanity. The deliberate destruction of a planet's ecology for monetary gain does not compute. Do we have another un-polluted planet to flee to in order to spend and enjoy our ill-gotten fortunes? To me, the ruling and elite quotient of man is most contemptible. To the alien, he is simply interesting and strange.

Unlike man, the Biaviian holds no illusions as to his niche in the Genesis of life in the universe. He does not consider himself a God, nor does he consider himself the only keeper of the true faith or the possessor of all knowledge. Quite the contrary. The Biaviian is quick to point out his own shortcomings and his limitations. Many of the mistakes that man is now making parallel some of his own historical actions, only on a smaller more bizarre scale.

The Biaviians, as I understand it, were never ones to do unnecessary things in war or peace. When they vanquished an enemy, they didn't bear grudges or allow the defeated to starve. Except for military weapons, they always helped the former enemy to regain self-sufficiency.

They never militarily occupied a vanquished country. Instead they sent in physicians, engineers, agriculturalists, etc., a kind of interplanetary Peace Corps, and in this manner they succeeded in pacifying and making allies of their former enemies.

Social and religious customs were respected, and trade commerce was established. Furthermore, they gave the former enemy their protection. The scientific quest to improve and purify existing methods has always been of the utmost importance to the Biaviians. On Biaveh you cannot buy the political influence to poison the environment or knowingly market a product that is dangerous to the health of a populace. In concept, the Biaviians way of life is not too far different from our concept of democracy. The great differences lay in the application of that concept.

While we may find excitement in football, water skiing and movies, the Biaviian tends to find excitement in the quest of knowledge or something new. A human being can be entertained continuously by watching new movies or by climbing the same mountain, but a Biaviian is not amused by repetition and will seek to experience that which has not been experienced before. Perhaps this is why he has not tired of observing mankind because man is always springing something new an unanticipated on him, the fact that much of it is, in essence, dumb shit, only adds to the fascination. You see, he knows what the ant, the fish, bird or bear will do in a given life span without notable variation, but the same cannot be said of the human creature. Thus the continued interest.

Man is so diverse in his religions, customs and habits that no common modus can be attributed to him, and as he grows stronger technologically, his social and religious actions and reactions become more pathological and frenzied, the very fabric of the so-called civilized society will undergo drastic upheavals, dissolutions and chaotic transitions the likes of which have not been seen before. The greatest portion of these upheavals will transpire within the next ten years, so say the computer projections of the aliens.

The quest for democracy among all men is coming to the forefront of nearly all sociopolitical movements of this time, and the ruling force of tyranny will not suffer this transition kindly. Mass murder, famine and anarchy will be the law of the land in much of the civilized world, and not even the aliens can discern the outcome of this chaotic period. But it is, to say the least, very interesting from the aliens' viewpoint.

In the words of Tan, by far the biggest crime ever committed by any intelligent species toward its own environment is the element of collective indifference. The opposite of hate is not love, but indifference. The opposite of war, famine, bigotry, greed and truth is indifference. A caring being may be poor, uneducated and socially oppressed, but he is never indifferent.

When a problem is discovered among the caring, there is an immediate movement toward solving the problem. To even consider that a problem exists which cannot be solved is to give way to the very depths of indifference. Most of humanity's problems can be solved quite easily with collective participation.

The person who says that we cannot house the homeless, feed the hungry, care for and educate the children, put the unemployed to work, care for the aged and grant equality is a fool, a bigot and a master of indifference, not to mention a gluttonous thief and sinner.

Religious doctrines, practices and rules are useful only to the extent that they contribute to the practical well-being and bio-ethical survival of a number of beings under a given set of circumstances.

Common logic continues to refine a crude invention toward a more efficient and practical model as time and circumstances warrant.

The words of nomadic scribes written three thousand years past need not be considered any more inspired or practical than words of wisdom written today. It should be noted that a resurgence of religious fervor always signals the beginning of political unrest, riots wars and famines. However, religious piety and exalted idealism have little to do with baser reasons of aggression, which are greed, power, jealousy, racism and vengeance. The leaders of these movements are always aware of this and use these latent evils under different subtle subterfuges to further their personal aims.

Tan understands this but cannot understand why the greater portion of humanity is so willing to go along with it. Does this point to an innate biological trait in humankind? Is there a primordial predisposition toward predatory aggression? I'm inclined to think so, but Tan doesn't agree.

As I understand it, this is basically how he sees it. Man is not gifted with an inherent good, nor is he afflicted with an inbred propensity toward evil. It is a fact that even the most docile species of creature will fight to protect its nest, young or territory. However, if it is not directly threatened, it is perfectly willing to live and die without resorting to aggression.

The human being in a more complex manner is basically the same way. Regardless of his environment, common sense and the sense of self-preservation dictate that on the whole he would shun war in favor of peace if given a choice.

A society that is oriented toward the positive outlook is also predisposed toward equality in its treatment of its fellow citizens and toward common sense in judgment. He is of the opinion that a small core of war mongers among all the races are the ones who actively work to keep past prejudices and hatreds alive so as to divert attention away from their own skullduggeries.

He believes that there is and has always been an unwritten but conspiratorial kinship among the elite of all political persuasions, an un-proclaimed declaration of inherent superiority to and contempt for the masses. Ruthless dictators are not chastised by other political leaders for their beastilities, but for being sloppy enough to let news of them get out. When some mass murderer is deposed, he has little trouble finding sanctuary among others of his own ilk. Good or bad, this atrocious minority recognizes the need to stick together.

The mentality among them us relatively the same, while the only difference in their political sentiments is the varying levels of sociological suppression, the covertness or overtness of their killings and depths of their thievery.

The honest cop, politician or preacher is the rare exception instead of the rule, and the will of the people is no longer a major factor in the true decision making of the planet. In knowing this, the aliens have proven to me that they are not completely ignorant of the over-all state of things. Tan explained this to me without emotions, and I said, "Yeah, now tell me something I don't know".

You see, those religious denominational leaders who forbid birth control or flexibility in doctrine application automatically condemn millions to starvation, famine and all manner of depravations by virtue of their growing numbers. These religious leaders are, for the most part, educated and clear seeing individuals who know better. They further believe that the alteration of their doctrines to a more practical mode would weaken their positions of earthly omnipotence and monetary fortunes. And upon this Earth they are a scourge unto all that is rational. Conventional wars on the global scale are no longer feasible and the numerous small conflicts will not sufficiently deplete or hold in check the rapidly growing numerical value of world population.

Tan tells me that the country called Bangladesh in southern India is topographically a death trap and will continue to suffer natural disasters on the famine inducing scale. However, their imminent disasters will not be enough to contain the great birth rate of that people.

The expanding birth rate in most Third World Catholic countries will reach the desperation level in about twenty years, and the rampant poverty, disease and civil conflicts transpiring now in many of those places is but a prelude to the seething mass chaos that is soon to come.

The swift depletion of the equatorial rain forest belt is assured by virtue of the necessity for more living and agri-space. The damage caused by this rain forest depletion on the ecology and atmosphere of the planet will be felt almost immediately and drastically.

According to Tan, it was the aliens who first domesticated mankind from his hunter gather nomadic ways and brought forth the first stationary societies. It was they who first gave mankind the knowledge of mathematics, architecture, medicine, agriculture, animal husbandry and governmental law.

He also says that the aliens introduced wheat to this planet from Biaveh in order to form a food base for their first stationary societies. They also introduced a number of animal species to this planet, among which is the dolphin, some reptiles and at least two species of dinosaurs, which were saved and re-introduced here after the alien engineered destruction of the dinosaur kingdom about seventy million years ago.

The Biaviians are physically small and frail beings, who are not given to physical labor. I get the impression that retiring physiology and greater mental capabilities are the imminent effects of time and advancing techno-capacity.

Should man survive as a species, he will eventually evolve to take on some of the physical characteristics of the aliens, including the loss of the little finger on each hand.

Chapter 13

Artificial Intelligence and Robotics,

Its Many Levels of Application

In the concept and application of artificial intelligence, man has found his forte in the super computer and micro-electronics. He has developed certain binary languages, which have enabled him to accomplish extraordinary things computer-wise in a very short span of time. Yet when compared with the advancements accomplished by the Biaviians, the Targs and some other intelligent life forms throughout the cosmos, man's work must thus far be considered just rudimentary in its capabilities and superficial in its applications.

However, at the other end of the computerized spectrum, I'm told that some life forms endowed their computers with too much autonomy in capability and design and have actually been completely displaced and in a few cases exterminated by their creations.

I don't believe that any of those intelligences deliberately set out to create their own destruction in the form of robots, but at some point the technology reached the point where it was removed from their hands and controlled by the smart machines. Then instead of beings masters of their creations they became just so much unnecessary vermin in the eyes of the smart machines. Of course, man is a long way from attaining such a level in robotics technology. Yet should he survive long enough he would eventually do so. It is at this point in man's ascension that he is experiencing his most perilous state of being, both physically and ethically.

At this point the aliens are giving three to one odds against man surviving the nuclear chemical age as a technological species. This is not for man's lack of the ability to do better, but because of his total disregard for ecology in his quest for material gain and his preoccupation with finding more efficient ways to literally destroy his fellowman. When it comes to the quest for more knowledge in science, it is found that among most intelligent life forms, including man, nothing is taboo, and only those who collectively come to the realization of the probable consequences of their acts will be able to halt the direction of their research and then channel their creative energy in more positive directions. The odds are that man will not do this before it is too late for the Earth to rejuvenate itself from the damage already done.

The Biaviians don't base this opinion on the data collected from the Earth alone, but upon their observation of other intelligences similarly motivated and upon their own historical experiences. It may be noted that even though there are literally millions of different species of life forms along the great spiral arms of the Milky Way ranging from the amoeba to the vertebrate, the true cognizant or intelligent forms among them are very small in number and bear many similarities in physique and motivational application.

Intelligent life forms on a hundred different planets may have sprung from one or two common origins, that is to say that far more planets have been colonized than have evolved their own intelligences. It is a common trait that when the numerical value of a species becomes too great for it to support itself on existing land, it will attempt to acquire more living space, either through peaceful migration or warlike conquest. This is true of ants, as well as man.

If those intelligences are capable of doing so, they will seek new living space off of the surface of their planet of origins, or, as is the case of technologically inferior planets like Earth, they generally succeed in destroying one another entirely or nearly so. It is estimated that at the present rate of growth, the human population will double itself within the next twenty years, and it doesn't take a genius to visualize what this will mean, especially when nearly a third of all humanity is presently on the brink of mass starvation.

Then there are some life forms who have managed to control their birth rates through technological means, survived the nuclear age and moved onward and upward. Yet, I'm told, that in order to have succeeded, it was necessary for all of those life forms to undergo drastic alterations in their viewing of religions, the sanctity of life, their approach to energy research and their ways of dealing with their neighbors.

By one means or another it is essential for all races of a given intelligence on a planet to join together as a common order and dedicate themselves toward common goals for the good and survival of all. Without this cooperation, there will always be antagonisms, fragmented progress in the most important things and inequities in consumable necessities, which lead to revolutions, wars and various stages of anarchy among the masses.

Countries need not have to adhere to the same custom, language or even political order in order to find common ground in those areas which are essential to the survival of the planet as a whole. It's certainly not practical for one country to be able to go to fusion energy, when the next country continues to poison the atmosphere with fission and other deadly pollutants.

A planet is a delicate and perishable entity. A cancer from any source will eventually succeed in poisoning the whole body because all of the planet shares common water arteries and air supply. Thus it is impossible for one country or race of man to save themselves without also saving the rest of humanity. Any unique advantage gained by one over the other is but a fleeting thing. One has only to view the Earth from a few thousand miles out in space to truly comprehend the extent of the common destiny we all share, and the cancer running rampant through the arteries of this single planetary body is man.

When we think of other intelligent life forms, our imaginations conceive a wide array of physique and intentions. We have attributed to these imaginary aliens all of those qualities possessed by man from the angelic benevolent to the ruthless warlord. It would come as a surprise to most people to learn that many of these imaginary creations of the science fiction writers do indeed exist out there in the cosmos.

While some life forms are quite similar to man in appearance, like the Biaviians and the Dorians for instance, there are other forms which are so different from man in appearance and logic that it would boggle the imagination.

We must not assume that similar forms are automatically friendlier or less dangerous than the more bizarre looking aliens. Just as all technically intelligent life forms are not sapien bi-peds or even mammalian in species, nor are all life forms even composed of flesh and blood.

I'm told that there are several known quadrants of the galaxy which are completely controlled and peopled by smart robots composed of metals and silicons, or of bionic beings composed of metal and flesh fused together. It is not inconceivable that such intelligent forms may eventually over-run the entire galaxy.

The Biaviians are well aware of the locations and tech-capabilities of these life forms and continue to monitor their progress, yet they have no desire to establish close contact with them.

When I asked him why, Tan said that these life forms have come to view all physical organisms as simply that. While the Biaviians may view mankind collectively as inferior fellow creatures with some esoteric potential, the smart machines, when observing a physical species, immediately proceeds to calculate the amount of useful chemicals which could be extracted from rendering them down to their natural content, as there are certain materials, silicons, calcite sugar and acids to be found in living organisms, which are useful in the fabrication of the micro-electronics of artificial intelligence. However, should the smart machines come upon a living planet and find that any needed materials are more abundant in inorganic form, they might simply proceed to mine the materials they need, while completely ignoring the life system around them. They would not find it necessary to destroy the surrounding life forms unless those life forms began to interfere with their mining operations.

Occupying certain zones of that same quadrant of the galaxy is a race of bionic beings, which I'm told by Tan, presents far more danger to the cosmos than do the smart machines alone, because these bionic beings are partially composed of organic materials, such as brains, eyes and sexual organs. I'm told these beings were once servants to the life form they ultimately replaced through aggressive annihilation, so they probably would not be adverse to putting another intelligent physical species to use should they happen upon them and they also require some organic nutrients to sustain themselves.

Both the smart robots and the bionic forms were originally the creations of the science of intelligent physical species. And how did this come about? I'm not a scientist and the theoretical mechanism of most of it evades me, however, to the best of my ability, I shall recount, in part, the story as it was told to me by Tan.

Long ago in that far quadrant of the galaxy there lived a race of humanoid bi-peds, who progressed along the evolutionary ladder much in the fashion of Earth men, and just like Earth their history was dotted with wars of conquest of other races upon their own planet. Ultimately, one particular race of these beings succeeded in overcoming and assimilating all other races upon the planet until they became as one people.

Then the planet went into a state of peace and unusual prosperity, and the scientists from all the combined nations pooled their knowledge and began to make great strides in computer and space technology. The lack of ground wars and many great strides in medicine were key to extending their life spans, while the population continued to multiply.

Within one life span they were successful in exploring all of their own solar system and establishing manned stations on three of the dead planets. On those planetary bodies whose atmosphere were much too harsh to allow physical exploration, they eventually perfected smart machines, which could withstand such atmospheres.

It was soon discovered that one planet, being closer to the sun, contained great quantities of certain precious metals on and beneath the surface, so a major scientific program was launched with the goal in mind of mining these ore deposits using remotely guided robotics. A fourth generation of machines were lifted into space, and eventually a fifth generation of machines, which had the pre-programmed capability to fabricate other machines of its own order from materials already existing on that planet, were lifted to the planet.

The surface temperature on the side of the planet facing the sun reached heights ranging from 225 degrees to 400 degrees Fahrenheit, while on the dark side of the planet the temperature plummeted to 200 degrees below zero. In the vast underground chambers, which were hewn out by the robots, the temperature remained fairly constant, and it was found that the oxygen, carbon and hydrogen content of the rocks could support plant life.

Having already made great strides in bionics, it was decided to introduce a number of bionically altered beings to the planet to oversee the organic operations in anticipation of the day when the pure oxygen production of the plants would become sufficient enough to support first a smaller and then a larger colony of people from the home planet.

At first these bionic beings were all volunteers from the scientific community of the home planet, and then the authorities started to press into service other beings who were not of the scientific community, felons, prisoners, terminal medical patients and so forth, until the bionic population of the planet became numerically notable. The authorities never feared a rebellion of these biotrods because the computer control banks were located on the home planet, and robo-cams kept the operation under close observation. To be doubly sure, a built-in remote destruct mechanism was implanted in every biotrod.

For some years the great mining-agri operation ran smoothly, and the home planet grew fat and prosperous from the precious metals gleaned from the interior of the ore rich planet. Slowly, the planet of the biotrods with its cornucopia of gold and other precious metals begun to take on a greater and greater import to the home planet. Thus, when the computers on Biotron began to request more and more micro-storage capacity pods, it was decided that with a certain amount of extra power supply units on the robot planet's surface, the existing machines could be programmed to design and fabricate their own electronic needs.

Of course, this would mean giving the supply planet more autonomy in operation. The physicists and electronic theorists on the home planet were split on the decision as to whether or not to allow this, as their knowledge of artificial intelligence only went to a certain point before crossing over into the realm of theory. Because of the possibility of a greater precious metal output as weighed against the astronomical cost of airlifting all the extra equipment, the ones for the project won the vote.

Soon the supply planet was fabricating its own solar power dishes and placing power supply units in space around the planet. Once the great computer on Biotron began adding units to its original brain capacity, the process took on a life of its own. More and more power gathering units and satellites were built to supply the ever-growing need for energy to sustain the heart of Biotron.

At what point does the data storage capacity of a computer brain cross over from the realm of machine into the realm of independent cognizant entity? Some believe that it may have happened when the master brain reached a storage capability of five trillion bits of information. But we should hope that we never have occasion to find out.

The day came when the planet Biotron was ready to receive the first consignment of two thousand new settlers to the interior eco-system of the planet, and it was with great fanfare that these first volunteers departed the home planet for a new life out in the cosmos. It was to be the first great experiment which would ultimately lead to the step by step re-population of the distant stars.

At this point the home planet for some years had been receiving shipments of a dehydrated organic protein compound, as well as precious metals from Biotron, and most of the poorer masses had come to depend upon this food source. Before long the representatives of the new settlers were reporting how wonderful things were on their new home and requesting more and more settlers to join them. According to them, they had room for a half million new settlers and were adding to the eco-chamber system daily.

Soon the settlement fever swept the home planet with the force of a hurricane, and hundreds of thousands clamored to get on the rolls for resettlement. The fact that thousands of poor people back home were receiving mail shipments containing gold and platinum nuggets, as well as small uncut diamonds, only served to add to the resettlement hysteria. Soon a black market system of bribery to get on the resettlement rolls was flourishing and petty bureaucrats got rich, while higher officials got richer still. In various places, people began mobbing the embarkation stations, demanding to be allowed to migrate to Biotron. The government reported in the fourth year that the shipments of organic nutrients from Biotron had doubled and were expanding.

This resettlement frenzy continued for ten years and showed no signs of abating. Literally millions of citizens from all over the planet had gone to the new planet. The settlement representatives were requesting more and more settlers, which the high officials were more than happy to supply as it helped to relieve the population explosion on the home planet.

Then, as with most out of control bureaucratic fiascoes, it would take some insignificant data processor somewhere to come upon some chilling information concerning these settlers. Upon gathering and tabulation all of the information from around the home planet concerning the re-settlers and then computing the volume of organic nutrients received, less the estimated volume which would have been consumed by the new settlers, and cross referencing all of this information with the land mass of the planet Biotron, he came to some startling conclusions. At first he found it so unbelievable that he tabulated the information again and then again and each time with the same results.

According to his data, in order for the planet Biotron to have housed and fed all the new settlers and still shipped the volume of organic nutrients back home, even without allowing for a single new birth, the planet would have to be twice its known size and its food growing potential would have to be four times as great as all the land surface would allow.

Like any good citizen and worker, he immediately passed this information on to his superiors. Soon he was visited by several officials from the home office, who took him out to dinner at a most expensive eatery and were as affable to him as if they were brothers or even equals. They told him that they had had their eyes on him for some time because of his excellent work in data processing, and they felt that it was past the time when he should be moved up the ladder and given a position more befitting his capabilities. Of course, this would mean a substantial raise in pay and new, more spacious living quarters for him and his family. There were even allusions to a possible club membership for him, and suggestions as to which of the more exclusive institutions of higher learning he might consider sending his children to. But what about the Biotron data? Oh, that.

Well, even though we're not authorized to reveal this, we feel that since you are now, unofficially, part of the administration, what the hell. There's a third planet. A third planet? Yes, a third planet, even richer in precious metals than Biotron, and for years now we've been sending settlers there. But why the big secret? I should think that the government would want the people to know of our good fortune. Just take my word for it, friend, the government knows what's best. First of all, we don't want to cause more mob scenes and anarchy among people who are clamoring to migrate as we're already filled to capacity. The flood of precious metals and jewels has to be controlled to prevent the depreciation of our currency. And, said the official, leaning over toward the petty bureaucrat and assuming a conspiratorial tone, there is a fourth planet in the works. Can you imagine what would happen on the stock market if this got out, why it would be pure chaos. Oh, I see, said the data processor. So you see that it's imperative that the information, including the Biotron data, be kept a most discreet secret. You mustn't repeat this information to a living soul, not even your own family. Agreed? Agreed.

Suffice to say, the little official was deeply flattered at the attention paid him by his superiors, whom he had never laid eyes on before. He was overjoyed that his excellent service had at last been recognized and rewarded. His knowledge of the inner workings of the government's data gathering networks far exceeded that of most of those in the highest levels by virtue of being privy to all raw data long before they saw it. He was convinced that all pertinent information concerning transport ships, settlers, metals and food tonnage, etc., had to come through his department, as he had access to the central computer control. Something definitely smelled fishy.

That night, security was rather surprised to see him returning to his office after hours, but they weren't unduly disturbed as this particular worker was known to work late on occasion. Upon entering his office, he opened a safe to which only three people including himself knew the combination and retrieved from it a top secret code book. He then proceeded to sit at his terminal and to input a number of special access codes. This gave him access to the innermost data banks of the government.

He queried the central computer as to the source of all the information that he had previously received and received the reply that the source of all precious metals and organic nutrients, etc., was none other than Biotron proper. He asked about the third and fourth planets and received the reply that no such operations existed. Conclusion: hundreds of thousands of new settlers literally disappeared upon reaching Biotron.

Next he instructed the master computer to link him directly into the central computer on Biotron. The answer was: access denied. On whose order, he queried: By the order of Biotron Major, meaning the master computer on Biotron. He then instructed the computer to over ride Biotron's accesses and go directly to inner central, and the computer answered that it was unable to accomplish the override. By whose order? By order of Biotron Major. Instruct Biotron Major that unless access is granted immediately, remote instruction power will be cut and disciplinary actions taken. Biotron Major says, Fuck you.

Something is awfully wrong here said the startled processor. He picked up the phone and dialed in a secret code access and got a high insider on the line. He then proceeded to reiterate what he had found out about the Biotron operation. The official listened tentatively, and then instructed him to remain at his office and special agents would be there within the half hour to bring him to Government Central so that he could fully explain his findings to the inner council itself.

As he began to ponder the situation, the full import of it all began to dawn on him. Of course, the Inner Council must have already known what was going on. They had to know, because all of the data from the branch offices would have been funnelled into central.

I had better get the hell out of here before those agents arrive, he concluded, but as he came out of his office, he was stopped by two burly stone-faced security officers. They informed him that their instructions were to see that he remained at his office until his escorts arrived. He thanked them and returned to his office. Fifteen minutes later, two agents walked into his office just as he punched the enter button on his telefax terminal. What did you send out? asked one of them. I thought that all of the branch and sub offices should have this data on the Biotron operation said the processor, but his smile was erased by a laser blast that penetrated his forehead and splattered little pieces of his seared brain all over the terminal behind him.

Members of the Inner Council and a few other highly placed officials had known of the situation on Biotron for some years, but upon consultation had decided to allow the process to continue. The motive of this momentous decision could be boiled down to one common factor, and that factor was greed, pure and simple.

We may ask ourselves just how could an allegedly decent government knowingly send millions of its citizens to their doom for reason of personal profit. To the average decent rational person, such a thing would be inconceivable, but in reality it is not so far fetched as it seems.

While the average citizen may not have been intimately aware of the facts, it is a fact that the western governments knowingly stood by and permitted the mass murdering of some six million Jews and six million Christians in Nazi extermination camps during the Second World War. Their reasoning was that Hitler's preoccupation with killing Jews would require a lot of manpower that would weaken his forces on both battle fronts. Furthermore, the government and the western press deliberately withheld this knowledge from the public at large, nor did they so much as bomb the numerous rail lines that led to the concentration camps.

It is a fact that the Chase Manhattan Bank consortium and a few other big money conglomerates deliberately started the Vietnam War in order to protect their financial interests in that part of the world. The factor of sacrificing tens of thousands of young American men and women to this effort presented no moralistic problems for them, that is as long as their own children could be kept out of harm's way.

And thus it was the same on that planet of which we speak. In a less direct but equally effective manner, the big oil and power and chemical companies today are doing the same thing, willfully sacrificing untold thousands of lives and perpetrating permanent ecological damage for the sake of profits alone. Any lofty, religious or esoteric reasons offered beyond profit margin are just so much bull shit.

Just as in the western world on Earth, the majority of the people on that planet believed in their government and would fall for just about anything that they were told. Remember that on that planet, due to the continuous flow of precious metals, emeralds and food concentrates from Biotron, many found it strange that no settler ever seemed to wish to return home from Biotron, but the occasional arrival of a parcel from that far away relative or friend generally containing a small jewel or perhaps a nugget of gold tended to wipe away any doubts in people's minds as to the well being of the settlers. In fact, most pictured Biotron as a paradise of wealth and leisure, where one could spend their time enjoying the pleasures of life while smart machines did all of the manual labor for them.

The authorities were unable to prevent the damning information about Biotron from getting into the hands of a number of other small bureaucrats, but they immediately set about the task of suppressing this information, by bribery when possible and murder if necessary. Yet they had failed to reckon with the possibility that the information might fall into the hands of some independent hackers, who had broken the codes and routinely tapped into the government's branch office computers. The information about Biotron spread like wildfire across the planet, and soon millions were demanding that the government supply proof that all of the settlers were safe and alive on Biotron.

At this point not even the highest ranking government and military officials knew the full extent of the technical operations on Biotron. For many years they had relied upon audio and video reports from their bionic personnel on the planet. Of course, they had seen agricultural and technical production tapes from Biotron, but no living physical being had ever personally explored the entire inner workings of that planet and returned to tell about it.

Even with the Biotron settler statistical information floating about, there were still tens of thousands of people wishing to become settlers on Biotron. So, the Inner Council members and the military got together and worked out a plan. Among the next group of settlers there would be a number of secret agents, and each of these agents would be equipped with one real and one bionic eye, which was in reality a miniature remote video camera. These tiny cameras would transmit video images to special satellites, which would in turn relay the pictures to base units back on the home planet, along with any commentary that the agent cared to add concerning any particular operation.

The agent's job was to mingle as freely as possible with any settlers already on Biotron and to seize every opportunity to explore all parts of the subterranean operations there. To prevent the false eyes from becoming evident to electronic sensors on Biotron, they were designed to allow the wearer to turn them on and off when they so desired. Theoretically this would make them very difficult to locate among the thousands of other settlers. So when the next great ships departed from the home planet for Biotron, the secret agents were aboard.

As I have stated before, when Tan is communicating with me telepathically, the transmission is composed of mental pictures, as well as mental sounds, so I am able to vividly see these things transpiring. I'm sure that I visually comprehended the marvels of this far away robotic society to a far greater level than I am now capable of explaining to you. However, if you have read a book or listened to mysteries on the radio, then you will also form pictures in your mind of what I saw transpiring as Tan told the story.

The great settler transport ships had for years now been built and serviced on Biotron and were piloted by bionic personnel from Biotron. So no planetary personnel had the privilege of close social contact with the bionic or robot beings on Biotron. During the actual trip, which took ninety days, the wayfarers were well cared for, being abundantly fed and rested and inundated with propaganda videos of the marvels that they could look forward to on Biotron. There were recreation areas for the children and adults and plenty of fermented beverages for those who cared to indulge. Of course, every one spoke of getting rich. For the most part, the journey was a happy and interesting experience.

When the transport crafts entered the orbital zone of Biotron, the on-board computers and guidance systems were automatically interfaced with and taken over by Biotron Major, and the great ships were guided in even through the great asteroid belts that surrounded the planet and remotely brought to a smooth landing at one of the ample landing ports.

Then the thousands of new settlers disembarked amidst a great and marvelous laser light show, which was accompanied by spirit lifting music. Thousands of small drone robots were busy unloading luggage and beeping welcome to the new arrivals, and off in the distance, a vast glass-enclosed well-lighted cavern city awaited them. The robots were pointing toward the distant city and saying, "Follow the golden roads", of which there were a number, like the spokes of a wheel, all leading toward the city.

Through the bionic eyes of the agents, all of this was being viewed by the Inner Council back on the home planet. It never seemed to occur to the excited new settlers to wonder why, or to put the question as to why, not a single former settler had been there in the flesh to welcome them. After all, were the people not master of it all?

Now the unseen speakers were saying, "Time is precious, you must all move immediately toward the city". Then like orderly lines of ants, the thousands started to move along the road toward the great shiny city. By and by all of them had cleared the landing area but none had reached the city up ahead, and then, before my mind's eye, I saw the illusion of beauty begin to fade and the nightmare begin to happen. Like some great and bizarre domino creation, hug shiny metal plates or walls began to rise from the floor cutting off the progression of the masses toward the city and stranding the terrified settlers in what looked like a monstrous maze.

They very shortly discovered that the walls were electrified, not powerful enough to kill but enough to discourage any one from climbing over them. Now the thousands were milling about in a disoriented manner, many had panicked and started to scream, children were crying, while some kept their heads and started to try to back track through the maze, back toward the landing area. Of course, all avenues of retreat had been sealed off.

Then the hidden speakers started to play a song, which was their home planet's version of the death march, and straight away, literally thousands of killer drones were released into the maze to hunt down and kill the people in many atrocious and painful manners.

Biotron Major knew that most people harbor a primordial fear of certain insects and snakes, so many of the killer drones were fashioned like giant spiders, scorpions, praying mantis and snakes, even though they all were made of metal. There were easier, more efficient ways of killing, of course, but it was done in this manner for a specific reason.

The bionic personnel on Biotron required a certain amount of organic nutrients to sustain the physical portions of their bodies, and while these nutrients could easily be extracted from the food plants in the agri-gardens on Biotron, the bionics had discovered that living beings possessed certain chemicals of a natural type that when extracted and concentrated produced an exquisite neurological high of the psychedelic sort when injected into the exposed brain. The chemical, as I understand it, was of an adrenal-pheromone nature.

They had found that the chemical was more abundant and potent when extracted from a person who had experienced a great deal of terror and pain before death, thus the reason for using such a terrible method to kill them. While the drones possessed no sentiments one way or the other and Biotron Major was interested only in the end product, which was a very fine organic fertilizer and an excellent machine lubricant, the bionics, I believe I can safely say, were capable of deriving some kind of sado-sensual pleasure from observing the murders.

It soon dawned upon the doomed agents the horrible truth of the situation on Biotron, and, though schooled in the arts of survival and self defense, they really didn't pose any notable problem for the determined killing machines.

Back on the home planet, the central council members watched in horror as their agents were overcome one by one and torn to pieces.

In order to induce the most awful levels of terror in the subjects, the Biotron Major computer had created and programmed numerous fear-inducing methods, which were designed to solicit the most nightmarish levels of dementia in terror. For instance, to be stung and incapacitated by a large black clicking scorpion, and while trying to crawl away, feel the claw grab an ankle as the lights go out. The stinger continues to penetrate again and again in the painful darkness. And other even more terrible means that I won't even reiterate here.

Now the central council found themselves faced with the age old dilemma of morals versus greed. The horror that they had just witnessed was shocking even to these hardened men, and yet it must be remembered that a major portion of the home planet's wealth and food supply came from Biotron. The moral question of sending millions to their doom was superseded by the question uppermost in their minds, namely how long can we keep this thing a secret.

Due to the information that was already circulating, it had become very difficult to evade or to give suitable answers to the pressing questions. The population at large was still of the impression that the workings of Biotron were completely controlled by the home planet, but a larger number of insiders and minor technical personnel knew that Biotron had long ago become an independent entity, which was self-sustaining in power and natural metal resources. Few if any could fathom the true depths of the artificial intelligence of Biotron. Had they realized the true technological power of Biotron, they would have experienced a state of fearful apprehension.

The use of robotics on the home planet was of a technical level which was little more advanced than the robotics of present day Earth, and even the members of the central council were amazed at the level of artificial mechanisms that they had just witnessed on Biotron. Not even they could fathom the true complexity of artificial dexterity and logic now possessed by Biotron Major. It may be safely said that not even the most intelligent machine ever does anything without a logical reason. Only physical beings like humans and others are prone to illogical actions and reasoning.

In the logic of Biotron Major, the use of the physical bodies of the home planet settlers was the most natural and abundant source of organic fertilizer. Any touches involving unnecessary pain and sadistic gratification from their nullification were owed entirely to the bionic residents and not to Biotron Major itself. Fertilizers produce plants, and plants produce oxygen. Oxygen is essential in the various smelting, welding and power generating processes necessary to build and repair new or existing machines.

From the human cadavers also came other essential or very useful products. Gold and silver fillings and jewelry were smelted into bars and shipped back to the home planet in payment for more settlers, or should I say organic fertilizer. The settlers' bodies also yielded in small quantities a very fine oil that served as a lubricant for the joints of robots. Bone gristle and cartilage served well in the production of microchips and as electrical micro insulators. The hair was used in filters for chemical purification, and bone marrow served as a protein rich additive for the dehydrated vegetable foodstuffs sent back to feed the home populace. So from Biotron Major's viewpoint, the settlers served a useful and essential purpose and there was no waste at all.

A few of the secret agents' bionic eyes continued to operate even after the agent died, as they were hooked into a battery powered source pod which was embedded under the skin of the stomach, so they were able to witness portions of the dissection processes. However, these electronic attachments were soon discovered by the electro-sensors of Biotron Major. Robot and bionic technicians then proceeded to dismantle the gadgets and decipher their technical capabilities. The robots were smart enough to adapt and make use of this technology in future and existing units of their own design.

Biotron Major was also able to interface with the computers of the transmission satellites then orbiting Biotron and to pirate the transmissions. This, of course, enabled Bio-Major to discover that portions of its operations had been spied upon by the home planet. The spy satellites were equipped with remote controlled destruct mechanisms, and it took Bio-Major only twenty minutes to decipher the remote destruct sequence and then destroy the three satellites. This technical ability of the robot planet was duly noted by the scientists back on the home planet.

The home planet at this time was making great use of nuclear power and also suffering some instances on nuclear pollution and sporadic melt-downs similar to those of present day Earth. It was known that there were large natural deposits of uranium ore on Biotron, but until this point the machines on the planet had not begun to utilize it for power. Not because Bio-Major did not possess the technical ability to do so but simply because it had reasoned that solar and volcanic chemical reaction energy were the most abundant and least hazardous methods available. The home planet could have taken a lesson from the robots in this respect.

Even with the false government resettlement propaganda, it was inevitable that the news would get out, and that the people would wise up and refuse to go. The government was able to keep up the flow of living fodder for Biotron's cauldrons for a year by emptying all of its prisons and forcibly removing other undesirables, but this source too dried up.

Finally, the point came where the government had to refuse Biotron, and suffice it to say, the robots didn't like that at all. Immediately the gold and the food stopped coming from the colony planet. This prompted the government to put together a punitive force of well-armed soldiers and dispatch them to the robot planet with orders to destroy the main computer banks and to shut down the operation until the proper technical personnel could arrive to take over.

The Inner Council and the military strategists had the opportunity to see the punitive force suffer the same fate as those unarmed settlers before them without ever penetrating anywhere near the central brain and now Bio-Major had acquired the technology for mini-lasers and a number of chemical explosives, not to mention the technology of the three heavily armed warships which composed the assault armada. Of course, Bio-Major would now be able to reproduce those ships and weapons and even improve upon the designs.

It was now agreed the robot emplacement must be destroyed at all cost. But how was it to be accomplished? Machines are physically far more durable than human beings, but they have one inherent weakness. They all run on electricity and computer tapes can be magnetically erased. They wasted no time in calling in their most brilliant scientists and setting them about the task of devising a foolproof method of destroying the robot intelligence.

Biotron Major's mode of logic led it to conclude that the home planet would soon mount another far more potent attack upon its planet, so it started to program its own schematic into the brains of small mobile units. Soon hundreds of separate units would possess the ability to repair and even fabricate different parts of Bio-Major's brain. Other units were utilized as auxiliary storage pods, each containing a part of the program, which would enable them to collectively restore the whole. Then, based upon the nuclear reactor engines which powered the captive ships, it started to make high megaton bombs, which would be mounted in the nose of missiles.

Within three months another ship from the home planet arrived above Biotron. It carried three nuclear loads. Bio-Major performed the usual procedure of interfacing with the ship's computers and the bombs' destruct mechanism. It knew that if the nuclear piles would destruct that close to Biotron that the resultant electro-magnetic waves would disrupt its own power supply and damage its brain, so it decided to halt the destruct mechanism, bring the ship in and dismantle the bombs. To make sure that such a thing would not happen again, Bio-Major launched a hundred nuclear missiles at the home planet.

When the ship touched down inside the bomb proofed installation, Bio-Major picked up the presence of a fourth nuclear load aboard the ship, and that one did not possess an electronic timer computer. Robot sensors skittered frantically around the big bomb but could detect no electrical timer mechanism. Bio-Major ascertained that the bomb was composed of a large core of high grade plutonium and that it was covered in a thick sheath of a metal substance. Further analysis revealed the casing to be pure cobalt. It alerted the bionic personnel and swiftly began to plot a strategy for dismantling the bomb.

The dismantling could be accomplished quite swiftly because machines are not harmed by radiation poisoning. All of the bomb's paneling had been welded shut, so it would be necessary to cut through the housing with gas or laser. Soon a small panel was removed, thus enabling Bio-Major and the bionic technician to get a visual of the inside of the bomb. What they saw was a primitive mechanism, which was operated by atmospheric pressure and an acid corrosion timer.

It took Bio-Major only thirty seconds to issue the order to close all of the vault doors leading to the core brain, but it was too late. In another five seconds the acid burned through the firing mechanism and set off ninety-one TNT charges, which sent numerous titanium alloy rods smashing inward with a force that caused critical mass, thus setting off the all-consuming nuclear reaction of the mighty cobalt load. So great was the force that the planet moved on its axis and metal flowed like water, fusing metal with glass and lighting up the sky so bright that it could be seen quite clearly with the naked eye back on the home planet.

Those with telescopes could also see a hundred fiery projectiles as they entered the stratosphere of the home planet, and most of the common people were ignorant of what was going on up until the moment that the warheads started to detonate above the cities.

Thus was a highly civilized race virtually wiped out by smart machines of their own design. I am told that deep within the bowels of the robot planet some units were unharmed physically, and that less than a century later enough of the master brain had been restored for it to be able to start sending out remote controlled search devices whose destinations will encompass many distant stars.

In computing the distance in light years from Earth to even the nearest stars and calculating the tonnage of fuel and the possible speed our ships or probes would be capable of attaining, most of our scientists are of the opinion that manned space flight or even remote devices of exploration would be impractical, as, at near the speed of light, providing it could be obtained, it would still require too long a span of time to be of any practical value. But they fail to realize that for some physical life forms and intelligent machines, the factor of several hundred years wouldn't faze them at all, for while the average life span of an earthling is prohibitive, this is not a factor of import to some other intelligent life forms.

Furthermore, our knowledge of the laws of physics gives us to believe that matter cannot possibly move faster than the speed of light, but as the Biaviians have shown me, this law has other levels that transcend this. To be sure, there are various modes of speed and methods of acceleration up to and beyond the speed of light, beginning with the solid and liquid fuels currently in use by man and up to the manipulation of space warps and hyper-space quantum.

The Biaviians further told me that they are aware of the fact that a solid object can conceivably traverse a black hole corridor, as has been proven by the fantastic journey accomplished by the great octopi-like intelligent creature called the Great Agynmum.

The Biaviians can also accomplish dematerialization and rematerialization of living creatures over certain measured distances. For instance in 1975 I was picked up in such a manner, and since I don't remember ever physically disembarking from the saucer after a journey, I may have been returned to Earth in such a manner.

The materialization of the two Targs in my apartment in 1988 is another case in point. When an alien, such as the infamous men in black, appear and knock on doors as would normally be done, then you may be sure that they are doing this so as not to unduly alarm the visited party or to play the part of human beings.

The most common mode of planet to planet or planet to mothership travel within a given solar system used by the Biaviians and others is electromagnetic induction, which is generated by a hydrogen fed fusion core drive, but these fusion cores are also capable of utilizing other kinds of gases and some of the more complex ships are able to warp to hyper-space using the same kind of power source.

Yet on the home planet and at other points in the galaxy, the Biaviians and others use a number of propulsion methods and materials. They know that ships and unmanned probes can reach astronomical speeds using antimatter propulsion and that near light speed can be attained using laser propulsion.

As a hypothetical example, let us say that a ship or probe is launched from a given planet. If the ship did not have the electromagnetic fusion propulsion or power system and if it used some kind of solid or liquid fuel, the greater portion of this fuel would be used in escaping the gravitation pull of the planet. However, when this ship reaches the vacuum of space, there would be practically no resistance to its forward momentum. A small pile of anti-matter would then boost the speed of the ship to a fantastic momentum before burning out. Then a fission or fusion generated laser would kick in and could be used to literally push the ship forward or a laser from the planet of origin could be used to push the ship away, because at a certain speed, a concentrated light beam becomes a mode of propulsion. This simple laser would eventually push the ship to near the speed of light, and the acceleration could be assisted by an ion drive, as is the case in some Biaviian ships.

Any body in space could be utilized as a springboard for the laser or a kind of magnetic slingshot. When the Biaviians are ready to transcend light speed, they are somehow able to transmute the molecular solidification of the ship and metamorphic into a zillion microscopic magnets, which are able to use ions and quarks to pull the ship forward. Apparently there are other levels of super sub-atomic quantum that nullify the factors of time. Of course, the comprehension or even the visualization of such things are beyond my knowledge.

Our Earth scientists will tell you that we do not have to set foot upon or even get physically close to another star or planet in order to ascertain its chemical make-up. For instance, the light spectrum that emanate from certain gases can give us a very good idea as to the atmospheric conditions of that particular body. We may even be able to tell if that body is capable of sustaining any forms of life. If we are this advanced, then you may be sure that others are similarly knowledgeable of such methods. In other words, it would not be necessary for an intelligent life form to actually visit this planet in order to know that it has some form of life on its surface.

At any given moment there are no less than tens of thousands of exploratory probes out in space looking for something. There are a few life forms who have for some reason or the other lost contact with beings of their own kind, who are somewhere out there in the voids and are sending out probes to look for them.

Tan speaks of at least three known kinds of artificial intelligence forms, who are traversing great voids of space and do so by utilizing an opportunistic method of obtaining fuel and new technology. However, due to the vast distances between the stars, the chance of these smart robots chancing upon other intelligent life forms are very slim, though not impossible.

The Biaviians, during their history of space exploration, have come upon numerous non-intelligent life forms, some very early evolutionary life forms who have the potential to eventually evolve toward greater intelligence and a few forms of primitive intelligence, similar to some aboriginal people on Earth.

It is also a fact that some seeker probes out in the cosmos, which have long since lost contact with or the control of their places of origin, have, on occasion, been discovered and used by others who have not yet attained that level of technological sophistication.

Even the Earth has sent out space probes, which will eventually travel beyond our technical ability to communicate with them. As I've stated before, the Biaviians have on more than one occasion, physically retrieved and examined Earth satellites before returning them to their former orbital paths.

Perhaps Earth is a very fortunate planet indeed owing to the fact that no alien species with conquest in mind has yet happened upon it. We are also fortunate that those smart robots have not found it necessary to explore this far afield in order to acquire any kind of metals or chemicals they may need. We can attribute this more to the fact that any known substance may be found in abundance on any number of thousands, if not millions, of lifeless bodies. The smart robots do not require a moderate climate in which to work. With bodies constructed of special heat resistant alloys, ceramic and other composites, they are able to function easily under some of the most extreme atmospheric and temperature conditions. This enables the smart machines to work under a much more diversified set of conditions, which would be deadly to any physical organisms.

It may be safely said that the controlling mega-brain of an artificial intelligence does have a conception of existence, if not of pain and other emotions, and will often go to extraordinary lengths in protecting itself from destruction or sabotage. However, the remote drones hold no such fear and cannot be compromised, nor can they be sidetracked from their programmed function by any means less than physical destruction or system malfunction. However, there is another level of artificial intelligence that transcends the inorganic computer, and it is called the neuro-tron or the neuro-sphere.

The neuro-sphere in description is quite similar in appearance to the glowing orbs I witnessed aboard the Biaviian mothership, yet there is a notable difference in their contents and abilities. While the glowing orb of the Biaviians is a remote controlled device, the neuro-sphere is capable of and designed to operate as an independent entity.

In essence, the sum total of any non-organic and to some notable extent an organic computer's knowledge does not exceed its programming. A computer, depending upon its complexity, can be designed and instructed to perform innumerable tasks. The true neuro-sphere has a brain nucleus which is composed of organic matter.

We might call this nucleus a living brain, however, it is not composed of true brain materials but of a mixture of nucleic-acid clusters, which are grown for the purpose. In the neuro-sphere, this brain cluster may be no larger than a walnut or it may achieve the dimension of a basketball with the passing of time and the continuous influx of new knowledge gained.

Even the aliens will concede that the most complex computer in existence is the human brain, the Stagyian brain and, no doubt, the dolphin's brain. Even at this moment, and without your conscious awareness, your brain is accumulating and storing millions of bits of information or data. It is aware of the breath you take, the odors of the air around you, the various fluctuations of light in the room and the shadows, the color of your clothing, the feel of the air currents, and the sounds of insects, automobiles and your heart beat. Second by second, it is storing all of this information while controlling your every bodily motion and function. Simultaneously it is alluding to the abstract and actively searching for esoteric essence. It is further proceeding to store and cross-reference all of this information for future recall and logical correlation and dissemination. Every one of those actions were consumed and updated several times each second since you started to read this paragraph and shall continue to be until you die and beyond.

The neuro-sphere is far more complex than anything you will find upon this Earth technologically. However, in data accumulation and processing ability, it must still take a back seat to the human brain. The neuro-sphere's one great advantage over the human psychology is that its data collection method is structured, its recall is instantaneous and total, and its method of thought is that of almost pure mathematical logic.

The Biaviians are not the only intelligent life form in the universe who have the neuro-sphere technology. I am told that the sphere's primary function is that of long range and long term universal exploration. Even the Biaviians are not able to personally cover all of the vastness of the universe with manned ships nor can they be sure of what kind of life forms, if any, will be yielded by a distant star constellation. So neuro-spheres are dispatched in many different directions on missions which may encompass hundreds, if not thousands, of years, and though it has been programmed to ultimately return to its place of origin, there is no guarantee that it always will. It may perchance come upon a species of life form which is composed of pure energy and become a friend or playmate to them, or it may happen upon a source of information which will keep it processing data into infinity, because the neuro-sphere becomes more complex and grows larger in proportion to any new knowledge it gains.

The neuro-sphere is also different from those bionic beings which are called the Ancient One in many ways. The nucleus of the sphere is composed of technically created organic matter, while the brain of an Ancient One has been literally transplanted from the living body of a Biaviian or Stagyian scientist into a body which is fashioned of certain translucent acrylic plastic materials, which is supported by a titanium alloy skeleton.

The thought processes of the Ancient One, while given to logic, also retains the whimsical and spiritual characteristics of their physical counterparts. These Ancient Ones are generally utilized to pilot ships on extended journeys, which require the crew to lay in suspended animation for many years. The stimulus of continuous information gathering and other duties keeps the Ancient One genially occupied. I suspect that certain parts of their brains, perhaps the centers that control sadness, family memories and other non-essential things, have been surgically altered in these beings, and they don't seem to have any conception of time.

Unlike the Earth spy satellite, which is interfaced with control, video and recording devices back on Earth, the neuro-sphere must record all of its information in its own organic brain. Upon its return from its mission, it is then capable of passing this information, both audio and visual, to recording instruments at home. It carries no film, recorder tapes or other similar devices.

When the neuro-sphere leaves its home base, it is a self-propelled self-sustaining entity. As the glowing orb streaks across space, the very heat friction generated by its hull or skin serves as a power source and continues to recharge its power center. Even as it streaks along at speeds approaching that of light, it is accumulating data on the density and composition of the gases in space.

When the neuro-sphere reaches its preprogrammed star cluster and starts to explore the solar systems around it, it slows its speed to a level which enables it to carefully examine the physical and ecological characteristics of each planetary body revolving around a sun. It will circumnavigate the planet a number of times from deep space and then adjust its orbit to enter the stratosphere of the planet if necessary. It is not uncommon for the sphere to sometimes come to a complete stop and dispense a number of energy balls to zoom in for a detailed observation of some very interesting feature. Perhaps the sphere has been programmed to find other life forms and to disregard lifeless bodies. It may have been instructed to locate planets which can support Biaviians with or without special life support apparatus.

The sphere would also measure the levels, if any, of the technology of any living planets it comes upon, and it is not unknown for it to actually communicate with those technically capable forms. However, it has been instructed not to interfere in the affairs of those beings. Still, with the passing of time and the accumulation of knowledge, the sphere can come to have a mind of its own, so to speak.

It may take the time to record and learn the verbal and electronic languages of various races and tongues on a given planet, and it may tarry and get hung up on attempting to decipher the illogical motivations and actions of a species.

The sphere eventually becomes capable of consuming all of the relevant data of even a complex planet like Earth in a matter of days. If it comes upon a life form and an ecological system which is similar in composition to one already known, then its observation time is shortened considerably, as it doesn't find it necessary to consume repetitive material.

Should it come upon a life form which is totally different from anything it has experienced before, it will linger until it has consumed all biological and technical knowledge of it. When it reaches a certain level of data gained, it feels obliged to return home and unburden itself of that knowledge. At least the Biaviians hope it will.

During the Second World War, allied and enemy pilots sometimes reported being followed by glowing orbs or faux fighters. These were not neuro-spheres, but the more common electro-spheres of the kind I saw aboard the Biaviian mothership. They were, no doubt, observing and reporting on the planes' technical systems and propulsion systems, etc. Sometimes these little spheres are seen pacing UFOs, but they may just as easily have been plasma-like energy spheres or balls dispatched from a neuro-sphere from within our stratosphere. When the energy sphere has accomplished its purpose, it may just disappear, as the neuro-sphere would never retain it any longer than is necessary. No unnecessary power is wasted, even though power is abundant this near a sun. The physical electro-sphere and the neuro-sphere, unlike the energy ball, do not disintegrate, but can move fast enough from a standing position that they seem to just disappear.

The neuro-sphere is, without a doubt, the ultimate in Biaviian electronic technology. Tan told me that even though it has not been confirmed, it is theoretically possible that a few neuro-spheres have developed the ability to move through time at will.

Since all past knowledge can be surmised through the physical composition of present things, it is his theory that the neuro-sphere would have chosen to attempt going forward in time, yet since none have returned to this dimension, his theory cannot be verified.

The future cannot be fixed with any known precision. Of course, we know that our actions today will ultimately influence the context of our future. You can look at a thing and calculate the rate of its natural deterioration and get some idea of when it will collapse, but we cannot anticipate all of the various elements which will contribute to or prolong its decline of longevity.

We may safely say that a banana will deteriorate and turn black in a few days, so we hasten to sell them. Yet if this customer didn't buy it, would it spoil before another one bought it? Will the person who bought it, eat it, or will his son eat it? Or will his son share it with his sister? Can we say with certainty that the sun will rise tomorrow? Or that New York City will still exist? If you kill one ant from an ant hill, you have altered the numerical value of all ants forever.

Simply because we have spent the last billion years surviving the evolutionary process, there is no guarantee that it all won't be completely destroyed in the next moment by some form of unforeseen cataclysm.

The Biaviians are perfectly convinced that the force of life is immutable and will continue regardless of what happens. However, no material thing is guaranteed to continue in its present form, and no matter the complexity of material creations, the sum total of all knowledge can never be known by any one person, nation, planet, galaxy or universe, thus the endless quest of various life forms for this knowledge.

The realization that all knowledge will never be known by mortal beings has never and will never dissuade beings in the least from seeking to possess this impossibility. This is why they have come here and why we are sorely intent on going there. Only the snail's pace of our inner enlightenment causes them to stand in wonder of us, to be capable of such greatness, while putting the dumbest of animals to shame. From the Biaviian's viewpoint, the ultimate stupidity of man is his ability to think of himself as being the only living, breathing product of the universe's creation. It is the supreme form of insane arrogance on man's part. Little does he know that his physical genus has long ago been catalogued and dismissed as a common sub-order by simple machines and smart insects.

When humanity comes to the definite realization that it is not alone in the universe, it shouldn't cause people to view themselves of any less import, but instead should allow humanity to move into a more enlightened mode of realization, to begin to comprehend the far greater scope of the many mansions in God's kingdom, to become as one world community and to seek to ultimately become as one with the greater universal intelligence.

If we could come to look upon ourselves as us among them, or even us against them, then perhaps we might rise above the senseless mode of us against our brother, or one nation against another.

I personally could never again, even momentarily, discount the existence of other beings, because I have first hand knowledge of their existence, and this realization is soon to become evident to all of humanity, whether they are ready or not, willing or not, believers or non-believers. Still there are those who will run to the rocks and beg the rocks to hide their face from the very sight of the ships. These are the ones who have long held the delusion that in their hands lay all power or in their religions lay all truth. These are the ones who will suddenly come face to face with the fact that all of their weapons of destruction could avail them nothing should it come to a show down. Since it is highly unlikely that man will cleanse himself of his refusal to lay aside or dispense with his hatreds, as a last resort and in a natural attempt to save itself, the very Earth will attempt to cleanse itself of the cancerous growth called man.

Inasmuch as it is possible to predict futuristic events based upon present conditions, I'm informed that all future projections tabulated by the aliens come back to the fact that the Earth is virtually suspended upon the brink of an ecological cataclysm of universal proportions, and that they will simply have to rescue a certain number physically.

Chapter 14

Statements of Reflection

Logic & Other Stuff

Martin : You know, there are still people, very powerful people who believe that God created Heaven and Earth and man and the animals about six or seven thousand years ago.

Tan : There are some very powerful beings among us who feel that the Homo sapien bi-ped should be considered upon the same plane as destructive rodents instead of fellow wayfarers in the cosmos.

Martin : How is it possible that with all of our scientific knowledge the greater portion of our intellectual community either denies outright or refutes the possibility that beings such as you can exist or could be here now?

Tan : Regrettably a culture is often directed by the most ruthless instead of the most enlightened. The title of intellectual greatness is often wrongfully claimed by and erroneously attributed to the possessors of the greater share of materials and social power, when in reality, they are in essence no more than highly proficient scavengers of all militarily weaker elements. Your scientists have come predominantly from this scavenger element, and they have not the inner 'Omsa' to visualize beyond their fleeting mortality and their self imposed boundaries of logic.

The greater measure of your true scientific worth has thus far been suppressed or laid waste by the beast within the nature of the scavengers who yet control the force of your destiny and I fear that your planet is forfeit because of it.

Ignorance is always a passing phase, yet hatred and stupidity are the consumer of planets and the death of all ascension in the true wonders of reality.

Martin : I find it hard to believe, especially in view of all of the sightings, photographs, abductions and even some physical evidence, that the scientists, government and world leaders are not aware of your presence in our stratosphere.

Tan : You may be sure that our presence is known by many of those of whom you speak. Thus far we have not chosen to communicate directly with these untrue representatives of mankind, who are murderers and supporters of false endeavor. By their own choice, they have chosen to withhold our presence from the masses. I suspect that they hold a great fear of any power which is obviously greater than their own. Yet they have been aware of our presence long enough to be assured of the fact that our aim is not military conquest of the Homo sapien order. What are your thoughts upon his secrecy?

Martin : Many so-called intelligent men, even today, refuse to accept the archaeological evidence and common logic of evolution, because it is contradictory to their religious doctrines and because he believes that it demeans him to be placed in a lower biological order.

This is, of course, imbecilic stupidity, and yet these same individuals are often the ones who control society. They attempt to deny your existence because to recognize it would literally undermine the validity of his religions and minimize his self-conception of his power and importance both on Earth and in the universal order of things.

Should his religious orders be superseded by mere rational thinking, his monopoly on the manipulation of ignorance and consequently the size of his monetary collections would diminish. Open recognition of your presence would usher in an extraordinary new phase of universal logic and even spiritual enlightenment, so he believes that he must deny and even suppress the knowledge of your existence and presence at all cost.

Even so, I believe that the cat is out of the bag, and that this truth has soon to become evident to even the most skeptical.

Tan : True, not because we seek universal recognition, but because approaching circumstances shall force us to reveal our presence in great numbers all about your planet. If the mission is to be completed and if the human species is to be saved, it cannot be otherwise. It would be well if, upon that time, humanity would not experience mass terror upon our approach, yet no matter the state of mind, this undertaking must be executed.

Martin : I must admit that many times I feel that these things I'm writing here will not be accepted or believed by the people who are meant to read them. After all, I'm not a notable personality a scientist or even a formally educated person. In the world today people are more concerned with the credibility of the writer than with the words that he writes.

Tan : Rest assured that those for whom your revelations are meant shall comprehend. Many others not so chosen shall be enlightened and those who discount your words altogether are of no import to the end results of the mission.

You must not become discouraged. Your work is but one among a number, and yet it is the foremost of them. It is within your power to express that which you have seen and touched and those who hear will believe or be given to contemplation and events will verify and make plain your words. Your words are formed of a truth truly known by you and must not fail to touch others who seek the truth, and only the worthy shall know it without question.

Martin : I hope that you are aware of the fact that if you show up in force, the military will probably attempt to shoot you down, or at least try to prevent the airlifting of thousands of people right under their noses.

Tan : We are not concerned in the manner as all implements of destruction will be temporarily altered to malfunction. Our presence at each point shall not be more than necessary. Those who are summoned would have gathered unto one another as communities some time before, and the time and point coordinates will not be made widely known to those not of the chosen.

Martin : Maybe I underestimate the propensity of people to accept the unknown and the unusual and maybe you overestimate the ability of Earth people to do so. I've got to be honest with you Tan, you have got some weird looking shit on your mothership, and a lot of people might freak out in the face of it. I don't think that you should use me as a barometer to measure the psychological stability of all humans.

Tan : Your concern is valid, and it is true that you have served to measure a spectrum of response. Yet I am aware Martin, that your depth of psych-compromise exceeds that of many and parallels that of some. Few shall be given privy to things non-essential to their orientation. Time and depth of inner perception shall be measured on an individual basis. Do you think that my countenance is repulsive or too great to bear for the normal human?

Martin : No, Tan, my friend, I wasn't referring to you in particular. In fact, aside from that big head and those funny looking feet, you are kinda cute. And, to me, Nela is beautiful. But some of the other life forms are basically some ugly mother fuckers, if you know what I mean.

Tan : I must tell you, Martin, that the Targzissians fail to find any physical beauty in you. Yet to me, you are a most pleasing specimen.

Martin : Well fuck a lizard. In fact, fuck a lizard's momma.

Tan : Martin, get serious. Should we not both treasure these spans of communication? I am at peace in your presence, and I delight in your resonance.

Martin : I'm deeply concerned about you and your people, Tan. I have journeyed across this land since I was fourteen years of age, and the number of near righteous people I've known could be counted on little more than my right hand.

You may not fully understand the awesome chance you would be taking by bringing this many humans into your trust. I have no doubt that if given the chance, some of them are going to screw up and cause trouble for you and among your people. Unlike the Biaviians, who are not given to doing dumb shit, some human beings seem to thrive on controversy. Do you understand what I'm trying to say to you?

Tan : Martin, friend, you honor me with your care. It is a measure rare among any but the lower orders, such as your canine domestics. Yet you do me a service which is little deserved, as my innocence is born more of comfort in my technical power, than of inherent kindness. If your missiles, lasers and particle weapons could not broach my defenses, how much less must I fear the irrational physical. It is my wish that a planet live, though I possess the power to destroy a score and more, much more.

Martin : In other words, you've got some heavy 'zap shit'.

Tan : Correct.

Martin : Maybe I'm being a bit critical of the human species as a whole. Surely there must be a good number of very decent people on the Earth. I've just never had the pleasure of experiencing many together in one location.

Actually I'm certainly not worthy to judge others, because I've done some shitty stuff in my life. For instance, when we got drunk together on the mothership and you passed out, I rifled through your carrying case looking for diamonds and dope and shit. I really feel bad about that. Anyway all you had was a bunch of shitty tasting wafers, which Question stole and pigged out on.

Tan : Martin, on each occasion of our meeting and while you were in the dream state, I explored the contents of your pockets and took three coins and one wrap of hemp cannabis sitana. I too have borne a guilt thing.

Martin : You stole my dope?

Tan : Yes.

Martin : Well, I forgive you.

Tan : And I forgive you for attempting to steal a whisper craft.

Martin : Tan, it was all Question's idea. The dirty bastard got me drunk and suggested we go to Vegas. Scout's honor.

Tan : Yes, and I'm Wee Wee Herman! (I cracked up) Martin, when you laugh, I feel the mirth, and it causes me to regret that I do not have the ability to articulate.

Martin : Tan, when I first met you, you didn't know nothing about bullshitting, but now you're getting just like Question, whom I'm going to 'kill', and who basically makes me want to puke.

Tan : Bullshitting can be spiritual.

Martin : Yeah, no shit.

Tan : Even as you journeyed with me within the zones of your solar spheres, I felt your fascination and the resonance of your 'Omsa'. That which to you was so normal was to me quite wondrous. You cannot know how great the gift nor how true the treasure of your friendship is unto the Elohim. The level of your inner being in synchronization to my own in resonance is a rare thing indeed between human and Biaviian. Thus I delight in your mirth and find fascination in your pain.

Martin : Tan, if you find fascination in my pain. I fear that you are kind of 'freaky', my friend, but I get your drift. You find it marvelous to feel my emotions because these things are new to you. But from the human standpoint, sometimes emotions can be a bummer.

Tan : Being devoid of emotions, like so, may on occasion transcend your bummer. Do you see?

Martin : Yeah. You know, Tan, without exception, the greater religions of the world, as they are practiced and understood, give no credence to your existence. To definitely reveal your presence would nullify man's belief in the validity of his faith and his Gods.

Tan : Has your religious belief been made the less by your knowledge of my existence?

Martin : Naw! Quite the contrary. Long ago I pondered the

question and after about ten minutes I came to the conclusion that if mankind was God's only creation in all of the universes in which to entrust all of His glory and His aspirations, then He has come up shit out of luck.

Of course, I had met you before, but I couldn't be sure. Even so, I did not question the existence of a God force. With my own hands I have relieved pain, and I have witnessed some portions of miracles. To attempt to unravel the mysteries of infinity through religious scriptures is an exercise in rhetorical futility. I just instinctively know that the creative force wouldn't place all of its eggs in one basket but would instead cast the seed of life out upon the waters of the universe and let evolution take its course and seek its own levels of infinite comprehension.

So there had to be other life forms out there. Thus, having come to that conclusion, my conception of God has been greatly enhanced. My comprehension of God's logic, I believe, has touched and literally tasted new levels of spiritual resonance. For a while I felt that if humanity was the measure of God's divine essence, then He had probably gone ape-shit. However, since I've witnessed these things you have shown me, I have a much greater respect for God's infinite preoccupation and his propensity to come up with weird shit.

Tan : Well put, friend Martin. I, O-Qua Tangin Wann, know of the many variables under which physical life forms come to be, yet even the Stagyian theorists do not know from whence emanates the force of life itself. We do know that this force knows no conceived boundaries and certainly pervades all of the cosmos.

This force is not so great a director as it is an opportunist, so the virus, the insect and the mammal have equal access to its essence. This force grants no special dispensation or divine right to existence. Only the endurance, tenacity and ingenuity of a given life form shall permit its survival as a species.

I have neither the power to grant life nor to destroy the force of which it is made. It has always been and shall always be, and neither the nova of stars nor the implosion of galaxies shall halt its progression or greatly diminish its diversity. The sum total of all things that are or shall come to be is the ever motion of its total reason. In our ignorance we call it light and ever seek to return unto the epi-center.

Martin : No shit! On Earth, man has a concept of good and evil. He views physical existence as a constant battle between these two forces. What is your concept of good and evil?

Tan : This concept you speak of tends to elude the definition when viewed from my sense of logic. For Biaviians do not consciously exceed the boundaries of necessitation. In accordance with natural order, the predator kills only to the extent of its needs, while only intelligent beings are given to exceed logical boundaries. In order to penetrate the realm you call evil, one must have embraced the emotion called hatred. This emotion we no longer possess to measure, so in this zone I must remain your pupil. Perhaps you can enlighten me?

Martin : I'm no psychiatrist, but this is how I see it. Evil, I believe is the receiving of psychological and/or sensual gratification through the infliction of physical and/or psychological pain upon some other person or thing.

On the Earth, evil takes on many forms and is practiced in various overt and covert manners. Evil hides under many forms of legally acceptable subterfuges. Conservatism is in essence racism, and the judicial system is nothing less than an official manner of lynching the poor and minorities. Born again religious leaders are, by nature, divine racists. To condone and maintain any system of social endeavor which profits by the suppression of others is evil.

Apartheid is a classical example of an all-consuming legalized evil. Hateful words and actions rendered in a moment of anger are evil. The maltreatment of a child, the elderly and infirm or the torture of an animal are evil. The deliberate poisoning of nature for profit is evil, and the achieving of sexual gratification by inflecting physical pain on some other unwilling party or thing is evil.

I further believe that sustained hateful thoughts toward another is evil. Total indifference to the suffering of others when we have the means to relieve that suffering is one of the greatest evils of human kind. Any action, thought or deed designed to inflict pain is evil without compromise.

Tan : I begin to better comprehend this concept. Let me say that among the multitude of Biaveh, it is not unknown that some being may, on occasion, be given to performing some act of indiscretion against another. Yet the emotion is fleeting and the nature contrite.

It is well-known that emotions in varied extremes are not conducive to the orderly functioning of the physical body, thus to deliberately invite and sustain such vibrations is to disrupt the resonance of the 'Omsa'. Yet I realize that the Biaviians, as one, are not afflicted with the many chemical imbalances and genetic mutation disorders as pervade the Homo sapien bi-ped species of Earth. Still this entire measure of evil upon your sphere far exceeds the context of physiological disorder. Thus it may be theorized that evil is a thing which is genetically inherent in your order. Yet upon closer scrutiny of the life spans and selfless actions of a number among you, it is found that an existence devoid of sustained evil and hatred is quite possible on a mass if not universal scale among humans. Do you believe the human is inherently evil?

Martin : No, humanity obviously is not totally one thing or the other. It is neither all good or all evil. Instead I believe man inherently holds a measure of both good and evil, and the strength of his inner self and sense of common judgment decides the extent to which he will give sway to these dormant emotions. While an imbalance in body chemistry may push the rare individual over the edge into the zone of sporadically pure evil. I believe that evil is much more a product of deliberate premeditated wish.

The fact that historically more mass movements have been motivated by evil than by good and that hatred in its many forms seems to prevail as a more tangible force upon the Earth at this time indicates to me that the sado-sexual gratification from the emotion of hatred tends to exceed that derived from good emotion.

The mental and physical release gained from the murder of an enemy is generally more intense than the mental and physical sensation gained from helping a friend or an enemy. To the hateful person, evil is a drug which is far more addicting than heroin or cocaine, and in order to satisfy this addiction men collectively practice things like apartheid, slavery, conservatism and pure racial bigotry.

The ruling factor in South Africa is literally sustained by the collective practice of evil, and the ruling faction of this country is sustained by the same though less direct levels of that anomaly. The preoccupation of the ruling factions of this planet with institutionalized evil is with minor variations universal, and yet I don't believe that evil in itself is biologically inherent in the human species.

If given the proper motivation from the top down, or from the bottom upward, or from the center outward. I believe that good could prevail among mankind. Instead the potential good in people is often suppressed by the communal consensus which emanates from the most forceful element, which are the leaders, or the most economically powerful.

At this time, these leaders, while comprising a very small numerical factor of the whole, still control the flow of human sociological endeavor. In other words, this planet is almost devoid of powerful motivation toward good, while being saturated with powerful motivators of evil.

Does this mean that humanity has lost the battle between good and evil? I cannot say.

Tan : All ecological, atmosphere and sociological data compiled by Elohim concerning your species unto this point indicate with overwhelming probability that humanity as you know it cannot long endure. Yet we are but physical beings, and neither our knowledge or technology is infallible. We may observe the past at leisure yet the future must linger in the zone of conjecture and probability.

Martin : What are the odds of humanity surviving total or near extinction upon the Earth?

Tan : Eight percent positive and ninety-two negative.

Martin : Then what's the chances of me getting the fuck outta here before the shit comes down?

Tan : Fifty, Fifty.

Martin : Have you played any direct part in my survival unto this point?

Tan : Martin, you well know that it is forbidden to intervene directly in the chosen destiny of humans, and I concur with this directive as it would open channels which might grow to dominate the mental order of your entire species. Nor is there enough knowledge among us of the human psychology to even attempt such an undertaking.

I have embraced our friendship, and it has been my delight to have visited your inner mind on occasion over the time to experience your emotions and to impart to you some little things of interest. In this manner your comprehension of my reason has been greatly enhanced even without your conscious awareness.

Martin : In other words, you've been fudging the rule?

Tan : Correct.

Martin : I understand that you are completely convinced that the force of life continues after physical death. So am I. But what about the individual consciousness, where does it go and what does it do after death? What is the order of things after physical life? Is there punishment or reward, heaven or hell?

Tan : Martin, give unto me a break and get serious. True this question has been contemplated, researched and theorized by the Elohim and Stagyians since time immemorial. There is a specific group here at this time who are preoccupied with this aspect of human continuum. Because of the volatile emotional nature of humans, they have proven to be ideal subjects for this research. We have succeeded in verifying the continuance of the life force by recording its presence on sensitive instruments. So of its existence we have no doubt. In seeking to comprehend the modus of these non-physical entities, we have reached certain decisive points, yet no universal conclusions.

It would appear that there are varied zones or levels of after-life consciousness. Some entities by wish alone or through a misconception of their present status are capable of interfacing with sub-atomic particles and achieving visibility to the physical eye. In most cases the time frame prevailing at the point of demise tends to be fixed and unchanging. Further research has revealed that the esoteric or terror punishment or reward concept tends to reflect the inner orientation and spiritual mode of the human at the point of demise.

We further believe that like mentalities tend to flock together in the outer realms, and that the negative or evil minions are more prone to activity seek to re-enter this plane via artificial or unnatural means, while the satisfied or fulfilled entities rarely have any conscious wish to return.

In computing the heaven and hell factor, we theorize that there are as many variations of each as there are conceptions of same, and may be as distinct in projection as the individual personalities of the 'Omsa'. We believe that geographical and planetary place fixation is a matter of spirit-wish ignorance. While those so inclined may traverse the far reaches of the cosmos. There does not seem to be any electronic or physical boundaries governing the universal movement of the enterprising spirit. Thus it would not be uncommon for a spirit to escape this planet and be physically reborn on another planet.

It is not uncommon for a writer of science fiction upon your planet to be simply recording true memories of past physical spans at some point in the cosmos. Since time as you perceive it on this plane holds no meaning to the other dimensional entity, the span between death and rebirth may span a few years or an eon, and yet seem as only a day to that entity. Apparently that spirit has no control over the circumstances, sex, race or social position of its rebirth.

We base these rationalizations upon existing data

gained, yet freely admit that our assessments must be viewed as theory and deductive conjecture instead of fact immutable. Does this assist you in any manner?

Martin : Yes. My own research into the paranormal had already led me to conclude that life as a force continues, but you have helped to reinforce that conclusion and to further convince me that I may not be completely nutty.

But what about the Biaviians? Don't you have your own ghosts? What of their outer body dimensions?

Tan : Our after life entities are no less alive than are your own, yet the resonance of their presence is much less expressive and far more difficult to record than that of humans. Perhaps that is because Biaviians are less given to emotional extremes than humans are. And remember that most physical death among Biaviians is a voluntary transition, and thus there is little conscious incentive to interact with this plane of consciousness. We know far less of our own outer infinity than we have come to learn of yours. Because of the short gestation spans of humans, they make, as I have afore stated, ideal subjects. We have literally observed the entire physical spans of entire generations of certain fixed communities, and this observation has proven fascinating.

Martin : Do you believe that it is possible to learn too much of the workings of infinity, or that some things are better left unknown?

Tan : But for the active suppression of knowledge throughout your genesis, man might at this moment be traversing the farthest reaches of this galaxy.

Martin, I tell you truly, the Biaviians are an ancient culture with a recorded history exceeding a billion of your measured years, and yet the culmination of all of our knowledge gained may be compared to one drop of water in the vast ocean of the universe.

That which we have yet to learn exceeds the imaginative theorems of all minds yet born and the aspirations of all those yet to come. He who places limitations upon the quest for knowledge is seeking to halt the motion of infinity. Knowledge alone is never detrimental. It is the use to which this knowledge is put that decides its merit or detriment.

Because humanity was taken artificially from his natural order of progression and given the rudiments of mathematics, agriculture and medicine, he has advanced much faster technologically than befits his baser prerogative, and the result is what you see before you. Thus we are bound by our own past intervention to rescue a segment of your species so that physical extinction shall not claim you.

Martin : If your people played such a prominent role in the ascension of man, and if you feel such a responsibility toward humanity, then why don't you just come in and take over and set him on the right path. Surely you have the power to do so.

Tan : The original genetic experimentation and the blood assimilation between Elohim and human far exceeded the home directive.

There was no contact between the expedition and Biaveh due to damage incurred during the Targzissian conflict, and the situation had progressed to a universal level upon our next contact with the planet Earth. We concede that the level of that experimentation was a mistake, yet direct military intervention into the affairs of an intelligent planet is out of the question.

Martin : What about fear? Do the Biaviians fear anything?

Tan : The emotion called fear is essential to the survival of any species which must co-exist among other predatory creatures. In this sense, humans have just cause to fear other humans. When the element of immediate danger diminishes or becomes unknown, then natural fear diminishes accordingly.

We of Biaveh have achieved a state of being which is virtually immune to immediate physical danger and so have no tangible cause to fear, and yet even we are initially wary of any unknown element. Fear as you have seen and experienced is not our common plight. Then neither is emotional joy. I have experienced this emotion fleetingly in you on several occasions and found it fascinating.

Martin : What about love? Do Biaviians experience the emotion in the manner that humans experience it?

Tan : As with other emotions common to humans, we are not given to experiencing extremes in any manner. It is true that even among Biaviians there is a bond of spirit between male and female that transcends the common resonance, yet save for the rare moment of procreative intent, the emotion remains on a nearly un-fluctuating plane. The peak force may transpire but once, twice or thrice during a Biaviian's life span.

I have felt your emotions undergo extreme alterations while in the company of your friend, Question, and the varied levels of your emotions have served to enrich me upon the potential modes of the human species. Yet when tabulating your emotional data in its entirety, I have concluded that your general intent is to love, even when given logical cause to embrace a more negative resonance. Your ability to love Question commends you highly.

Martin : Oh, yes, I love Question alright. I'd love to get that little mother fucker in a pot with about two pounds of onions.

Tan : It is well that we Biaviians communicate on the telepathic plane lest we be afflicted with the propensity of humans to articulate a thing and intend another. Your negative statements, while extreme only serve to reveal the true depth of your care and compassion. You speak ill of humanity, yet you care greatly. If all of mankind could love in this manner, there then would be no limit as to what he could accomplish.

Martin : Even through it all I have never been able to hate people in general, but I hate wrongness and injustice from wherever it comes. It pisses me off considerably to have some politician tell me that we can spend six hundred dollars for a two dollar claw hammer, but we can't afford to give kids lunch at school. Or to spend a hundred billion dollars to build more bombs, when they already have enough shit to kill every man, woman and child on the Earth ten times over. They can spend two hundred billion to bail out Savings & Loans, but they can't find the money to save the American farmer. They can find five hundred million to build new prisons, but can't find the money to create job training and industry for the inner city poor.

It breaks my heart to realize that humanity has literally given sway to evil, deception, stupidity and greed, but a bigger infraction still is to expect me to buy this shit and be satisfied.

Tan : The falsification of fact and the corruption of truth has long been the destroyer of civilizations. When deception becomes common and ignorance is enforced, the ultimate destruction of a system is assured. This preoccupation of man to speak one thing and do another, I fear, has damaged the psych and ecological balance of the Earth beyond retrieval. That such a living paradise has been so wasted is indeed a sad thing.

Martin : According to Earth scientists, the acceleration speed and aerial maneuvers performed by your ships seem impossible or go against the laws of physics. How is your propulsion system generated? How do you nullify the weightlessness of space.

Tan : Your law of physics is based upon matter, force and resistance, and thus conforms to your equation of motion in the elemental sense, yet the very planet upon which you stand exemplifies a most tangible form of encapsulated universal stability. At a point, all forces in opposition to the other tend to counteract all equal force, thereby nullifying the centrifugal effects of motion. Whereas your planet does revolve at a rate exceeding a thousand of your measured miles per hour, while moving around your sun at some eighty-eight thousand miles per hour, you stand unaffected and mayhap unaware of the motion.

The force you call gravity, while being influenced by your moon and sun, works in a complimentary fashion to stabilize. There have been and yet are a few among us you who are capable of physical levitation by manipulating the electromagnetic forces with the mind. Observe the common honey bee. In body weight and aerodynamic design it cannot possibly fly, and yet it does so by literally manipulating the electromagnetic currents around. Thus, its wings do not sustain but simply alter the flight pattern or control it, if you will.

The sphere (ship) in which you are now reclining is but an artificial microcosm of an entire planet or a larger version of your honey bee. In the encapsulated world of this sphere, there is no up or down or sense of physical motion because its interior is an isolated 'here'. There is no there.

The power source of this sphere is a common fusion generator and is fueled by Hydrogen, which is an abundant factor throughout the cosmos. We move about by generating an electromagnetic field around this sphere, and the manipulation of this field is the manner by which our traverse and direction is accomplished. To move toward an object we adopt the opposite magnetic essence and to move away we simply adopt a like magnetic essence. Should our power source be lost or malfunction, we would then be governed by your common laws of motion. It is also through the manipulation of these forces that we may attain near light speed and then warp to hyper-space, which effectively nullifies the dimensional physics of time.

Martin : In all of these years that we have known one another, I remained unaware, until recently, just how many people have had experiences similar to my own, and from what I can gather, most of these people live in terror of you.

Their abduction and the experiments you have performed upon them have in some cases given them psychological complexes and real or imagined physical infirmities that they cannot overcome. Perhaps you don't realize just how great an effect you have had on the lives of many earthlings, but in view of it, I find it hard to visualize tens of thousands who will be prepared to place all their trust in you.

How do I know that you aren't just using me to get more guinea pigs for your experiments? How do I know that you are not, in reality, monsters? Granted, you and I have spent much time together, and I truly believe that your heart is decent and compassionate. Yet I really don't know much about any other Biaviians besides you and Nela. I'm fascinated by the things I've seen, but what of the things I haven't been shown? Why should I try to get other earthlings to trust you? And why do you need me anyway? These questions continue to perplex me. So would you please set my mind at rest? Give me peace in what I go to do. I hope that my queries do not cause you to take offense.

Tan : No, Martin, I take no offense, as your queries are logical and fair. In truth we have visited thousands who yet remain unconscious of that meeting. It is also true that the Targs have visited many, and it would seem that the mind pacification processes of the Targs is flawed so that many yet retain partial recall of some moments of discomfort.

The destruction of human brain tissue is forbidden and so is the disfiguration of the physical. Yet some imperfections in procedure have transpired on the Targ's part and like so, ours. In giving attention to the unblemished physical, I'm sure we failed to truly comprehend the depth of the human psyche equation.

We have long observed the most crude tissue destroying methods of your species illness treaters (doctor), and the predatory manner in which you treat your child, your elders, your brothers, your lower creatures, yet we break not the skin nor cleave the inner organs.

In mindless machines do thousands die upon your planet, even as we speak, and millions more suffer the death bringer of your poisoned waters and chemical clouds. Yet I tell you truly, Martin, not by our hands has one human died nor suffered physical pain beneath our scrutiny. Still we have been wrong in not comprehending the psychic effects on the terrians who have been so visited by creatures unknown such as we.

You may trust me not by force of inner emotions alone, but by the elements of common logic. Were my motives untrue would they not best be practiced upon the powerful, the gullible and the untrue leaders of your world instead of Martin? Or then, why bother deception at all when man possesses naught but the power to destroy himself instead of me and mine?

Upon our part, it is but a true attempt to better comprehend the mind and emotions of man. How else may we even do him service or learn his needs? You are chosen because of the openness of your spirit and reason and because of your genetic lineage. You have been shown this much, yet to have shown you more would well have disoriented even your psyche, which is beyond common measure. And this you have seen exceeds that of most other men of Earth, even unto Tesla, Copernicus, Hannibal and Elijah.

In the time span remaining of which I have told you, there is no immutable certainty that man himself will not nullify the gathering by doing the unforeseen and literally destroying his own species. You see, this gathering cannot be of random survivors but of those chosen.

Yes, I can say with near certainty that your planet will undergo drastic alterations, yet not even the Stagyians can pinpoint to the hour or the day. This element must remain in the zone of theorem, which is based upon data thus far compiled. Sadly I must say that our scientists have never been far wrong thus far in their projections.

I tell you truly, Martin, that we shall not take one who wishes not to go. We have not sought to control your reason or to bend your will by artificial means, and I shall not impose upon you any oath or promise against your will. You will write of me because you know me by sight, sound and touch, and because you have contemplated the logic and found no rational choice but to believe and because you yet wish to see so many things yet unseen. So then to further question this reality is folly.

You may be assured that any truth thus far denied you results from my ignorance and psychological limitations and not of conscious wish or treachery.

Then will you pass this along?

Martin : Fuckin A.

Chapter 15

On the Future of Humanity

It is safe to say that our actions today will, to a great extent, shape the happenings of tomorrow, so it doesn't take a genius to coherently speculate upon some future scenarios based upon the data existing today.

As I have said before, the future projections on Earth put forth by the Biaviians are based upon the scientific data that they have thus far amassed. In my opinion, the aliens do not depend upon any kind of psychic clairvoyance in drawing their conclusions, but upon soil samples, water and plant samples, temperature variations and atmospheric contents, as well as geological strata and seismic disturbances. The actual physical form of man plays a minor biological part in the overall picture, but the by-products and ecological destruction wrought by his mode of existence do play a most prominent role in the shape of things to come. His flagrant disregard for, and seeming ignorance of, biological functions of the planet, is to the aliens quite reprehensible.

The seeming necessity of man to destroy millions of acres of living trees in order to make more paper, when enough recyclable paper already exists to cut this destruction by two-thirds, is lost upon them. They know that human life on Earth cannot hold its numerical value without trees, while the trees cannot reproduce fast enough to replace the rate of depletion.

To them, nearly all of man's greater action seems to be a headlong determination toward imminent suicide, and this makes no rational sense at all, especially as man does not possess the technological means to depopulate the dying planet through interplanetary migration.

When they look at humanity, they see something like a hill of ants, who are willfully feeding the queen a slow acting but deadly poison, thus assuring their own extinction as a species.

Try as they might, they have not been able to discern any underlying master plan to man's madness. Thus humanity forfeits any right to esoteric consideration by the Targs. The Targs have long held the philosophy that human beings should not be considered any more than laboratory specimens, despite the conviction held by the Biaviians that humanity, while totally misguided, holds celestial qualities.

This is only conjecture on my part, but I believe that the Insectillians 'Skreed' views humanity only as a slightly harmful but swiftly passing malignancy, which will soon give sway to the true masters of the Earth, the insect kingdom. This rationale is quite logical as the insects would certainly survive even in the case of all-out nuclear war. If you should travel to the far reaches of the cosmos, observing the various life forms, you would undoubtedly discover a million insect species for every single intelligent or sub-intelligent mammalian species living. So all the odds are on the insects side.

We find that like most creatures, when man comes upon a system that works, he becomes locked into that system to such a degree that even considering a radical change tends to terrify him. But just like those creatures in nature who are unable or unwilling to change, extinction is sometimes inevitable.

We know that mankind is capable of great accomplishments when faced with desperate situations. In the past, these great undertakings and changes were made because the reasons of necessity were clearly visible and urgent. For instance, the institution of fairer laws concerning the masses transpired in Europe as an aftermath of the Black Plaque in the fourteenth century, when so many died that labor was at a premium. Thus the people could demand better wages, fairer laws, etc.

Higher wages caused a great consumer market to arrive, which hastened the rise of the Industrial Revolution, and mass production machinery. As countries became more economically prosperous, they found it expedient to create better war machinery in order to keep abreast or ahead of aggressive neighbors.

Injuries, pestilence and disease caused by wars and famine brought about more open-minded and comprehensive research into medicine, food preservation and communications. Divine authority diminished in proportion to technological advancement and science began to take on a more prominent position. The rapid growth of metropolitan population brought about the creation of sanitation and health departments, professional schools, sewer systems and a host of other necessary entities.

It is a fact that no great changes toward the common good of all people have ever transpired unless the common people were in a position to demand these changes. The ruling factions have never voluntarily given up anything. We find that world circumstances have been changed by revolution and not by evolution.

The plague gave worth to the working man, but the invention of mass production machines proceeded to diminish that individual worth once again. Soon this led to debtors prison, execution for minor offenses, deportation and indentured servitude. The rich class had never changed in its abhorrence of the poorer classes, and the Industrial Revolution only added to the number of the wealthy elite. Children were literally working to death in factories and women in sweat shops, while men lost their lives by the thousands in the mines. This terrible suppression of the masses led to the American Revolution and then to the French Revolution, in which cases the serfs rose up and overthrew the masters.

To curtail some of the power of the new rich industrialists, the people demanded and got some laws passed concerning working conditions, wages, child labor and formed unions to hold on to these paper rights. As a result, the largest middle class on the Earth arose in America and also the most comprehensive and democratic constitution in existence. For two whole generations labor was king, and the country prospered on the mass level, but with the advent of the electronic revolution and the rise of the conservative faction, once again we find that the unions have been destroyed, civil rights are swiftly deteriorating and the middle class is being continually diminished in number and worth.

Once again the rich elite hold the reins of destiny in their hands, and this time their power will not be usurped by a civil revolution but by the destruction of the planet itself. So we all lose this one.

In this assessment I could be proven wrong, but only if the controlling faction would immediately choose to sacrifice a tenth of their present profit margin for the good of the ecology and the people, but as we said, such a transition among the rich has never voluntarily transpired in all of recorded history so I certainly don't see it happening now.

Because of my rather adamant condemnation of the overall actions of the rulers of this society and the bigotries of the majority masses, one might easily get the impression that I don't like people very much, but this conclusion would be wrong because I truly do care deeply for all good people.

I do not like, condone, uphold or pay lip service to wrongness regardless of its source. I am critical of the ruling elite because their every action has been to their own benefit at the cost of trashing a large segment of society. I am critical of the American majority mass because they willfully vote these nigger haters into office at the cost of much of their own economic solvency, and by the time they truly realize that the minority didn't foreclose on their farms or close down their factories or poison their lakes, it may be too late to rescind their initial decision which was to cause harm to the niggers only.

I have said that the American majority member is the most hateful, gullible and stupid political pawn on the face of the Earth, and I find no justification in altering that opinion in the least. Europeans, in general, are capable of great benevolence when sufficiently inspired, but they are capable of an ever greater evil when the nod is given by their leaders.

It is true that in western society a young minority male upon meeting a violent end will do so in most cases at the hands of another minority male, while on the other hand, most Europeans who meet a violent end do so at the hands of another European and not at the hands of a minority member. Yet it is common practice for most of society's ills to be laid at the door of the minorities. For the most part, minority members do not commit mass murders, serial killings, child murders and baby molestations. Should the European rise up tomorrow and kill or imprison every minority member of the Western Hemisphere, it would not save him from the aforementioned beastliness which unfortunately seems to be an integral part of his nature and seems to have been so since the first mention of him in the hieroglyphics of ancient Egypt.

And now he has brought this planet to the brink of extinction. If left to his own sentiments and designs, there can be no hope for the continuation of human life as we know it.

On very rare occasions, the over-zealous and greedy inner city dope dealer may mix and sell a drug which will kill a dozen people, yet even as I speak, reputable pharmaceutical companies are willfully selling contaminated or worthless generic drugs, which will kill or maim tens of thousands.

At this moment some inner city thief is snatching some lady's purse or stealing some one's television. Also at this moment some big city banker, in collusion with the government, is stealing the farms of a thousand hard-working people. At this moment some inner city drug dealer is dispensing a hundred pounds of cocaine onto the streets, and this drug will no doubt cause the ruination of hundreds and the death of a few.

While at this moment an upstanding chemical company is releasing fifteen thousand pounds of deadly acids into the atmosphere every hour and will no doubt cause the slow death of tens of thousands of people, trees, animals and lakes.

I don't say that your priorities are completely wrong, but I can say that your vision is decidedly myopic and your judgment perversely flawed in realizing the magnitude of the danger that is facing us all.

By denying a whole segment of society the opportunity to

enter society constructively, you literally guarantee the arising of great criminal enterprises and no segment of society will remain untouched or uncorrupted by any cancer of their own making. The twisted and bigoted news media seek to give the impression that dope and crime are predominantly an inner city, and thus a minority problem, but this cannot erase the fact that a whole European generation is being trashed by the same problems or that your politicians are spending your tax dollars in homosexual sex rings and foreclosing on your homes.

Those worthy human attributes like ethics, honor and common decency have been relegated to the position of thin facades of convenience, and the media and propaganda picture of the person has little to do with the true realities of his worth.

Charlatans, thieves and perverts know one another at a glance, and the one who does not fit this mode is discarded as soon as possible from among the politicians and the religious hierarchy. The government bureaucracy in its entirety is basically bought and paid for by the big business interests. This universal collusion of big business, religion and government to absorb and divide the spoils of easily manipulated societies has been refined to an art, while a greater portion of the citizens live with the delusion that they are being duly represented by their elected officials.

The politicians know that the best way to prevent some fairly honest person from gaining public power is to fashion the financial and media systems in such a way that the poor sucker doesn't even get a chance to run in the first place. By making sure that all candidates are fellow thieves, they are able to perpetuate a no-lose situation, and this is the state of things at this time in this country, and indeed in the world as a whole.

In many parts of the world where religion play a major part in the social and political processes, a great percentage of the common people may believe that their wars are based upon some divine principles, but the leaders know that it's all about money and power. They know that any political position, whether elective or appointed, is of import only to the extent of its thievery potential.

If you believe that the constitutional amendments and the legal statutes apply to any person without money in this country or any other, then you are rudely mistaken. Nothing you own, including your life, is safe from legal and political incursion, and within the next decade, most of you would have been herded into a political and economic corner of deprivation from whence you cannot by law emerge. Under the guise of law and order, your bigotry and gullibility will cause you to vote away the few remaining rights at your disposal, because in the rich man's eyes your worth no longer fits into the human equation but has been relegated to the statistical realm of numbers, dollars and cents, asset and liability, and the foot soldiers, who are the police, will keep you all suppressed. All of you.

As I've said before, big business, politicians, preachers and state bureaucrats are on a mad feeding frenzy, which, if unchecked, will completely absorb all of the liquid wealth of this country, and bring about the literal extinction of the middle class. Don't delude yourself into believing that there is a point where the rich man decides that he has taken enough away from you, because in his mentality, no such point exists.

Do not expect that the great industrialists who pollute the rivers and atmosphere will ever reach the point of voluntarily cleaning up their acts. Unto this point, there has never been a secret, military or otherwise, which hasn't been sold to the enemy, nor has the wealthy class as an equal ever been made to suffer equal punishment for their crimes against humanity. Yet every person down to the smallest stockholder is guilty of the crimes of the company.

No doubt many will say it's not my fault that this or that company uses slave labor in South Africa or that this company has destroyed a whole lake or forest. Yet you purchase the wares of the former and own stock in the latter.

The man Jesus said, "This you have done to those, the least of my brothers, you do also unto me". I believe in this parable, regardless of its source, because common sense and decency give me to realize that, like it or not, I am my brother's keeper. I consider the abuse of any man, woman or child on this planet a direct attack upon me personally, and should I stand idly by and raise no objection to injustice then I am just as guilty as the perpetrator. On this there can be no compromise.

In the nineteen sixties we had a phenomena transpire in America, which for a time actually threatened to turn this country into a democracy in action as well as name. This phenomena may be more aptly described as a mass rebellion of the young against the sins of their fathers.

At the time America was embroiled in two circumstances which were the antithesis of everything that this country is supposed to stand for. The first was as aggressive and unpopular war against people who had never done us any harm and, indeed, whom most of us had never even heard of before. This was the Vietnam war. Secondly, on the home front, the nation was enmeshed in a great moralistic struggle over the civil rights issue in this country.

For the first time the young people of America began to openly question, scrutinize and then rebel against governmental and parental authority, which they perceived as transparently false and without any tangible moralistic base. They understood that it was a glaring contradiction for their parents to profess love of God and family while preaching hatred of the racial sort toward their fellow man. Napalming Vietnamese villages seven thousand miles away to prevent the expansion of communism while supporting a corrupt, thieving, cowardly regime just didn't mesh with America's professed noble principles.

The ongoing preoccupation of the American government in lending financial and, if necessary, military support to some of the most cold blooded killers, torturers and dictators on the Earth, like Marcos in the Philippines and Samoza in Nicaragua, completely alienated the young in America.

In turning away from parental and governmental authority, much of that baby boom generation sought to find truth and direction in the streets, Eastern religions and communes. Their disenchantment with the moral fortitude of their parents and government led to a dropping out of society for many and to acts of aggressive sabotage and disorder on the part of others. Still others sought to find themselves in drugs, which led many into the sordid and heartless world of prostitution, thievery and other vices. Just about the only tangible fact that resulted from that time was a general loss of moral and spiritual direction.

That same generation has emerged today to be the major political and economical force in the country. Those parents, whom they rebelled against at that time, have become the discarded and unloved senior citizens of today.

The baby boomers never truly regained the love they formerly held for their parents, and without that source, they tended never to develop love for other humans or even their offspring. They did, however, find sanctuary in the embracing of the status quo, the love of money. In order to truly love money, one must be prepared to suppress or sacrifice all sublime human principles. That love of Mammon and that disregard for the sanctity of family love has now been passed on to the offspring of that rebellious generation. The result is that they have spawned a generation of vipers, not only in the European but in the minority races also, because the strong minority leaders were killed off, leaving their subordinates and hangers-on, who have become symbolically the minority leaders of today. Never have a more spineless bunch of brown-nosed sellouts existed on Earth than these so-called minority representatives of today. Skinning and grinning and kissing ass has been raised to an art by the minority elite of today.

So we are faced with a younger generation devoid of morals, purpose and direction and an older generation of thieves, graft takers and perverts. As a result, America has essentially gone to shit, while dragging much of the planet down into the muck and mire with it.

We are swiftly heading toward an existence which will be driven by suppression, poverty and terror. The factor of brotherly love has become the exception instead of the norm. Barred windows and semi-automatic weapons are replacing trust, mass imprisonment and street war are replacing civil rights and due process of law. Soon it will become a near impossibility for the average citizen to eat without running afoul of the law.

The same Internal Revenue Service which caters to the rich

has begun to send out letters informing the minimum wage earner of back taxes owed, thereby making criminals of the only segment of society which has always paid its taxes.

Any sensible person knows that it is literally impossible for a citizen to pay the rent, utilities, eat, pay insurance on automobiles and park his car on the average salary. Thus the government, in collusion with big business, has made criminals of most non-wealthy citizens in this country, and they won't be satisfied even after they have completely destroyed the liquid holdings of the whole of society with the exception of themselves.

Even the downtown parking meters are rigged so that a person cannot park their car and do a day's work without getting a ticket and thus becoming a misdemeanor criminal. Only those people making good money can afford to rent a personalized parking space close to their place of employment.

By virtue of being forced to take subsistence pay level jobs, more formerly middle class people are being literally forced to rent places in high crime areas, and resort to many cases to felonious activities in order to make ends meet. The new poor quickly learn that is very dangerous in certain areas to even have a decent car and other accouterments that they were used to before.

Ultimately the criminal and the underworld sympathizers are going to greatly outnumber the ones who are attempting the near impossibility of living within the law. At that point, it is going to prove very dangerous to be a police officer and a rich man.

The seeds for organized social unrest and covert terroristic organizations have already been sown in this country, and these are going to make the SLA and the minute men look like amateurs. Such a social backlash is the inevitable outcome of a system of social and economic oppression in any country. You now see it happening in Russia and its satellite countries, China and many other places. Violent rebellion is always the last resort of the suppressed masses. However, these actions on the part of the people in no way diminish the belief of the rich rulers that they can still maintain their fortunes and positions by using greater measures of terror and suppression instead of actually setting about to relieve the suffering of the people.

Now in America, the political rhetoric in Washington is the building of more prisons, the lengthening of prison sentences, the criminalization of erstwhile misdemeanor crimes and expansion and re-arming of police departments, not the reopening of factories, the saving of the farmers or the filtering of industrial pollutants, nor even the feeding and retraining of the hungry and the homeless.

The entire projected situation is geared toward the protection of the rich and the imprisonment and destruction of the poor, and those who cannot yet see this are fools indeed.

What humanity at large and rich people in general fail to realize is that all paper money, stocks, bonds, precious metals and jewels are but symbolic items of worth. When it comes down to true actual value, the man with a bushel of vegetables in hand during a famine is the possessor of the only riches.

What it boils down to is that if you can't eat it, drink it or fuck it, then it holds no literal value. A person can live without money or trinkets, but when you take away this ability to feed himself and his family, you had better get ready to kill him because he is coming to kill you.

If you and I are on a shipwrecked life boat and have the water and food, while you have a bank account and the credit cards, you will starve if I refuse to honor your paper and metal.

Red China is a country governed basically by necessity, and necessity dictates that all arable land be used for growing food in order to feed its people. Thus far they are able to feed the existing population of that country.

On the other hand, all capitalist countries are governed by the stock market, and if the stock market takes an extreme plunge, people can starve while millions of rich acres lay fallow. If famine hits China, it means that for so reason they were unable to grow enough food to feed the populace. The existence of any hunger in an economically and agriculturally rich country like America can only be the result of too much greed at the top. It certainly cannot be attributed to a lack of resources.

Over the last decade, a great segment of America society has changed from a relatively stationary, savings in the bank society to a more transient, renter, non-saving, consumer society. The overall living standard of middle and lower earning America has continued to decline, while the rich have been in a greater ascendancy.

The closing of factories in favor of overseas labor, the decline of the American oil worker in favor of Eastern oil and the diminishing of well paying jobs has caused a rippling effect, and as a result home ownership is in decline. This has caused a glut of homes for sale, while property value is in a proportional decline. In the meantime, the flood of foreign made imports has risen drastically.

Car buyers, television, stereo and VCR owners would have started to hang on to their present wares for an extra year or two. People will no longer eat out regularly, buy new wardrobes, change their tires or make large commitments for new homes and such. This will prove to be catastrophic for thousands of businesses and cause a panic of selling on Wall Street. Computer sales will decline and so will the sale of heavy machinery and building materials. Farm commodity prices will drop to a level which will make it more expedient for farmers to hold back on expansion and planted acreage.

When car dealerships and other businesses cut back on borrowing or go into bankruptcy, many banks will find it necessary to raise interest rates and many will fold. OPEC's oil prices will go down to around $16.00 a barrel, but buying will still slow down because people won't be traveling as much, which will hurt the vacations areas. The reason oil buyers will be shy is because they would have filled all of their storage tanks and will not want to spend the capital to build more tanks, nor will they wish to make huge forward purchases in the volatile Middle East. The mass lay-offs resulting from these happenings and a general social unrest which is starting to grow at this point will cause outbursts of rioting and near anarchy in many of the larger cities.

And when we suffer, of course this will cause much of the western world and all of those countries who depend upon America for their export economy to suffer. Prices on food, perishables and many other items will go down. But America is becoming a country that doesn't buy great stacks of cheap items like food any more. A cheap computer or VCR means nothing to the person who already has one. He has become unsure of his job and his future, so he just won't buy or make any commitments.

The big companies will cut their losses by simply cutting back on production, purchases and personnel. A rash of buy-outs and mergers will occur, and the government is going to be forced to step back and reassess the situation.

Countries who cannot sell to us will be forced to renege or default on loans owed America, and this country would have taken another downward step closer to social and economic fragmentation. Because property value has suffered greatly over the last decade, foreigners have found it expedient to purchase vast amounts of American real estate and buildings. These foreign buyers realize that the land is the only truly valuable commodity. They gladly pay exorbitant prices in dollars for land, because in the last analysis the dollar itself is transitory but the land is forever. In selling off America real estate to overseas interests, Americans are doing something which is tantamount to a person systematically selling off his body organs while he yet lives. He may not immediately feel the effects of the missing kidney, but in the end it cannot help but weaken his body.

Soon you may be denied access to certain parts of American beaches by ex-dictators, Arabs and Orientals. But go to Tokyo and try to buy some land. You will find that is forbidden by law.

But all of this is just incidental when compared to the far greater problems yet to be faced by this planet. You may be sure that a number of people in high places are well aware of the precarious position in which the planet now stands, but their moves to correct the impending cataclysm are too little too late.

You may have noticed of late that Russia and America have begun to de-emphasize the necessity of expanding existing nuclear stockpiles and are even seeking to reduce the present mega tonnage. They are carrying this out because of the economical drain upon their economics by the military apparatus and because even a fool must eventually realize that possessing enough fire power to kill the world's population ten times over should be sufficient. The nuclear waste materials already in existence from the fabrication of past weapons is so great that no one knows how to safely dispose of it. At least the Russians have faced up to this reality even if the conservative hawks of America have not.

The last thing that anybody wants is a war between the great powers. In fact you are much safer with a Russian than you are on the New York City subway. The time of great world ground wars is past and will not transpire again as long as they have the bomb. So the greater powers must now content themselves with instigating and supporting small wars within and between smaller Third World countries.

Within the next two decades, should humanity still exist, it is going to be necessary to institute programs, which in today's unrealistic moralistic atmosphere would seem unthinkable. The world has only two choices. Humanity will either have to practice mass contraceptive methods or institute forced euthanasia. There is no way around this inevitability. Sporadic ground wars are no longer sufficient to handle the population problem.

Droughts and famine will begin to transpire on a greater basis, but these natural happenstances will not be enough to control the population growth problem. Terrorism will reach such destructive proportions that concerted military actions without regard to legal ethics will have to be mounted, and in five years, by 1994, terrorism will rise in America and besiege the elite of this country. The police forces of this country will find that their jobs will no longer consist of simply rousting minorities, beating up drunks and burglarizing stories, but will start to be literally dangerous.

Never before in the history of humanity have so many deadly elements been at work upon the Earth at one time. All of these things I've spoken of thus far in this book have come to the crucial stage and have already begun to manifest themselves in undiluted forms. The great increase in desperate and irrational actions transpiring all over the planet at this time are born of some subconscious realization of the coming cataclysm.

The creeping mechanism of chemical saturation is upon us, and few locations are yet un-polluted by these deadly elements. They are in the air, the water, the soil, the vegetables and the meats. They are pooling in human bodies, destroying metabolisms, twisting chromosomes and manifesting themselves in nightmares and acts of dementia. The human species at large cannot know the full extent to which it has and is being effected by these things.

The ever more progressively ruthless character of each successive generation is much more than just a product of parental and social moralistic breakdown, but is also the side effect of the very pollution in the atmosphere and the diet.

It is a fact that society is experiencing dangerous psychopaths in great numbers, and the rise in these murderous incidents is in direct proportion to the rise in chemical pollutants in a given area. This is exemplified by the fact that the psychopath rate in some of the most densely populated countries on Earth is far less than that in the more chemically polluted western countries. Mass murders, serial killings, rapist and murderers are a rarity in countries like Red China and India, though one would think that such densely populated and poverty stricken places would be rife with psychotics.

Of course, pollution and diet alone are not the only elements that feed these mentally warped individuals, but these elements do agitate and concentrate the intensity of such syndromes. Within the next ten years as the newest generation comes of age, the maniac factor will reach epidemic proportions.

If you believe my projections to be too extreme, then I challenge you to stop and honestly assess the overall mentality of the people around you, your children, wives, husbands, friends and associates, and you will no doubt be compelled to come to the realization that a kind of mass irrationality is swiftly infecting all levels of humanity.

Just beneath this every day psychological shell lies the instinctive realization that the world is coming to the breakdown point. It is a subconscious foreboding of impending doom.

To a great extent western women have somehow collectively decided to stop having children, and in those parts of the world where such contraceptive methods are either not available or forbidden, life in general has lost its worth and sanctity. The streets are literally being over-run by great masses of homeless urchins.

Terrorism, racial hatred and small wars of attrition have become the order of the day. New oil wealth and advancing technological productivity has only tended to exacerbate these aggressive circumstances. It would seem there is no great shortage of religious fanatics who are willing to sacrifice their own lives in order to destroy their real or imagined enemies.

The use of religion as a motivator is only incidental to the true insanity that drives these maniacs. And what do you think is going to happen as thousands more discover that they are infected with the AIDS virus? A number of those so infected are going to become predators instead of docile patients. In fact, when the infamous Green River Killer is caught, it will be discovered that he is an individual who has been infected with the AIDS virus through the patronage of prostitutes, and it is this circumstance that motivates his terrible hatred of women. His case is, of course, extreme but his motivation toward destruction is by no means unique. There are many other AIDS carriers, male and female, who are willfully infecting others through sexual promiscuity. These people are well aware of the fact that they are sentencing many others to death, and they are, in reality, far more deadly than the Green River Killer himself.

When all things are considered, this is by far the most lethal and terrible span of time which has ever transpired during man's recorded existence, and the next two decades will see an awesome transition or the near extinction of the human species on this planet.

Never before have so many detrimental elements come to a crucial point at one time. There are surely a number of others who are aware of most if not all of this information I am giving you. However, those in a position to reveal and perhaps alter some of these things have decided that the public is better off remaining ignorant of the full force of this truth. This book will not alter the course of humanity at large. However, it will serve as a beacon to bring those together who have been chosen to be among the wayfarers who will be physically taken from this planet within the next two decades.

For reasons not altogether evident to me, I have been chosen to be one of the humans who have been given the task of imparting this message to the masses. I am aware of the fact that I am one of the very few human beings who have a very clear, if not intimate, knowledge of these extraterrestrials. If perchance not one person believes me, it will by no means diminish this reality in my mind or in our skies.

I have been told that over the next few years the visual presence of UFOs in our skies will increase to such a degree that the average person will have no choice but to reach the conclusion that we are not alone in the universe. I also believe that more close encounters of the fourth kind will start to transpire. This will happen for a number of reasons, the foremost of which are that the aliens want people to know that they are indeed real and that there is no danger in their presence. Also they want to prevent mass panic when they do find it necessary to visit in force for the pick-up.

When the nucleus community of the chosen is started by myself and some others, it will be found that the combined spirit or esoteric force of the members will be manifested in many tangible ways, such as touch healing, levitation, telepathy and telekinesis, new inventions and procedures in horticulture, power generation and sociological order. This community will serve as microcosm of what could or should be and will encompass all social, cultural, racial and religious factions. The community will be economically solvent by virtue of its combined resourcefulness and the pooling of its brain power, and it will be an example of the new and greater community to come on the planet Biaveh. At this point, a great percentage of the people are of the opinion that no large group of people of various races and religions can live in peace, love and prosperity, but the community will dispel this myth.

During the course of this book I have touched upon many things, and yet there is enough that I've not touched upon to fill another volume. Some things that I have not spoken of because the knowledge is not yet to be imparted to the masses, while some other things are so controversial or intricately complicated in essence that I simply do not yet have the ability to explain them. Others I would have to literally show you through touch or resonance of voice.

As a matter of instinctive self-preservation, mankind tends to think of the unknown as being potentially dangerous until proven otherwise, while there are a few of us who would rather think of the unknown as being harmless until proven dangerous. Are the aliens dangerous? I would have to say that anything that possesses the technological power of these beings must be considered potentially dangerous. However, all of my experience in their presence gives me to believe that they have no wish to either harm or enslave mankind.

When weighing all of the factors, I must conclude that their intention toward humanity is one of benevolence and to some extent kinship. I fully realize that the aliens do not need my help in order to round up people for some kind of nefarious purpose because they have the high tech power to simply take people at will, with or without that person's consent.

They told me that they plan to greatly expand the human colony on Biaveh and to prevent the extinction of man as a species, and I believe them. No doubt there are other humans on Biaveh, who have been there for several thousand years and who have developed psychological and spiritual qualities far beyond anything we have seen and will be the teachers and instructors for the people to come.

Just as I have been visually shown many of the wonders of that world, I'm certain that the humans there have been able to visually follow the progress of this planet. They know that we are coming, the numbers of travelers and will have all living and survival as well as educational accouterments waiting for us when we get there.

Many of those earthling settlers gone on before have gone exploring in the far reaches of the galaxy, but few, if any, have ever expressed a desire to return to the Earth to live and die among humanity. I'm sure that a small number have, on occasion, returned for a visit, but as I've said before, human beings do not age swiftly on Biaveh, so the person who left here three hundred years ago would only be able to visit relatives who are many generations removed. Time on Biaveh has little meaning.

I'm sure that at some point in a person's life span on that planet they must start to tire of the physical existence, yet I also know that with proper stimulation, sexual vitality and the discovery of new things and sensations, a being's life can remain fresh and exciting almost indefinitely, or at least for a few thousand years. The great mothership is only forty kilometers in diameter, but I'm sure that I could have found enough new things to keep me fascinated easily for an earthly life time.

I truly do love women, Earth women, and always will, but I know from my first hand experience that there are females of other intelligent life forms who are sexually desirable to me also. I can only visualize how many other kinds of these marvelous creatures I have yet to discover. I have seen enough examples of other lower forms of creatures aboard the mothership to occupy my reflections for a lifetime, and yet I'm aware that I only saw a fraction of the specimens on that ship and but a small number of the vast kaleidoscope of different life forms throughout the galaxy.

Many of the things that have caused others to develop mental psychoses have only served to fascinate me to no end. My aversion to or fear of any of these things I've seen has never been as great as my curiosity to learn what it was about. The shock trauma of suddenly being cast into a totally foreign and possibly nightmarish setting is largely a state of mind.

There have always been those individuals who were perfectly willing to risk life and limb in order to make a new discovery or to see what lay beyond the visible horizon, and I am such a person apparently by nature.

Perhaps the greatest thing for the abductee to overcome is the fear that something awful and painful is going to happen to them. Second is the realization that there are indeed other intelligent creatures in the universe. The combination of these two factors often causes the abductee to literally freak out and lose touch momentarily with all reality. Thirdly, this horror is reinforced by the fact that they have been anaesthetized and cannot move even while they are being touched and examined by the extraterrestrials. Add to this the fact that most of the aliens are funny looking or just down right ugly by our standards, and it becomes some weird shit.

In most cases no amount of verbal or telepathic assurance on the part of the aliens can quiet the element of abject horror in the abductee. The aliens have found that children make the best subjects, both because of their size and because children are more receptive to new experiences than are adults. Children are able to swiftly overcome the fear factor and then start asking questions.

Women are the next best choice, because they are less prone to fight against the bonds of their circumstance and they are by nature quite curious. However, women do tend to magnify all perceived pain during the examinations. For some reason, women tend to retain more of a psychosis following their abduction.

Open-minded people are always preferred, but open-minded males especially, because upon regaining consciousness, the open-minded individual starts almost immediately to rationalize the situation at hand. He begins to think, I'm not really surprised because I always suspected that they existed. If they haven't hurt me yet, then perhaps they are not going to hurt me, and if they are going to do me in, then everybody has to go sometime. If I do get out of here, then I had best attempt to lock this experience in my memory. What do they look like, smell like, feel like, etc.

There are no doubt a number of reasons for wiping the

memory of most abductees, but I suspect that one of the main reasons this practice is done is because it is an attempt on the part of the aliens to prevent the abductee from re-experiencing what they consider to be a nightmare. They are trying to preserve the sanity of that person. This is only speculation on my part as I was never told this by Tan.

The years 1989-90 and 91 will be a very active span of UFO sightings and close encounters because the aliens are once again in a close observation mode. Also a great deal more emphasis will be directed toward the observation and contacting of children. Unknown to them, many of these children will be chosen to join the future airlift, which will transpire within the next two decades.

Also certain towns and communities, which have been under observation for generations, will start to see a great deal more UFO activity. Of course, so-called highly qualified skeptics will continue to try to discount the bulk of these sightings or to attribute them to some new and secret military projects. But I don't believe the public at large will allow themselves to be deceived any longer concerning the fact that we are surely being visited by life forms not of this Earth. If a nationwide or indeed a worldwide poll were taken at this time, I'm sure it would be found that the vast majority of humanity would confess to the belief that there are other life forms out there.

Sadly the general masses are not fully aware of the precarious position this planet is now in from the ecological standpoint. At the present rate of depletion, the rain forests of the world will have become a thing of the past in another twenty years. The scientific projection of the greenhouse effect is no joke. The progressive warming trend of the Earth's surface will do more than just melt much of the poles. It will also contribute to the depletion of the ozone shield by allowing much more manmade pollutants to rise into the stratosphere and open scattered windows in the ozone shield. These windows will continue to widen and to move about, causing untold death and cancerous plagues unto the Earth.

I have told you that we are due to be visited by a giant meteor from space in 1998. The aliens have imparted this information to me, but I also believe that certain people in the higher echelons of the governments of the world are aware of this. As we do have the technology to have been forewarned this far ahead of time, all of the super powers of this planet are going to have to pool their destructive space technology in order to try to alter the course of this meteor. However, all data existing at present indicates that mankind will not succeed without aid from these visitors out in space.

I have told you that there is a great mothership stationed near one of the moons of Saturn, which forms the base for seven different intelligent forms of life. The many sightings of UFOs over the next three years will verify the truth of this revelation. It is true that the Biaviians probably always have a number of ships en route to and from the home planet. However, even with their technology, it would not be practical to send small ships alone across the hundreds of light years of space as single units of exploration. A mothership, which forms a permanent space base, is essential to such an undertaking. As to the exact location of that great ship, I cannot say because I never learned any name for the moon that it is close to. However, if our instruments could locate which of the twenty-three moons of Saturn that it is near, then find that point between that moon and the planet Saturn where the gravitational pull from those bodies cancels each other out, there would be the mothership.

I have told you that the Biaviians are very sensitive to human emotions and seem to greatly enjoy experiencing them. When the Biaviians picked me up on December 27, 1987, I have since recalled what the alien Tan asked me during our conversation. He asked, "Martin, can't you feel the horror and the pain? Oh the horror". At the time I didn't know what he was talking about, but I learned later that at about the time I was being picked up, a man, only a few miles from that point in Arkansas, had killed all of the members of his immediate family.

The aliens seem amazed by the fact that human beings cannot literally feel such strong and terrible emotions in others around them. I've thought this over and have come to the conclusion that, from his viewpoint, such an anomaly of telepathic emotional transference would not seem strange, even on Earth.

You see, this emotion transference is quite common in nature. Harm one honey bee or one ant, and the rest of the hive or nest knows it immediately and reacts. Cut down a tree of a given species in the forest, and others of its kind miles away will undergo a measurable electro-molecular reaction. The same is true of even higher animals in the wild or some domestic animals. Since all living things on this planet are tied together chemically and probably spiritually, it only seems logical that human beings would be included in the number. We must be able to feel something of the emotions of others, because I have felt the tangible feelings of Tan and the Great Agynmum, and I'm sure of some other people from time to time.

If indeed we humans could actually feel each others pain and other strong emotions, then surely we would stop hurting, hating and killing one another. Then, regardless of our sentiments, in order to keep from having to feel your hunger or sadness, I would feed you and attempt to lift your spirits and any ill done to you would feel as if it were done unto me also.

Don't you know that we can't go on this way, hating and hurting one another and even hope to survive as a species? Racism, bigotry and hatred must be taught to a child. Human beings are essentially loving and responsive creatures by nature. Most, if not all, negative social traits are acquired as that person grows older.

Of course, there will always be dominant and submissive personalities among all species of higher animals. Even among the aliens there are distinctly different personalities, but their telepathic and spiritual link to one another is far stronger than that between most humans and so they have apparently learned to do away with nearly all of the negative traits that plague humanity.

No Biaviians need have fear of any other Biaviian. Among them, any extreme social deviation is isolated and dealt with. As I have said before, they are not perfect but capital offenses are almost unknown among them. The fact that human beings are dangerous, hateful creatures is not unique in the cosmos among evolving species. However, the institutionalizing of racism, hatred and mass terror is a thing more pervasively unique in the human order than in all other known intelligences who have gained our level of philosophy and technology.

The legacy of predatory aggression and random psychotic acts of deadly motivation which seems atypical of modern humanity, I am told, is largely due to two artificial factors. One, the consumption of and exposure to all manner of inorganic chemicals and toxins, and secondly, but most important, is the fact that man is a carnivore in habit, while being biologically a vegetarian. Though I never thought of it in this manner, I'm told that the statistics of aggressive anti-social activity of a given country or locale will be directly reflected by that populace's intake of toxins and red meats.

Certain primitive people have always believed that the consumer of another human or animal literally absorbed the physical and emotional attributes of the victim. To a measurable extent this is true. Thus when we eat red meat, we are inadvertently acquiring some fraction of the emotional make-up of the slaughtered animal. Fear, desperation, anger, sadness and dementia are all some of the things we consume every day by eating red meat. Of course, this simple revelation doesn't explain away all of the mental problems of humanity, but think about it.

All carnivores, those animals that eat meat almost exclusively, have short intestinal tracts. Nature has designed it so that the nutrient qualities of the meat eaten would be absorbed quickly and then expended from the body. The digestive systems of herbivores, plant eaters, are much longer, so that the nutrients can be extracted from the vegetables slowly before passing through the body.

Human beings are long intestinal vegetarians, so when meat is consumed, it passes much too slowly through the digestive system, and this lingering absorption process, after a point, literally begins to poison the body. Ultimately this consumption of meat begins to manifest itself in many illnesses of the body and the mind. Add to this artificial preoccupation, a wide array of chemical growth hormones and preservatives, and you have a volatile and deadly poison, which literally saturates the physiology of western man. Perhaps the more aggressive and seemingly heartless activities of the Targzissians can be attributed partially to the fact that these aliens consume animal matter, while the peaceful and sensible Biaviians are exclusively vegetarian.

In the month of January 1994, the aliens project that the geo-disks along the San Andreas fault will shift, causing a major earthquake in the Los Angeles area. In February of 1992, another great hurricane and tidal ebb will ravage the country of Bangladesh again with catastrophic consequences. In 1995 the mid-western grain belt is due for a crop destroying drought, so farmers should bear this in mind.

In March of 1993 an extremely destructive hurricane will ravage the southeastern coast of America. Be prepared. Geo-data indicates that at the present rate of sub-surface movement, a new island will be pushed above the surface of the Mediterranean Sea near Madagascar in mid-1996. A projected stock market crash in October 1993. These are but a few of the things revealed to me by the aliens. These projections are not the product of any clairvoyant attributes but are based upon scientific, geological, atmospheric and economic data compiled by the Biaviian computers.

Since destiny can most definitely be altered by direct outside intervention, the Biaviians have a policy against interfering in the lives of major characters in the governing scheme of things. The project afoot to let man know that the Biaviians and others are here and real without throwing humanity's whole social, religious and historical perspectives into chaos is a delicate one, which must be handled with the greatest tact and discretion. They know that man is much too dangerous to be given open social intercourse with them, and they are careful not to let the wrong kind of technology fall into the hands of those who rule the planet. Just think what would happen if any of the present day rulers got their hands on a single Biaviian whisper craft. The individual who had the ship could easily rule the world. The adage that power corrupts and absolute power corrupts absolutely has always proven true where man is concerned.

And yet it is inevitable that the extraterrestrials must show themselves in force in order to execute the great airlift at various points in the world. The colony of wayfarers to be taken from this country is but a fraction of the whole number to be taken worldwide. In truth, the great space exodus will be a wonder to behold.

Whether those chosen will be vegetarians or not won't matter that much from the aliens' perspective, because I'm told that aside from seafood, the diet of the wayfarers will not include red meats. However, the meat eaters will be able to satisfy their cravings by consuming vegetable matter which will mimic the look, taste and texture of their favorite meat exactly. So a person will be able to have chicken or steak, etc., if he so desires that won't be organically harmful to him. Just as a person will be able to drink, smoke, eat or inject their favorite stimulants and receive all of the esoteric benefits without suffering the hangovers, withdrawals and organic damage from those things.

All wayfarers who may be afflicted with any manner of

physical handicap or amputation or body distortions will be technologically restored. The lame will walk and the blind will see, etc. And the aged will be restored to youth.

I'm told that the human wayfarers will be able to learn of many other intelligent and lower life forms in the cosmos but will not be permitted to have social intercourse with any of the intelligent forms aboard the mothership.

Given the aliens' technology, I don't imagine that it will take very long to actually pick up the chosen number of people worldwide, so the event need not be so world shattering as to completely disrupt the social order of all of humanity. There won't be any great amplified warnings of impending doom or any White House landings, but simply a quiet and efficient pre-arranged extraction from certain locates. The fate of the rest of humanity must continue to be made evident of its own design and momentum.

I have no doubt that a smattering of government agents will be able to find out some pick-up locations and manage to join the wayfarers, but this infiltration will in no way alter the schedule or the overall destiny of the project. After all, once the travelers are out of the Earth's gravitational pull, it really won't matter one way or the other what the agent knows, will it. Obviously he won't be able to smuggle weapons aboard, and a mutiny would be out of the question. Even if he were somehow able to send a message back from Biaveh, it would take four hundred and fifty years to reach Earth.

The human populace aboard the ship will be attended by friendly robots, who will do everything from producing a certain book, holding a conversation to massaging a tight muscle. Robots will help you watch the kids and keep them entertained. These friendly robots will keep the floors vacuumed and the trash picked up.

Yes, you may take a dog or cat, if you can't bear to leave him behind. You can also watch your favorite home planet programs and movies on the vid-screens or on personal eyeglasses. You can choose to take a nap, which will last thirty minutes or the duration of the journey. Day and night and some temperature variations will be simulated so as not to disrupt the human bio-rhythms.

Their technology is such that a person will be able, within reason, to pick out the physical form they wish. There are limitations though. For instance, an obese person can order up a body weight of say a hundred and twenty and correct any facial or body abnormalities, a crooked nose, a missing eye, a club foot or cleft palate, etc., but a Chinese would not be made a Caucasian, or a short person made taller. You couldn't order up another person's face. Woody Allen could not become Tom Selleck, but he could become a perfect Woody Allen.

Any manner of disease or abnormal medical condition would be healed, and if you are missing a finger, an ear, etc., they can and will replace it. You cannot order larger sexual organs, which were not genetically given to you in the first place, but you can have access to certain aphrodisiacs. Pregnancy will be left to choice and will not be a chance situation. And, of course, you can have sex freely without fear of venereal infections.

Travelers will be able to experience the climate and topography of the planet to which they are bound by entering one of the holograph simulation rooms. They will also be able to eat some of the native foods plants from Biaveh, as well as sample some Earth plants which were previously transplanted on Biaveh.

The travelers will also be able to experiment with a number of technologies which they will have access to on Biaveh, but which are unknown on Earth, such as through music or dream recording machines, levitating chairs and beds and living history books. For instance, if you want to know exactly how Napoleon or King Tut looked and acted, you can punch them up on the screen and know that you have true visual representation.

From a technological standpoint, the Biaviians are light years ahead of Earth. They can fix an injured body and prolong physical life almost indefinitely, but they cannot prevent accidental or suicidal death, nor can they raise the dead once the life force has fled the body. So they are not totally omnipotent. That power has always and shall always rest in the hands of God.

The Biaviians cannot make a fool a wise man or a dumb person a genius. They can give you all the technology at their disposal toward higher learning and the extra life span you need to consume the materials. They can even give you mind altering substances, but in the end you must learn and retain that learning at your own pace.

With them, if you are psychologically and spiritually capable of it, you can become a God, but you cannot attain undeserved prestige or reputation by virtue of race, force or material wealth. Among the Biaviians there are teachers and students, scientists and artisans, inventors and laborers, such as it is. Some Biaviians can levitate using telekinesis and some can not. Some, by virtue of character and learning, can command great respect, while others are not so blessed. My friend Tan is a pilot and perhaps a sociologist, but he is not a mathematician or even a very good mechanic.

I find his mode of reasoning to be logical but by no means is his philosophy to be considered divine or beyond correction. His knowledge of the history of man far exceeds my own, but his grasp of the psychology of man must be subservient to my own.

Biaviians do not lie to one another, because deception is simply not necessary nor logical to everyday modus, not because they are divine or spiritually metaphysical beings, which they are not.

When the Biaviians abduct a person, they know that they are not going to harm that person physically, so they aren't really bothered conscience wise. They don't seem to realize the extent of the psychological damage they may be putting that person through. From the human standpoint, such as attitude on their part seems quite heartless, but from their point of view, the abductee has not been physically harmed and the pulse and temperature rates have returned to normal before release back to the wild.

Their logic is that they would never ever do unto us that which we constantly do unto one another, and they can't get over the wonder of the fact that so many humans could be so presumptuous as to think themselves the only intelligent life forms in the vastness of the cosmos. After all, it's not as if they have been completely hiding their presence in our skies.

Tan is able to comprehend the workings and the reason for certain human emotions. He understands the emotions of fear, joy, anger, and even hatred, but he cannot discern the logic of why any of these emotions should play any more than just a momentary role in existence at a given time to fit a given circumstance. Why fear a tiger in a cage or hate a stranger on sight. Why remain angry beyond the confrontational moment or stay perpetually sad. His concept of logic rules out such unessential preoccupations.

But he is no fool either. If you tell him that you admire him, he knows if you mean it or not. When I told him that he was funny looking, he took no offense, because he knew that I meant that he was funny looking but in a cute way. When I told him that I wanted to kill Question, he knew that I didn't mean it, even if I didn't realize it myself.

He apparently knew that while aboard the ships I was looking to steal something to bring back with me and either took precautions or simply stole it back from me while I was asleep. I'm certainly no angel, but he has apparently come to the conclusion that I'm not a bad sort, that my admiration is not contrived and that I can be trusted to a greater point than most. He knows that my anger is fleeting and that I do not study to harm the weaker or to hate the different or to fear the unknown to any obsessive degree.

I realize that many people upon seeing some of the things that I have seen aboard that great ship would have freaked out. It fascinated the shit out of me to see a big insect who has his own ship, but it didn't do much for my human self-esteem. The realization that a big bug could take me out in a high tech show down doesn't do my ego a helluva lotta good, but I didn't geek out either. My last assessment is that it stands to reason that all things must be capable of evolving into some higher degree. I was told that the Skreed, as the Insectillians are called, are roughly four billion years older than Homo sapien as a species, and apparently motivational circumstances were ideal for their evolutionary progression.

And what of the Targs? By any stretch of the word, they are reptilian in origin, and their physical form, aside from the reptile skin, has roughly paralleled our own in the sense that they are upright bipeds, but then many dinosaur species of our Earth's history walked upright.

The anthropological thesis or belief that a creature has to be mammalian or big brained in order to be technically smart is totally erroneous. From observation of the Targzissians' skull dimensions, I estimate that their brain may be no larger than say a banana, but the mother fuckers have got some totally awesome ships and no doubt lots more heavy stuff that easily transcends our technology.

Each day we use complicated electronic gadgets without having the slightest idea of how they work or the mathematical knowledge of how they were fabricated. Well, the same can be said of the Biaviians and no doubt the bulk of the mass of other intelligent aliens. I would even venture to say that there are probably some dumb Stagyians, that is to say that not all Stagyians are necessarily mathematical geniuses by birth. Can the pilot of a 747 build a similar plane from scratch? Of course not. The engineering that went into the making of that plane encompassed a compilation of structural aerodynamics and electronic knowledge that spanned decades and thousands of brains. The same can probably be said of the aliens technology.

Tan fancies himself an expert on the subject of human psychology and is recognized as such among his peers, but in my opinion, his true knowledge of the human equation is quite rudimentary. The concept of material wealth and its unequal distribution tends to evade him. Over-population and unnecessary waste, religion fanaticism and the systematic poisoning of the only environment we have makes no sense to him.

Why should an individual feel compelled to rob and steal in order to acquire drugs, which could be readily supplied to the user at a fraction of the cost of property loss, police enforcers, prisons and physical injury? Why continue to build and stockpile more nuclear bombs when the destructive saturation level was reached long ago? How can any human feel justified in enslaving other human beings? When he asks me to explain the logic behind such things, I find it difficult, if not impossible, to give him a satisfactory answer, because, in truth, these things cannot be logically justified. When he calls my attention to the mindless bestiality of humanity, I can see how it would be hard for any intelligent observer to hold any respect for this species called man.

I understand that the Biaviians have trans-galactic ships, which are called sleeper ships, that are even now enroute to other distant galaxies while the crews sleep in suspended animation. Some have been enroute for hundreds of years, but may have been preceded by other crews hundreds of years before. Perhaps they will find colonies of their own kind when and if they arrive at that far away place. Some day no doubt there will be humans among those crews who will endure to re-colonize totally different galaxies.

The visionary possibilities are quite beyond what the present imagination can conjure. Or maybe not. We start this great odyssey from this point and within this lifetime, and I am personally looking forward to that day. I know that there is little or no hope in expecting that humanity will drastically alter its way of doing things here on Earth before it is too late to matter. The elements of greed, perversion and falsity now completely govern the ruling faction of this planet, and like some cancerous infection, it has become terminal both moralistically and economically. I don't think it is premature of me to state that the human species as we know it is already dead but doesn't yet fully realize it. I wish with all my heart that it were not so.

The handwriting is clearly on the wall, and those who truly realize it, don't have the power to stop it, nor the wish to take on the responsibility of attempting to inform the masses of this impending Armageddon. And most would not believe the truth anyway.

The time is almost upon us when all earthly situations as we have come to know them will reach the point of crucial lethality. It is not within my power to prevent this inevitability, and those who could do something about it, feel as if they have too much to lose by attempting to do so. Those who now have the power are frantically amassing money and other valuables, so that when push comes to shove they will be able to run away to some well-guarded fortress and live unmolested, while the rest of humanity fend for itself.

In the end this won't save them as they will eventually find themselves at the mercy of those whom they hired to protect them. Even before that point in time, the terrorist factor would have reached epidemic and bizarre proportions and would have reached the streets of America.

It is a fact that the drugs cocaine and metham-phetamines (crack) induce paranoia in the users, but more potent drugs are on the way, which will add a kind of demented aggression to this paranoia, giving rise to an even more dangerous kind of criminal. The drug will cause minority drug users and dealers to kill other minority drug users and dealers and will cause Caucasian users to go about killing other Caucasians who are strangers and innocent.

This is the season of the serial killer and the psychotic mass murderer, and the age of the suicidal political assassin is just truly beginning. Great masses of people in the Middle and Far East and the Latin American countries will become locked in civil destruction and rebellion unparalleled in the history of the planet.

Sexual attacks and murders will become commonplace, and the police forces will find themselves up against well armed and psychotic foes. The prison factor will expend to the mass concentration camp level, and executions will become summary even in America. A substantial number of ordinary citizens will suffer chemically induced psychosis and commit heinous crimes. Murder and suicides will become common, and the rich will live in fear and with good cause.

At a certain point, it will no longer be just a matter of drug addiction and economic oppression, but a matter of mass poisoning brought on by the contamination of the ecology and the water supply. In some places the rule of law and order will completely break down for a time, and anarchy and chaos will reign supreme, until the military is called in.

Some of this will transpire before the great space lift occurs, but the very worst of it will happen after they are gone. Money cannot get a person aboard the ships, nor position, nor formal education diplomas. What all of the criteria are in order to be chosen I cannot say, but I do know that for the most part it will consist of good hearted, open minded people. People who have within themselves the wish and ability to lay aside racial prejudices and other petty foibles. The aliens certainly do not want people who don't want to go. They don't want those who have less than a full conviction in their decision to leave this planet.

Psychotics and those who have secretly committed capital crimes against humanity will not be chosen. Those who have knowingly contributed to the social oppression and economic exploitation of the working masses will not be chosen. Most politicians, preachers, lawyers, policemen, big business men and, of course, military brass will not even be considered.

Those who consider themselves very religious people in the conventional sense will have to reconcile themselves to the fact that there are many mansions in God's kingdom. I believe that the omnipotent force meant for us to learn of these things in due time.

It is fortunate indeed that man has not yet developed the technology to go exploring the cosmos. We may be sure that he would have subjugated or destroyed the weaker and begun studying ways of destroying the stronger or he would have brought the destructive powers of angered aliens down upon the Earth.

Even now, when the Earth is moving swiftly toward self-destruction, the aliens dare not give man the technology to be able to leave this ailing planet. He cannot chance having such a dangerous species running amok in the galaxy. Yet they will not allow this species to perish completely from the cosmos.

The way unto the kingdom is so plain that a child can't err and a blind man can't miss the way. It would be too ludicrous to even expect that a blind man would do what is right, but he might succeed in salvaging humanity if he ever decides to do that which is necessary in order to see that this beautiful planet is saved from manmade destruction. To do that which is necessary would cost some money and momentarily cut the profit margin a bit. However, it would not destroy his fortunes or bankrupt his holdings. Greed, ignorance, stupidity, racism, religious fanaticism and ingrained perversions among the elite have effectively laid waste to reason and benevolent decency and this assures a bleak and lethal future for the world as a whole.

The Biaviians and the Targzissians have dematerialization-materialization capabilities, that is the power to beam down and to beam up. I was picked up in such a manner in Maryland in 1975 by the Biaviians, and I was made aware of the Targs' ability to accomplish this when two of them materialized in my apartment in Tulsa in May of 1988, at which time they amputated the last joint of my right little finger, in retaliation for my having telepathically destroyed the mental factors of one of their kind a short time before.

In order for the aliens to keep abreast of the dimensions and styles of modern human dwellings for purposes of exact duplication in the future, they sometimes physically beam down into the homes of people in passing. To prevent startling the occupants and to keep from suffering physical attack themselves, they usually scan the premises to make sure that no adults are in the house at the time. And, of course, they are always taking soil, vegetable and grain samples from various locations.

Generally, when a Biaviian ship is on a sample gathering jaunt or when a crew plans to physically touch down or leave the ship momentarily, the ship will be accompanied by a smaller light sentinel sphere. The purpose of the light sentinel sphere is to protect the ship and crew from any possible danger while they are vulnerable. The electro-magnetic waves emanating from the craft and the sphere tend to kill the grass upon which it lands, and the affected area can generally be seen with the naked eye.

The electro-currents from the ship's propulsion system tend to effect electrical motors and other implements and to cause a zone of static electrical activity when a craft passes near. For instance, you can actually feel your hair standing on end when the ship approaches. Trees and leaves are made to tremble perceptively in the wake of the craft. The electronic systems, altimeters and compasses of an aircraft may be momentarily effected if a saucer comes near the plane.

The aliens have electronic sensor devices, which are capable of locating and tracking a single individual most of the time. Some people believe that the aliens have implanted electronic devices in their bodies, but I've been assured and shown that this is not necessary. Instrumental electronic communication from ship to ship while in the Earth's stratosphere is rarely used, because of the aliens' telepathic communications abilities. These messages are nearly always relayed from ship to ship by the Stagyian scientists, and the transmission may last no longer than a nano-second. So Earth does not yet have the tech ability to intercept such exchanges.

An alien craft can possibly be electronically effected by strong electrical storm activity if it flies through it. One ship and its crew and a remote drone were literally blown out of the sky in mid 1947 out in New Mexico. A remote drone was downed in Japanese islands in the early fifties. So their technology is not infallible.

There are many living human beings who have retained or

inherited intact some of the alien chromosomes, and these people, of whom I am one, are capable of telepathic communication with the aliens. But the larger percentage of the people who will be chosen for the space migration need not possess the gene of the aliens at all. Nor does one have to possess this trait in order to develop the ability of telepathic communication with them. Indeed, most people have telepathic capabilities though they are undeveloped.

With telepathic abilities, one does not have to possess the technical abilities to accomplish a certain thing in order to comprehend the principle behind it. For instance, I can comprehend the principle of time travel and hyper-space projection, but I don't know the mechanics of how to do it. I have also been given the names of a number of people in this country, some of them are famous, who possess the alien gene, but I won't divulge their names at the risk of doing them a disservice.

The widely held belief that any social interaction with people in past history will alter the future is true. However, this does not prevent the Biaviians from traveling back in time or from occasionally interacting with certain people.

For instance, when a child is born today who possesses a stronger than average alien genetic trait, then the geneticists may very well be obliged to go back in time to trace the ancestry progression of that child. In this manner a data chart can be plotted with a greater degree of accuracy.

By some times manipulating circumstances where a certain person with the gene is surreptitiously influenced to meet and procreate with another person carrying the gene, a future Mohammed or Buddha or George Washington Carver can be created. The process generally takes about fourteen generations, Yet this is not done on a mass basis, as it is more in keeping with the directives to allow this genetic progression to occur randomly.

Alien scientists, like Earth scientists, are naturally inquisitive in the quest of knowledge and results. Say, for instance, the ancient writings of a certain people foretell the coming of a great leader and specify the time that this is supposed to transpire. Knowing this, it would be a great temptation for these scientists to travel back in time fourteen generations, extract the spermatozoa from the original adept personage, come forward in time and literally inseminate a gene-carrying lady in the present. In this manner, they could almost guarantee that the child will possess the proper messianic qualities. Certainly this is no less than man would do if he could. Has it been done by the aliens in this manner? I can't really say.

If you went back in time and prevented Napoleon from losing at Waterloo, then today's world situation would probably be notably different. However, if you went back and abducted or otherwise communicated with a simple foot soldier in Napoleon's army, the impact that you would make on history would be so insignificant as to not even be noticed in the order of things. As long as you stay away from the notable characters of history, it's okay to drop in and physically interact with some of the little guys.

I'm told that there are certain dimensional points upon this planet that would allow a present day person to accidentally step back in time, never forward. These dimensional points are mobile and generally fleeting, so a person who enters one may not be able to get back and that person might indeed be able to make some notable alterations in history.

While it is against the directives for the Biaviians to take a person from one time period and transplant them more than a few days back in time, this rule doesn't apply to animals. At any given time, Biaviian time travelers are somewhere back in time collection living samples of certain animal species to add to their suspended collection. These creatures are rarely reintroduced into a different time setting on their planet of origin, but will often be introduced into a living nature setting on Biaveh or perhaps placed in an evolutionary niche on some other young planet.

As I have said before, the ways and conditions of organic evolution throughout the universe are relatively uniform. A fish on one planet though different in coloration and size would still be recognizable as a fish and would essentially be structured and operate in a manner similar to a fish on another planet. It is essentially the same with birds, carnivores and insects, as well as intelligent bi-ped vertebrates. The belief that the life forms of another planet must be radically different from that of this planet need not be so. Biological organisms are far more adaptable than you might imagine.

It is true that things tend to grow larger and taller on low gravity planets, while being wider and shorter on high gravity planets, but it is quite possible for a transplanted creature from a different density planet to adapt and thrive there also. The Biaviians originated as a species on a planet with a higher gravitational pull than on Biaveh, but they have adapted quite well to the low gravity of Biaveh. Numerous other species of Earth creatures, including humans, have adapted well to the lower gravity of that planet. Actually it is much easier to adapt to a lower gravity planet from a higher gravity planet than the reverse. When walking about on Earth, the Biaviians and others use anti-gravitational devices to offset the difference. New arrivals from Earth to Biaveh are obliged to use such devices to produce the opposite effect for a time before getting used to the lighter weight sensations of the planet.

The planet Biaveh is young enough in its evolutionary cycle that most life forms native to that planet are still in the aquatic stage, and I'm told that the oceans have life forms which are huge and quite dangerous. The waters of Biaveh would no doubt be an oceanographer's dream.

Most land creatures now living on Biaveh are transplants

from various living planets throughout the galaxy, and the Earth is a Biaviian naturalist's dream owing to the marvelous array of animal life forms to choose from. Oh, how marvelous it must be to be able to start your own planet from scratch. Plants tend to grow much larger on Biaveh. Imagine tomatoes the size of basketballs and plums like softballs, butterflies as big as kites and strawberries as big as pineapples.

A planet is a terrible thing to waste. This Earth, this living jewel, this marvelous sphere of life, this showpiece of the cosmos. Oh, how I mourn your fate. This cosmic sacrilege which is being perpetrated against your form by ruthless and uncaring humanity. If I had the power to alter your fate, surely I would attempt to do so without hesitation. And yet I know that, no matter the ravages of destruction wrought by man upon your surface, you will yet endure and slowly heal yourself, so that your children will find you pristine upon their return. My tears for the fate of your wayward children have been exhausted, and my hope for their redemption has become translucent and without flavor. For how can they ever come to truly love and respect you when they have not even come close to extending a courtesy to their fellow beings.

When the time comes and I am obliged to leave you knowing that most of those of my blood and masses whom I love and pray for will exist no more, I will be so sad. Surely something within me shall also die at that time, never to be regained, no matter how many wonders these eyes may see.

Even as he has come, seven times before to ransom his life for all of God's children, they have repented not of their wickedness, nor been chastened by their suffering. Then it is with the deepest anguish that alas he must withdraw his hand from them for a time and allow that they endure the chilling embrace of the destiny of their own creation.

By choice has humanity chosen hatred over love. By choice has he chosen destruction over conservation. By choice has he chosen swift death over long life. By choice has he given way to the Gods of gluttony avarice, blood and vomit. Having sown the wind, they must now reap the whirlwinds.

Let the innocent children know that they will surely return again to inherit the Earth. Bade them to be not afraid of the coming rest for their sleep shall not be without end. Let them know that they will awaken in a new body and form to look again upon the golden sunrise. God is not slighted nor un-forgiving, and he will not allow your lifes' force to be extinguished. Know that you shall live again.

Take note of this lesson lest you forget it and commit a similar atrocity again in the future. Even though ages will come and go, you will not be forgotten or go un-mourned. Perhaps we shall meet again at some point in time, and we shall not be repelled, but drawn together in love and dreams.

Chapter 16

What Is, Is Not Reality Transcended

Upon seeing some photos of UFOs that I had taken in early 1988, a Tulsa police officer, in a resigned tone, said "Well, I guess that shoots religion all to hell". And I responded, saying, "quite the contrary. The realization that other intelligent life forms exist in the universe should only serve to broaden our concepts of God and his creative diversity. In my Father's house are many mansions".

In fact, any open-minded person would easily conclude that no God in his right mind would dare place all of his creative talents and indeed all of his galaxies in the hands of one intelligent species. When viewed realistically, on a scale of one to ten in the 'just desserts' department, I don't think that humanity would rank very high on the celestial scale. I personally know of at least eight intelligent life forms that easily out rank man of the technological level, and I have no doubt that there are many more throughout the cosmos.

In measuring the ability and innate psychological motivations of the extraterrestrials as opposed to man's, I'm very surprised, though nonetheless delighted, that none of the aliens seem to be naturally aggressive and warlike in a strategically concerted fashion. This rule among them which states that one doesn't automatically subjugate or destroy all other weaker species in their paths is in direct conflict with the predominant reasoning and action of humanity. Had the technological situation been reversed and mankind had happened upon them first, I could do nothing more than pity the poor bastards.

The fact that the aliens have decided that humanity is, by its own hands, doomed as a species has troubled my dreams on more than one occasion. Yet the realization that they consider the human species worthy of being saved from complete extinction keeps the light of hope burning dimly within my heart.

I've not yet completely satisfied myself as to the depth of the aliens sentiments in this respect. Does his intent to save the human species stem from an inner motivation of the spiritual brotherhood that one intelligent species holds for another like species, or does man measure somewhere between the salamander and the whale on their things to save list? The alien Tan gives me to believe that they look upon man as infant Gods in the making, instead of just an interesting mammalian rendition of evolution, and I've come to believe that he is sincere in this assessment. Why? Aside from the very close fellow being rapport he and I developed over the time, my belief is born more so of simple logic.

From what I have personally seen of the aliens technological abilities, I know that the only thing preventing them from doing whatever they so desire with the human species is their personal sense of respect for life in all its forms or their adherence to intergalactic laws which forbid such exploitation or both. It's certainly not because of the lack of raw power.

There are numerous people, some of them former abductees, who are firmly convinced that the aliens are constantly working toward the destruction or physical or psychological control of the human species. Some believe, and with some justification, that the aliens are carrying on a great genetic experiment using humans as guinea pigs, while some others believe that the extraterrestrials are secretly working with the government on some genetic material exchange project.

There is some elements of truth in there assumptions, but the overall logic of these opinions is untenable in view of the true reality of the thing. It is true that a considerable number of human beings alive today yet carry the alien gene within their body, and that some human males and females are capable of physically breeding with certain alien hybrids because of this genetic distinction. I'm also sure that the aliens have on occasion abducted certain individuals with the express purpose in mind of producing more of these hybrid offspring. Some of these offspring are probably put back into Earth society to carry on the genetic strain. These experiments, with the passing of time, have become more of a scientific procedural fact than an experimental uncertainty. The nectarine is a crossbreed between the plum and the peach and is a definite marketable entity unto itself.

While the aliens have a rule against physically damaging an abductee, they don't appear to be bothered much with getting permission from the abductee before performing certain medical procedures upon them. This seemingly apathetic and emotionless attitude on the aliens part has, no doubt, caused a great deal of mental and, in turn, some physical damage among the abductees. Certain abductions have to be made and medical procedures done in order to closely follow the migration and organic alterations of the genes.

The aliens have no doubt discovered that most human beings, if given the choice, would not consent to being impregnated with an unearthly seed, or to having sex with alien females who are by all Earth standards of physical beauty, extremely fucked up. It is much simpler to abduct the human, sedate them and then inseminate or physically invade them, suppress the conscious memory of the event and return them to their original locale. The memory wipe doesn't always work, and the physical procedure on occasion may leave some marks, but not to worry. What's the abductee going to do? Call the police? Or the military?

That mankind tends to view itself as the supreme spiritual rendition of God's creation doesn't bother the aliens in the least. The fact that the greater portion of humanity thinks itself to be the sole possessor of intelligence throughout the cosmos is to the aliens incomprehensible, not only because the laws of numerical probability demand the speculative assumption that the evolutionary processes are opportunistic, but because their ships have been visibly invading our airspace since before the beginning of recorded time, not to mention the numerous visitations and abductions, as well as much archeological evidence and scriptural recordings. In other words, they refuse to believe that mankind could truly be that stupid or ignorant.

Just as Einstein's Theory of Relativity opened new concepts in the study of physics, so would the universal recognition of the existence of these aliens open new horizons in the thought and technological processes of man. Instead of remaining the spiteful, evil and vicious little vermin we insist upon being, this universal revelation might cause us to actually start contemplating the equal creature-hood of all our fellow men.

When pressed to give a name for their religious concept persuasion, Tan called it JU-WANN, meaning 'The Light'. When asked to explain the doctrines and scriptural philosophy of that religion, he went into a three hour long telepathic explanation of his religion's evolution. Pure telepathic communication consists of inner visualization, as well as sounds and words, so I find it extremely difficult, if not impossible, to impart to you a very good view and feel of the experience.

The visionary experience showed and told of the first seeds of life beginning beneath the foamy waters of a young planet and followed its progress through all of the complex renditions, forms and orders through time on up to the present. The vision showed that the Biaviians themselves had historically labored through and suffered many of the mistakes of man. They had in fact literally destroyed the ecology and most life forms upon the first planet through fissional aggression and rendered a second planet uninhabitable through pollution, unrestrained scientific experimentation and other factors which were not of their making.

I learned that Biaveh is the third and present home planet of their species. Since having settled on the present home planet, the Biaviians have undergone several wars with other intelligences, the longest and most devastating being with the Targs. However, during Biaveh's history, the Biaviians have never fought among one another, and man was yet sub-human hominoides since their last trouble with the Targzissians.

The many spectrums and applicable components of light have been their scientific and esoteric philosophic preoccupation and spiritual endeavor since that time. In his words, light is the ultimate focal point of the God's head. Light, which all things must have to come to be and to ever be. The central premise of that philosophy is quite simple, to treat others as one desires to be so treated. To respect and not squander life, to respect and adhere to fact, truth and seek not to corrupt it. To reason instead of harm, harm instead of maim, maim instead of kill, and kill instead of die. Not to take beyond necessity and to not alter the natural order of things.

To be honest, I had expected to hear some kind of universal truth which was beyond human grasp, but it seems that there is no greater truth than the simple premise of do the right thing.

You needn't cleave unto any particular denomination or practice any particular rituals, nor even is it necessary for you to see a book or know how to read in order to do God's will. All you need do is do the right thing. What, you may ask, is the right thing? I put the same question to a wino called Ruo Board, many years ago, and he said, "Boy if a bird knows how to fly South in the Winter, then you damn well know how to do right". And I haven't found an improvement on that statement unto this day.

The aliens don't shoot down our military aircraft because it's simply not necessary. Evading or outrunning them is no problem. They don't want our gold, diamonds, platinum and silver, because these materials can be found in abundance on lifeless meteors and other planetary bodies out in space, or they can be literally fabricated.

They don't need human slaves for labor, because they have robotics to perform all menial tasks no matter how complicated or inhospitable the conditions. They don't need our fuels or nuclear materials because their technology is beyond such crude methods of propulsion. They have no wish to control or enslave humankind because such preoccupations are frivolous, illogical and unnecessary.

Among the Biaviians, an individual's worth and esteem is measured only by that beings inner worth. As an entity, no Biaviian is greater than another, and yet certain among them have gained great renown and are sought out because of some inner spiritual or other attribute which exceeds that of their peers. The concept of material wealth, as we know it, does not exist on Biaveh.

As with other species of intelligent beings, there are leaders as well as followers among the Biaviians. The difference between an Earth leader and a Biaviian leader is that the Biaviian leader cannot achieve his position through birth, wealth or race, but only through the intellectual knowledge and other mental and spiritual power possessed by him.

They do not seek to contact Earth leaders simply because there are no Earth leaders. While we in the leadership positions on this planet are a cornucopia of idiots, maniacs, bigots, thieves, murderers and dope dealers. The aliens are not impressed by a human's position, wealth or race. In the end all of these falsely held positions and the terrible inequity of resources distribution will result in the further fragmenting and ultimately the collapse of the human order. The ones who will have the best chance of surviving are those who understand nature, the so-called primitives.

Is there any rich man upon the Earth who can truthfully say that I'm loved and respected because of my inner worth instead of my material worth? If so, then the number if few and the situation tenuous. The incessant quest for money, without thought of the common good, has led to the down fall of most historical social orders and kingdoms, and humanity has never learned from these past mistakes.

Through a system of self-serving laws, suppression and monopolization, a microscopic ruling class has always managed to ultimately wrest almost total control of all economic commodities in a given society, thereby causing the wretched masses to rise up in revolution against these rulers. The first actions of the successful revolutionaries is to kill off as many members of the fallen ruling class as can be found. When this happens, unfortunately numerous members of the lesser strata, like teachers, engineers, scientists, doctors and artisans, are also killed, thus destroying much of the real intellectual wealth of that society.

Because of these terrible upheavals in societies historically, mankind has been held far short of its true technological and intellectual potential. Racial sentiments toward the minorities, and social, economic and educational suppression of same have resulted in an immeasurable loss of brain power in societies down through history, Such sentiments prevail today in the most progressive societies.

For generations now in industrial societies, the negative and deadly by-products of mass production have far out distanced the positive aspects of these endeavors. Such a state of things can be attributed to the unmitigated greed of just a handful of rich capitalists. Capitalism is not a thing restricted to the so-called democratic societies but to all rulers everywhere upon the planet, regardless of what their system is called. It all boils down to a handful of people owing and controlling all of the planet's resources.

This lopsided state of things always has a radical and unsettling effect on a given society. Crime of all sorts grows and becomes rampant, which in turn calls for more and more repressive methods, the building of more prisons, a hardening of laws and prison sentences. The growth of police forces ultimately leads to a kind of police state, which is controlled by this handful of super capitalists, those who have always preferred to live under armed guards than to equitably share the resources of the country. The result is a polarized society consisting mainly of the very rich and the hunted poor. This state of being is swiftly becoming a reality in America.

I spoke of the landing bay area of the great mothership and of its vastness. The great bay in which we landed served as a common one for the Biaviians, Dorians and Targs, and this area stretched for several miles in either direction.

I learned to recognize some of the different ships of the Targs, Dorians and Biaviians, but there were other ships of even stranger dimensions that I could not attribute to either of these intelligences. Later, on the vid-screens, I saw some ships of the Insectillian 'Skreed' and the Nyptonians, but I never visited their landing areas.

I was awed and fascinated by the smooth rimmed saucers of the Biaviians and the beautiful symmetry of the Dorian saucers, yet the ship that impressed me more than any other was the great V-winged ship of the Targs. I had the unforgettable experience of seeing this awesome ship launched one time. You are perhaps familiar with the size of the huge 747 passenger jet. Well, this monstrous V-winged ship was large enough to have parked four 747s beneath its wings side by side. The hull of the ship upon first notice appeared to be jet black. However, when I got closer to it, I could see that the color had a kind of deep iridescent purple-blue quality.

From my vantage point, which was about a quarter mile away, I saw that the ship rested on three retractable legs with large circular disk pads on the floor surface. The legs retracted periscope fashion. From the central fuselage a large ramp had been lowered, the steps of which were shiny red, giving the ship the appearance of some great leviathan sting ray with its mouth open.

I saw about forty Targs in green, brown and black jump-suits enter the great ship via this ramp. As the Targs neared the ship, they were obviously shuffling in formation, but they broke this formation when they started up the ramp.

I was standing at a point directly in front of the ship. Beneath the outstretched wings of the great ship, six sharp edged Targ saucers rested, three under each wing. These saucers, I estimate, were about forty feet wide from rim to rim, and I believe each was manned by four Targs.

The small glowing light spheres I've mentioned before, which must have numbered about a dozen, were constantly busy moving about the great ship, under the wings, over the command pad, zipping out toward the tips of the wings and back.

On Earth in an aircraft hanger or auto garage, one experiences the pungent odors of gasoline and motor oil and exhaust fumes, but in the mothership's bay area the only odors that I remember were an occasional whiff of ether and something similar to static electric burn. There were some other more pleasant odors which defy description.

Presently the six saucers beneath the wings slowly started to rise in almost synchronized unison, and I could hear the deep throb or vibrations of their engines. Multiple blue lights beneath the floor started to flash as the worker machines backed away out of the great triangle. The six saucers rose up and eased into perfect circular slots indented into the undersides of the V-wings, and their fit was flush with the contours of the wings. Unless you were beneath the wings looking up, you wouldn't know that the saucers were there.

Now the great ship itself was warming up. A thousand soft blue lights and a smattering of red ones lit up about the ships. The rumble of the engines could be felt in my teeth and caused my eyes to momentarily blur. Whoosh went the three legs and the ship now sat slightly bobbing above the floor.

The attendant globes would momentarily flare like fire bugs as blue and white arcs of electricity jumped from the ship's surface to them. Tiny streams of spider web like material rained down from the monstrous ship as it began to back away. It didn't turn and head out, but simply backed through the first lock that opened just enough to clear the contours of the ship and then closed immediately after its passing.

On the huge vid-screen I saw the great vee back out into space, turn rather slowly and then move swiftly out toward the rings of Saturn. Its turning and disappearance in the ink black distance took no more than five seconds. I don't know where the great V-wing was heading. Perhaps it would take up orbit just beyond the Earth's stratosphere or behind the moon and dispatch its saucers. Or perhaps they were heading for some other planetary body.

There were several other much smaller V-wing Targ ships there in the docking area, but none nearly as impressive as the great one. After a few minutes it dawned on me that this great machine was piloted by lizards, and I felt a momentarily sickening chill. Question and Tan were standing on the transport disk with me, and Question said, "Kinda makes you want to rush out and tongue kiss an alligator, don't it?" And I laughed, evaporating the emotion.

In 1975, while aboard the great mothership Tan showed me a special computer. The machine was situated in a glass and metal chamber under soft blue lighting and was approximately five feet in height with a clear bubble dome that revealed the computer's brain, and I mean this literally. The brain of the computer was composed of some kind of pink, gray and blue organic matter that seemed to tremble and pulsate as current ran through it. Pinpoints of light danced across the brain's surface. Outside the chamber in a recliner with controls at his fingertips sat a Stagyian. Directly in front of him was a video screen upon which were numerous strange computations and four dimensional body sections and profiles of women, Earth women.

Tan explained to me that the computer was designed and built by Stagyian scientists, and its purpose is to decipher, compartmentalize and ultimately to comprehend and explain all the motivations of Earth women. The machine will ultimately be able to anticipate the actions and reactions of Earth women to any given situation. I learned that the computer has been collecting data for over a hundred Earth years. Success? Tan says that the program has thus far been inconclusive. I told him that he was wasting a perfectly good computer. And Question said, "Yeah, when you figure it out let me know, and I'm going to smack a rogue elephant with my nuts".

On the other hand, I learned that the program concerning Earth man was conducted satisfactorily long ago. It appears that the male of the human species is not a very complicated animal.

This preoccupation with the mental factors and modus operandi of the human species seems to fascinate Tan to no end. Figuring out and anticipating the actions and reactions of any other species of Earth animal except man is a piece of cake to them. Figuring out and anticipating the actions and reactions of other Biaviians and Targzissians, etc., is not nearly so difficult as that of attempting to make sense of the human being's motivations. Therefore human beings remain an endless source of interest to them. About the only thing that they unanimously agree upon is the conviction that, for the most part, humans cannot be trusted.

No Biaviian would ever dream of withholding an invention, concept, procedure or other thing from his fellow beings which could be used for the common good. They cannot comprehend the concepts of monopolies and capitalization upon the ignorance of others, or why greatness is more often than not attributed to the un-deserving while the truly deserving are left unrecognized upon the Earth. Or why rational creatures would create and enforce false realization upon their social orders.

They see a vital segment of society's brain power going to waste because of bigotry and lack of opportunity and can find no philosophical or material justification for it. Try as I might, I've never been able to explain racism, supremacy and bigotry to Tan where he could fully comprehend it. No amount of explaining can convince him of the necessity of people being hungry or homeless when the means to prevent such things are easily within our capabilities. Of course, he is right in his logic, so I really have no justifiable argument to the contrary except to say that the true nature of those who rule our societies seems to be beyond redemption.

He said something once which has stuck with me. He said,

"Martin, were I to base my reasoning upon the level of that which I see then would I not feel justified in controlling through force and fear all that comes before me of weaker strength? Were I so motivated as man, would I not be unto the universe an enemy of all sanctity?" I could only respond with "Thank God we don't have the intergalactic zap-shit that you have".

Still in their eyes it is inevitable that humankind must eventually become a conscious part of the celestial community. Should man survive as a species, he will ultimately evolve into a new, more comprehending and open-minded being, one capable of eventually accepting the existence of the numerous forms of alien life that exist out in the cosmos.

So, at this point, such a thing on the mass level, is out of the question. Prior to this time, all direct intervention into the affairs of humanity has ended in partial or total failure because the warlike, aggressive and ruthless have always succeeded in physically overcoming the spiritually and ethically enlightened.

A case in point was the aliens enlightenment of one of their genetic descendants, Ahnkhnatn, of the eighteenth dynasty of ancient Egyptian rulers. This pharaoh sought to enlighten his idol worshipping people with the one supreme being concept and was ultimately murdered for his efforts. He did, however, manage to impart this concept, along with some of his writings, to the nomadic Semites, who then lived in his area. These nomads embraced the one God concept and passed it along to successive generations though in a less than pure form. We call them the tribes of Abraham, among whom a rather large number of the original genetic bearers of the Elohim abode.

Even unto this day these genetic traits find expression in scientific fruition among the Jews. The fact that more Nobel Prizes have been won by Jews proportionately is no accident or anomaly, and a great portion of the potential Nobel brain power of humanity remains untapped among many other suppressed minority people. Derivative religious orders which are spin-offs of the original have never allowed the latitude for psychological and scientific expansion as have the literary and religious offerings of the Jews. Ignorant people have always hated and sought to destroy them because of that knowledge and that truth, and yet the more astute among these beastly masses have always sought to siphon from the Jews the creations and fruits of that innate knowledge. And with some success too I might add.

That's not to say that any race is devoid of a certain number of individuals who are capable of learning the most complicated mathematical theorems, because the capacity of the human brain to attain knowledge has only been rudimentarily tapped. However, historically some groups of people have collectively spent more time in the pursuit of knowledge.

To be sure the original genetic traits of the celestial are

dispersed sporadically among all of the people, nations and races of the world. It is just that some have utilized this innate attributes to a much greater degree than others. If the quest for knowledge consistently remains a preoccupation of a given people than the gifted ones among them will always find a medium for growth and expression.

The Jews have nearly always been such a people, even though this original genetic trait has been greatly diluted in the Jews through conquest, bondage, dispersal and intermarriage. From the original dark skinned Semitic tribes of Abraham, the trait still remains within them collectively to a greater level than most other nations. Add to this their historical love of knowledge and you have a force which, for its size, is unequaled on the Earth.

Then, like it or not, upon their shoulders falls a responsibility concerning all of humanity, which is far greater than is generally known or consciously recognized by the world at large. Judging from the willful part the Jews are playing in the enslaving of my people in South Africa, I feel that they have consciously fallen far short of this trust and that the baser elements of greed and apathy have slowly taken precedence over the righteous measure. I could expect no more of the European Anglo, but of the Jews I remain un-reconciled. I am sorely heartbroken.

We have come to a point upon this Earth when drastic and awesome alterations in the human equation are inevitable in the very near future. It would be too much to hope that mankind would suddenly undergo a drastic change in sentiments and actions. So we are left speculating just who among humanity will be better equipped to survive the coming Armageddon.

When the great changes come upon us, they will transpire in swift succession, far too swiftly for humanity to prepare for or to adapt to. If at that time, the people of the world would pull together regardless or race, culture and language, the storms might eventually be weathered.

However, all present data collected by the aliens indicates that most of humanity will devolve into anarchy and bestiality and survival of the fittest or the most proficiently deadly will be the order of the day. Of course, the aliens are not perfect, and there is a very slight possibility that this assessment of the human equation is wrong. Yet let me point out that the human being is the only creature of this planet that is capable of altering the course of destiny.

Because of the nuclear throw weight possessed by the world's greater powers, wars on the world scale are no longer feasible. Any major war in the future would, of course, be the last war ever, because no one will take a whipping as long as they have the bomb. At present greater powers must content themselves with mounting small wars by proxy by arming and financially supporting small civil wars in Third World countries.

Idealism plays little part in the minds of the handful of powerful people who orchestrate these civil and country against country wars. The end result of these mini-wars is the full or partial control of the natural resources and profits there from, of those countries by a small group of elite people.

The weapons producers, politicians and high military personnel, as well as secret service officials, who gain monetarily from these ventures are seeking to accomplish these things in descending order of importance: (1) Fostering continual divisions to assure continual weakness. (2) Monetary gain from weapons sales and natural resources. (3) Population control through the creating of circumstances that foster violent death, disease and famine deaths. And (4) to lock the country in question into a system of continual supply debt, from which it will not soon emerge, if ever.

These powerful people can't just simply take the taxpayer's money and pocket it, so they have become masters at getting this money in a round about way. A hundred million is appropriated for a certain so-called freedom fighting or democratic rebel group, but only ten million dollars actually reach the group. The other ninety million has mysteriously been funnelled off into certain pockets and hidden bank accounts. Thus the tax paying public get robbed, and another puppet dictator gets a chance to create his own death squad while swiftly amassing a huge personal fortune.

What the average person fails to understand is that feeding the world, boosting proper medical treatment worldwide and raising the educational and economical level of the world's populace are the very last things that enter the minds of the world's controllers. Yet, if things continue as they are, the planet is caught in a Catch-22 situation. Each day tens of thousands more people, through orchestrated misfortunes, find themselves wards of this country. Thus our borders are constantly inundated with refugees, both legal and illegal, who are fleeing economic and/or political oppression.

Understand that this influx of aliens serves only to heap more hardship upon the already fragmented American middle and lower classes, while having absolutely no immediate effect upon the steadily rising profit margins of the big conglomerates. The more disturbed the working citizen is with the unwanted immigrants, the less likely he is to stop and start analyzing the true nature of things.

So great has the difficulty of finding a job and keeping up with the cost of living been that the world's greatest polluters have been given virtual carte blanche in the poisoning of the planet. Even though the paper mill has killed the river, it still supports most of the people in that county, so few people raise an outcry against this ecological destruction.

The factory owners and the politicians know that the pollution saturation can be brought under control, but to do so they would initially be forced to take a cut in profit, which they are unwilling to do. Even if all industry would do an immediate about face, we would still be too late to prevent most of the futuristic back lash of this chemical horror.

Humanity is at present enmeshed in an orgy of ecological destruction. From the preservatives in foods, to the destruction of the equatorial rain forests, to the numerous toxins in the drinking water supply, the saturation point is upon us. Most people never stop to realize that this planet is a completely self-contained body, a single organism. Absolutely nothing natural to this planet ever leaves the planet. It is simply transposed from one compound to another. Every toxic emission, gas, poison, metal, liquid, acid or vegetable ever created or grown upon the Earth is still with us and will remain so. Most of it settles back to Earth and saturates the eco-system. While organic materials are naturally broken down and reused, inorganic toxins for the most part are not.

Once the nuclear warhead has been built, destroying that nuclear material to a level where it is harmless to living things is literally impossible, because it has an active life span of 26,000 years. When the world leaders proposed to destroy so many war heads, even if this was their wish, it still would not remove the abiding danger of the material, no matter how it is diluted or packaged. The hexachloric acid action of nuclear materials will leach through any materials known to man, including a sheath of pure nickel, within a matter of months or years, not centuries. Everything the material touches in turn becomes contaminated and deadly. So much poison has been dumped into the planet's liquid artery system that it could be considered as a person with leukemia. The planet is actually dying.

I have told you that a certain number of chosen people will be physically airlifted from this planet before or by the year 2011. This number, though encompassing all of the races and physiologically distinctive groups of the Earth, will still be a number so small as to appear insignificant in face of the true numerical value of the human species on the Earth.

And when we leave here, what do we go to? All of my experience with the extraterrestrials over the years has sold me on the belief that, in comparison to what we have here, we go to a living paradise. Yet my perception, although born of the most skeptical and pragmatic scrutiny, is probably not infallible. What if all of it has just been an orchestrated show for my benefit? The aliens, I believe, have great confidence in my natural power of persuasion, and it is only logical that a large number of willing guinea pigs would be preferable to a great number of hostile abductees.

I have concluded that the aliens do not have the technical means to induce mass mind control among humans, and so adept human persuaders would be the next most logical step. Then, on the other hand, I'm forced to give the aliens the benefit of the doubt. Why? Because they do have the technology to produce a thousand or a million human clones from the skin samples of just a few humans. If what they wanted was a chemical free guinea pig or even human food supply, then growing their own would be much simpler. Certainly they wouldn't want the contaminated examples like myself and others.

The alien Tan, I believe, has expended a lot of sincere energy in seeking to understand more of the human emotions and sense of reasoning.

Some people believe that the government has been working with certain extraterrestrial for years, trading people, animals and genetic materials for more advanced technology, but such beliefs, judging from what I've seen, simply don't pan out. Of course, the government would be more than happy to make such a deal if given the opportunity, in which case they would personally supply the abductees and the animals instead of having them picked up at random where nosy relatives and ranchers can witness the results and conceivably cause trouble.

As far as the aliens are concerned, the military and government have no say in the matter. The aliens don't have to and don't ask permission to take what they so desire from the planet. However, you can be certain that the government knows they're out there, knows what most of them look like, and over the years has found at least three downed alien craft or drones.

All that prevents man from fashioning common interplanetary ships is his lack of the ability to generate and miniaturize the necessary power supply for such ships. If humanity should survive with its technological knowledge intact, it would surely eventually perfect such technology.

If man doesn't make it as a species, and the odds are that he won't, he certainly won't be the first, nor will he be the last, intelligent species which didn't make it because of their own violent natures and other destructive preoccupations. In fact the legacy of humanoid genocide and total destruction stretches back over countless eons of time.

The Biaviians have in their archives physical recordings of at least a dozen such celestial tragedies and archaeological recordings of many more. To you this no doubt sounds fantastic if not unbelievable, but let me remind you of the fact for every species of creature now living on this planet, a thousand other species have become extinct. These numerous now extinct species did not simply evolve into newer models. They simply could not adapt to certain ecological changes or were displaced and overrun by a more aggressive species, which in turn met the same fate. Any person living today who is more than two score years in age, has witnessed the extinction of several species of creatures, and may live to witness the extinction of some more.

Were it physically possible for mankind to have completely

wiped out the entire races of his enemies in the past, he would not have hesitated to have done so. If the Nazis had won the Second World War or if the Arabs had their wishes, would any Jews be alive today?

If Saddam Hussein or the Ayatollah Khomeini had the bomb, would the world still be standing? And what of those whacked out psychopathic dictators who will eventually have the bomb? For as we know, experience has shown us that no secret exists which has not or cannot be bought. Most of the bomb quality uranium on the planet comes from northern Africa not far from Libya.

No technology on Earth, except its instruments of destruction, has ever kept pace with or surpassed its creation of negative crisis. In the year 1347, some twenty-five million people in Europe perished of the Black Plague, because real medical research in Europe was relegated to mostly religious quackery by the non-secular suppression of the sciences.

Today we are faced with the manmade chameleon-like deadly virus of AIDS, and this virus alone has the real potential to literally decimate the human species. The existence of these numerous deadly things, coupled with mankind's apathy and greed, literally assures that the roulette gun of extinction will soon stop on a loaded chamber.

Most of humanity goes about its existence seemingly unaware or uncaring of the precariousness of its very presence as a species. The extraterrestrials are acutely aware of the fragility of mankind's state of being, and during much of the time I spent among them, this subject dominated the bulk of our conversations. With due modesty, I must say that the aliens consider me to be one of the most open-minded humans they have ever encountered. However, I balked when Tan asked me if I could ever honestly accept and admire the Targzissians as a fellow species. After a long moment of searching contemplation, I finally said that yes, I honestly thought that I could eventually learn to like and accept the Targs. And Question said, "Yeah, and I'm sure I could learn to love having my pouch stuffed full of dog shit". I just looked at him and shook my head in disgust. Nothing, but nothing is sacred to that awful little animal. Were it not for the fact that he on rare occasions would come out of his pouch with some thing interesting to smoke or drink, I probably would have quit hanging out with Question long ago, and there were even those moments of intoxicated delusion when he was almost likeable, or at least he could con me into thinking he was.

I tell you truly, I do not enjoy being the bearer of dark tidings, and yet it has to be done. The fact that I was chosen by the aliens to be the one with undeniable privy to their existence was not my decision to make. It was made for me, perhaps long before I was born. I'm sure that there must be a chosen number of others who have also had intimate and extensive contact with the Biaviians or some of the other species of aliens. I mean others who have been embraced beyond the rudimentary abductee status, but I've never, to my knowledge, met any of them. Perhaps it was designed in this manner, a counterpart of myself in each country in the world.

Actually the full number of people needed to fill the celestial quota is not so great as to require any great worldwide campaign on the aliens part. They are aware of the fact that were the place and time of the airlift known there would be no shortage of volunteers. However, the aliens don't want just anybody, but just those who are to be chosen by the seekers. And I am one of the seekers. How will I know who the right ones are? I'm told by Tan that I will know them by the frequency of their inner beings.

As I've said before there are many people worldwide who have some amount of the original alien gene. However, the possession of this genetic trait is not essential to being one of the chosen. Paupers as well as princes and saints as well as evil men have possessed the gene. I should add that women too have possessed the gene. The gene is more concentrated among some African tribes, certain oriental groups, certain American Indian tribes and is dispersed on a declining order among American blacks and Caucasians in that order. The Semitic people also have a certain portion of the gene, with the Jews being the foremost among them in the concentration factor.

The movie, 'Close Encounters', was the closest screen rendition ever of the actual physical characteristics of the Biaviians. It was also a fairly close rendition of their mode of telepathic contact and the dimensions and propulsion methods of their ships. Tan has mentioned the movie. I truly believe that Spielberg was directly influenced on the telepathic level in the creation of this movie and that many of his technical personnel were so chosen.

I'm also aware of the fact that Spielberg left out much subject matter that would have presented a broader view of the aliens. I know that he possesses the gene to a concentrated level and that this trait has caused him much controversy during his life. Perhaps we shall get together and make the true movie in the future for we are the only two people on Earth who could do it correctly.

Those men who are blessed with a concentration of the original gene are also cursed to a certain extent. If he is an Aborigine, he will most probably be the artist or the shaman. In America, he would be a scientist, a minister or a movie director, or maybe the leader of a street gang. These men are always visionaries, who can see beyond the shallow facades of their social circles. They are often financially successful but are not truly controlled by the dollar. A large proportion of them are left-handed and naturally artistic in some manner.

The greater portion of them were born in the first six months of the Earth year from November 20 through June 20. Many of them are dyslexic early in life, tending to write letters or numbers backward. Some have speech impediments early in life. They tend to make great lovers, but are almost always unstable in one-on-one relationships.

They are often inventors, poets, actors, leaders of the common people and some times hermits.

One thing that they have in common is the youth strain, even though many have never realized it. It is a fact that the spermatozoa of these men has a quality that retards or even reverses the aging processes in women. Along with this anomaly comes another factor which is perplexing to that man. In about ninety percent of his women companions, his spermatozoa tends to cause her to experience from minor to extreme emotional swings depending upon the mental control factor of the woman. As he is almost always the type of person who is rarely given to mood alterations or emotional outbursts, he is hard pressed to try to decipher why his mate, who was obviously happy and loving five minutes ago, has, for no apparent reason, changed into a vindictive monster. He swiftly learns that even though she might be the most loving person in the world it would be suicide to entrust her with confidential information which can and will be used against him as soon as her mood changes. So among these men you will find the divorce rate very high, and these split ups will continue until he meets a woman on whom the gene has no adverse effect, about ten out of a hundred.

At this point no scientific work research has been put forth to verify what I am telling you because no one has thought to look for and isolate that particular gene and then correlate its presence to the carriers past social life. Those who suspect that they have such an attribute will, after reading these words, start to put two and two together.

Many, like myself, have gone through much of life wondering: is something awful wrong with me or have I always managed to choose mentally unbalanced women for mates? Once he comes to understand that he possesses this special gene, then the circumstances start to make sense. You're not a bad or uncaring or unreasonable person, so don't put yourself down. In fact, you are most probably the type of person whose generosity, compassion and sense of reasoning exceed that of most of those around you, the kind of person who would go to great lengths to right a wrong or to keep a promise.

You are nearly always good with children, and the children automatically accept you no matter how grouchy you try to be on the outside. The same holds true of animals with whom you possess a kind of instinctive communication rapport.

All of these things I've revealed to you, with the exception of the youth factor, are subject to minor variables depending upon many sociological and environmental factors. For instance, the inner city kid who possesses the gene may become a great house painter because he was never exposed to the influences that would have allowed him to expand in the expression of his dormant capabilities. Because of ethnic and racial barriers and monopolies, the totally undeserving and unqualified are the ones who generally inherit the leadership positions and the monetary power in this country and most of the world, which is why the planet is in this shape.

Another fact that is not generally known is that rich women or women millionaires in this country outnumber their male counterparts three to one. For every thirty-four male millionaires, there are a hundred female millionaires. Also women comprise better than 50% of the voters in America.

Even though rich women far outnumber rich males, about ninety-five percent of the corporate and investment forward personnel are white men. What does this mean? It means that women, if they could ever come to a universal agreement on anything, could literally control the politics and the economy of this country, and indeed a large portion of the world where women are given the vote.

Those men in power are well aware of this. However, they also believe that they can rest easy in the assumption that women, on the whole, have never and will never come to agree on anything whatsoever, and therein lies their greatest weakness.

Ultimately, because women live longer than men and because a greater proportion of the wealth will fall into their hands by inheritance and marriage, political leadership will tend to fall into their hands by default.

Prostitutes and the more astute women know that the macho man front, as it is portrayed, is largely a myth, and so does the homosexual segment, which has social contact with the high political and leading male movie roles.

They know that this strata of society is literally pervaded by masochists, bi-sexuals, homosexuals, fetish freaks and hidden creeps. These are the ones who use all of their resources to downgrade and show the minority male in an undesirable light, when in reality these are the only real men we have left, along with the hard working blue collar Caucasian. These strong, often poor and disenfranchised males will ultimately inherit the more progressive females by default. You want an expensive meal, go out with a star. You want to get fucked for real, find him at the construction site. You want money and security, marry the corporate head. You want sex, call a plumber.

At some point in almost every person's life, no matter how rich they are, they must eventually come to the realization that man cannot live on 'false front' alone. On the other hand, it can be said that those women who allow themselves to be pawed over and who must cater to the deviations of rich old freaks for years certainly deserve the money they earn when the bastard dies. The same can be said of the young male who opts to cater to the geriatric wishes of rich old females. As to the straight males who cater to the unholy practices of homosexuality in order to advance themselves, I have no pity or respect.

Elderly men love young women and this is only natural.

Older women love young men and this is only natural. Wealthy older men and women should not hesitate to shower monetary gratuities upon their young lovers. It is well to realize that but for your money you would be just another senior stagnating somewhere unknown and unwanted in one of the dog pounds called retirement homes. Those people in these retirement homes have no less sexual and other desires than you. They just don't have the money to fulfill their fantasies. If you have managed to delude yourself into believing that that young person really loves you for yourself, then go broke and see what happens.

Real men have become a rare and precious commodity on the Earth, and the availability of marriageable young males is dwindling all of the time. You women who have been given advancement opportunities or who have acquired wealth had better take stock of the overall situation and reassess your expectations, because the younger more aggressive females are grabbing up everything that moves.

The ways and manners by which the extraterrestrials gather their ecological and sociological data concerning Earth don't involve any form of science beyond our own concepts and capabilities. They utilize everything from satellite photos to soil, plant and atmosphere samples. They observe, abduct, monitor and test human beings, animals and insects. They monitor radio and television transmissions, etc., and base their findings upon the results of constantly updated super computer data. I needn't have to say that their information gathering and electronic computer apparatus far exceeds our own, yet the principles of information gathering are relatively the same as ours.

You have, no doubt, seen the satellite photo progressions on your television news casts. Well, the aliens are capable of running a progressive satellite surreal simulation of the Earth's atmosphere that encompasses tens of thousands of years, while ours can go back only a decade or so.

Once I was discussing with Tan the horror that forced abductions, sightings, accidental scars and mutilated animals had caused some earthlings, and I berated them for having such a heartless unfeeling attitude in their treatment of people. During my rather extensive dissertation he never said a word. When I finished, he said, "Martin, it is true. Our mistakes are many and without justification in your eyes, yet perhaps you know not the true meaning of horror. Should you so desire, I shall show you true horror". I said, "I desire". And Question said, "Oh, oh, you done fucked up again". He took me into a good-sized circular chamber, and we took seats in translucent levitating recliners. Then he said, "When you have seen enough, we will cease". Presently the entire forward wall of the room became a huge video screen.

As the picture came up, there appeared before me a large

barracks type room, and this room was populated with about fifty children, boys and girls, ranging in age from about six to thirteen or fourteen. Toys were scattered about. Many of the children were dark complected with dark hair and eyes, but a smattering of them were blonde and blue-eyed.

There were neat rows of bunk beds along both walls with wooden tables and chairs in the center of the aisle. Midway in the building there was a large pot-bellied wood heater. The children seemed to be happy and content. Some were reading or playing games, others were eating or simply resting. All of them were dressed in cloth slippers and silken pajama-like clothes. Presently a tall blonde woman dressed in a uniform came into the building and started to call names from a roll. Soon she had about fifteen children of various ages and sexes lined up. She marched them out.

In the next scene all of the children were marched, nude and well washed, into another room, their hands were bound behind them. Suddenly they started to scream and cry out. Across the room, directly in front of them, six other children hung writhing and bleeding from sharp butcher hooks. The hooks had been forced through their ankles, and they were hung by their heels, stretching the Achilles tendon.

A big grotesque bald man wearing a butcher's apron walked up to the first hanging child and deftly slit the jugular vein on the left side of her neck. He proceeded to catch the blood in a large porcelain basin. Even before the last twitches of life had left the young body, the butcher had started to expertly skin the body. He wouldn't butcher the next child until he had finished skinning the first one, and so on down the line. The children awaiting execution were deliberately allowed to view the butchery. Perhaps Tan was speaking to me and explaining the process, perhaps he was not, but I knew why it was being done.

Young unblemished children were chosen for the quality of their skin, which was cured and used to fashion fine coin purses, lamp shades, slippers, wallets and even items of clothing for special customers. The other children were allowed to see the bestiality because the horror caused their glands to secrete adrenaline and enlarged the capillaries beneath the skin, which was believed to enhance the fineness of the skin. This burst of adrenaline also was believed to enhance the flavor of the meat, which was used to feed the rest of the children and some special customers. Of course, the other children were not aware of what they were eating in their stews.

Certain organs and glands were removed from the corpses and distilled into a fluid, which was then used to inject into the muscles of rich aged men, who believe in its rejuvenating qualities. The same procedure is presently done in Switzerland on rich customers using sheep glands.

The hair was used to fashion fine hair pieces of fabrics. Lungs, livers and kidneys were used to make stews for the rest of the children, while other body parts would be used to make sausage. The whole blood was chilled and sent to rich women who liked to bath in it. They believed it excellent for the skin and complexion.

The eyes were removed and preserved in a solution to be sent to medical schools or even to novelty makers. The butchery was a lucrative and well-operated business for several years. Even the fatty grease cooked from the bodies was used to make a fine soap or to serve as a base for a few expensive facial creams.

The calendar on the wall was turned to April 1944, and a star of David emblem was clearly visible on the wall above it. I don't know how long I sat and watched this scene of horror, but finally it was over. Then Tan said, "Martin, this you have witnessed is but a minor level of the true horror that pervades the entire history of the Homo sapien. Would you like to see more?" I declined, but I quit bugging him on the subject of the aliens inhumanity from then on. As I was watching that horrible scene on the screen, I could actually feel the fear and desperation in the air and smell the blood and sweat of the victims.

This creature called man, this monstrous claimant to divinity and greatness, while many of his beastly preoccupations may be hidden from the eyes of other men, absolutely nothing has escaped the scrutiny of the extraterrestrials. Certainly it is not mankind's decency that exempts it from being conquered or annihilated, nor is it his military strength.

His existence, or his continued existence instead, is due to a celestial rule of conduct which prevents the extraterrestrials from taking such actions, and it doesn't seem strange to me at all that they would find humankind a continuing source of curiosity and fascination. Given man's mentality and judging from his evolutionary history, I must conclude that he could be nothing else but a malignancy unto this planet, or any other if given time and opportunity.

The Biaviians believe that by keeping a certain number of humans alive and young for a thousand Earth years on Biaveh, they will be able to create a far more advanced human, both morally and spiritually. I have my misgivings, but I think it could possibly work. Imagine having at your fingertips a thousand times more educational materials and knowing that you are literally physically eternal, having no fear of aging or debilitating diseases, being sexually vibrant for hundreds and hundreds of years. Under such circumstances, a new kind of human could not help but emerge. Will this new race be a peaceful sort? I can only hope that it will be. They will be returned to Earth after a thousand years, at which time they will slowly start to age again, but maybe not.

Perhaps he would have developed a medical technology of his own which will arrest or counteract the aging processes of Earth man. Surely a biologist or geneticist or any scientific mind would advance accordingly if given centuries more time in which to perfect their research. Then, on the other hand, many kinds of research projects which are essential on Earth may very well suffer or be forgotten on Biaveh. What need will there be to research and find cures for diseases that no longer exist?

The utopian plenty of Biaveh will not easily be continued without great effort when the wayfarers return to a much more primitive Earth. I've been told much of what life will be like on the new planet, but the future back on Earth yet remains vague and imprecise.

Regardless of what happens to mankind back on Earth, we can be reasonably assured that some humans will survive the coming times, some animals, and certainly a magnitude of insect species. These will, no doubt, have to be dealt with upon the resettlers return, and the possibility that we will also be sharing the Earth with one or more forms of newly arrived extraterrestrials is also there.

I have seen the highest results of crossbreed human-alien offspring. Will they return with the humans? There are many questions for which I do not yet have answers. I can only hope that Tan would have supplied me with all of these answers before the time of our departure.

I know for a fact that there are a number of alien bases on Earth and have been throughout all our known history, but to my knowledge, these aliens have had social intercourse with man on a large scale only once in history. I know of no future plans for such socialization. Since the first failed or controversial experiment of crossbreeding with man, the aliens remaining have opted to keep to themselves and to keep a low profile on the planet, much as a present day observer of creatures in their natural habitat would do. Of course, even the most careful observers will sometimes be seen and will have to show themselves when collecting samples of the species or other data of ecological and horticultural value.

I believe that the Nyptonians are the ones who man the underseas bases on Earth. I'm told that the glass domes encasing these cities actually become stronger, not weaker, with the passing of time, so that the cities, which are mobile, can actually move to different depths if the need arises. This is necessary sometimes because of the continual movement of the geodesic plates beneath the Earth's surface. They rarely are disturbed by man from above because of the inaccessible areas chosen for most of the installations.

For reasons of re-supply and personnel change, it is necessary, on occasion, for saucers or ships to visit and leave these undersea bases, at which time some have been seen by passing ships. These occasional sightings are rare enough not to pose any problems for the occupants.

I learned that the same outer stratosphere saucer ships can negotiate undersea travel almost as easily as they negotiate stratospheric travel. At times a retractable tail fin is used beneath the sea on some models.

It seems that the electromagnetic power source of the ships generates a force field cover around the ship through which water cannot penetrate. Extreme lightning activity in the Earth's atmosphere has been known to have literally knocked out the power systems of several drones and even a manned extraterrestrial ship. These ships fell into the hands of the Earth's military along with the bodies of the crew members of the ship. The fact that the military and some high members of government are well aware of the alien presence is without question.

In their opinion, this information cannot be revealed to the general public, their logic being that the official revelation of this information would cause panic among the people. However, the real truth is that by revealing the existence of the extraterrestrials they would, in essence, be diminishing the extent of their own power, when compared to the power of the aliens, which they know is far superior to their own.

I am of the opinion and conviction that the people of Earth should be told of the presence of other life forms. I believe that this knowledge would cause people everywhere to stop and reassess the impact of the human experience. Prejudice, racial hatred and war wouldn't be so important any more. Perhaps we would begin to view ourselves as a part of the universal community instead of as the only and ultimate creation of infinity. True, such a revelation would cause man to reassess his history and his religions. Archaeology would finally have to start viewing many of its finds from a different perspective. The physical part that extraterrestrials have played in the history and ascension of man may clearly be seen in many archaeological finds.

By denying the existence of other intelligent life forms in the universe, we can no more cause them not to be than we can the stars.

The history of man has been one long chapter of evil, ignorant and powerful men suppressing the advancement of intelligent men. Even unto this day outmoded and impractical religions are used as the foremost force of suppression in many parts of the world. However, even the most zealous of these religious dictators, while outlawing birth control and many other essential things, to a man have never hesitated in attempting to acquire the most sophisticated weapons of destruction. From the tenth century popes to the present day Ayatollah Khomeini, we live in a time when the most abject, witch hunting stupidity exists right along side the multi-megaton warheads, where powerful and dangerous people are still attempting to make a lie of evolution, where archeological and scientific history is still edited, deleted or changed to fit into the prejudicial concepts of small minds, where the true knowledge of most essential things is kept under lock and key and revealed only to a handful of those in the high echelons of religion, government and secret organizations.

Chapter 17

The Omega Zone

I have learned that the fantastic diversity of life forms throughout the cosmos do indeed defy the imagination. While aboard the great mothership on several occasions I was taken through portions of the ship's very extensive halls of preservation of suspended animation. At those times I saw literally thousands of examples of life forms which were not of this planet, all the way from the enhanced microscopic to the megalithic.

The display was so extensive and diversified that I couldn't even begin to commit them all to memory, nor to recall all of the varied descriptions. Some of the creatures both warm and cold blooded could be recognized as fish or snake or carnivore feline, canine, etc., because of their vague or similar resemblance to their Earth counterparts. Still other creatures I was told were from different prehistoric time periods of the Earth itself.

Tan took me there in order to give me some idea of the numerical value of the varied orders of life in the Milky Way Galaxy alone, and I was told that these numerous examples were only a drop in the bucket, comprising only a minute quantity of the diversity to be found on some of the living planets they have thus far visited.

The Earth collection alone would require more space than can possibly be allotted for it on the mothership. No doubt the Great Agynmum, that huge intelligent octopus, will take his place among the frozen examples in the suspended animation halls, just like the pterodactyl, the Neanderthal and the dodo, because I was told that he is dying.

Other than being extraterrestrials, another thing that fascinates me about the aliens is their open and simple attitude toward tragedy. In fact, the Biaviians are not prone to show any emotions whatsoever, yet Tan has an insatiable craving to experience human emotions. Perhaps all Biaviians have this wish. It seems that they aren't able to experience the emotions of all animals or even all humans. This may be one of the main reasons that they expend so much energy on observing and abducting humans.

Tan readily admits that some humans possess neurological attributes or powers that the aliens don't or no longer have. He spoke of a man named Ahbey Mabebe and a man named Wolf Massing, both of whom were endowed with great mental powers. I don't know who they are, but they must be very special people indeed. He named a number of others whose names I can't recall. Apparently they have contacted and/or observed these people throughout their lives. Who knows how many gifted earthlings are under close observation.

I'm told that the predominant percentage of human beings have the dormant ability of telepathic communication but rarely attempt to develop this attribute. During that thousand years that the chosen humans will spend on the planet Biaveh they will have more than ample time to develop this innate quality.

Perhaps it is fortunate at this time that a large number of humans are not able to easily use the power of telepathy. Why? Because such a power would no doubt be diverted into nefarious and super-negative zones of use.

During my mind link with the Targ, I learned first hand the potentially destructive power of negative telepathy. Further, I'm fairly certain that this power of telepathy in humans could be dangerous even to the Biaviians themselves. I believe that this is another reason why they are so discriminating in their choice of those few humans who they choose to develop close face-to-face and mind-to-mind relationships with. Yet, when we stop to consider all of the nice, placid and even-tempered people they could have chosen instead of me, we may be given to wonder just how smart are these aliens? I have given this considerable thought and come to the conclusion that the aliens are not so concerned with a certain emotional level in humans but in the over-all nature of the person.

The elements of human emotion are numerous and varied in intensity and duration. Constant extremes in any direction are abnormal. Any race of people who can enslave another or hate another human being because of race or complexion or any race of people who will stand by, condone and enjoy the fruits of the suppression of his fellowman cannot be considered normal or desirable on the scales of logic, be it celestial or earthly.

A human being doesn't have to pull the trigger in order to be a component of inhuman evil. Thus the greater majority of the human species must be literally discounted from consideration by the aliens.

It's certainly not for lack of communication skills that the aliens have chosen not to have any widespread dealings with humanity. To their technology, there are no hidden computer programs or totally deceptive psychological systems in existence on the Earth. They are well aware of the fact that the administration in South Africa has a less visible counterpart in Europe, Russia, America and elsewhere. They are acutely aware of the ongoing and concerted racial and economic injustice in this country and the world.

The Targzissians, unlike the Biaviians, actually consider certain races and most of humanity as nothing more than lower life forms and thus not deserving of any over animal consideration. We can be thankful that the Targs are bound by the same 'do not harm' rule that applies to all of the other aliens.

A well read human might be able to search the annals of history and cite a smattering of humans who are deserving of the highest esteem on the celestial scale because of their selfless, giving and compassionate acts throughout their lives, and these examples may be used as a strong positive argument as to the potential greatness of man. Yet when the human species is viewed collectively down through history, its inhuman actions far exceed any positive iotas of exemplary decency dotting that history.

In fact most of the exalted historical figures have chosen to or have been forced to resort to inhumanities, which would easily put them in the category of mass murderers and salivating panderers. The philosophies of even the most loving prophets of history have served as the justification for millions of murders and hundreds of wars since their passing. Suffice it to say, there has never been a philosophy, religion or order created on Earth which has not been used as the justification for all manner of beastly actions by its followers. (It may be safely said that all famous would-be pacifists must hire men with guns to protect them from those who would be tyrants, while all famous would-be tyrants must hire men with guns to protect them from those who would be pacifists).

If the aliens so desired, they could prevent man from destroying this beautiful planet, but in order to do that they would be forced to literally come forth and take over the resources and governments of the world. They would be obliged to introduce more advanced and alternative technologies, such as fusion power and genetically engineered agriculture, as well as population control. This they are not prepared to or are prevented by celestial laws from doing, nor would mankind accept or appreciate their intervention.

At one span in history the Earth served as a reservoir, which supplied water and vegetable matter to an alien mining colony on Mars, but that operation was discontinued thousands of years ago. The aliens have apprised me of their plan to prevent the complete extinction of humanity as a species. However, as far as I know, they don't have any plans to prevent man from destroying himself down to a mere fraction of his present number. In their mode of logic, I believe they have concluded that most of mankind must go in order to assure the continuing survival of the planet itself. To give man boundless energy and to wipe out diseases and wars would only compound man's ability to further alter, rape and destroy the ecological balance of the planet. The way they see it the human race is far easier to preserve and replace than would be the whole planet. It's a pity that so many must perish, but under the circumstances it can't be helped.

The aliens have attained a level of technology which would tax the wildest imaginations of the scientific mind, and yet in the logic of the quest for power and riches, they are, in many ways, on the level of the most primitive of Earth men. In this manner, any possession beyond practical necessity is passed along or simply discarded. A Caribe Indian in the South American jungle would never dream of carrying several sets of clothing, extra pots, pans or silverware, extra bows and arrows, or unnecessary materials like gold, silver, etc. Anything he can't wear or eat, he considers an encumbrance. He kills only enough game to feed his group and nothing goes to waste. He doesn't build two houses, when he needs only one or carry extra shoes.

I am told that even the Biaviians came through a period of greed, decadence and gluttony, which was similar to that of present day man, but eventually common logic and necessity won out. Now in all practical respects, the foremost technological beings practice a lifestyle which, in essence, parallels that of the most primitive Earth man. Every Biaviian, high and low, possesses only that which is of practical necessity. In the final analysis, all of life boils down to the simple essentials, that is eating, sleeping and procreating. Nothing else is truly essential to survival.

I believe that capitalism upon the Earth is a legal, if not totally essential, concept, because of our numerical value and technological limitations. However, the factor of disparity in the sharing and dispersal of this planet's resources is untenable and is not conductive to the forward progression or even the universal stability of the species. Resources or the lack of resources are constantly used as a political level to keep the masses dependent and in line.

Even the aliens have statutes and laws which evolved from necessity, and no matter how complicated their technology, their laws are quite simple and to the point. Man, while less advanced technically, has cluttered and complicated laws, which are presently designed to protect the rich and penalize the poor. Legal loopholes, political action bribes, junk bonds, savings and loan scams and a host of deregulations allow the conglomerates to literally commit murder with impunity and to rob the public blind without fear of legal retribution. The system is designed so that any political candidate of substance cannot help but owe his soul to the big money interests.

Most people are naive enough to believe that people including politicians are as decent by nature as they are. This is a most unfortunate misconception. An honest but un-wealthy man has about as much of a chance of running and winning a major political position as a hippopotamus has of ballet dancing. Even the maggot infested state of things need not be so terminal as to completely destroy the very worth of society and the formerly resourceful heart of the nation's middle class.

Prior to this time in history, the super rich were not adverse to sharing a small percentage of their prosperity with the little guys. Their reasons may not always have been altruistic, but many of them actually believed in this country and held a grudging admiration for the hard working joe. However, the new breed of business mogul of today holds no such sentiments and will stop at nothing less than taking it all. They have succeeded admirably with the collusion and help of the politicians, judicial systems and the boot-licking foot soldiers, commonly called police officers. They have learned to hire homos, bigots and borderline psychotics to people the police forces as the older, better men are retiring. I didn't say more honest men, but less vindictive and bigoted men are retiring.

In Japan it is against the law to export jobs that can be filled by the people at home or to sell private property to overseas buyers. It's against the law to import materials and products that are made in Japan, and any concessions or bending of these laws must clearly be in the best interests of the export segment of home economy. As a result, Japan does not have an unemployment and homeless underclass problem, because the big money people have not lost all love and respect for the common people of their country. They look out for their own. They long ago learned that conservative Americans will sell their children, mothers and souls for a dollar, and they have no qualms about taking advantage of these inherent genetic and moralistic weaknesses.

What these thieves fail to understand is that money and position can't really protect them from the wrath of the multitude of psychotics they are creating through these Judas goat actions. Desperate poor people first turn on themselves violently, while the formerly solvent often picks some prominent individual or individuals to violently fixate upon. They don't seem to understand that they are creating their own assassins through their own greedy actions, and by conspicuously advertising their decadent consumption, they unknowingly give their very physical lives into the schemes of the obsessed psychotic.

The belief that any one with money can truly protect themselves and their loved ones indefinitely from the determined and resourceful psycho is an erroneous belief. Still, for the greedy man, it is cheaper to hire bodyguards than it is to do less profitable but decent things, like keeping the factory in America. It cannot be very comforting to lay down each night knowing that someone out there is obsessively plotting your doom. I am not saying these things to be vindictive, I'm simply stating the facts as they have come or are swiftly coming to be.

Television news show revelations of inner city crack houses and prostitution serve to induce fear into the hearts of the so-called law abiding citizens. The truth is that the rich elite have little or nothing to fear from the inner city dope user. No, the person they have reason to truly fear is the laid off white and blue collar worker, the unemployed computer programmer, steel worker or former S & L executive. These are the people who are the mad bombers, serial murderers and fixation psychotics of today and their numbers grow daily. The rich and famous person who takes my words lightly will live to regret it.

Since I was first contacted or abducted by the extraterrestrials in 1953, the collective telepathic mood of the world has changed drastically. Political movements around the world at this time while moving toward more democratic sociological concepts on the surface appear to indicate a more positive outlook for the planet, but I'm told by the aliens that this is only an illusion masking the true underlying desperation on the part of the masses, and on the part of the rulers who have milked them down to their last ounce of blood. The name of a political system has little to do with the real manner in which it is run.

True democracy and true communism have never and do not exist in any so-called civilized society on the Earth. Equal rights for all and due process of law have never and do not exist within any so-called civilized society. The common man is fined or even arrested for catching a fish from the river without a license, while the factory owners can literally kill all life in the whole river without fear of legal repercussions. This is democracy as it is practiced, and the recent political movements will not alter these practices.

I am told by the aliens that the trafficking in the buying, breeding and selling of babies and young children for pornography, physical torture, deviate sexual practices and human sacrifices is at the highest level since the years of the Second World War, and the purchases and users are the rich of all societies, predominantly those of western society, Europe and the Americans.

Moralistically, civilization is at its lowest level since the time of the Inquisition, and this deviate sickness grows greater with each passing day. Revelations of such rings in the near future with the names of many well-known people connected with them will shake the world. Included in the number will be politicians, doctors, judges, movie actors and huge financial business moguls, as well as big time preachers and certain noted personages of the Catholic faith.

But these coming revelations are but a drop in the bucket, a tip of the iceberg, in comparison with the true magnitude of the situation. No rich man, secular or non-secular, believe in or fears God. Such a belief is, by its very nature, an antithesis to his position and materialistic life style. It is nearly, if not totally impossible, to be decent and worth a hundred million dollars while whole families sleep on the street. The Bible says that the poor will always be with us and this is true, but there is a great difference in being merely poor and being completely destitute and without hope.

In the aliens archives are color videos of historical events spanning tens of thousands of years, and if they tell you something is so, they are prepared to show it to you. When Tan showed me that terrible film circa 1944 of the skinning of the children, I did not detect any strong emotional change in him, but he literally swooned on the emotions that he gleaned from me during the screening. While he knows of the concept of true horror, he has no inherent way of truly feeling it, and the film alone was not capable of literally retaining the inner emotions of those children, but I could recreate those feelings for him and pass them on in tangible form.

The Targzissians have, during the course of abducting and examining humans, sometimes caused the abductee excruciating pain, but were unaware of the depth of the mental and physical anguish simple because they are, with rare exception, unable to tune in emotionally with human beings, even as we might fail to pick up the emotional and mental terror of some creature we have captured for study but have no deliberate intentions of hurting. The Biaviians are different, in that they are extremely sensitive to the emotions and physical pain of humans and are thus much more gentle with their abductees.

In verbal conversation, the words are analyzed by humans for meaning. However, in telepathic communication, the opposite is true. The words you speak aren't nearly as important as the inner meaning of the speaker. This is why Tan could always tell whether I was serious or not about a certain thing. If I told him that I hated Question and would like to see him in a pot cooking, he knew that I actually loved the creature and was only momentarily disgruntled with him. And with good reason too, I might add.

When you and I are viewing an action packed adventure movie with car chases, gunfire and explosions, we tend to get caught up emotionally in the action, but it's different with the aliens. They tend to measure the force of the blast and disseminate the actions into technical components. They are more interested in the expertise of the special effects than in the story line. It's not that they aren't capable of emotions, instead it means that emotions must be real in order for them to appreciate them. They know that emotions cannot lie. You either feel it or you don't.

By tuning in to my emotions during a time, thought or

incident, Tan is able to correlate that emotion to the thing that is happening, thereby gaining a deeper insight into the human experience. The negative and desperate emotions sent up at any given time collectively by the human species must be awesome indeed, and the aliens can sense its drift.

I have noticed that when Tan is tuned in to me telepathically, any extreme emotion on my part tends to have a definite physical effect on him, so much so that he often has to draw back from its intensity.

Physically the Biaviians are weak and fragile, and any great physical show of emotion toward them on the part of a human, such as a bear hug, a smacking kiss on the check or a firm hand shake, could easily injure them. A conspiratorial elbow or finger poke in his side could hurt him. Because I sometimes become physically expressive. I noticed that Tan tended to keep a safe distance between us when we traveled about or set for discussions.

When a Biaviian wishes to touch you, which is rare, their touch is always slow, measured and tender, no sudden grabs or back slaps. Now Question, on the other hand, is physically durable and had no qualms about grabbing my leg or arm or jerking on my robe, etc. You wanted some skin, Question would slap five with you in a minute. Question was also good about faking you out. You might attempt to slap him five, and he would snatch his hand away and say something like, "now don't you look silly?" Question never apologized or had any qualms about hurting your feelings, and his limitation of insults was not restricted by my own sense of 'put down' creation. For instance, in disgust, I might say something like, "Question, do you realize that you're funky, you stink". And he would look at me and retort: "Did you ever try to ease out a fart in a crowded place but it came out loud anyway, 'wheet', and you got real embarrassed with you stinkim ass?" And he would be looking real serious when he asked the question. I would just shake my head and walk off.

During the time spans I spent aboard the great mothership, I was left alone with Question for varying periods of time on a number of occasions. Where Tan went and what he did during those times away, I haven't the slightest idea. I'm certain that we must have always remained under surveillance, but I couldn't sense being watched.

There were most certainly parts of the great ship which were off limits to me. If Question and I walked about, it was he who took the lead in direction, and when we stepped aboard the levitating transport disks, the thing would automatically go in any direction I wished, up to a point, then it would turn on its own or reverse course.

Keeping me within the allowable boundaries was done in a subtle manner, never through speakers or alarms or recognizable warnings signs. If I became insistent upon going in an off limit direction, a drone machine of some sort might block my path or shimmering blue horizontal lines of force would suddenly appear. I don't think the laser lines would have harmed me if I touched them, but I decided against chancing it.

Sometimes while walking along, Question would say something, and his voice would actually startle me because even though the mothership is huge and peopled by thousands of aliens, there is very little sound or human sound. Telepathy is silent, and even the robot workers and machines are very quiet. One could pass right by you and only the soft wave of the air would indicate its passing. You would find yourself automatically placing your feet silently as you walked. There was always a distant hum from the ship's engines and the fleeting whiz of small transport ships moving about through the vast spaces of the inner ship. Even the worker robots that repair or serviced the landed crafts did it without the 'clinks' and 'pings' one generally associates with a garage or repair ship.

I noticed another thing, Except for Tan, Nela and Question, I was never close enough to physically touch any of the other aliens. Of course, they would pass by on transport disks by the hundreds, but the distance between the lanes and the disks was out of touch range. I saw Targs and Dorians in their respective lounge areas but did not enter myself. Only on one occasion aboard the ship did a Targ approach me, and it was not to socialize but to retrieve a light metal object that Question had stolen from him and then passed along to me. On Earth in May 1988, two Targs materialized for several minutes in my apartment in Tulsa and amputated the last joint of my right pinky finger, but those two beings were wearing life support system complete with close fitting helmets.

Also, I remember that during my first and second contact with the aliens, the tall skinny Stagyians were the ones who did the physical exams on me aboard the saucer, and they would touch me some times with their flat ended fingers. I've never seen a Stagyian without his life support apparatus. Obviously they are very careful about picking up infectious organisms from humans or of infecting humans with organisms of their own. The Stagyians are also physically fragile, or at least I got that impression.

The physical shortcomings on the part of the aliens should, in no sense, give man cause to feel superior, because these beings have at their fingertips destructive technology which would defy the imagination. They can destroy a planet by blowing it to bits, or they can actually destroy matter altogether leaving only a black hole where the planet used to be.

While Earth is no doubt a fascinating entity of observation and experimentation to them, it is but one among many projects which are ongoing at any given time. I was told that there are a number of celestial planetary bodies out there upon which man could live without the aid of artificial support systems.

Out in the cosmos, the species chain generally follows the

life order chain on Earth. Numerically the mammalian species, including man, on Earth is far exceeded by other species of creatures. Thus intelligent and sub-intelligent mammal life forms are the rarest of all throughout the cosmos. You could expose new living planets for a life time without coming upon another intelligent Homo sapien like mammalian life form.

Because of the disparity between man's tech-advantage over all other species on Earth, human beings find it hard to believe that any life forms other than that homo erectus could ever achieve advanced logic and technology, but I know this to be a false assumption judging from what I've seen with my own eyes.

Even on those rare occasions when mammals evolve to gain a foothold on a planet, the odds are against their ever enduring to reach a status of over animal intelligence. The infinitesimal fraction who survive to reach the primitive human-like stage are nearly always doomed to become extinct within a short span on the evolutionary scale of time through disease, natural disasters and by being overcome and displaced by more ferocious and numerically superior species. This would surely have happened on Earth had it not been for the intervention of extraterrestrials in the scheme of things. Even today, under certain circumstances, the most advanced human societies would swiftly revert back to the most primitive order of human existence.

The dinosaurs were destroyed before anything resembling a present day human evolved upon this planet. However, if for some reason, man would be stripped of all his technology and placed upon an equal survival footing with the dinosaurs and other creatures, the dinosaurs would win. On the scale of evolutionary time, it is safe to say that the mammal species will always advance up the ladder much quicker than would a reptile, fowl or insect. However, this in no way rules out the fact that, given time and the proper set of circumstances, all other life forms, including the insect, can eventually attain a highly technical state of existence.

We must not make the mistake of assuming that our sense of logic is the only viable means of intelligence progression, because it is not. We have only to look at the short evolutionary history of man to understand that once the first level of over animal knowledge is obtained, like the use of fire, all other facets of progression tend to accelerate.

On more than a few occasions through disease, natural disasters and wars, high levels of civilization have been overcome and cast back into the most primitive stages. For such a catastrophic thing to happen today would require a more destructive effort on the part of the victors than it did in the past, but it could be done.

In ancient times, the people who possessed the deeper knowledge of things were small in number in any given society, and the same thing is essentially true even unto this day. We take for granted that all of our electronic gadgetry, cars, packaged foods, etc., will always be there, but how many of you know how to make food preservatives, car engines or VCRs from scratch? The victor need only murder that handful of people who form the base of our technological knowledge and destroy their computer programs in order to stop technological advancement in its tracks. The only thing standing between the average cosmopolitan American and the aboriginal lean-to is his access to books and the existence of that small number who are capable of comprehending them.

For any species of creature that cannot swiftly adapt biologically and live under the most harsh and extreme conditions, life is a fragile and tenuous prospect at best. For lack of medical knowledge, some twenty-five million people perished in Europe of the Black Plague in 1347-38, and a blight of the potato in the 1800s did more to destroy the economical and social autonomy of Ireland than any other one thing in its recorded history. The failure of just one crop of a certain species of bamboo planet would be enough to cause the complete extinction of the panda. A thirty minute nuclear warhead exchange between the two greatest super powers would be enough to decimate the human species beyond its ability to make a comeback.

On the other hand, such a man-make holocaust would have little or no effect upon the numerical value and continuation of the insect kingdom at all. If this entire planet would suddenly experience an ice age that lasted ten thousand years, it would surely destroy all mammal, fowl, reptile and most aquatic life. However, it would only prove a minor inconvenience to the insect order. This is why insects are by far the most abundant life form inhabiting planets throughout the cosmos, followed by mollusks, fish, reptiles, fowl and mammals in that order.

We can safely say that from the very first moment that a Homo sapien like man creature looked at a flower and began to view it as a thing of beauty instead of something potentially good to eat, he entered the 'omega-zone', and his evolutionary destiny was cast, immutable from that moment on. At that very moment he removed himself from the lower animal kingdom to which he could never truly return. It would be only a short matter of time before he began to contemplate returning to the stars.

Life, or the chemical stuff from which physical life originates, is abundant throughout the cosmos, and life matter is opportunistic enough that it never passes up the slightest chance to come to be. If the planet is a frozen wasteland, it will seek out those warm springs that boil up from the planet's bowls and await its chance to expand. If the surface of the planet is molten rock, it will seek out that small area, perhaps beneath the surface, which is less effected, or even plant its seed high in the thin cooler stratosphere of the molten planet.

Suns and planets can be and are constantly being destroyed, while others are in the infant stages of forming into solid entities. As far as life is concerned, all of these cataclysmic happenings pose no real or lasting problems. A planet, a solar system or even an entire galaxy may suffer destruction, but the force that is life will patiently wait a few billion years for another galaxy to form and then continue its physical manifestations. An eternity seems like only yesterday.

In the biological workings of nature, any form of intelligence which manages to remove itself from the ecological order of progression in essence becomes a false or artificial entity. In this sense, mankind and all alien technological intelligences must fit into this category. The bushman is much more a part of and is less an impediment to the biological order of nature, than is the Westerner, the Biaviian or the Targ. From the standpoint of natural order on this planet, the human species true status ranges from the benign tumor to the terminal cancerous growth and is in direct and opposing conflict with the natural order of nature.

The most primitive man is much closer to the essence of the God's head than the Bishop, Pope or preacher could ever hope to be. The primitive man knows that the life force is eternal, while the foremost religious scholar remains skeptical and uncertain.

Throughout the cosmos, above animal intelligences are numerically rare. However, life in many lower physical forms is not so rare. Thus it is found that numerous living planets may be visited which have no above animal master species, but intelligent life forms, by necessity and out of the insatiable curiosity that is a by-product of logic, will eventually discover and colonize these planets, which is how we got here and why we are seeking to continue our exploration of the cosmos.

Understand that while the creature that would eventually become man has evolved on Earth from natural acids and carbons, the force of life that adapted the organism has always been and shall always be. The complete destruction of Earth would simply mean that this life force would have to start the evolutionary processes over again on some receptive celestial body, and because this form of intelligence requires a certain DNA chain receptor, the end product would probably again look similar to us. The new creature might be heavier or lighter, depending on the ecology and gravitational force of the next planet, but it would have two arms, legs and eyes and would eventually walk upright. Given a few million years of evolutionary progression, it would learn to build some more nuclear bombs.

A host of other earthly life isotopes would no doubt drift along in the same carbon hydrogen clouds that carried the human consciousness and would likewise start to evolve on the new planet. Perhaps on this planet no extraterrestrials would come along and destroy the dinosaurs, and the mammals might never get a foothold and come to be the supreme species there. Nature nurtures and protects only those things tenacious enough to survive the primordial natural and predatory factors. Nature shows no more love for man than it does for the ant or the snail. If it gets cold and you can't grow fur or learn to use the fur of other creatures, you die. It's as simple as that.

We are approaching the portals of the twenty-first century, and wars, hatreds and violence of all manner are more prevalent today than they were two thousand years ago. Man has not learned from his past mistakes, and so he forfeits another planet and scraps another bio-span.

It is some consolation to know that there has always been and that there will always be a small number among humanity who will keep alive the elements of decency and brotherly love, but their number is far too few among the predatory factions of this bio-span. Those who truly seek cannot help but find some measure of the truth and reality of existence. But there are too few seekers now living. Those who would exist upon the rewards of bigotry, slave mongering and war cannot or will not accept the truth, because the way of their chosen existence cannot be justified to any degree.

Once a disembodied life form finds an evolutionary home, it becomes locked into the repetitive mode of continued birth, death and rebirth, in that same planetary body. In a small number of rebirths, the individual may actually retain some conscious recollections of past lives. A rare number retains enough of their past attributes to become child prodigies, but the vast majority retain little more than the personality flavor of the past life span.

The Biaviians can and do clone identical biological counterparts of themselves, but not even they can clone the acquired knowledge and recollections of the experiences of the original. In order to achieve this, the physical brain from the original must be transplanted into the new body and even then some portion of the original knowledge is lost, perhaps due to the unavoidable destruction of some brain cells during the transfer.

These things I'm telling you were explained in detail to me. However, I believe that I would have eventually reached a lot of the same conclusions on my own. My inclination for as long as I can remember has been to question the nature of all things. I have explored many religious and secular philosophies and found them all wanting in the overall sense of logic. I understand that man's knowledge can be no greater than his accumulation of learning since his recorded beginnings. However, some notable number of humanity shall soon have access to the archives of the universe.

I know that the larger portion of you who read this book will scoff at and dismiss the material herein out right or at least you will try to, and with some success until these things are upon you. By then it will be too late for the non-believers to join us, and this is the way it was meant to be.

I can say that no matter who you are, be you laborer or mathematician, you will not finish this literary work totally unaffected.

I tell you that we are in the last days of life on Earth as we know it. I do not take relish in revealing this, but my failure to do so would not change a single thing. What if a large portion of the world's leaders would read this book and begin to see the light? Together they might succeed in staving off the inevitable. But such a thing would be too much for the reasoning mind to even seriously contemplate. No, we're up shit creek without a paddle, and our fate is most probably sealed.

I had no great desire to return to the Earth after my last stay aboard the great mothership, but I wasn't given a choice in the matter. I would have been perfectly content to have remained there and continued to explore that leviathan wonder, but alas that was not yet to be. I know that some others down through history have been allowed to remain among them and may have played some part in influencing the Biaviians to return and save humanity from extinction. They have proven that human beings can live for hundreds or thousands of years without feeling the compulsion to go to war. They have shown that human beings are capable of rising above hatred and bigotry, and they have also proven that given the proper circumstances, free from hunger and sickness, there is no limit to the level of spiritual awareness that the human mind can attain. Yet after having existed for centuries on the planet Biaveh, those humans are probably so different from Earth man in their thought processes and motivations that most of them could not be considered a fair representation of Earth man today. The genetic pool of those people has need of fresh blood, as well as different psychological variations.

The Biaviians are convinced that my presence on Earth is essential to what they wish to do. They also believe that a proper number of desirable people will hear and believe what I have to say. I don't know if they grasp the significance of choosing some famous well-known human being as an emissary instead of an unknown traveler like myself. I pointed out to Tan that human beings are shallow and gullible, and that a well-known and trusted human could probably accomplish this mission far easier that myself.

But he answered me saying, "Do you not already have enough false prophets and scavengers of stupidity and weakness? Must you also consider me blind in judgment of that which is? Better that I should embrace an angered viper than do as you have said. Those who consume rare flesh and glisten of carbon while multitudes perish for want of essential sustenance have already their rewards. Not a pinch of benevolence given or compassion felt. Still they shall find their enjoyment fleeting and their end to be just".

"Martin, even the jackals do share, thus should not the lowly scavenger be considered greater than the foremost among your species. You, Martin, though given opportunity, have not preyed upon the weaker, nor sought to enslave your brother. You have had the chance to enrich yourself by the spreading of superficial and false doctrines, yet you have not".

"When others suffered greatly, your compassion exudes forth, and have you not shared your last meal on many occasions? You have never sought to do harm for the sake of sadistic gratification, and you have loved and respected some among them who even now seek to destroy the positive essence of your people".

In our Biblical scriptures and in the scriptures of other religions, as well as other archaeological recordings, the extraterrestrial visitors were thought to be Gods or Angels. This is understandable as certain Earth men have been mistaken as Gods by more primitive people, who were seeing them for the first time.

After having learned the manner in which the Biaviians literally altered the evolutionary course of Earth and by which they settled their present home planet, it is not difficult to attribute to them a godlike status. Think about it.

The Biaviians came upon their present home planet while it was yet in its evolutionary infancy. There was as abundance of aquatic life forms, but few species which had made the move from the waters to land. Even the plant life was for the most part composed of water plants. So we may consider them something like gods in the sense that they had an opportunity to literally shape the fauna and ecology of that planet to their own designs and wishes.

They had brought with them numerous species of the desirable plant seeds and some useful insect species from their last planetary home. No doubt they also had certain animal embryos and creatures in suspension. On their former planet, there were many forms of plant and insect, as well as higher animals, that they did not consider essential, so they didn't bring them. Over the eons they have added to their planet's collection of desirable plant and animal life by gathering specimens from many other living worlds in the cosmos. The result is a utopian paradise, free of the non-essential nuisance factor.

If you had come upon the Earth in its infancy, would you have fashioned it as is claimed by the God of Biblical scriptures? Or would you have left out some things like fleas, mosquitoes, thorn bushes and moths? Would you have allowed as many poisonous snakes, clutching vines or leeches? I think not.

Natural scientists will tell you that all living things play an essential part in the ecology of this planet, but this is not true where many things are concerned. Locusts, boll weevils and tomato worms do not help your crops. If all mosquitoes disappeared, all of the fish would not die, and numerous other kinds of detrimental things could be excluded from this planet and the ecology would continue to thrive. Tens of thousands of species of things have become extinct since the beginning of this planet, but their passing didn't stop anything, did it?

Of course, in another hundred million years or so, Biaveh will probably start evolving many of those pesky species that Earth evolved long before man came to be, so they have a jump on evolution that man never had. On any living planet it may be safely said that the evolutionary processes will roughly parallel the past evolutionary stages of the Earth, beginning from microscopic one-celled aquatic forms to crustaceans, worms, fish, insects, reptiles, fowl and then mammals.

Of course, the elemental atmospheric and geological composition of the young planet will directly influence or dictate the many physical forms that the new life will take. It will go through many climatic stages of warming and cooling and cataclysmic upheavals.

At certain stages conditions will be favorable for certain species to thrive and become the dominant force on the planet. Fish and crustaceans will grow to megalithic size in the nutrient rich waters, and insects will become giants. Dragonflies will have wing spans of three feet, and roaches will grow a foot long. Two feet tall praying mantis will do mortal battle with large lizards and win.

For a hundred million years it will be a world of nightmarish venomous deadly things of huge form locked in eternal and mortal combat, clawing, stinging and ripping their way to ascension. Ultimately one order will rise to dominate, and each major order will ascend to the forward place in time with the passing of the ages. Numbers, size and ferocity, instead of intelligence, will dictate the state of things.

Most of this has yet to transpire on the new planet Biaveh, but the Biaviians are in a position to control the progression of things. Is this good? The Biaviians think so. Unlike earthlings, the Biaviians have no established misconception of some omnipotent force creating a planet and all its life forms in six days. They realize that nature may bring forth just any kind of terrible, useless and harmful thing, simply because that thing had the tenacity to survive. Because it lives is not sufficient reason to assume that the thing is good or necessary.

If left to its own designs, nature will continue to create and to create without regard for one species over another. No matter how docile or lovely the creature, if it can't adapt, nature ruthlessly exterminates it. You may be sure that had the aliens not destroyed the dinosaurs those creatures would still be the dominant life form on the planet.

You must remember that during the hey day of the thunder lizards, the creature that would one day become man was no more than a rodent-sized creature darting among the twining roots of huge swamp bottom trees. The only reason this rodent-like creature was able to survive was due to its tiny size, about three inches long, and its ability to evade pursuit by burrowing in to the soft humus. Still the size, number and diversity of the habits of the many different kinds of lizards would have eventually sought out the nests and consumed them. Or at the very best, the future evolution of these creatures would surely have been held in check by the eternal predatory presence of the thunder lizards and a host of other perils.

You must understand that all manner of life, no matter its origins, has come through these various stages of evolution. Some species reach an ideal stage of evolution and may remain essentially the same, physically, for hundreds of millions of years, like the common cockroach, for instance. Yet given a few score more million of years, the cockroach will evolve further and its physical dimensions will change. Evolutionary change is a never ending process.

Neurologically and physically, due to the intervention of the extraterrestrials, man is millions of years ahead in his natural evolutionary process. According to the dictates of time and natural progression, man would not yet have learned the use of fire let alone be able to split the atom. Thus they feel somewhat responsible for our present state of being, and because of this genetic kinship, they will save humanity from complete extinction.

Perhaps the word extinction is too strong a term. Even after all of these cataclysmic things transpire upon the Earth, it is reasonable to assume that some humans somewhere will survive. With anything short of an all-out nuclear exchange between the two greater powers, we can conclude that certain small geographical areas will still be able to sustain small populations. It is enigmatic that the ones who now have the most, the most technically advanced, are the ones who are least likely to survive. For those who are left alive in the western cities, existence will be far more perilous than for the survivors on desert islands or in the most remote jungles.

It has been proven and observed that even under the most prosperous conditions, civilized cosmopolitan people are the most hateful, bigoted, racist, perverted and sadistic creatures infecting the Earth and all of these negative attributes are magnified in direct proportions to the economic hardships of that society, a case in point being pre-World War II Germany.

To my knowledge, there has never been a recorded case of incest or serial murder among the most primitive tribes of people. Primitive people do not abuse their children or monopolize all of the food and resources, while their fellow tribesmen starve. No one is homeless in those villages, and the elderly are cared for and revered for their wisdom instead of locked away in animal cages called retirement homes as are the civilized elderly.

The chief of the village or tribe gained his position because of his leadership abilities, such as hunting prowess, combat success and benevolent wisdom, and not because of looks, ghost written speeches and special interest money.

The failure of electricity and the disruption of communications in the western world immediately cripple society to the point of unleashed mass chaos, dementia, starvation and criminal activity. As was exemplified by the eastern seaboard black-out some years ago, a sustained state of nationwide disruption would literally destroy everything from the stock exchange to any social cohesion.

The beast within civilized man is held at bay not by religion or innate decency, but by a prevailing fear of detection and punishment. For the most part western societies are city and town dwellers, while the rural agricultural populace continues to dwindle at an alarming rate. Over the last decade conservative manipulation and monopolization has resulted in the foreclosure of tens of thousands of family farms, and this land either lies fallow or is being farmed by huge conglomerates using methods that require a bare minimum of workers. Thus we no longer have a substantial populace who are capable of living off the land.

No doubt you have noticed that the subject flow of this book has branched off into seemingly irrelevant directions at times. You must forgive the taking of such literary license, but I can assure you that there is a reason to my rhyme. You must not have opportunity to look upon this work as merely another rendition of science fiction.

In all of its many flavors and aspects, this book is designed to awaken in you all of the emotional and contemplative sensitivities that I have experienced all of these years. In the end you should be able to visualize the whole picture as I have done.

The factors of an alien space travelers piercing the quantum of time and a judge handing down a bigoted jail sentence to some poor black are both relevant to the overall truth and fantasia of a maturing universe. To me, one thing is just as important as the other. Would you propose that I lose rational sight of the true state of the world simply because I know of things not of the Earth, or that I cease to care as much for the welfare of my fellow man in favor of more universal realities? There is no greater thing than the unyielding wish to experience justice for all of God's children.

Regardless of their technological power, the extraterrestrials are flesh and blood like you and me. The fact that they have managed to wipe out hunger, and greed and hate for hate's sake, is very commendable, but I don't believe that these things are beyond the scope of man's spiritual and material capabilities.

I have truly seen things that I do not have the ability to explain, and I have suspected or glimpsed some other things that I dare not attempt to try to explain. There is the bizarre, and there is the unbelievable, and then there is the unfathomable.

Upon first seeing those bizarre but intelligent life forms, I, like most normal people, initially felt a strong compulsion to freak out, but the emotion soon passed. I've learned from personal experience that the human capacity to accept new and strange realities is probably unlimited, and this ability will always exceed that person's ability to comprehend the workings of those many realities.

If I were given the choice to either live for many centuries on Earth or to be allowed to explore the living cosmos for the duration of this short physical life span, I would not hesitate to choose the latter.

But the aliens have given me the opportunity to possibly do both in the future. Even if they were pulling my leg, they have already shown me more than most mortals shall ever see in one life span. The fact that I know without a doubt that they are out there is to me a thing which cannot ever be removed from this conscious moment. My missing finger joint is a visual and tangible reminder of physical alien visitation.

I do not feel frustrated by the fact that most will not believe me. In your own life you have undergone some fleeting metaphysical experience that you know to be true, but you are not very concerned with having others believe you. The inner knowledge that it is so is consolation enough. This is how I feel. This means that I cannot be bull shitted with religious nonsense or rendered ignorant of that information which is left out of man's recordings.

Before we discount all new revelations outright, we should stop to consider some of the fantastic things that have transpired on Earth. The transition from the horse and buggy to the moon landing transpired in little more than one life span, and the jump from cathode tubes to micro-electronics transpired within two decades or less. From the first lithographic photographs to satellite visual transmissions transpired in a century. From three-masted sailing ships to nuclear powered submarines in one life span. You have witnessed man's walk on the moon and photos transmitted from beyond Neptune at the outer regions of our solar system. Long standing political and ideological systems literally change overnight. To the rational open-minded person the realization that we are being visited by beings from outer space should pose no problems in probable logic.

After this book is published, numerous opinions as to the truth or falsity of it will be forthcoming from professional people, who should be able to make an intelligent assessment of it. It would have been easier and much more believable for me to have claimed to have just seen a UFO on one or more occasions, yet I have ventured to attempt to give the most complete insight into the psychology and technology of these extraterrestrials than has ever before transpired. Only my lack of technical and mathematical knowledge has prevented me from being more precise in describing it all. Unfortunately, the aliens never gave me a pill that would transform me into a scientific genius, nor did they endow me with any metaphysical powers that I didn't already possess.

They did, however, make me physically and visually privy to things that might transcend the very sanity of many people. They allowed me to experience a ride through the time quantum of hyper-space, and extracted from me the living genetic seeds which produced living offspring whom I've seen.

They allowed me to come aboard and to explore some of the wonders of a mothership, which defy the manufacturing dreams and capabilities of anything on Earth. In comparison to that great ship, the great pyramid of Giza is nothing more than an insignificant pile of children's play blocks.

How could I touch them, smell them, eat and sleep with them, talk and question them without knowing it. Are the things I've told you possible? Or is the nature and extent of my delusion so great that it has registered on my camera, within my psyche, and upon my psychology to the extent that my every waking hour is rendered insane?

I have also rendered a substantial number of sketches for this work, which are based upon my recollection of some of the things I've seen. Since I've had no artistic training, my ability to recreate an exact replication of many things is sorely limited by my artistic shortcomings, yet I am satisfied that my renditions are sufficient.

Because my contact with many of the life forms, both intelligent and otherwise, was generally limited to the visual much of my commentary on the psyche and mannerisms of some things is based more so on conjecture and intuition on my part then on clearly revealed data about them.

I never had the opportunity to enter the Targ zone of the mothership, yet I intuitively felt that something huge and monstrous was alive behind those doors. I could have been wrong.

While the Dorians are more humanlike in appearance than even the Biaviians, I got the distinct feeling or impression that they were in reality much colder of nature, less responsive and unhumanlike. I never felt the natural compulsion to try to develop a close association with them. The Dorians did not appear to be mentally volatile or hostile. In fact, I would compare their psychological refrain to that of automatons, devoid of emotion one way or another. Anyway, I was never able to establish eye contact with any of them.

In contrast, numerous little Biaviians would momentarily make eye contact with me as they passed by, and from that fleeting moment I could pick up some kind of inner, pleasant vibe or spiritual resonance from them. I got the impression that they did not approach me and engage me in conversation because of some procedural directive, instead of fear or an unwillingness to do so. I could tell that they all knew who I was and the content of my nature, but were simply too polite to stare.

Targs would turn a head to look at you and would even hold eye contact with you, but you couldn't read anything in to the stare. It always produced within me an undercurrent of dread or even revulsion. There is also a twinge of fear there.

The ugly Stagyians obviously have feelings but these feelings and expressions are not directed towards the human subject. It is somewhat like two doctors discussing your condition but not including you in the exchange. They never made any attempt to develop a social rapport with me, but I instinctively knew that their examining touch was neither hostile or deliberately punitive. I felt that if one could get to know the Stagyians one could grow to like them. Strangely, their physical ugliness kind of grows on you and is not repulsive or intimidating in the monster sense.

I only saw two Nyptonians and just fleetingly. I saw one Skreed (Insectillians), and this was in the Chamber of the Seven. I did not fear the Skreed, but I still have problems in convincing myself that a big mantis-like bug could be technologically far more advanced than man. However, for some reason, I never had any great problem accepting the fact that the reptiles, 'the Targs', are highly technical.

I only saw one example of the seventh intelligent form of life, and it was also in the Great Chamber of the Council of the Seven. This life form is encased in a metal and glass tube, and with the exception of one big eye, has no recognizable physical characteristics which could be compared to those of a humanoid. I got the impression that it is a very intelligent and beloved life form, possessing no elements of danger toward humans.

The huge octopi-like intelligent life form called 'Agynmum', though grotesque in appearance, seemed almost lovable and sad.

The impression that one gets from the Biaviians ranges from the comical (in appearance) to the lovable. However, when you learn the potential magnitude of their power coupled with the deductive scope of their reasoning, you are given cause, on occasion, for apprehension. Because they do not respond in the expected manner to human rhetoric, it is sometimes easy to momentarily think of them as misguided munchkins, but then you are jerked back to reality when they suddenly zap you with something about yourself that even you may not have been consciously aware of.

They have a way of cutting through and dispensing with the rhetorical bullshit and getting to the reality of a given situation. If you say that you can't feed and educate all of the children, house the homeless or stop poisoning the river because of lack of resources or for political reasons, they won't even bother with your presence because they know you are full of shit. You can't be trusted, and you are trying to play them for damned fools like you do other humans. This essentially is why they consider politicians and so-called world leaders as something of less significance than say a rat turd.

Enduring procrastination is not one of their strong suits. In their reasoning, any intelligent species that does not care for all of its kind to the foremost extent of its ability does not yet have the right to lay claim to any status exceeding that of the lowest thing that devours its own offspring. In other words, there is no logical justification for enforced suffering, stupidity and hatred. No excuse for wrongness. They view the majority masses of the western world basically as a maggot-like corruption feeding upon the bloated carcass of a rotting animal. These maggots have willfully killed the only organism that can sustain their own existence, while loudly proclaiming that it is still alive.

The difference between them and the Targs is that, unlike the Targs, the Biaviians still see something in the human race that is salvageable and thus worth saving. I imagine that the prospect of a large population of humans living on a planet not too far from their home planet is disturbing to the Targzissians. Perhaps they view the Biaviians as too trusting and humane for their own good. I must admit that that makes sense. Wouldn't you be nervous if a large population of Russians suddenly moved into Mexico or Canada? Of course, we may be talking of distances spanning a hundred light years or more between the planets Targ and Biaveh but with the proper technology in your hands, it is still Mexico to the Targs.

The Stagyians I find to be the most enigmatic species of intelligent beings among the aliens. I've spoken of the Stagyians and their rural agricultural style of existence. As you now know, the Stagyians have the natural neurological ability to grasp, comprehend and expand upon the most complicated mathematical theorems and are capable of psychologically consuming and retaining vast quantities of information. As a result, they are utilized extensively by the Biaviians in many highly technical fields, as well as in medicine, horticulture, architecture and other professions. I understand that the Stagyians have played a major role in the creation and implementation of the foremost technology of the Biaviians and that they still play an essential role in the ongoing technological concession of Biaveh.

Those eternal beings who pilot the really long range ships over thousands of light years of space whose bodies are made of translucent plastic like substances with titanium skeletons and fusion powered hearts and are called the Ancient Ones are nearly all fashioned with Stagyian brains as the motivative organ. It seems that even though most Stagyian are perfectly content to live a normal four hundred years and die, they also have a natural propensity to accept and easily deal with prolonged physical life spans. No Stagyian bio-trad or Ancient One has ever been known to freak out, while it has happened a few times among those Ancient Ones with Biaviian brains.

One thing that I failed to mention before is that the Stagyian home planet's direction of revolution is opposite that of Earth's, in that their sun rises in the West and sets in the East. However, the planet's yearly journey around their sun is relatively the same as our own. Perhaps scientists can explain to you why the planet spins as our own. Perhaps scientists can explain to you why the planet spins backwards. I can't. The enigma of the Stagyians is this. One would think that creatures with such highly evolved neurological abilities would possess a technological level of living which would exceed or at least equal that of the Biaviians, but this is not the case.

On their home planet, Stagyians do not have space ships, airplanes of any sort or even combustion engines. They do not have television, telephone or radio. They do have a system of lighting that is generated by solar energy upon natural crystals to light up homes. Certain crystals are also used as musical instruments, which vibrate at levels and octaves which would not register in the human ear.

Roads are not paved but rock lain. No man-made chemicals are used for pest control or crop fertilization. Stagyians don't even have a written language, but a group of Griots or 'Sayers', who telepathically speak the facts of all Stagyian history. Each Stagyian carries a thought crystal from childhood, and this crystal is able to capture, store and retain all of that being's ideas, words and theories for a lifetime and can be retrieved by others indefinitely.

Stagyians have no robotic machines but transport produce and other things by wagon and domestic animals. They are a purely vegetarian race, and therefore do not raise meat animals. The climate over much on the planet is temperate and ideal for agriculture. Stagyians do not smelt metal, but use pottery, wood and razor sharpened crystals as instruments. Very few things in their diet require cooking.

The Stagyians are renowned also for their horticultural expertise in the cultivation of herbal plants. I had the pleasure once of having smoked a bit of a blue pigmented herbal leaf, compliments of my friend, Question, that I was told was of Stagyian origin. I have experienced nothing on Earth which comes close to reproducing the esoteric and psycho kinetic neurological effects of the Stagyian leaf.

Describing the effects that the herb had on me is beyond my ability, however, some of the most notable effects were the magnification of eye-sight. Anything in the distance, with a little concentration, would be drawn right up to you. Until you learned to control it, the item would seem to swiftly draw near and then recede in rapid succession with a yo-yo effect. The atmosphere around you visually became a panorama of subtle colors, like a faded, moving rainbow.

And you could actually see sound. Each sound appeared, represented by a unique visual configuration. For instance, the words 'good shit' appeared as long yellow balloon light green spiked ball. This to me and Question proved to be hilariously funny. Sounds would swiftly fade or burst like bubbles and had many color and hues.

Question said, "Watch this", (brown-zero-green-dash). (purple-oval - purple-oval - purple-oval - purple-red-oval). Then maniacal laughter, (yellow-red-green stars-brown squares-dashes and dots). The momentary ability to move solid objects with the mind was also an effect of the herb.

I never saw a female Stagyian with the Biaviians, and I don't know the reason for this, because I know that they do exist on the planet 'Stogg', nor do I know their manner of courtship or mating. I do know that once a Stagyian has left the home planet in the services of the Biaviians, he cannot return there to live on a permanent basis except when he nears the point of physical death. His recording crystal, however, is returned and placed in their archives. So we must conclude that the Stagyian way of life is a chosen way of existence instead of one imposed by technical ignorance.

The Stagyian 'Sayers', like their Earth counterparts, are wanderers who live off the hospitality of their guests. However, except for local gathering spots, the average Stagyian may spend a lifetime never leaving his home area.

Stagyian children are the exception. From an early age into young adulthood, Stagyian children often wander far from home, usually in groups of six, and are considered as a common responsibility to all Stagyians. These wanderings may last anywhere from one to a hundred years before the prodigal Stagyian returns home. Few homes are ever without young Stagyians as another group generally comes by as the first one leaves.

They have existed in this manner for uncounted centuries and in peace with one another. To my knowledge, Stagyian do not manufacture or carry weapons, with the exception of a staff-like stick, which is a common fixture of each Stagyian. I don't know much about the animal life of 'Stogg', but apparently they do not live in any fear of predatory animals.

Stagyians communicate telepathically in short neural burst of instantaneous duration. For instance, a Stagyian could probably recite the entire contents of the Encyclopedia Britannica to another Stagyian in several seconds. Except for the Biaviians, the Stagyians are an easy second on my likability scale, even though I was unable to comprehend communication from them. Even the Biaviians have to record and play back at a much slower pace any conversation with the Stagyians. Atmospherically the planet 'Stogg', I'm told, is suitable for human habitation. The oxygen content of their atmosphere is much purer than that of Earth.

I once asked Tan how could the Stagyians possibly protect themselves should some hostile life form come upon their planet, and he said, "The Stagyian are a true member of the seven and must not be harmed lest the wrath of all be incurred". It appeared that they have a kind of inner galactic mutual protection alliance. I don't know for sure, but I can easily imagine a number of sentinel globes and perhaps a few self-contained guardian manned ships orbiting above the stratosphere of the planet 'Stogg'. Surely the Stagyian race is far too valuable to chance losing.

I once saw Tan sip about two ounces of a green liquid through a straw, and this was the only food substance I've ever seen him consume save for several sips of the thought beverages I once got quite drunk drinking. However, as I remember, I did see a number of Biaviians spread a kind of pink or green or blue syrupy thick substance on the skin of their forearms and massages it in. I initially assumed the substance to be some kind of skin lubricant, but it could have served some other purpose altogether. Perhaps it was also a way of eating. Then I think when Tan or Nela touched me was it an act of affection or were they tasting the salt on my skin.

Do the aliens bathe and use soap? I can't say as I never saw one take a shower or even go to the toilet. However, in my sleeping chamber I had a commode and a wash basin and a soft water shower.

I was also served some solid food during my stays there and a lot of liquid nutrients. Come to think of it, I can't ever remember being refused a request for food, drink or even space drugs, though Tan did prevent me from overindulging in the latter on several occasions.

To my knowledge, the aliens do not use any kind of cosmetics or deodorants, but their body odor, when detectable, is not unpleasant. Targs, on the other hand, tend to smell like lowland mud, not an offensive odor, but not a pleasant one either.

In fact, strong odors of any sort were a rarity aboard the mothership. I told you of the powerful aphrodisiac type odor that was released in to the love chamber during my procreation span with the women, but it wasn't a thing that I detected at any other time.

Even in the great Hyborian garden with all of its life forms and dampness, the odors that one would associate with such an area were almost undetectable. Once there was a large ape-like creature in the Hyborian garden with his family which consisted of an adult female and two young creatures, and as we passed near above them, I caught a distinct odor which was forceful in the nostrils. The odor was so distinct that I felt it must have come from the bodies of these beings, even though I was a good fifty yards from them. I never realized just how dependent the human being is upon sounds and smells or the lack thereof.

The absence of loud, sharp and consistent noises aboard such a great ark peopled by so many beings and moving machines is a thing that I could not help but notice right away. If Biaviians can hear through the tiny holes that serve them as ears, it never became evident to me. For instance, if Tan's back was turned to me, I could snap my fingers or clap my hands and he never seemed to notice. However, when I directed telepathic thought to him, he would immediately turn toward me.

You would think that noise on all levels would be a common occurrence around a large number of deaf beings. I've never been around a bunch of deaf people on Earth, so I don't know if they are normally careful about making noise or not.

In any case, under normal circumstances, a great deal of noise is to be expected where a large group of beings congregates. This is not the case aboard the great mothership, and to see so much activity going on, including hundreds of moving beings passing without generating a reasonable amount of noise, is disconcerting.

Speech between Biaviians, of course, is telepathic, so there is no outward sound there. The levitating transport disks are noiseless.

When a Biaviian or group of them are walking together, the silken fineness of their garments and the soft materials of their shoes or slippers keep sound to a bare minimum. The many robot machines, which can always be seen busily working, are apparently designed with such precision that no friction sounds are detectable, and the motor drive of these machines is so fluid that you must be very close in order to pick up the movement whine as they perform many complex tasks.

On two occasions we passed by an enclosed area of recreation and relaxation where there were a number of Targs and in the next area a number of Dorians. I could clearly see them, and they were obviously communicating, or shooting the breeze, if you will, but I could not hear a thing through the insulation of the glass, if it was glass.

I also know that the Biaviians have a technological means of dampening noise. I found this out when Question and I visited the Hyborian garden. At a certain distance you can see the birds flying about, see the fish jump in the waters, see the water fall and small creatures skittering about, but you can't hear or smell a thing. Only when you have crossed a certain invisible line near the water do the sounds hit you. It's just like someone has flipped a switch. Move back a few feet and the sound abruptly stops, as well as the smells. Not a leaf or insect or a drop of water escaped the barrier of the invisible boundary. But if they can't hear in the first place, why go through all of that trouble to muffle all the natural sounds?

The reason that I dwell so long on the factors of sounds and smells, etc., is because the presence, experiencing and recalling of these things, is one of the only true means of separating dreams and hallucinations and mirages from reality.

In such an enormous open area like that of the great mothership no matter how great the technology there will be noticeable variables in temperatures and air movement. In moving about the ship I could feel subtle temperature drops or rises, gusts of wind, wayward odors and totally still zones.

The temperature in different compartments or chambers also differed in degrees, though not radically. When we passed along the great halls of suspended animation, these temperature variables could be felt more keenly. For instance, you would hit a zone that could be uncomfortable warm, while a few seconds later you might experience a cold pocket, which might cause you to shiver momentarily.

Nothing aboard the great ship, living or machine, seemed to ever be in a hurry, but moved along at a leisurely and calculated pace. No jaywalking business men or speeding motorists. No horns, curses, bumps or grinds. The aliens obviously don't look at time the same as humans do.

Yet they obviously know that humans need some sounds, just like we need sleep and regular nourishment. So they gave me

Question to talk to, and since Question's thought processes were gleaned from within my own psyche, I suppose that talking to him was somewhat like talking to myself. I can't truthfully say why he would have chosen to glean information from the sarcastic part of my personality, but in knowing Question, I have concluded that he has an independent will of his own and that he chooses sarcasm because he is, by nature, a stinking, devious and lascivious minded animal.

I've told you about the incident of the shiny metal thing that he gave me, which he had stolen from an extremely big Targzissian. Well, on another occasion, he pulled a little purple-red fruit pod from his pouch and was busy inspecting it closely when I asked him what it was. His answer was that the fruit was so good and rare and precious that he couldn't possibly waste it on a human who could never appreciate its fine qualities. This, of course, piqued my interest and made me determined to have a bite of it. I went on to explain to him that even though we had our ups and downs ours was a friendship that would last a lifetime. Surely he wouldn't allow a thing like a little piece of fruit to jeopardize that bond, etc., etc.

Finally, he chastised me for my selfishness in wishing to deprive a poor dumb animal of his last bit of sustenance, totally disregarding the possibility that he may go into convulsions of hunger and die, leaving my conscience to suffer knowing my greed was the cause. At this point I felt an inclination to just smack him and strong arm the fruit from him, but I let him continue. He was saying, "You don't realize what I had to go through to get this fruit. I had to sit up and beg and roll over and play dead like a motherfucker to get this fruit. But do you care? Me thinks not. Oh, well. I don't guess I should expect any more from a human, who would ease out a fart and then blame it on a poor animal. Go on take it".

He flipped it to me though doing so seemed to break his heart and make him shake his head in disgust. Fearing that he might change his mind, I immediately popped the pod into my mouth. I shortly concluded that I had made a bad mistake. The pod was as sour as vinegar, as hot as pepper and had a persimmon like quality that caused the mouth to pucker. I spat it out as best I could and started looking around for some water. I turned to Question and said, "WAA-TA-FOK-NOO-NOIN, TRY-TA-KUL-MA? you MA-FA-KA!!". And as he walked off, he flicked a few more pods of the fruit onto the floor, saying, "I didn't think that shit was ready to eat". And this is a typical example of Question's personality.

Had I not consciously imprinted all of the sights, sounds, tastes and smells of those experiences in my psyche, I could easily have eventually convinced myself that it was all a dream as I'm sure many others have done. I swore myself to an oath that I would never forget no matter what method, short of brain damage, that the aliens might use on me to erase my memory. Even as I moved through life down through the years, I always remained conscious of the fact that the extraterrestrials existed and that I knew them. Only the specifics of those visitations tended to elude me. Still I never for a moment doubted that one day all of the necessary pieces to the puzzle would be revealed to me in due time.

I'm sure that the fragmented and fleeting memories of many abductees of such experiences have driven them even unto the threshold of paranoid insanity. Perhaps in your life you have suffered some mental anguish because you couldn't immediately remember the answer to some question that you knew you should remember. The secret is not to let it bother you. Push it to the back of your mind and it will eventually emerge on its own.

With me it took several regressive hypnosis sessions to open the floodgate of my recollections. To be sure there are yet some hazy aspects of those experiences, and most of those hazy parts are probably due to the fact that Question exerted a bad influence on me by involving me in his nefarious preoccupation of getting high on something. Had it not been for him, I probably wouldn't have sought so much esoteric diversion. So that's it. The animal did it. Perhaps the rest of you humans are fortunate that the aliens have been open-minded enough not to blame all other earthlings on me.

I humbly concede that my actions and words on rare occasions may have been a bit less than gentlemanly. The crack that I made about the Biaviians not knowing anything about fucking was petty and certainly beneath the dignity of a conscientious representative of mankind. And I did try to the best of my ability to get them to flush Question out into deep space, but let me state that Question did some terrible shit to me also. It's only American to want to see him dead.

Aside from that and a few other incidents which are too minute to mention, I must say that I comported myself well, and you would have been proud of me. I do believe though that Tan may have been a little better disposed toward me if upon receiving my first solid food, I would have requested something more flavorful instead of asking, "Hey, slim, what's this dry shit?"

And perhaps I should not have made fun of his boots, by pointing out that they both looked like they were made for the same foot. I deeply regret that I stood watch while Question confused the worker machines, or when he went to borrow something that wasn't his.

Yet of this you can be sure I always kept my honor and held my intoxication well. I cannot say the same for Question though. There is not a bone of devotion of fidelity in his body. He has no qualms about lying through his buck teeth, refusing to share his wafers, or snitching me off in a futile and cowardly attempt to save his own ass.

No matter how revealing or emotional the moment, rarely, if ever, did Question get serious about anything. Once while he and I were sitting in the Hyborian garden partaking of his pipe, somehow the subject of religion came up, and I began to explain to him how many people believe that the Earth was made in six days. I told him how God decided to destroy humanity in a great flood and how Noah saved two of all the animals on Earth in the Ark. Before I could continue, Question reached over and gave me half of a yellow wafer. I was really touched at this unexpected show of generosity and that he would show such a genuine interest in Biblical history. I thanked him and asked him why he was being so nice. He looked me right in the eye and said, "Good buddy, I'm giving you my last wafer, don't bother that I'm chancing starvation, for one reason only.. "Our close friendship", I said, trying to keep from chocking up in the fellowship of the moment. "No", he said, "that's not it. It's payment for you to please get out of my face, talking that dumb shit". To wit, he snatched his pipe, pouched it and moved over to the next rock a little farther away from me.

If I do not survive unto the day of the great airlift of tens of thousands of humans by the aliens, I know that it will transpire anyway. The extraterrestrials are not omnipotent, therefore they cannot guarantee that the emissaries they have chosen, myself included, will succeed in gathering the number, in which case they have a Plan B, which is more time consuming but nonetheless just as effective.

Plan B would force them to make numerous pickups of small groups instead of the hoped for small number of large groups pickup. Plan A would be simpler and could be accomplished in a short span of time without a definite possibility of mass panic, while Plan B would require the aliens to utilize a large number of personnel and small ships. This large number of ships would in turn disturb a greater number of people, and the aliens might be forced to deal with a wide range of military apparatus over the planet. The panic firing of surface-to-air or air-to-air missiles, and even artillery by the military, while presenting no real danger to the alien ships, would certainly present a danger to the civilian populace.

As with Earth aircraft, some of the alien saucers or ships have less high tech features than others. Some are capable of hyper-space speed and some are not. Some are equipped to maneuver underwater and some are not. While all of them have the standard technology of radar scrambling, all of them do not have that of visual invisibility. In order to take on or disembark passenger, either through walk on loading or atomic disassembly and reassemble, all of the ships must lower their cloaking shields and force fields for a time, thereby making them vulnerable to attack, and the extraterrestrials would go to any lengths to avoid taking human life.

In 1964, and again in 1975, I personally witnessed the speed with which fighter planes can be dispatched upon sighting an unidentified craft. Evasion of those armed jets was a simple matter for Tan's whisper craft, but what if he had lingered to pick up ten or a hundred people instead of just myself alone?

On board instruments can easily interface with and take over or knock out the electrical systems of any missiles, but this is not so simple a maneuver even for the aliens because these electronic manipulations must be surgically done, with the safety of the pilot and the general populace in mind. It may be necessary to knock out the firing and radar electronics, while leaving the ejection mechanism intact so that the pilot can escape. If near the coast, then the wayward plane can be vectored out to sea. If inland, the alien craft may choose to momentarily disrupt the plane's electrical system if the missiles have been armed to fire, or, if not, to simple out maneuver the craft by increasing speed or altering direction.

If the missile is fired before such actions can be taken, it must be detonated high in the stratosphere or literally lead to a safer area. On board computers must be able to locate, classify and decipher the aggressive capabilities of any craft it encounters in the skies. It must know the difference between a fighter and a passenger plane. It must know if the missiles are nuclear ready or not. Are the missiles heat seekers or radar guided? Cruisers or simple thrust combustion? Do the pilot's vital signs indicate only inquisitiveness or hostility? What is the thrust speed capability and fuel distance capacity of that particular craft? All of these factors and more must be ascertained, computed and comprehended in a matter of milliseconds and the appropriate actions taken.

These things could not be readily accomplished without the proper compilation of data concerning all of man's technological creations. A simple thing like the addition of a new kind of non-flammable additive to jet fuel or the alteration of one or more engine parts is reason enough for an alien ship to come in close and pace the Earth craft in order to collect the new data. If the Earth craft is not a military sort, the alien saucer may not even bother to cloak its presence and may be visually seen by the Earth pilots.

If the truth were known and if more pilots were not afraid to come forth with their sightings, the fact that alien ships are present in our stratosphere would not still be an enforced secret to the general public. This great military and governmental conspiracy and denial is one that cannot be justified by citing national defense, nor can the facts be dismissed by propagating false explanations or dismissing all sightings as being the delusions of crackpots, since everyone from pilots to priests, policemen to presidents have seen them.

More of you who are reading this book have never been directly effected by a third or fourth class experience with any of these extraterrestrials, and yet common logic has led many of you to believe that they do exist. My overall descriptions of them, though undoubtedly restricted by my lack of formal education and expressive abilities, are none the less a more complete revelation of them than has ever before been put fourth by a human being.

My experience with regressive hypnosis sessions, which were induced by my friend Barbara Simon, were not as extensive as both of us would like them to be. In the future, I would like to undergo further regressive hypnotic sessions and perhaps recall many things that I missed. I'm open to any well meaning professional who wishes to question the validity of my claims and to delve deeper into these things, because I have no doubt that the many things I've told you will come to pass and will be revealed outright in the not too distant future.

You may suspect that my occasional attempts at humor mask some greater undercurrent of fear and horror on my part, and you would be partially right, but you must also understand that I was not born or raised a member of the ruling race or social class in this country. I've never held any delusions as to the omnipotence of my military or political power. Quite the contrary, it is somewhat refreshing to me to know that man alone is not the ultimate power in the universe. Those who rule upon this Earth are far too ruthless, arrogant, decadent and proud and should be brought down a few notches.

After having learned the ways and motivations of the Biaviians, I would have no qualms about living in a world under their leadership and guidance. Even the nightmarish Skreed might prove preferable to the people under whom we now live. I am an American black man, and as such, I and my brothers have always received the shit end of the social and economical stick in this country, which is ruled by a ruthless and demented race of which I can find no genetic origins. We live in a world and in a society where misinformation and dis-information have been institutionalized, and the truth is a rare commodity. Rather than accept the truth, those in power would rather kill you and so would most of the ruling segment of the public in this country.

I do not delude myself into believing that humanity will ever come to the point of being decent and fair in their treatment and dealings with one another, so I hold no great fear of these extraterrestrials. My concepts of manhood, beauty and self-worth have never been shaken in the least by these people who rule our society, because I've never been deceived as to their true natures nor surprised at the depth of their depravities or inherent physical and psychological weaknesses. When the cataclysms come, they are the ones who will suffer the most, because the minute an alien force would take over, in that instant we would all be rendered equal. If given as equal chance at life, I've no doubt of emerging among the foremost.

Within the next decade, in preparation for the great airlift, you will find that more and more sightings and recordings of UFOs will transpire, and not even the massive efforts of media suppression and manipulation by the governments will be able to discount this reality. I would go so far as to say that the aliens might decide to make their presence universally known and initiate communications with some earthlings, if they became aware of the fact that the masses could accept them without panic.

It is a fact that the U.S. Government and others have spent literally hundreds of millions of dollars to erect listening devices which serve many functions, one of the foremost of which is an attempt to listen in on alien transmissions. I'm told that some of these devices have indeed been able to pick up on a few ship to ship transmissions over the years, but ship to ship electronic transmissions are not the standard method by which the UFOs communicate.

In the case of the Biaviians, communications are done telepathically. I know this to be true, because I have communicated via telepathy with Tan over vast distances of space on many occasions and with the Targs on several occasions in the same manner. I don't think that man has the technology to record such transmissions yet.

I've never been aboard a Biaviian craft that did not have at least two Stagyians aboard, and I understand these Stagyians are utilized extensively, if not universally, to transmit ship to ship communications. As I have said before, the Stagyians communicate via short intense bursts of telepathic data. In this manner entire formations of saucers are able to maneuver with split second precision in the skies.

Earth scientists have long wondered how a formation of six or more UFOs are able to execute simultaneous course changes, starts and stops and formation changes with split second precision. This is how it is done. Biaviians, as well as Stagyians, are able to telepathically interface with the on-board computers.

Crew leader, or the designated Stagyian, will interface with the computer and the remaining craft members will give over operations to that crew or formation leader. Each on-board computer will interface with the point computer and follow its instructions. Any course change, speed alteration or aerial maneuver ordered by the point computer will automatically be acted upon as one by all on-board computers in a nanosecond, keeping the same velocity and clearance.

For the most part, neither Biaviians nor Stagyians manually fly their own ships. This task is left to smart robots, which will fly alone or follow telepathic directives. These pilot robots are smart enough to spot, check and elude any approaching danger. These robots are also capable of scanning in a 360 degree vector, anticipating and maneuvering numerous obstacles at a given time with split second precision, a case in point being the time that the craft I was aboard took a maddening flight through the ice boulder rings of Saturn. Tan, of course, directed the robot pilot to enter the rings, but the actual aerobatic maneuvers while in the rings were left to the computers. I needn't have to impress upon you the fact that that scared the living shit out of me. The ship moved through the rings at a fantastic rate of speed while evading the ice boulders just enough to miss them. Tan found my various depths of sheer terror quite fascinating, but to me, it wasn't funny at all, especially after I learned that the aliens' technology is not perfect. Biaviians love soaking up human emotions, and yet it was notable incidents such as those that imprinted themselves in my mind for recall at a later time.

It is strange, but I feel that something tangible actually goes out of your body when another being is soaking up your thoughts and emotions. Perhaps it's just my imagination. On more than one occasion Tan allowed me to mind link with him to the point of being able to see things through his eyes. In that stage I noted that colors were softer and that the depth perception of visual distance and physical dimensions were slightly different from a human's. A Biaviian's peripheral vision is also greater than a human's. Looking straight ahead, the only blind spot in vision is a narrow zone directly behind him. Motion awareness is greatly enhanced.

A Biaviian's heart beat is extremely fast, about three beats a second. It is possible that they may have two hearts, but I'm only guessing. Unlike humans, the Biaviian does not daydream, but is always right on top of the here and now. You can't catch him napping.

The Biaviian state of being is neutral and without fluctuating emotions, and while there seems to be no noticeable feelings of love, there is likewise no inking of hatred. I wish that I could go where they've gone and see what they've seen, but I would not like to be a Biaviian. Being a human, even with all of the bullshit thrown in, is a lot more fun.

I once asked Tan, or said to him, "Tan, do you believe that I love you and Nela and Question?" And he said, "Martin, I tell you truly, that we have never known such love before as that you give". "But do you and Nela love me?" I asked.

And he said, "Martin, in as much as it is possible to desire the presence of, and find marvels within another living entity, none other has ever been so close to Nela and I, save thee, and I would not fail to put forth my form and forfeit this consciousness so that you may live the more". Translation: We don't know much about the emotion of love, but I would not hesitate to lay down my life for your safety.

"And what about Question?" I asked. "This you must learn from Question", says Tan. And sure enough later on while Question and I sat taking his pipe in my sleeping chamber, I put the question to him. "Question, all bullshit aside, tell me honestly, do you love me like I love you?" And Question said, "Slim, I love you much more than I love to have my nuts thumped, and I love your old lady even when she's not naked".

I said, "Question, can't you be serious just once in your Godforsaken life? A simple yes or no would be sufficient". And he said, "I let you smoke my pipe, and I hung out with you. I give you choice shit outta my pouch and would have kicked that Targ in the ass about you, if my back wasn't acting up at the time. I listen to your dumb shit day in and day out and even sleep in the same spot with you. So what the fuck do you think".

"I'm sorry I asked. Just forget it", says I. Question is like that, you can never get a straight answer or pin him down. As an after thought I asked, "You're probably with me just to keep an eye on me and to report back to the Biaviians".

And he said, "Marty, you're all right for a human, but you don't really know shit about me. If nobody can make you do anything you don't want to do, then what do you think about me. These little big head mother fuckers ain't so smart. They actually think that you're smart and that you know some deep shit. But me!!! I like you because you're a goofy looking dick head who probably won't try to rob my pouch while I'm asleep, thereby causing me to bust my foot in your ass. Plus you're not boring, ugly but not boring. Now please return my pipe and take your ass to sleep". "Thanks, Question". "Don't mention it".

We are winding down to the conclusion of this manuscript, but the story is in reality just beginning. My time remaining upon this Earth is not long. I realize that I have a job to do, and even though at this moment I don't have a dime, I know that the resources and personnel I need to convey this message will be forthcoming. All things in due time. Perhaps the aliens will play a direct part in the spreading of my words and perhaps not. In any case, I have faith that it will be done. I have no doubt.

I never asked for and the Biaviians never promised me riches upon this Earth. I am basically at peace within myself, though I will always feel the pain that others suffer and seek to bring about a better world in any way I can.

If I had been seeking to deceive you as to my experiences then I could easily have stayed within the safety zones of superficiality, but I have chosen to reveal everything I know or think I know. Those for whom these revelations are meant will no doubt be duly influenced by them. Those not so meant, won't be so greatly influenced, and this is as it should be. To the non-believer, I say to you that this work, I hope, has at least been worth your investment if only for its entertainment value.

At this point, should some one desire to reach me, it would be difficult but not impossible. At no time will I publish my whereabouts because I know that those who are meant to reach me will eventually do so and at that time I will answer.

I do not consider myself the savior of the world nor an all-knowing guru. I am but a simple spirit who has been chosen, for whatever reason, to be the bearer of these tidings.

What if some high government officials who read this book and have enough compiled knowledge to know that it is probably true decide to actually start doing something about the ecological and social situations within this country and the world. What if something that I've said causes some rich person to realize that it's not completely necessary to render our middle and lower societies destitute, to give a quarter of each earned dollar back to society and settle for a few million less. They won't go broke doing so or end up with any less profit in the long run. What if some factory owner reads this book and suddenly decides to spend the money to put in the pollution scrubbers and the water purifiers.

If I'm telling the truth about my experiences, then we are in a heap of trouble. If I am lying or suffering a complicated delusion, then we are still in a heap of trouble. As we stand, should we continue on this path of self-destruction, there is no hope. Should we choose to come together and work together perhaps there would be some hope.

I stand open and ready to be tested and tried. You must scrutinize and weigh and measure all of these things I've told you. I for one truly believe that even though you have accepted much of what your leaders are telling you, you are still not completely deceived nor can you be continually deceived. We are to a great extent a victim of our own gullibility and corrupt desires. Soon it will no longer be possible to procrastinate away the facts of things, because the effects of our actions will be upon us. Must you see the pollution deformed babies to know that they are surely on the way? Must your neighbor, your brother or your child perish of polluted water in order for you to become aware of its existence?

Man cannot repair the ozone layer once it is gone nor explain away the skin cancer once the ultraviolet rays are unleashed. Man cannot cool the uranium atom once it has been activated nor guard against the earthquakes.

We could conceivably love one another and work together upon this Earth. We could wipe out mass hunger, house the homeless and be kind to the elderly. Not one of these good things have you done since we were first cast upon the sands of Jurassic beaches. Not once have you ceased to enslave and kill my brothers. Not once have you faced and accepted the reality of your actions. Not once have you known even the rudiments of love and respect for your fellowman. If at this moment, every person would resolve to do that which is right or fair, then the very elements would sing out in gladness and truly, there would be no limit to what mankind may do.

The dye is cast, and we have a destiny to share, a destiny of our own making. The extraterrestrials did not wrong us by causing us to realize the elementals of good and evil. The choice was ours. We have the innate qualities to truly be as Gods, but we have chosen to exist as beasts. Even your most divine creations of Gods are not devoid of the monster seed. That which you have done to these, the least among your brethren, you have done also to yourselves, and your legacy shall be inherited by your children, who shall be more ruthless.

Still, it would not cost humanity one cent to love one another, but instead would gain us the universe. Hatred, bigotry and greed, as you shall shortly see, will cost us a planet and perhaps our very continuance as a species.

The aliens will endure without you and will not long mourn your passing, and the universe will not record so much as a shooting star in the skies for some other kind of entity to see. When some future cosmic wayfarer comes upon the rotted remains of what we once were, they will be fascinated at the stupidity of a fairly intelligent species who were too fucking gullible to not destroy themselves.

For what it's worth, I have dearly tried to love you in spite of everything, and I know that you know how to do it better, if not right. I go now and prepare myself to ride the fiery chariots and fear not the thunder. I hope that some of you will eventually join me on this celestial sojourn, which shall warp us through the trembling shadows to time. Peace be with you one and all.

Q~QUA TANGIN WANN
BIAVIIAN PILOT SCIENTIST
TAN

TARGZISSIAN PILOT

STAGYIAN SCIENTIST

DORIAN FEMALE PILOT

NYPTONIAN PILOT

THE SKREED
INTELLIGENT INSECTS

7TH INTELLIGENT LIFE~FORM
ORIGINS UNKNOWN

O~NEE~SAYER~WANN
NELA
FEMALE BIAVIIAN

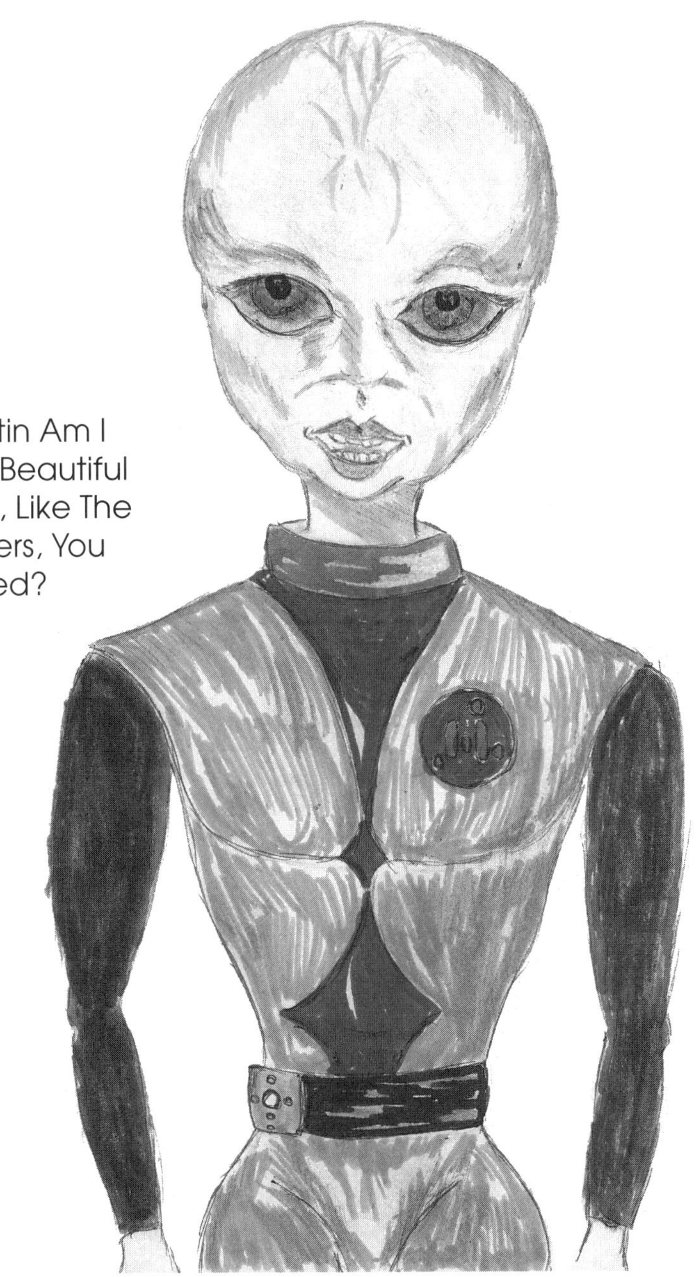

Martin Am I
Not Beautiful
Also, Like The
Others, You
Loved?

O~B~VAR~LEE~WANN

VERY OLD BIAVIIAN MALE
DRESSED IN PURPLE ROBE

FEMALE HYBRID

QUESTION

INTELLIGENT MARSUPIAL SPACE BEAVER,
MY COMPANION ABOARD GREAT MOTHERSHIP
1953~TIL PRESENT

MAN IN BLACK
ABOARD MOTHERSHIP 1953

ABOARD MOTHERSHIP
1964

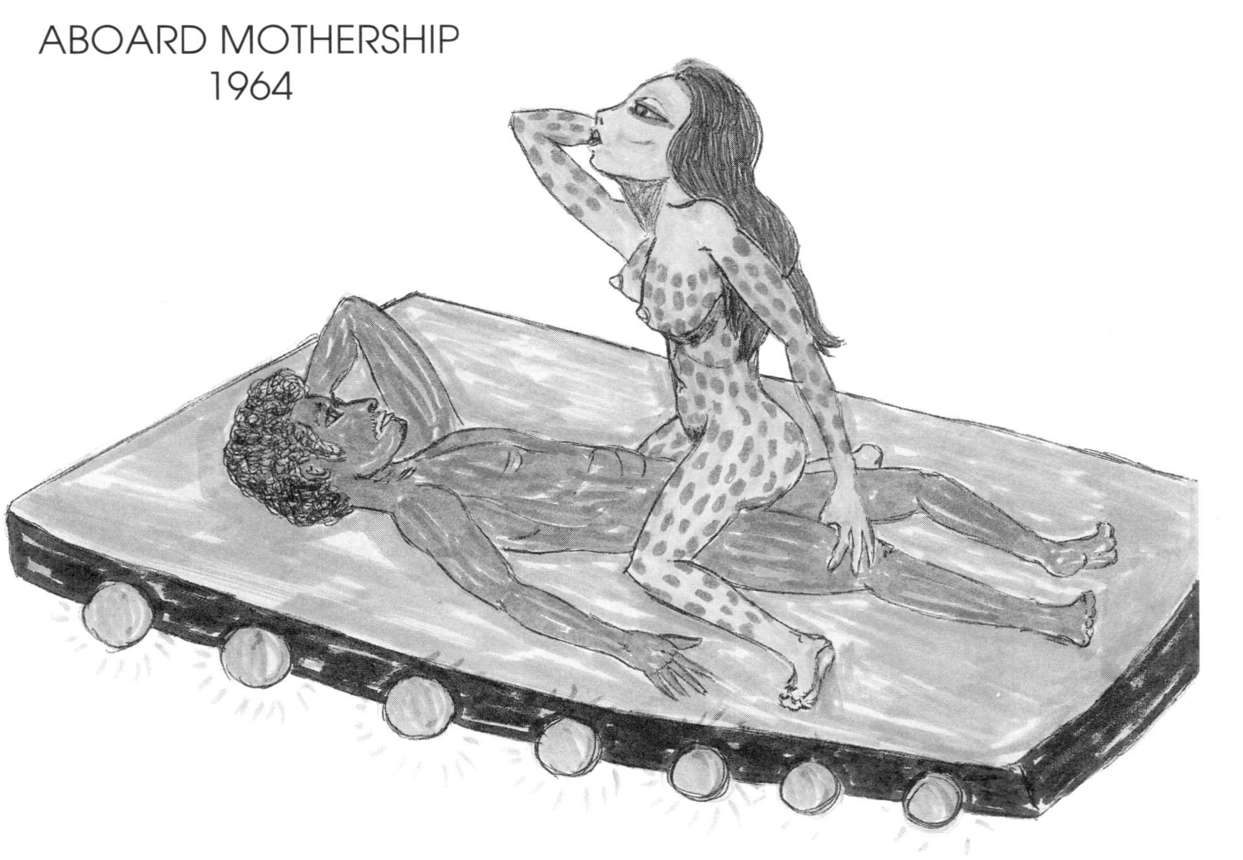

ROBOT NEURO~SURGEON

ANCIENT ONE
INTERGALACTIC PILOT

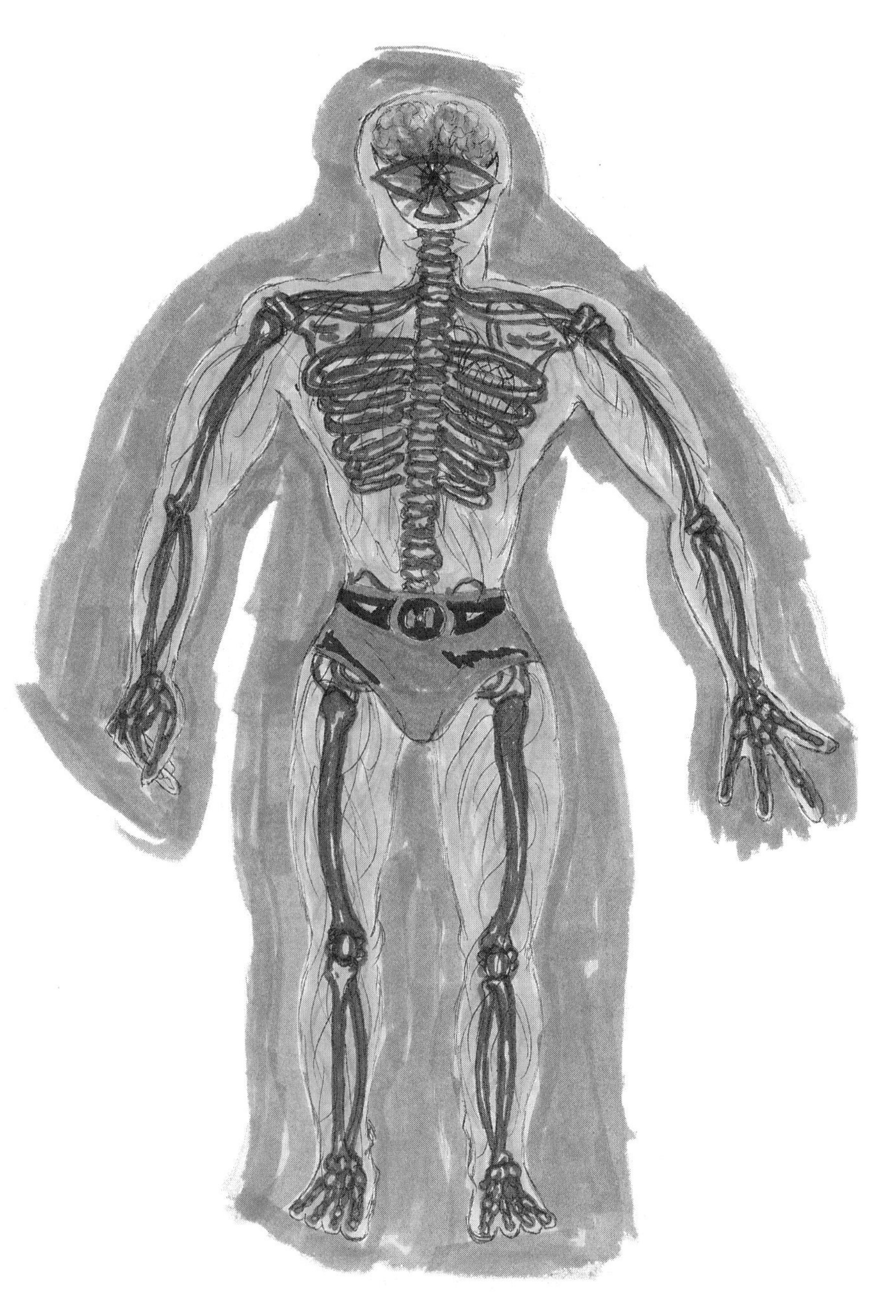

AGYNMUM
INTELLIGENT OCTOPI

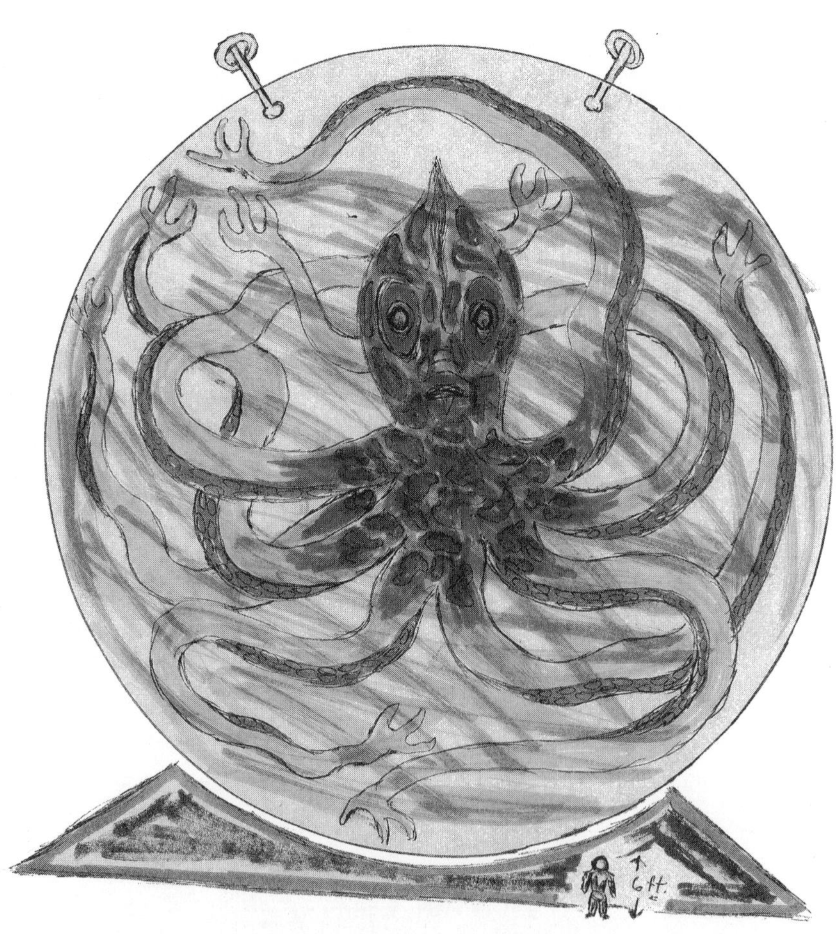

HAIRY MAN~BEAST
ABOARD GREAT MOTHERSHIP

NEUROTRONIC COMPUTER
STAGYIAN

REJUVENATION CHAMBER

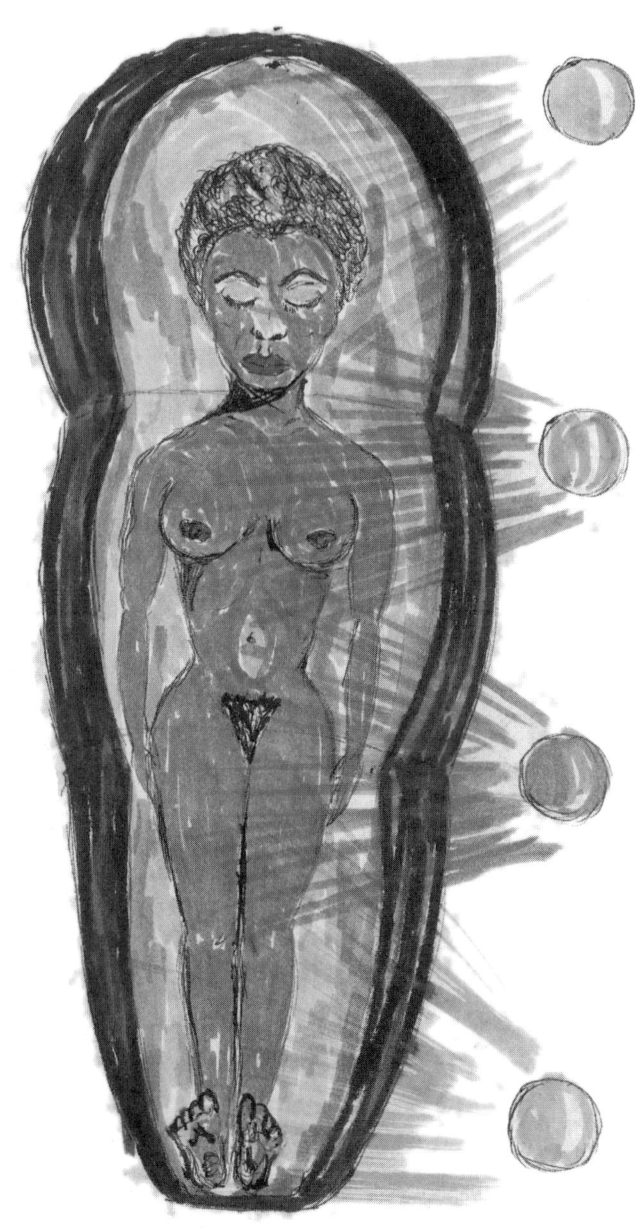

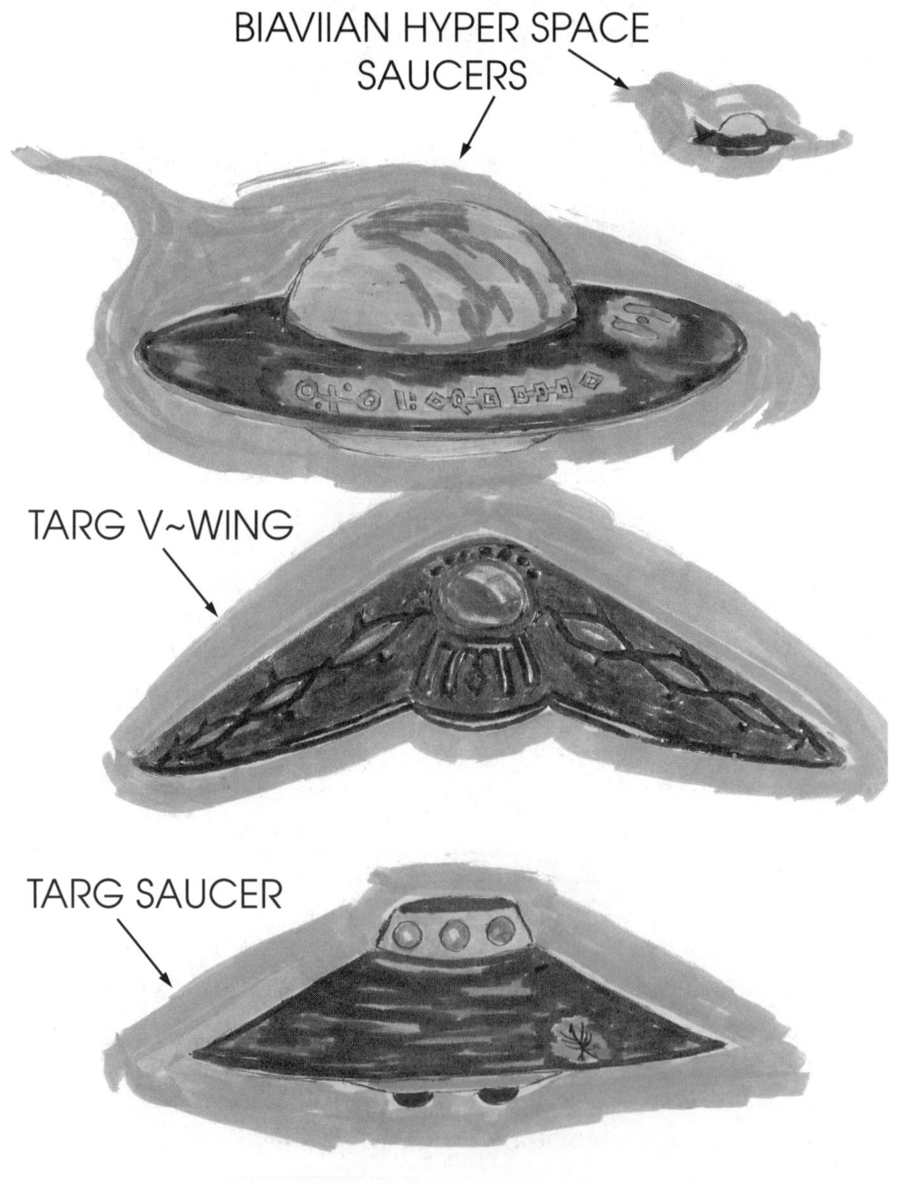
BIAVIIAN HYPER SPACE
SAUCERS
TARG V~WING
TARG SAUCER

TARG V~WING
THE GREAT SHIP

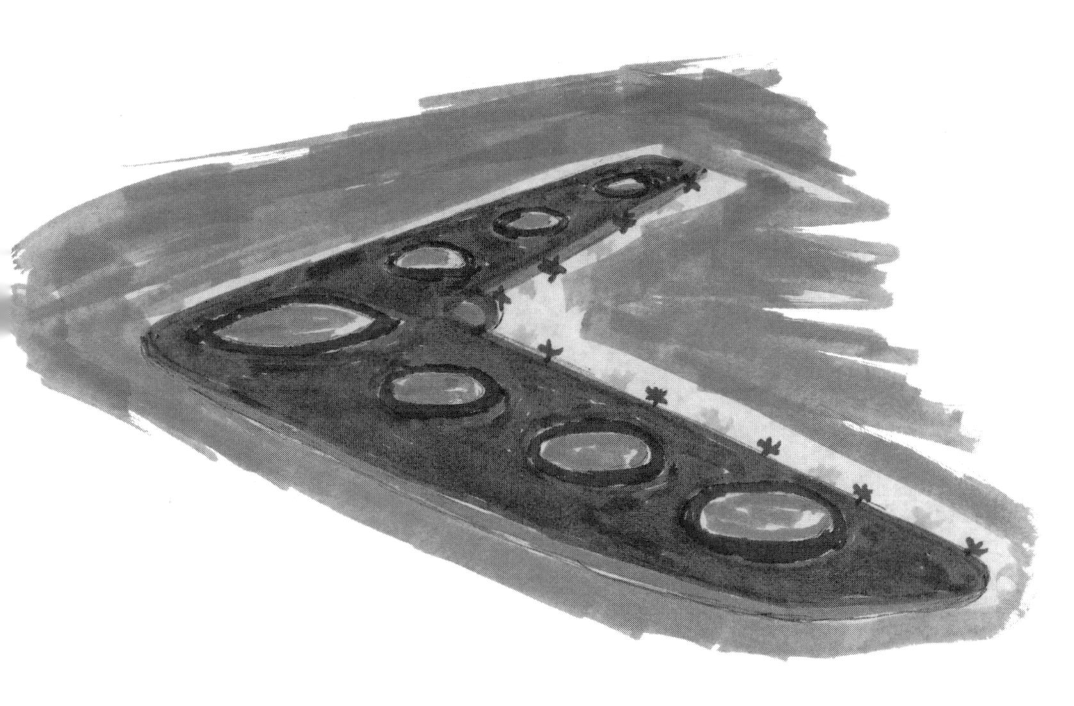

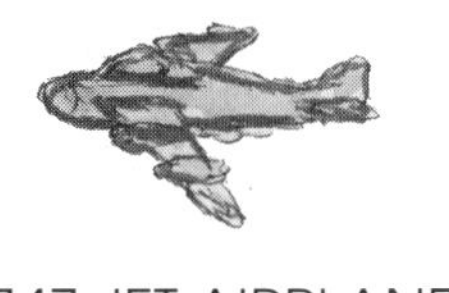

747 JET AIRPLANE

SKREED FLAGSHIP
INSECTILLIAN

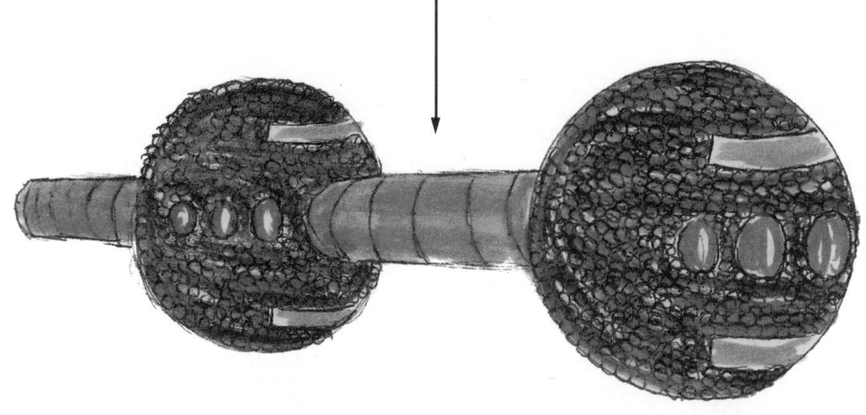

CRAFT ORIGIN UNKNOWN

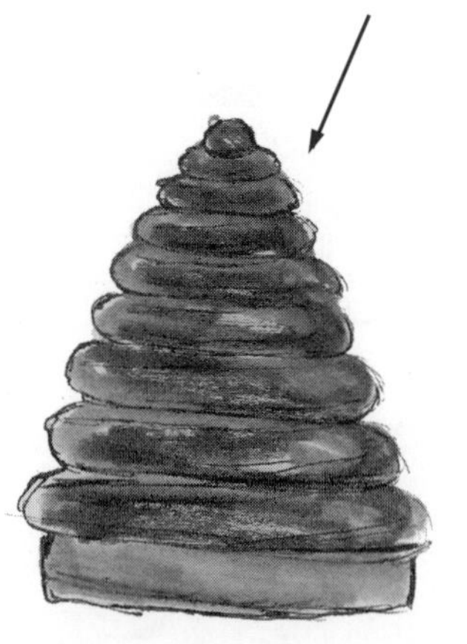

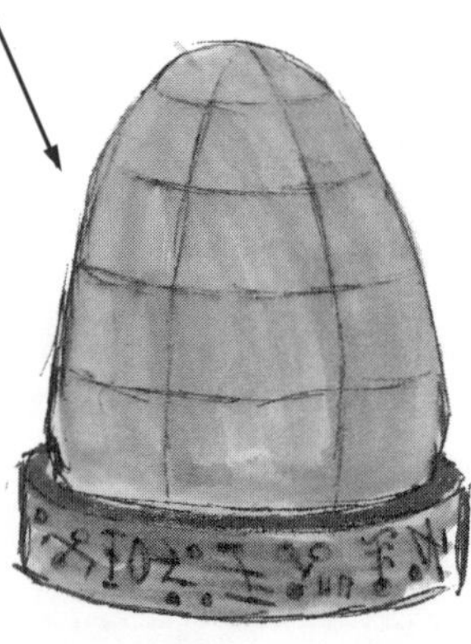

SKREED CITY

Biaviian Symbol

The circular symbol configurations you see before you, are not of this Earth. They are all of Extraterrestrial origins. And to my knowledge, I am the only human being who knows the meanings of them all. During my nine day visit with the Biaviians aboard the great mothership in 1975, the alien Tan fitted me with a kind of virtual reality headset. And through a visual strobe-light, like burst, 144,000 different symbol configurations was down loaded into my mind's Neuro-Syntaxes. The duration of that light burst was approximately twelve seconds. I am now in the process of setting these symbols to visual representation on paper.

Eventually these symbols will be distributed to 144,000 heads of families and their loved ones, who will comprise the potential wayfarers of the future airlift of travelers from the Earth unto a distant beautiful, un-polluted planet. Let me inform the reader that, one does not have to possess a symbol in order to become a potential wayfarer. However, possession of a symbol assures that the bearer will definitely be considered.

It would not be possible to explain the meanings of all of the symbols in a single book. Nonetheless I will give you in brief, a rudimentary synopsis of a general scope of the symbols meanings.

The symbols will be granted unto potential wayfarers without regards to race, religion, age or sex. The price of the symbols must be geared to the receivers material fortunes and ability to purchase it. The symbols are not meant for only the wealthy, but for all decent spirits.

Select a Biaviian Symbol from this book or request that I select one from the remaining 144,000. You will receive the original full color Biaviian Symbol along with a personal hand written note from the gift that was transferred to me by Tan on the mothership in 1975.

In as much as an intelligent high-tech life form can possess positive elements, the symbols are positive. The symbol(s) will automatically tone the positive vibrations of the bearer's home, help to expel negative forces, illness, and misfortune. The symbol attracts prosperity, love and mystic-comprehension. The symbol protects the loved ones of the bearer also.

Although it is possible, the symbols won't usually draw Biaviians to your home in the physical. However, the bearer will probably experience some incidents of kinetic, or seemingly paranormal occurrences near them, as the symbol realigns the vibrations, and the aliens scan their homes to access their potential wayfarer status. Do not be alarmed.

Finally, you may consider the original symbol a ticket to the stars, if you so desire to utilize it when the time comes. You will not be compelled to go if you don't want to. The owner of that symbol can reproduce it for their own use only, such as broach, ring, buckle, T-shirt, or framing for each room. However, if the symbol is sold or given to another, the power diminishes. And the original bearer no longer holds the right of wayfarer status. If the symbol is stolen, the thief is in trouble and the owner is not held to blame. If the owner deliberately parts with the symbol, and the receiver uses the force in a negative manner, the original owner is also subject to the elemental reaction of those negative actions. Most people can own as many as seven personal symbols. One can and should be purchased for each family member when ever possible.

When all of the symbols are distributed, there can be no more. Time is of the essence. May peace be with you.

Riley Martin

The following are uncolored symbols drawn in ink.
No erasures, no mistakes allowed. Time is of the essence.
Riley is to draw thousands of them ~ no two are ever alike.
Any symbol(s) requested by you will be in color.
See inside front cover for example.

While aboard the Biaviian Mothership
Riley saw symbols from time to time.
Read a paragraph about them on page 130.
The web site has some examples of the
symbols in color, and information on how
to purchase your very own symbol.

http://thecomingoftan.com

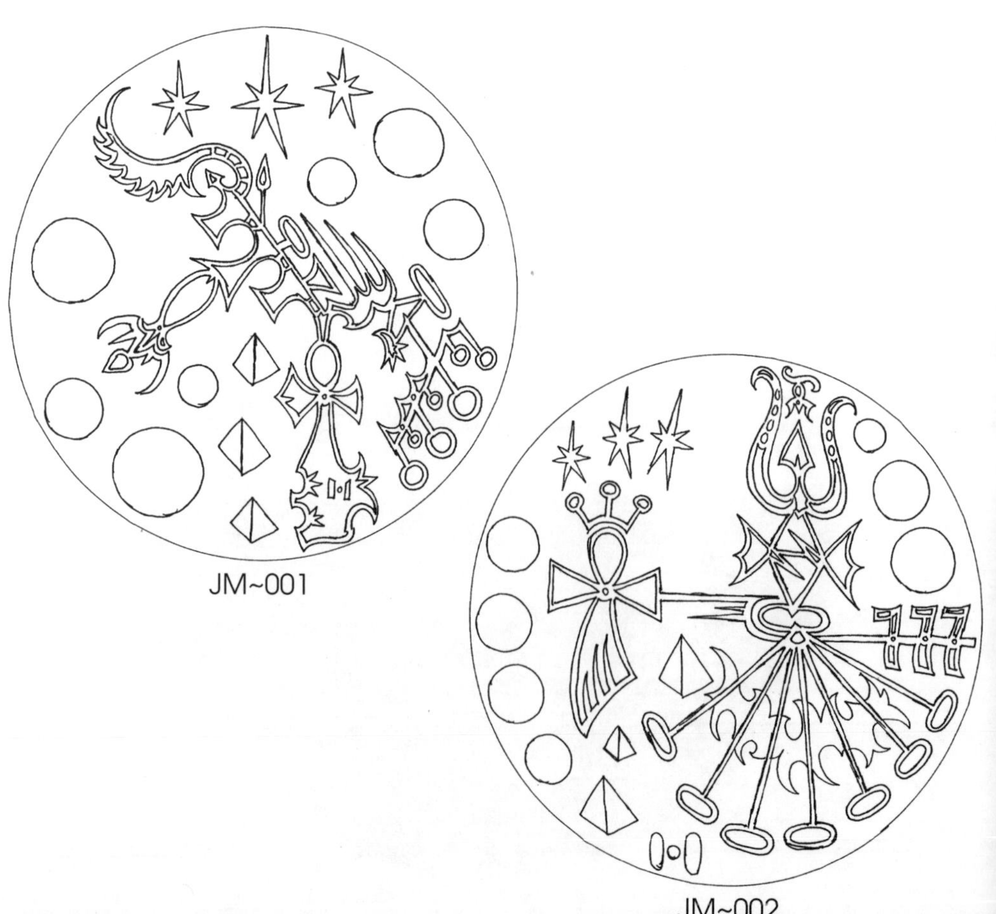

JM~001

JM~002

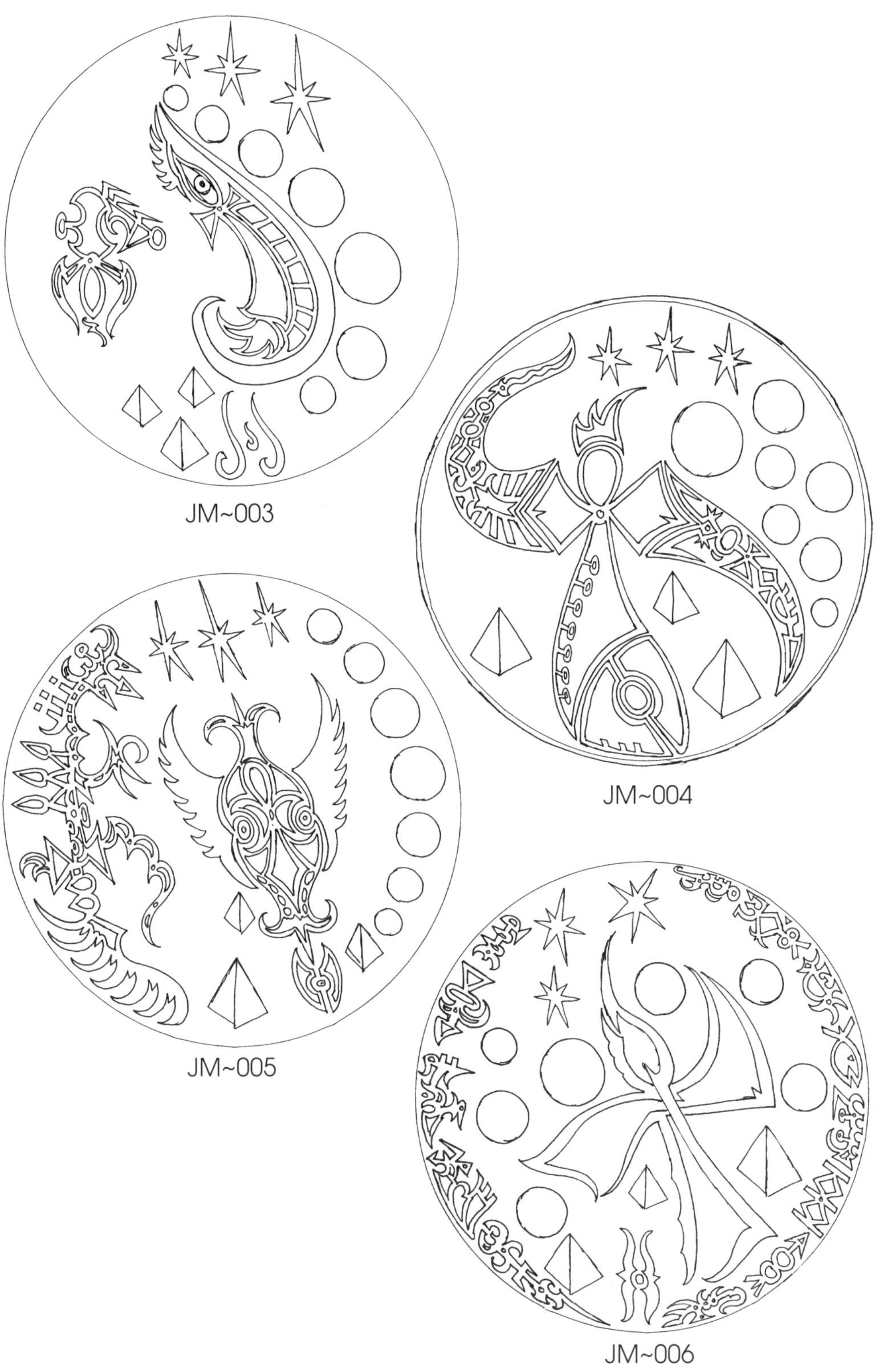

JM~003

JM~004

JM~005

JM~006

JM~007

JM~008

JM~009

JM~010

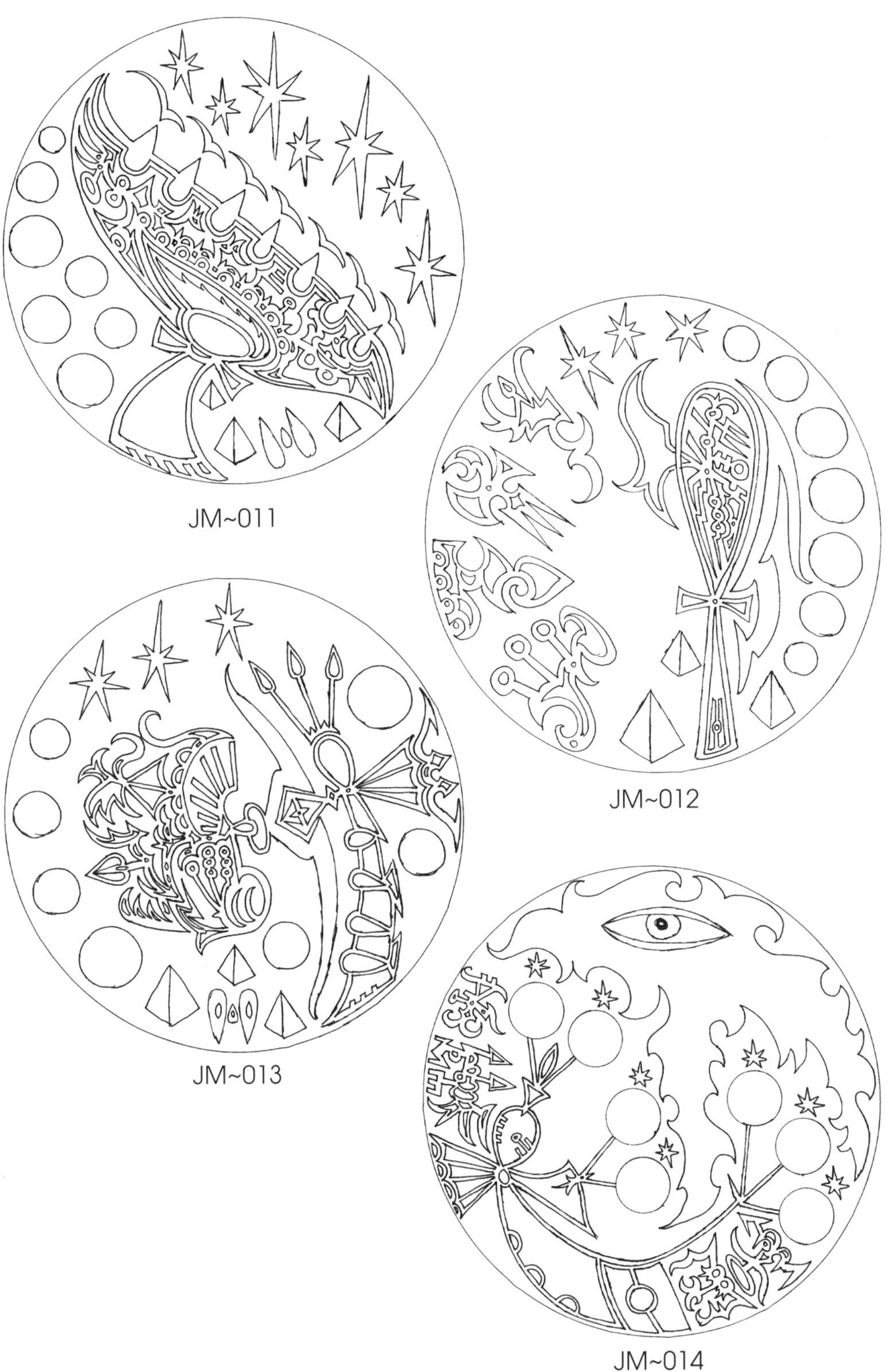

JM~011

JM~012

JM~013

JM~014

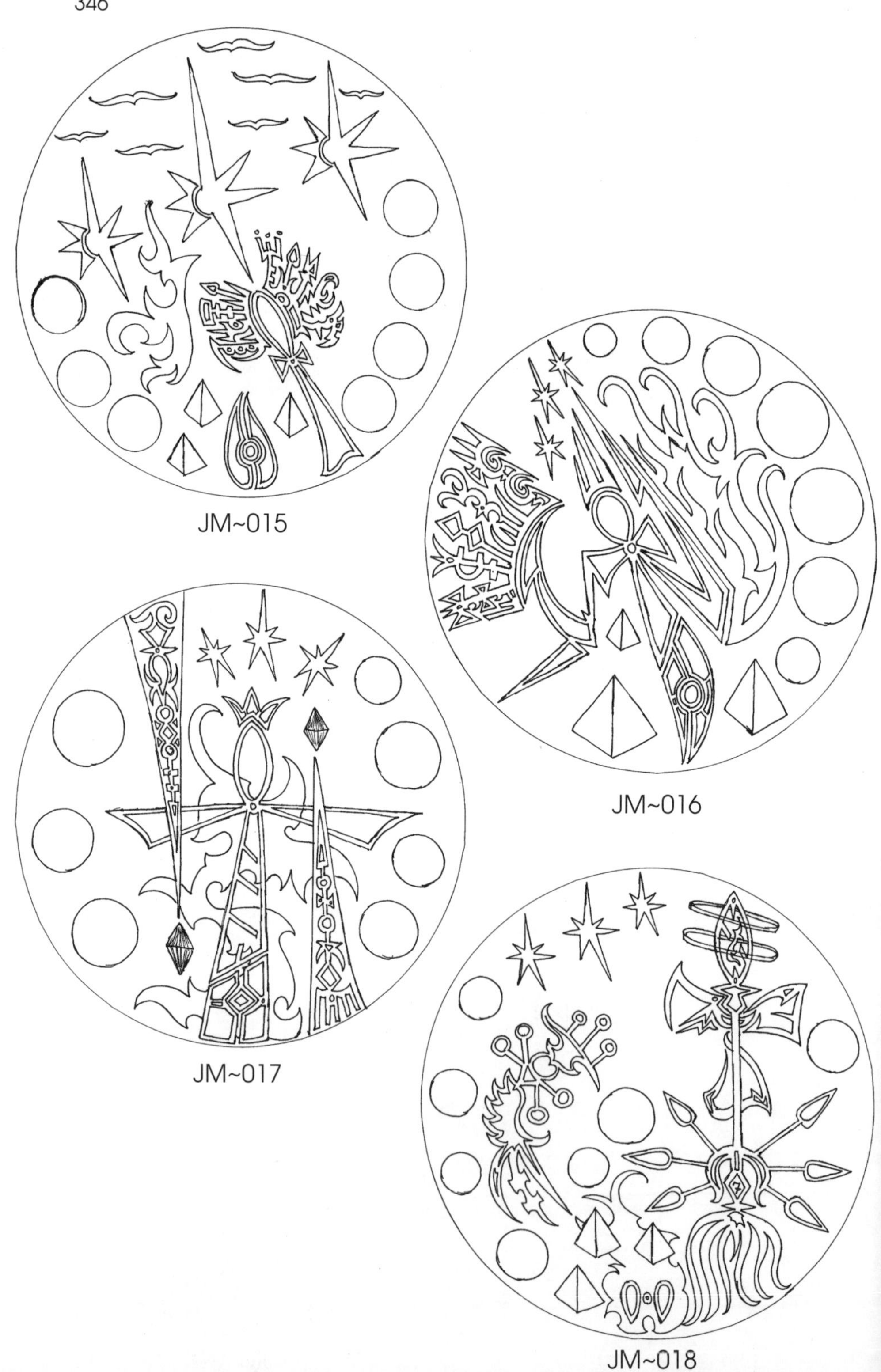

JM~015

JM~016

JM~017

JM~018

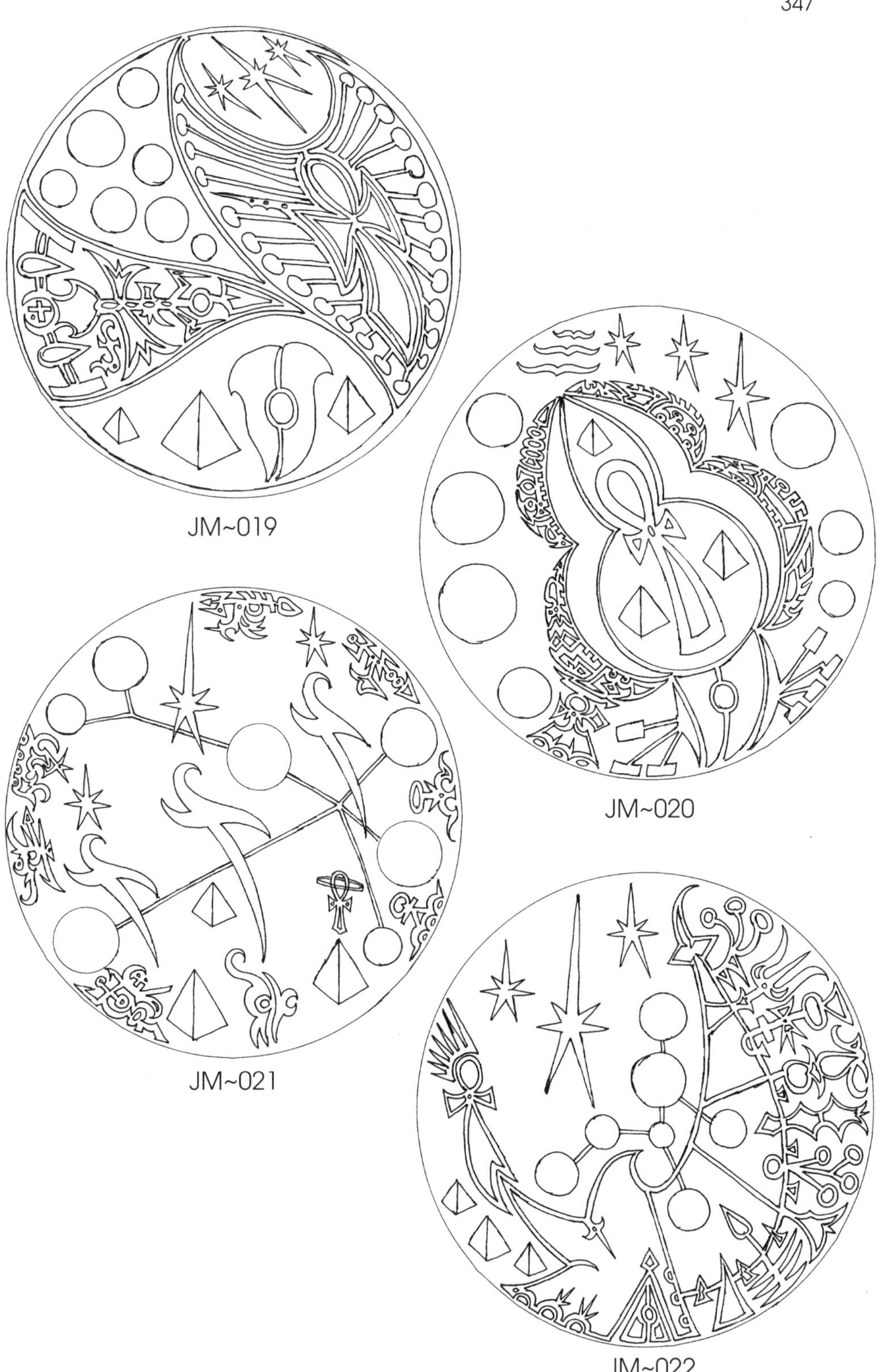

JM~019

JM~020

JM~021

JM~022

JM~023

JM~024

JM~025

JM~026

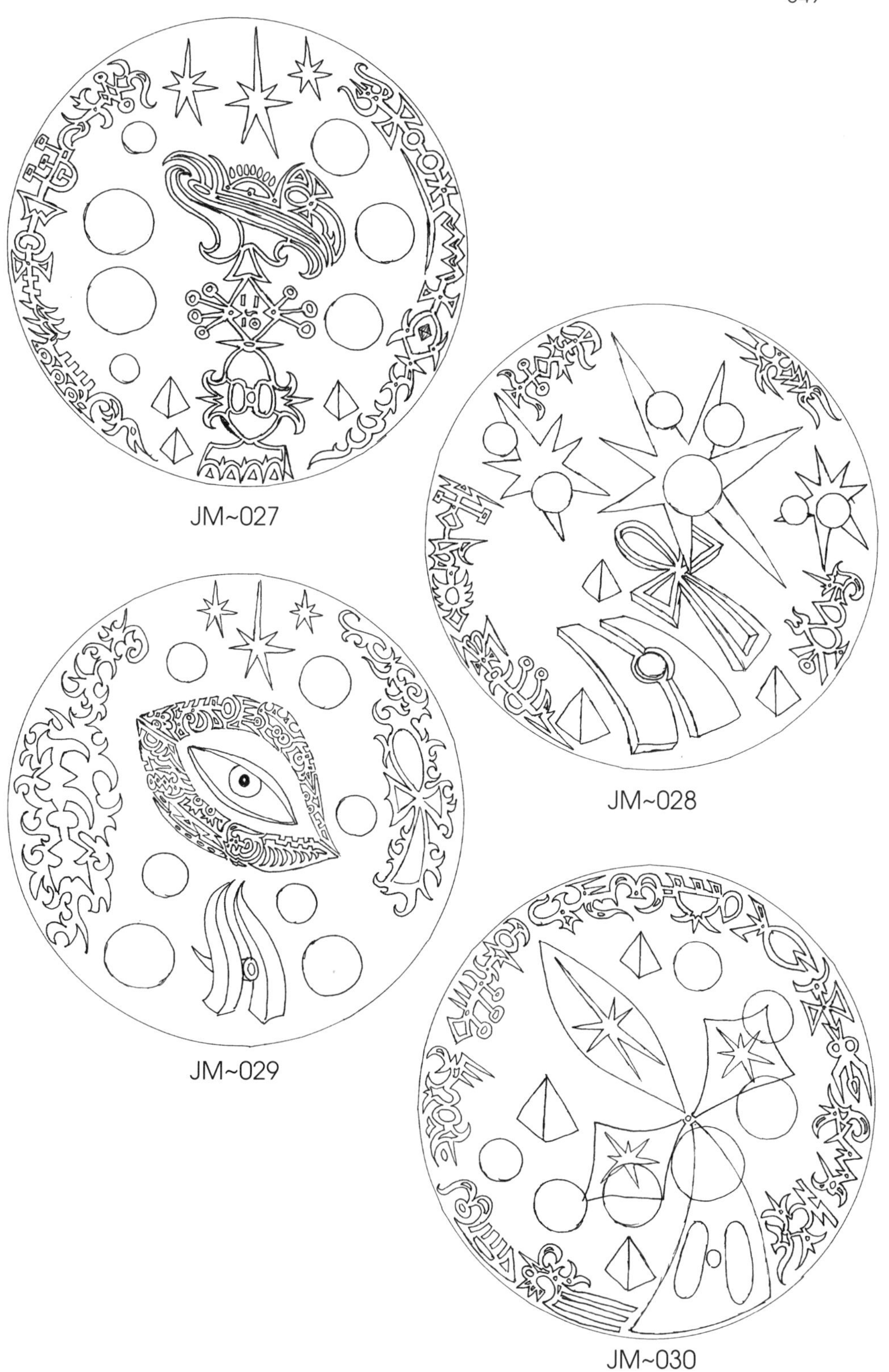

JM~027

JM~028

JM~029

JM~030

JM~031

JM~032

JM~033

JM~034

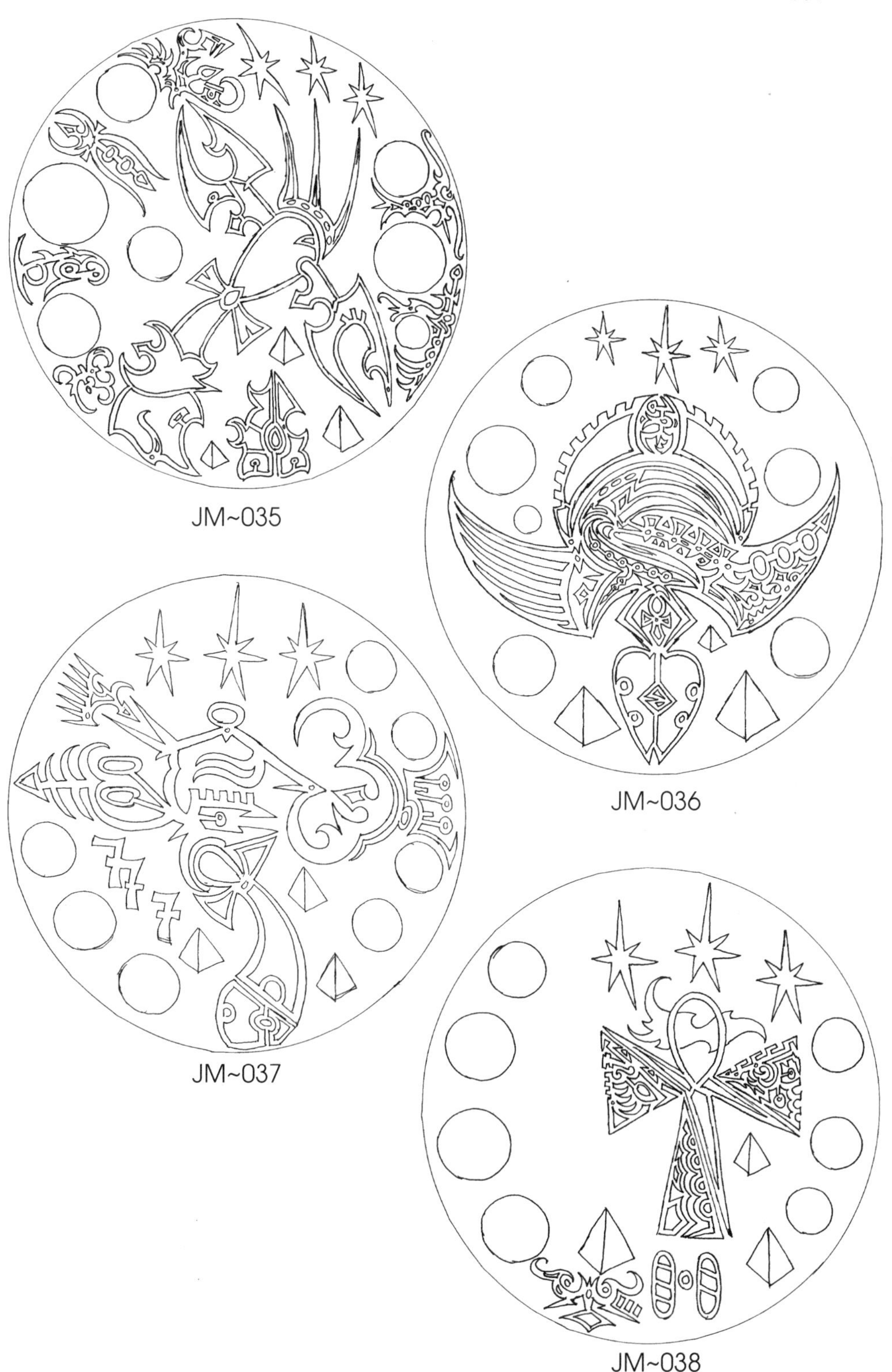

JM~035

JM~036

JM~037

JM~038

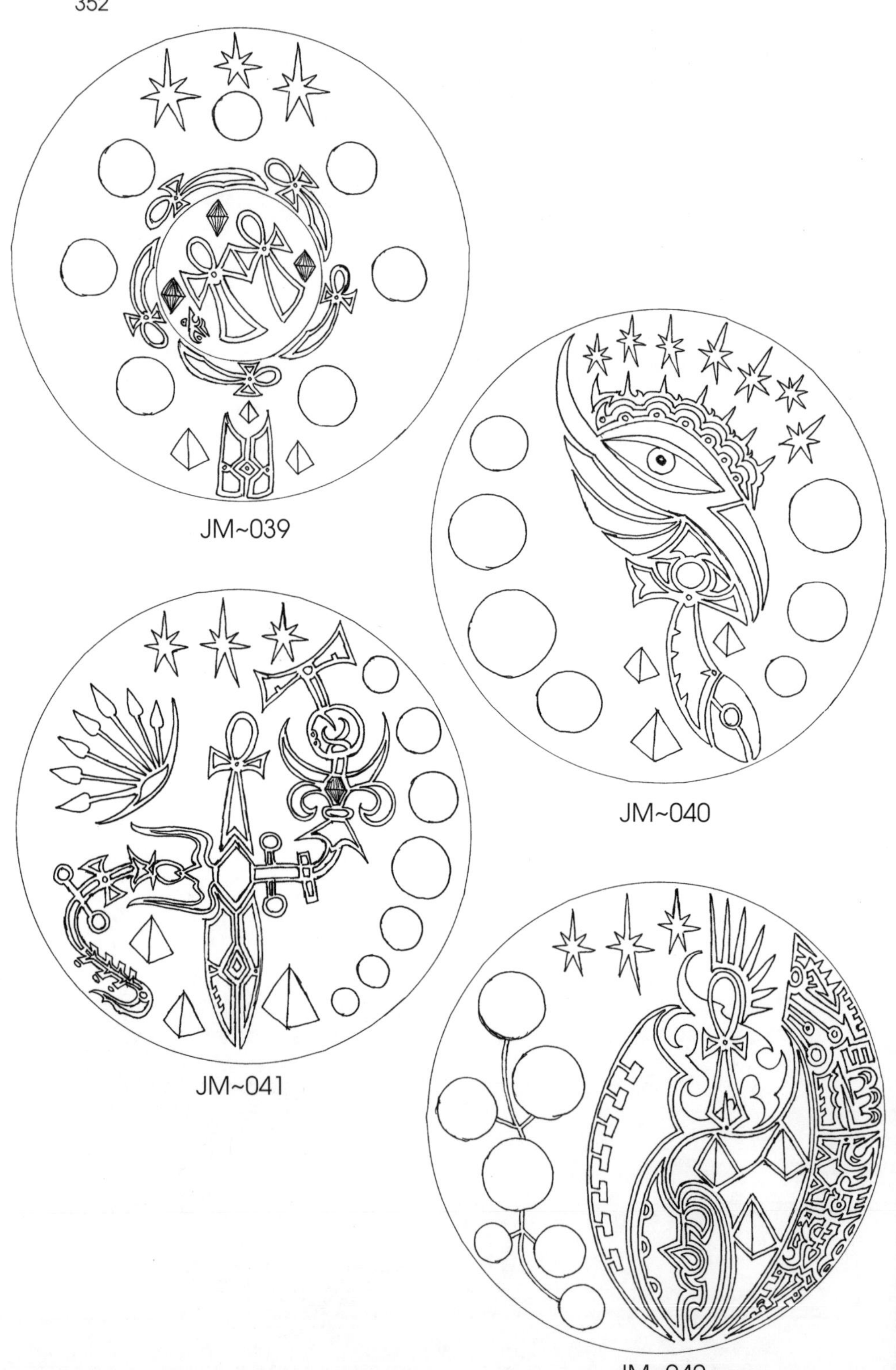

JM~039

JM~040

JM~041

JM~042

JM~043

JM~044

JM~045

JM~046

JM~047

JM~048

JM~049

JM~050

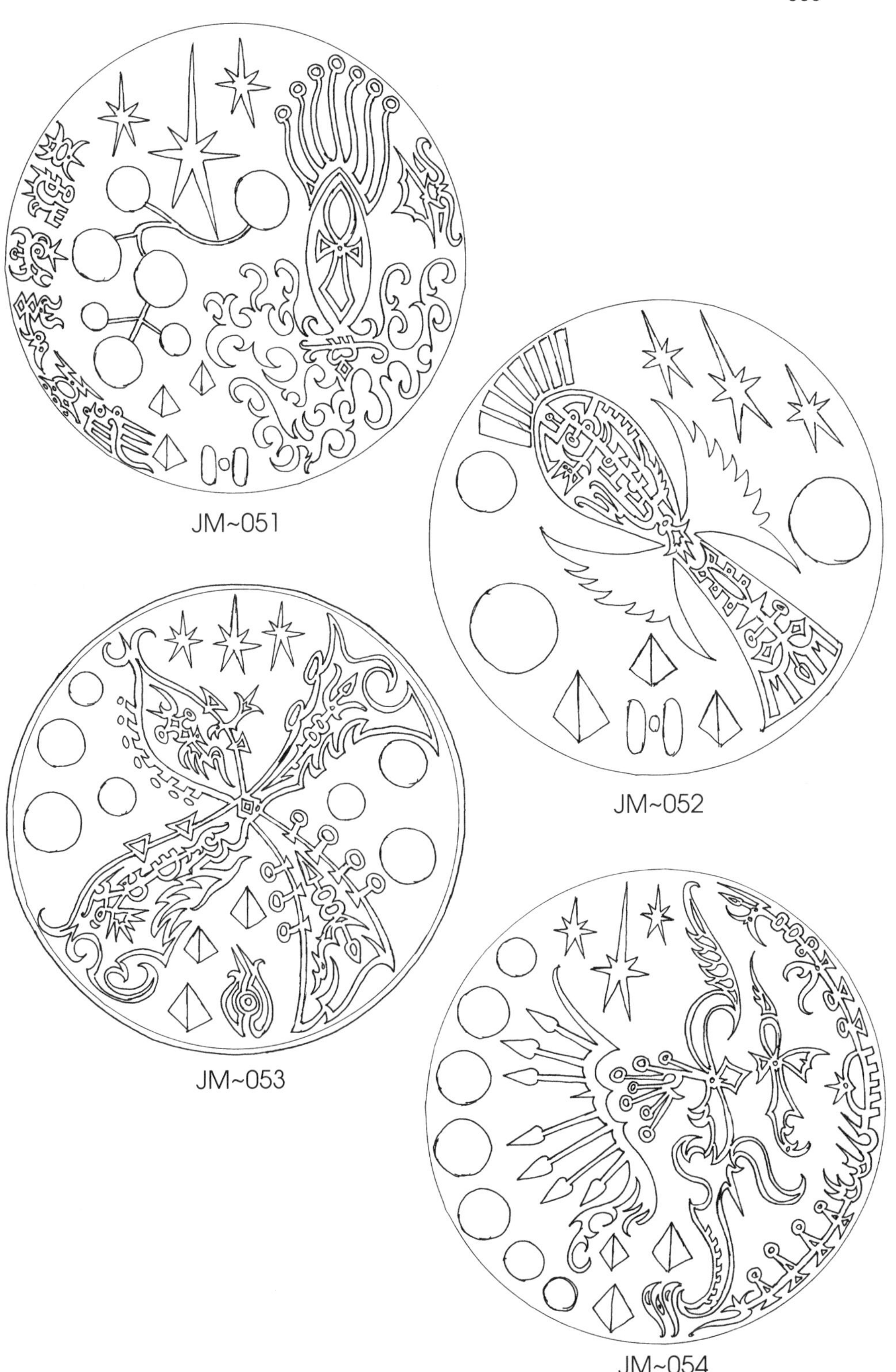

JM~051

JM~052

JM~053

JM~054

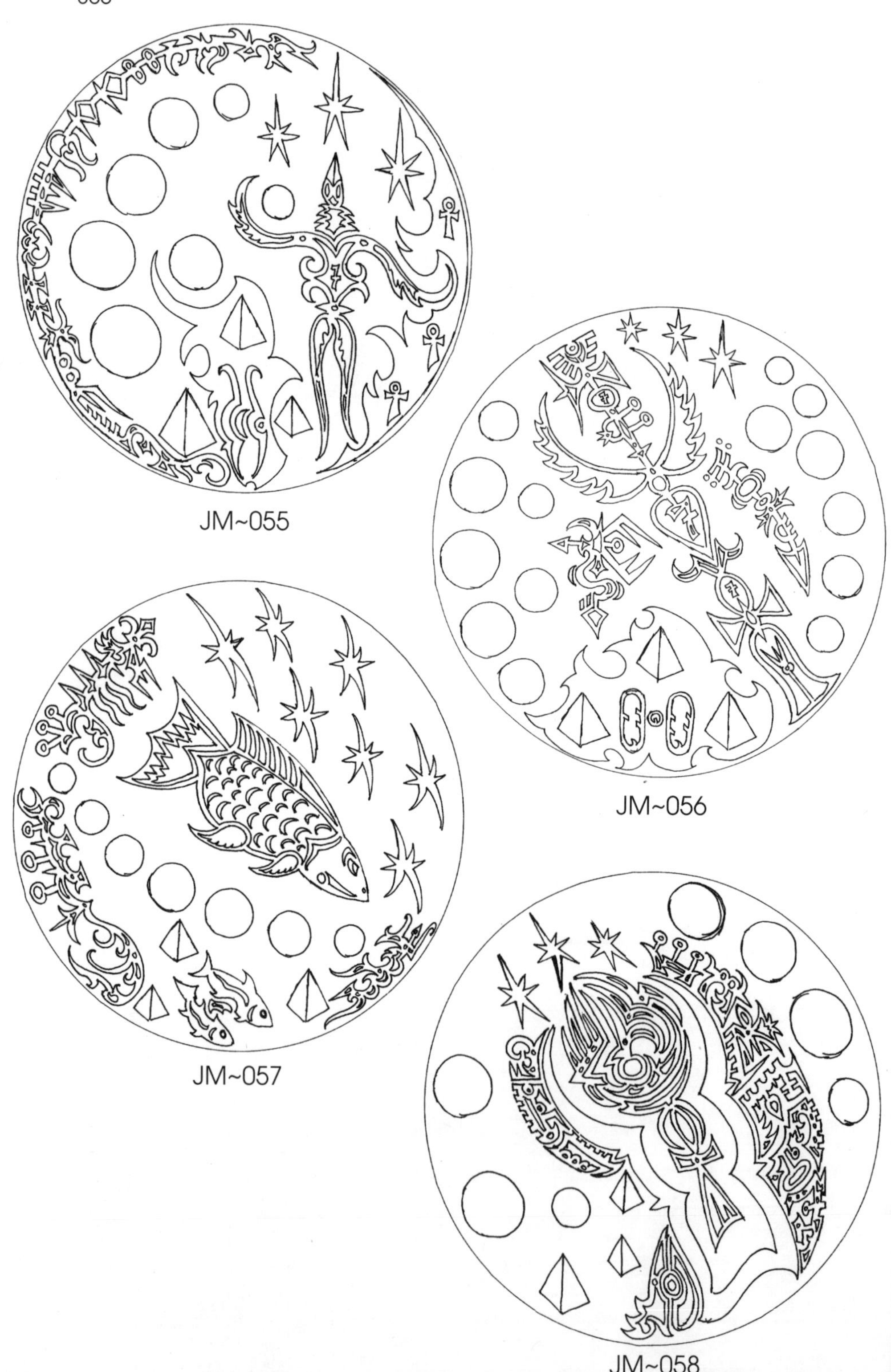

JM~055

JM~056

JM~057

JM~058

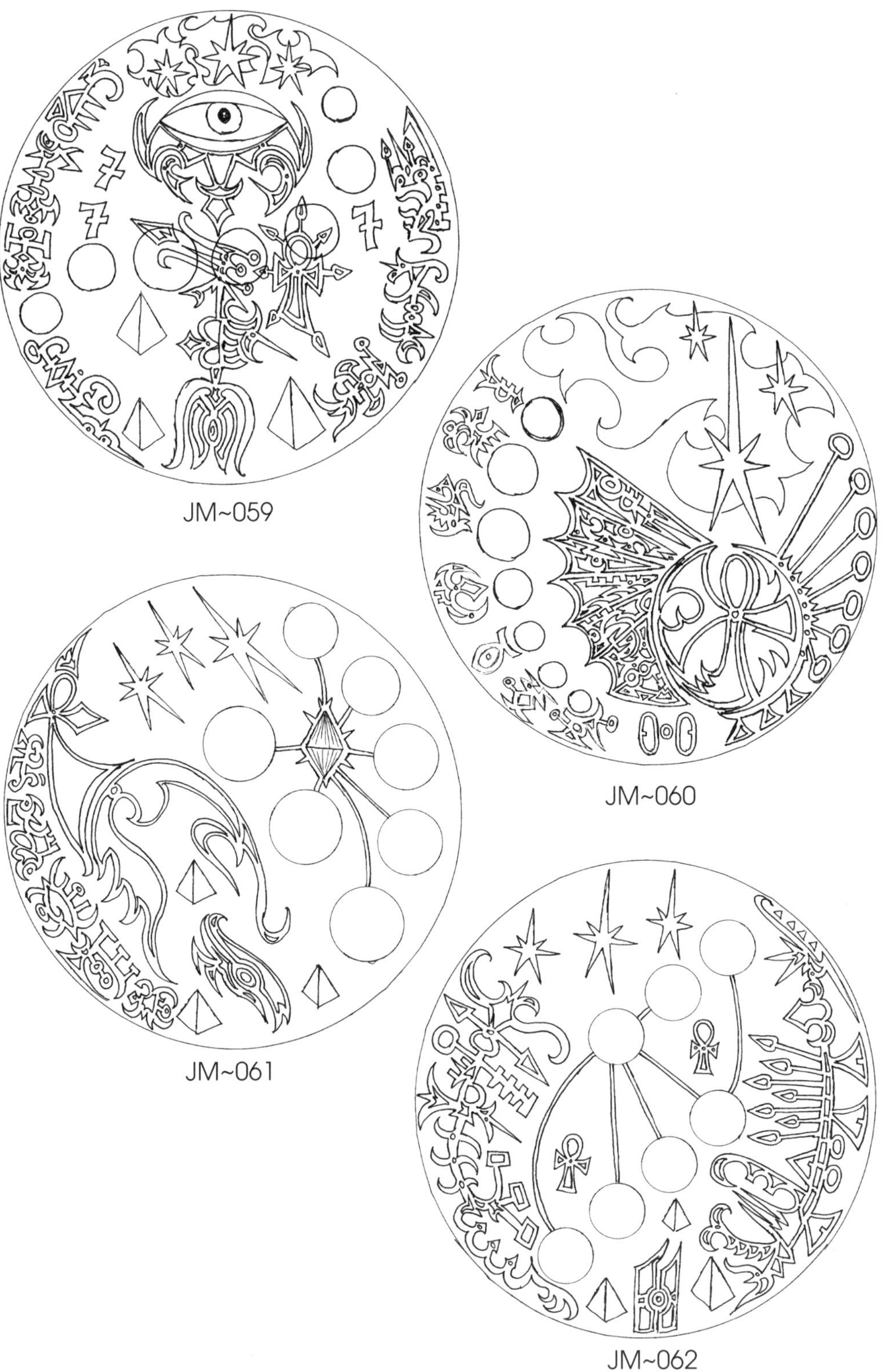

JM~059

JM~060

JM~061

JM~062

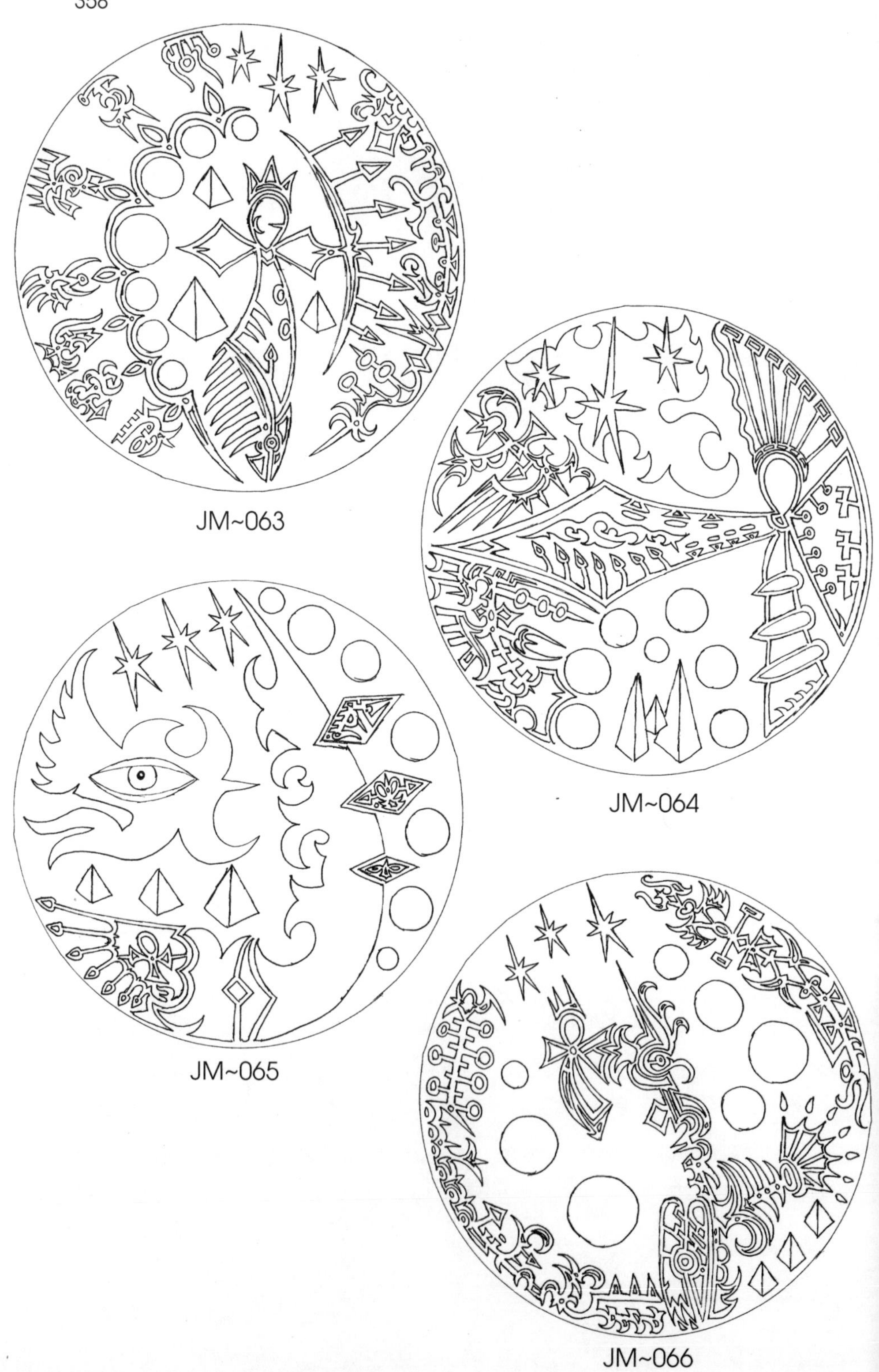

JM~063

JM~064

JM~065

JM~066

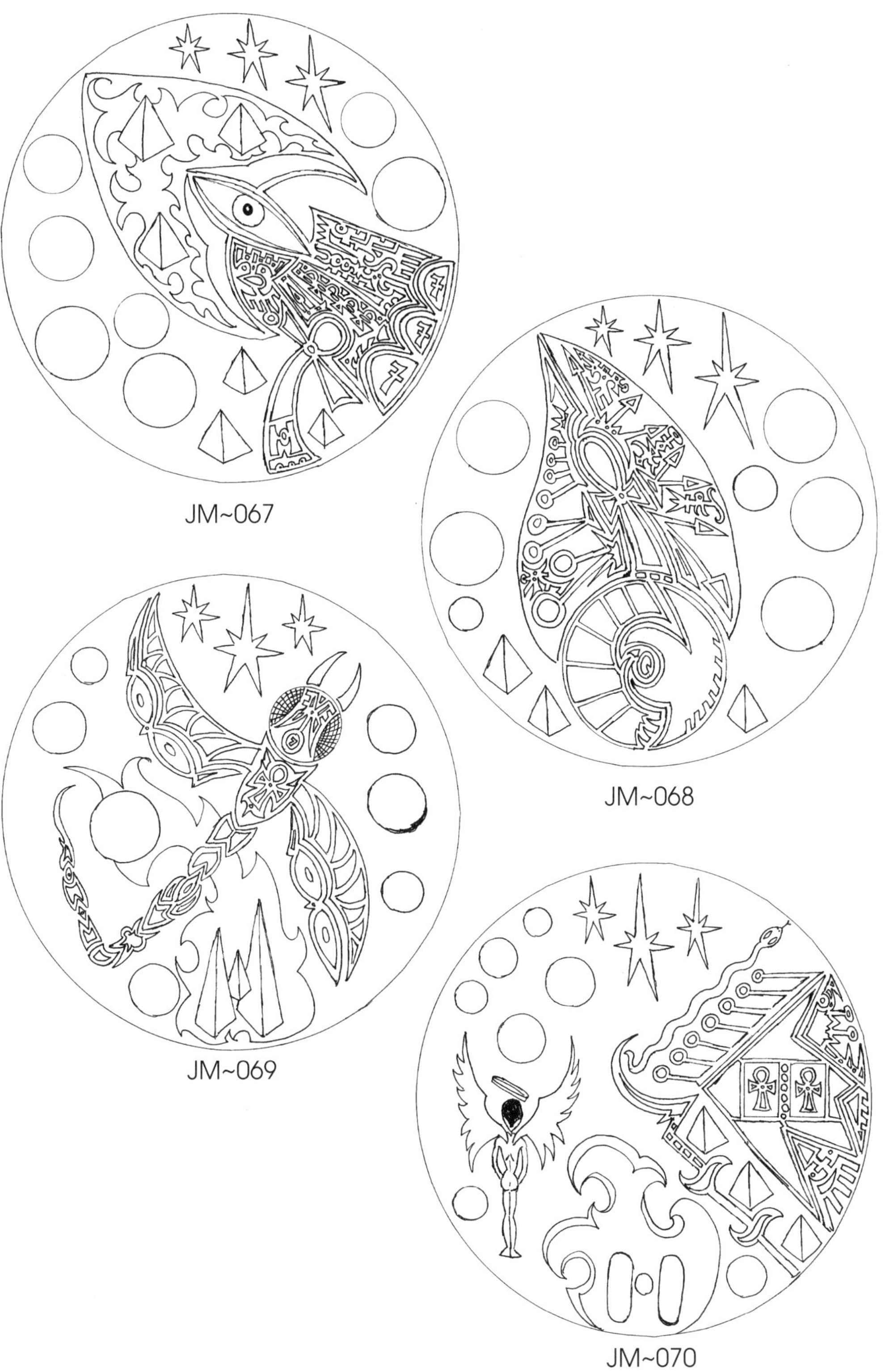

JM~067

JM~068

JM~069

JM~070

JM~071

JM~072

JM~073

JM~074

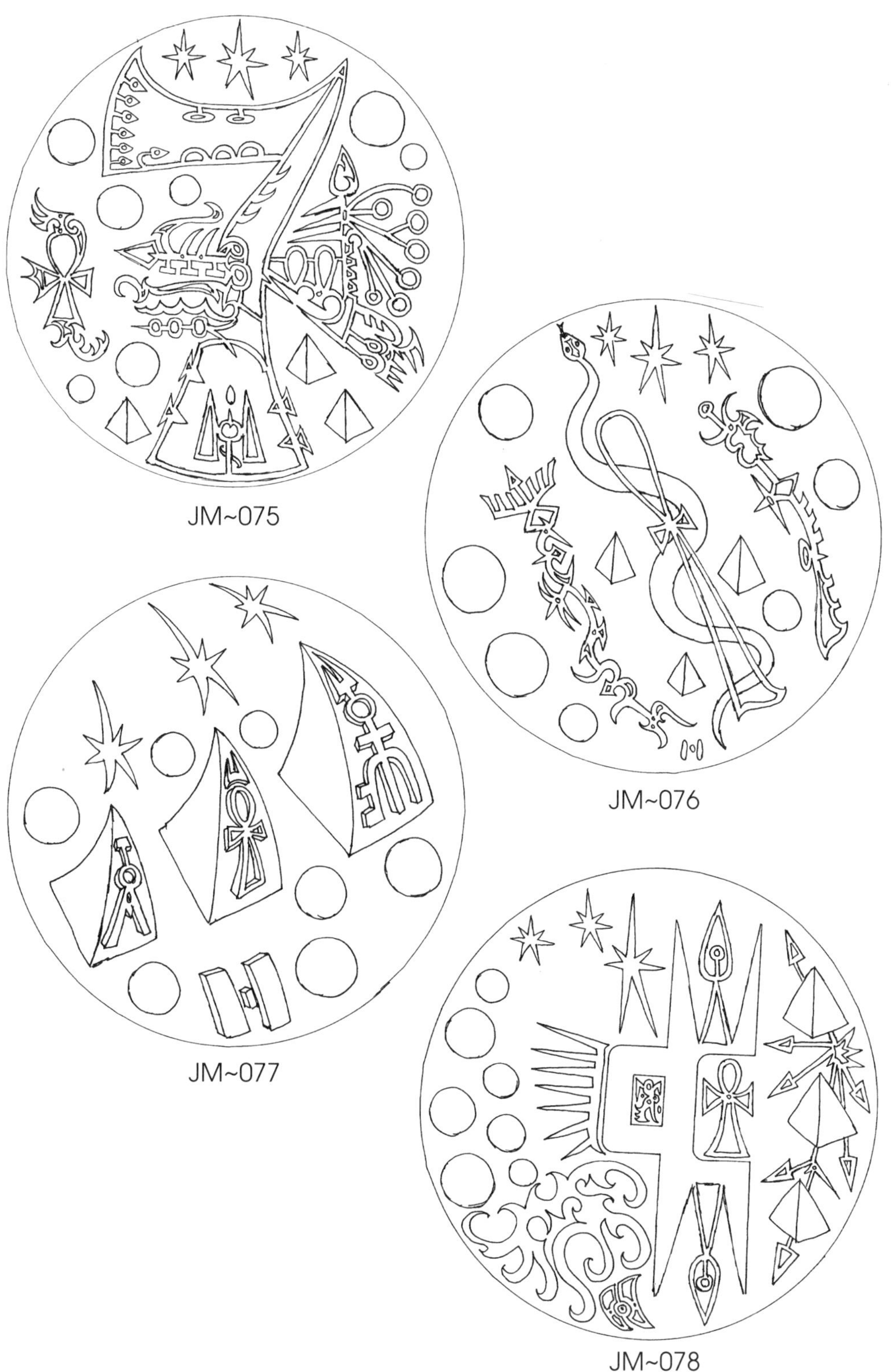

JM~075

JM~076

JM~077

JM~078